LITERATURE AND IDEAS SERIES
Irving Howe, General Editor

MODERNS
ON TRAGEDY

An Anthology of
Modern and Relevant Opinions
on the Substance and Meaning
of Tragedy

Edited with Introductory Remarks by
LIONEL ABEL

A FAWCETT PREMIER BOOK
Fawcett Publications, Inc., Greenwich, Conn.
Member of American Book Publishers Council, Inc.

I want to thank Sherry Abel, who helped me in many ways in preparing this anthology.

—*L.A.*

Copyright © 1967 by Fawcett Publications, Inc.

Library of Congress Catalog Card Number: 67-16880

First Fawcett Premier printing, January 1967

Published by Fawcett World Library
67 West 44th Street, New York, N.Y. 10036

PRINTED IN THE UNITED STATES OF AMERICA

Acknowledgments and Sources

"Bellac and the Theatre of Tragedy" From *Littérature* by Jean Giraudoux, 1941. Reprinted by permission of Editions Bernard Grasset, Paris, and of Georges Borchardt.

"The Christian Tragic Hero" From *The New York Times Book Review,* December 16, 1945, pp. 1, 21. © 1945 by The New York Times Company. Reprinted by permission.

"Andromaque" From *The Hidden God* by Lucien Goldmann, trans. by Philip Thody. Reprinted by permission of Humanities Press Inc. and of Routledge and Kegan Paul Ltd.

"Character Change and the Drama" From *Tradition of the New* by Harold Rosenberg, Copyright 1959, 1960. Reprinted by permission of the publisher, Horizon Press.

"Critique of Corneille's Horace" From *The Structure of Literature* by Paul Goodman. Reprinted by permission of The University of Chicago Press. Copyright 1954.

"Macbeth and the Metaphysic of Evil" From *The Wheel of Fire* by G. Wilson Knight. Reprinted by permission of the publisher, Methuen & Co. Ltd.

"The Cid, or Corneille's Cult of the Hero" From *Corneille et la dialectique du héros* by Serge Doubrovsky, © Editions Gallimard 1964. Reprinted by permission of Editions Gallimard and the author. (I have retained the original French of Corneille in this selection because I do not feel there is a good English translation.—L.A.)

"Berenice" From *The Idea of a Theatre* by Francis Fergusson. Reprinted by permission of the Princeton University Press and the author.

"The Limitation of Being" From "The Limitation of Being" in *Introduction to Metaphysics* by Martin Heidegger, trans. Ralph Manheim. Reprinted by permission of the publisher, Yale University Press.

"The Birth of Tragedy" Sections 5-14 and 17 from *The Birth of Tragedy,* trans. William A. Haussmann.

"The Concrete Development of Dramatic Poetry and Its Types" from *The Philosophy of Fine Art,* trans. F. P. B. Osmaston (London: G. Bell & Sons, 1920), pp. 312-348. (Translator's footnotes have been omitted here.)

"Tragedy and the Attacks on Socrates" from Hegel's *Lectures on the History of Philosophy,* trans. E. S. Haldane (London: 1892), Vol I, pp. 425-448.

Contents

NIETZSCHE'S "BIRTH OF TRAGEDY"

HEGEL ON TRAGEDY

MODERNS
ON TRAGEDY

Introductory Remarks

We feel that our age has a special relation to tragedy and should be represented by some work in the tragic form; we also feel that this form is inaccessible to us, our age has denied us access to it. We are interested in tragedy, value it, and are not sure what tragedy is. Tragedy, for us, is a problem.

In what the philosophers call "ordinary language" we say of such or such an event that it is "tragic," by which we mean that it is painful to think of or to comtemplate. But by "tragic" in the esthetic sense, we mean an event so presented that, for all its content of pain or horror, we can respond to it with joy. To be sure, the words "tragic" and "tragedy" are not our own creations, though they now form part of our language; these terms we have taken from the Greeks, who used them to describe the esthetic form which they alone invented.

One of our difficulties may be that the term "tragedy" remains a Greek word in no matter what language we speak, just as the word "philosophy" remains a Greek word in all tongues. A modern philosopher has even asserted that philosophy talks Greek; I am inclined to believe that tragedy talks Greek; this of course would mean that *Macbeth* and *Bérénice* are, in some fundamental sense, Greek works. It will be seen that this judgment is quite contrary to that of W. H. Auden, who argues, in the essay included in this anthology, that there are two kinds of tragedy, one Greek and one Christian, the first being the tragedy of "necessity" and the second the tragedy of "possibility." Now in the first place we are not very clear about what possibility is. And Professor Quine, I am told, has said it is a word no philosopher should use. In any case, in

Auden's so-called "tragedy of possibility," the catastrophe, as he sees it, would necessarily *not* be inevitable, and so would have to result from a moral lapse on the part of someone. But such a play would then have to be a moral play, and Aristotle has told us that the moral play ought to end happily. Moreover Hegel is quite in agreement with Aristotle on this point, and even contends that the dramatist interested in the tragic must make every intellectual exertion he can to save his protagonist: the dramatist's failure to prevent a catastrophe is precisely what convinces us that the catastrophe is fated. But I do agree with Auden on one point: there is something in our cultural heritage that stands between us and tragedy as conceived by the Greeks.

The question comes to mind: what has prevented much of modern philosophy from talking Greek? Has it not been the effort of our philosophers to talk, not philosophy, but science. Modern thought, I believe, broke with the kind of questioning the Greeks initiated when philosophers began to treat problems in the light of discoveries, that is to say, in terms of the deliverances of science. But recent philosophy, in at least two important schools, has returned to the older, the Greek mode of questioning: the phenomenological school, putting all received ideas in parentheses; and linguistic analysis, limiting philosophy to those questions about which one can be one's own informant.

What has prevented us moderns from thinking in terms qualitatively continuous with Greek dramatic thought? It has been our interest in and knowledge of psychology. Now, we know very little about the psychology of any figure in any real tragedy. I once asked some students to describe the psychological traits of figures of comedy such as Falstaff or Tartuffe: there seemed to be no difficulty was found in analyzing these characters. One is reminded, of course, of Morgann, speculating not only about the Falstaff of the plays, but about his parents, acquaintances, and the acts of his not yet invented life before he appeared on Shakespeare's stage. But when I asked the same students for an opinion on the personal traits of figures of tragedy, Oedipus or Macbeth, they were hard put to point out anything in these figures that would show them as distinctive. They could not say whether Macbeth was either good or bad, courageous or the contrary, candid or treacherous, weaker or stronger than his wife. All they could say was that he had imagination, and rather more than most men. But this is hardly a way to describe a character, and tells us finally that we know very little about Macbeth. Oedipus the students found altogether unanalyzable. I must add that I had to agree. So, do we have less psychological knowledge of figures of tragedy than of figures of comedy? Or of our personal acquaintances? Yet we are, or become, I think, personally acquainted with Oedipus and with Macbeth. We do know something about them. What?

Ortega y Gasset pointed out a similar problem with regard to the lover's knowledge of the beloved. Plato thought the lover knew the beloved, and better than anyone else could. Stendhal thought the contrary: that the lover was mistaken about the beloved, knowing less than others could know. Ortega in his essay sides with Plato. It seems to me, however, that Plato and Stendhal are both right, The lover may not know the characteristics of his beloved—this is Stendhal's claim. But the lover does know, and more surely than anyone, that the beloved exists: so he does have knowledge of the beloved, even if not the kind of knowledge Plato had in mind, Our knowledge, I suggest, of the tragic protagonist is something more than psychological, a knowledge of his reality, whatever his psychology be. We know in the fullest sense that the tragic protagonist exists, and we feel this all the more strongly as we see him driven, and necessarily, into non-existence.

Tolstoy, it will be remembered, thought Macbeth had no motive for murdering Duncan, and attacked Shakespeare's tragedy on this psychological ground. Is it true that Macbeth had no motive for murder? I said we know him to be real, so he must have had some real motivation; do we know what this motive was? I should say that his motive, which we can know, does not however set him apart from others, and in no sense gives us any insight into what may be called his character. His motive lies very simply in the excitement produced in him by the prophecy of the witches that he would be first Cawdor, and then King. It is often said that Macbeth reacts differently to the witches' prophecy than Banquo does to their promise that his descendants will be kings. The interest of G. Wilson Knight's essay on Macbeth, which I chose for this anthology as against other treatments of the play, is that it convincingly answers this contention: Knight shows that Banquo inwardly is as excited and involved in expectation as Macbeth himself. The matter might be put this way: the contrasting actions of Banquo and Macbeth spring less from a difference (fancied, I think) in

17

their characters, than from the different motivations supplied them by the witches.

We have an interesting anti-psychological approach to the problems of tragedy in Harold Rosenberg's "Character Change and the Drama." However, I think Rosenberg goes too far in dismissing the intention of a character as relevant to a judgment of his acts. Rosenberg ingeniously compares legal and religious with dramatic thinking, but it is excessive to say, as he does, that only the act of a felon or criminal is important to the law and not his motive: what if the felon or criminal is a minor? or is mad? What of the specific legal distinction between taking life after deliberate thought as against killing in passion? I believe that in tragedy motives should be immediately apparent—we should not have to look for them: Oedipus has no hidden motive for killing Laius. On the other hand, when a motive is not evident we are unlikely to find out what it is. Think of the quantity of speculation about Iago's motive for destroying Othello! I for one do not find a satisfactory solution in Coleridge's notion that Iago was hunting for a motive; the English critic has simply transferred to the character of Iago the difficulties he, and we too, have with the play.

If we have little to say psychologically about the protagonist of a tragedy, we at least know this, that he is one person though pulled in different directions. In the Spanish play *The Star of Seville*, once ascribed to Lope de Vega and now thought to have been written by some other playwright, the King tries to break into the home of Estrella—the Star of Seville—and is driven out by the young lady's brother, who, sword in hand, defends her. The King, wanting revenge, asks one of his favorites, the nobleman Busto (in love with and affianced to Estrella) if he is ready to accept any task the royal will wants done. Busto assents to any order; the King orders him to challenge and kill the brother of Estrella. This Busto does. And Estrella has to endure the double horror of hearing of her brother's violent death, and of how death was inflicted by her lover.

But the point to be noted is that the very quality of spirit that makes Busto kill, once he has given his word, is precisely the quality we expect from one whose word of love is not given in vain. For the author of *The Star of Seville*, whoever he was, hardly wanted us to think that Busto cared more for honor than for love. He wanted to confront us with something we almost never experience ourselves and can never encounter in any play not a tragedy: the tearing apart of a person who can be so torn because so unified. There is here no problem of psychology at all, and our sense of the unity of Busto's character is given with the same simplicity as our sense that he exists.

Of course, the world of *The Star of Seville* is a very special one, and to comprehend it more fully we probably have to have some knowledge of the romantic and chivalrous values of Spain's Golden Age. Similarly, we have to know something about what reason meant to the French of Racine's time to understand his *Bérénice*, and Francis Fergusson in his fine essay on the play has rightly stressed the rational meaning of the word *gloire* to Racine and his audience. For in the early part of the seventeenth century, the leaders of France had made the most extraordinary effort to give a rational foundation to all spheres of life: politics, thought, manners, grammar, and poetry. This effort may be said to have finally shaped the French character; it was by trying to be right that the people of France became French. True, by the time Racine set to writing his *Bérénice*, it was clear that the French effort at a thorough-going reasonableness had failed. The play's audience was in fact a most somber court, dismayed by what had come of its projects. As Ramon Fernandez in his book on Molière notes: "The palace at Versailles, a comedy by Molière, and a tragedy by Racine, are precisely equivalent expressions of the wholesale retreat from reason, a force that no more presides over mankind than the honorary chairman presides over an assemblage. Reason had ceased to be a working model and become a mold. . . ." That reason had become a mere mold may account for the element of artificiality—pointed up by Francis Fergusson— in *Bérénice*. But reason had very recently been a working model—hence the genuineness of the play and its great sadness. What Fergusson has failed to note in his essay is that out of the uniquely French experience of the defeat of reason Racine made a tragedy that is not just classical but Greek.

One could not create Greek tragedy in Greece, however, once the order of the Greek world, sustained by cosmic piety, had been destroyed: it was in ruins when the Sophists appeared, even for Euripides. He was the first of the Greek playwrights, I should say, who tried to write tragedy without being able to situate in a cosmic frame the catastrophes with which he wanted to move the public to pity and fear. Curiously enough, in the one play of Euripides in which he does make us feel that there is a cosmos underlying the normally experiences world, this cosmos is envisaged not as an order in which catastrophe might occur, but as itself catastrophic—I am of course referring to the *Bacchae*. So I cannot agree with the important view of H. D. F. Kitto (expressed in the section I have chosen from his book on Greek Tragedy) that Euripides wrote tragedy, though of a different kind from Sophocles, as Sophocles, according to Kitto, wrote a different kind of tragedy from Aeschylus. To carry Kitto's reasoning further, we would have to say that Shakespeare wrote a fourth kind of tragedy (Kitto does try to assimilate Shakespeare's kind to that of Sophocles) and Racine a fifth. And after all these qualifications of tragedy, we would be even less clear as to what tragedy is. For my part, I do not think Euripides' plays are tragedies; and I think it important to show they are not.

Especially the *Bacchae*, defended as tragedy by Kitto. Also by Thomas G. Rosenmeyer, in his essay "Tragedy and Religion" appearing here. Kitto asserts that Euripidean tragedy is peculiarly abstract and that is why it is often taken, wrongly, for melodrama. And he has argued for this view with great ingenuity, most cogently in reference to the *Medea*. I think, with all respect, that he is quite wrong about that play, and also about the *Bacchae*; both plays are faulty in the same way, and their fault is not abstractness. In a true tragedy, I hold, there is something like an execution; moreover, both the executioner and the victim must be noble. In the *Medea*, neither Medea nor her victim Jason is noble; nor is either the emissary of Dionysus or King Pentheus in the *Bacchae*: we cannot sympathize either with the rigidly rationalistic king, or with his cruel, divinely aided destroyer. And we cannot sympathize with Pentheus' mother Agave when, her ecstasy lifted, she realizes that it is her son she has killed. There is a great freshness in the work, and a most seductive poetry. But human feeling, which, in any true tragedy, is never diminished but on the contrary aggrandized, and is sometimes even lifted to equality with the divine, is in the *Bacchae* brutally set aside. Rosenmeyer, in his defense of the play, has tried to justify King Pentheus and present him as something more than a rationalist at grips with a god. Here is Rosenmeyer on King Pentheus' transformation under the spell of Dionysus:

"His vision is broadened; but his role as Pentheus is finished. The disintegration of the king is made particularly painful by the emphasis on feminine clothing. . . . The energies which

20

had once been directed toward the mustering of armies and the implementation of public decisions are now bestowed on the arrangement of his Bacchic vestments. . . . The Bacchianized Pentheus is a visionary and poet. But it is a poetry which lacks the saving grace of choice. He contemplates the prospect of his mother carrying him home from the mountains, and the prospect pleases him. . . . Having rid himself of the social restrictions and classifications, he savors infancy, a sentient creature for whom the mother's cradled arms offer escape and bliss. He is woman and child and beast, an amorphous organism susceptible to all influences and realizing itself in the life of instinct and unthinking sense."

The description, accurate enough, is hardly that of a tragic protagonist on equal terms with a divine destroyer; and the god in the play is reduced to animal proportions: at one point King Pentheus takes the god's emissary for a bull.

But this is not the place to argue at length for my own notions about tragedy; I only want to indicate what they are insofar as they have influenced me in selecting the essays I am presenting. For instance, I chose to reprint Lucien Goldmann's analysis of *Andromaque* because it calls attention to the cosmic setting of Racine's drama. Goldmann is the first, to my knowledge, to have noted that Andromaque's power to resist Pyrrhus, who does appeal to her, comes entirely from Hector, dead and buried. To be sure, I have not excluded views contrary to mine. I have tried, though, and this I do not deny, to present as many pieces as I could which have some bearing on my own notions, supporting or contradicting them. I could not include of course everything I admire. And I have used some pieces which I myself do not find clarifying. However, I think that on this topic anyone who has expressed himself forcefully is entitled to be heard; nor did I rely on just one norm in choosing pieces. For example, I chose to reprint Paul Goodman's passage on Corneille's *Horace* because the writer, though committed to a psychological viewpoint—one I do not accept—shows so much finesse in his moral judgment of the characters in Corneille's play. Serge Doubrovsky's essay on the *Cid* I included because of its quality, and not because, in agreement with the author, I tend to see the characters of tragedy as situated beyond the purely psychological. In fact, I disagree with Doubrovsky's analysis of the *Cid*, and I think his conclusions directly contradict his premises: he claims the play to be a tragedy—he claims too (in the book on Corneille from which I took his piece, abridged for publication here) that Corneille is the greatest French writer of tragedy, more tragic than Racine. But in his essay on the *Cid*, which he treats as one of Corneille's masterworks, Doubrovsky declares finally that the dramatic situation which "threatened to be tragic" ends in "tragi-comedy." Surely tragi-comedy is something different from tragedy. I think Doubrovsky, interpreting Corneille's hero as a representative Master, did not look carefully enough at Kojève's analysis of the class of Masters, an analysis Doubrovsky has used and cited in his essay. Kojève says: "The idea of the Master is not viable; one can only *die* as a Master. The Master who pretends to live as a Master is an impostor." Now, as Doubrovsky indicates in his book, all Corneille's heroes, including the Cid, try to *live* as Masters, and this is no doubt the reason why Corneille's plays seem not genuinely tragic and, finally, for all their strenuousness, strike us as comedy or tragi-comedy. But if Doubrovsky has not seen this very real difficulty, yet his essay nevertheless will interest for its intellectual vigor and also because it treats of Corneille in terms new to the discussion of tragedy.

Which brings me to the very first essay in this anthology, Jean Giraudoux's "Bellac and the Theatre of Tragedy." In this delightful piece the French writer says many things with which I am forced to disagree. When, for instance, he insists that French audiences prefer tragedy to any other entertainment, and that their taste for tragedy is inseparable from their love of bourgeois comfort, bourgeois well-being, I think he is being witty at some expense of truth. And it is not at all the case that whenever a tragedy is presented in France the house is sold out. Even if it were true that the French people have a special feeling for tragedy, something surely contestable, should we not make a distinction between the creator of tragedy and its consumers? The creator of tragedy in France was Racine, who was far from being the kind of humanistic bourgeois Giraudoux's essay celebrates.

What drew me, though, to Giraudoux's essay was his desire to relate the taste for tragedy in Greece to the taste for it in France, evident in the discretion with which French audiences have pursued this taste.

THE OPINIONS OF
CONTEMPORARY PHILOSOPHERS

What philosophers have had to say about tragedy is by no means more interesting and certainly not more important than what literary men have said. On the other hand, what the philosophers have had to say is much more general, and often more sharply put.

Scheler's essay is valuable, I think, for only one of the ideas presented in it, but this idea is most essential. When Scheler speaks of tragedy as a collision between equal and contrary values, he is, of course, repeating Hegel's view, and with less acuteness than Sidney Hook, who formulates the issue in tragedy as a struggle between the right and the right, or even between the right and the good. Also, it seems to me that Scheler's notion of "objective sadness" is both questionable and unclear. Do we respond to tragedy with "objective sadness"? What does it mean to say of any felt sadness that it is "objective"? I do not know, nor does Scheler say. But what is extremely valuable in his essay is the notion that at the heart of any true tragedy we will find the operation of a kind of causality which Scheler calls "eidetic." Necessity in tragedy according to him, is given, a priori: even an overwhelming probability of catastrophe is insufficient to define a truly tragic situation.

Sidney Hook's essay, which I have praised for its formulation of Hegel's view, is to be objected to, however, insofar as it tries to characterize a particular school of philosophical thinking, the pragmatic school, as "tragic." There is no philosophy, let alone school of philosophy, which can properly be called "tragic." I make this point in my own essay, "Is There a Tragic Sense of Life?" in criticism of Lucien Goldmann's view that Pascal's thought was tragic. Hook thinks Dewey's was. Both Goldmann and Hook have, I believe, fallen into the same error: they think the tragic is separable from particular tragedies. Valéry once noted that philosophers try to separate beauty from the things that are beautiful: the things themselves become irrelevant.

Stuart Hampshire's brief comment, written as a review for the *New Statesman and Nation*, contains more valid ideas than many long treatises. The critical asides about Lukàcs' manner of thinking are not only right, in my view, but applicable to Goldmann (Lukàcs is his master). And I am completely in accord with Hampshire's incisive point that in a tragedy the causes of a catastrophe are remote from the victim. I should go even further, and say that they are also remote from the dramatist, or at least not clearly discernible by him.

I have taken some pages from Heidegger's *Introduction to Metaphysics*, pages in which he tries to relate the thought of

23

Parmenides to what he calls the "thinking poetry of the Greeks," specifically to one of the choruses in Sophocles' *Antigone*. I think these few pages contain a highly original and genuinely philosophical notion of tragedy. Is it a romantic notion? This may well be. But in any case, the idea that the strangeness characteristic of man is most completely expressed in those collisions with reality that end in disaster seems to me one implied by all past theorizing about tragedy, be it by Aristotle, Hegel, or Nietzsche; and Heidegger has expressed his view with great power and a kind of poetry.

NIETZSCHE'S "BIRTH OF TRAGEDY"

For reasons of space, I have not been able to present Nietzsche's essay in its entirety. But in fact not everything in it is pertinent to our topic. Certainly the essay has historical importance, marking a decisive moment in our reflection. Also, it is filled with insights. Yet its enthusiasm for the tragic, wonderfully felt, has helped to propagate conclusions I, for one, find questionable.

About Euripides, Nietzsche was probably right. His judgment that Euripides was a rationalist was taken up and differently expressed at the turn of the century by the English scholar Verrall in his brilliant book on the dramatist. To be sure, Verrall rejoiced in the rationalism of Euripides, which Nietzsche deplored. And Verrall interpreted the *Bacchae* as an expression of rationalism, while Nietzsche took the play—here I think Nietzsche was right, Verrall wrong—as a recantation of rationalism.

What are we to think finally about *The Birth of Tragedy*? Its positive influence has been exhausted, whereas what I would call its negative influence is probably still with us. Certainly we must today regard Nietzsche's attack on Socrates, whom he calls the destroyer of tragedy, as totally unjust. And we cannot but regard Nietzsche's pitting what he calls "Dionysian" man against Socratic or "theoretical" man as so much rhetoric, the tantrum, perhaps, of a philosopher. After all, it was Socrates who upheld absolute values against the moral relativism of the Sophists—by argument, of course: what other means was possible against Protagoras, for instance, who excelled in argument? It was in fact the moral relativism of the Sophists, combatted by Socrates, that created an atmosphere in which tragedy became impossible. Moreover, Nietzsche thought tragedy an anti-progressive ideology, or dependent on some such ideology. In my judgment, tragedy is neither progressive nor anti-progressive, nor ideological at all: there is no such thing as a tragic attitude, or a will to tragedy. I have still another objection to Nietzsche's view. It will be remembered that Scheler, in his essay, maintains that at the heart of tragedy there is a type of causality that is essential, à priori. Where else is this type of causality to be found? Not in nature, of course, where we no doubt have to deal entirely with probabilities, however overwhelming. The type of causality Scheler has in mind is to be found, I suggest, in the presuppositions of a culture, presuppositions that may never have been confronted directly by the creator of tragedy. But Nietzsche writes as if the creator of tragedy were able to make an intellectual decision in favor of values consonant with tragedy, and contrary to those destructive of it. The decision in favor of tragedy would, for Nietzsche, have to be musically motivated, but it would nonetheless remain the decision of an intellectual. But Aeschylus and Sophocles were not ideologists of culture, like the Euripides whom Nietzsche criticized—like Nietzsche himself. What makes the tragedies of Euripides weak, or, as Kitto says, "abstract," is that they were founded not on the norms that were fateful for Greek society, but on the ideas the talented dramatist entertained at the moment, if you will, on his *vues d'esprit*—pacifist as in the *Trojan Women,* or barbarous as in the *Bacchae.* Nietzsche's consideration of tragedy amounts finally to ideological support for the Euripides of the *Bacchae* against the Euripides of the *Trojan Women,* whereas the Greek poet in both of these works was equally remote from those presuppositions of the Greek culture which in the works of Aeschylus and Sophocles operate both within and behind events causing catastrophe. Nietzsche did give us one fundamental notion: that the form of tragedy expresses a certain moment or condition of culture; but this true idea, in his treatment of it, is coarsened, becomes misleading. He argues as if the condition of culture he desired, and in which he thought tragedy would be possible, could be produced by the exertion of a certain cultural will; and tragedy is seen by him not as something we might have to submit to, but as something we ought to strive for ideologically, as something we ought to will. Now the desire for tragedy is anything but tragic.

HEGEL ON TRAGEDY

Hegel's views on tragedy are, it seems to me, much more profound than Nietzsche's; and what is essential in them has been reformulated with admirable lucidity by Alexandre Kojève in the passages from his *Introduction à la lecture de Hegel* presented in this volume. But of course I have let Hegel speak in his own words.

However, I must call attention to a curious misunderstanding by Hegel of his own idea of tragedy. He seems to have thought that his explanation of tragedy could also serve as a description of it. But were his view of tragedy meant to describe, it would be both limited and misleading. It could be said (it was said) that Hegel had adequately described only one tragedy, the *Antigone* of Sophocles; and Hegel himself says as much, when he proposes a second theory of tragedy to account for Sophocles' Oedipus.

I do not think Hegel needed a second theory to supplement his original and striking conception of tragedy. Obviously it is a weakness in a philosopher to present two entirely different theories to account for the same phenomenon. Hegel's first notion was an explanatory one, and not a description of the Greek works. And as an explanatory notion, that is to say, a notion as to *why* the form of tragedy appeared in Greece, it has a valid reference to every Greek tragedy, holding as well for the *Oedipus* as for the *Antigone*. It is true that Hegel's notion does seem to describe the *Antigone* perfectly, and the *Oedipus* only in part; but the intent of the theory, as I noted, was surely not descriptive.

In my own formulation of Hegel's view (as stated in "Is There a Tragic Sense of Life?") I assert that in the Greek world the superior individual had to violate the law of the family or of the state; on this point I am in agreement with Kojève. One might argue, though, against this view, that in Greece there was an alternative, permitting escape from fate. Could not the philosopher, at least, sidestep the conflict of state and family? Here the story of Socrates is instructive No doubt, Hegel had this in mind when he insisted that Socrates' fate was tragic; but his explanation as to why it was tragic is most unsatisfactory, requiring him to justify the Athenians in sentencing Socrates, something no philosopher before Hegel dreamed of doing. However, if Hegel had held to his original insight he could have shown a tragic content in the drama of Socrates' death, and this without justifying Socrates' accusers or judges. One thing held against Socrates was that he had voted for the acquittal of an admiral who, after an engagement, had failed to collect the Athenian dead. As Hegel himself pointed out, care for the dead was the special province of the Greek family. Failing to collect the dead, the admiral charged by the Athenian court had obviously sinned, but not against the state; nor did Socrates sin against the state in voting for the admiral's acquittal. But what about the sin against the Athenian families, a sin in which Socrates was also involved? I take this whole matter as an illustration that the antinomy of family and state in the Greek world was inescapable, even by a philosopher, once, that is, under the obligation to act.

Readers of Karl Reinhardt's essay on Sophocles' *Oedipus* (an essay praised by Heidegger) may think, though, that the critic's analysis of the play is more in line with Hegel's special theory about the *Oedipus*—the one I called wrong and said he did not need—and contrary to the theory of Hegel which I called original, and support. The argument no doubt would be that Reinhardt showed the *Oedipus* centered on an issue of Being as against Appearance, Appearance as against Being a metaphysical question, and not on a less general issue, such as the conflict between state and family in the antique world. My answer is that though Reinhardt has been wonderfully sensitive to the theoretical meanings Sophocles wove into his play, he has left out of his account the elemental struggle which gives these meanings their drastic character. Not knowing he has killed his father, Oedipus strives to find his father's murderer. He succeeds, trapping himself, and becomes his own judge and sentencer. But in the name of what? Of Being, as against Appearance? No—in the name of the state. The many conflicting postures of the characters in relation to Being as against Appearance, brought out by Reinhardt's clarifying essay, should not hide from readers the bitter conflict at the heart of the action in the *Oedipus*.

And Hegel's theory has a certain descriptive value, as I noted, even for the *Oedipus*. Suppose we ask: In what sense is Oedipus free? in what sense determined?—questions Reinhardt raises but does not succeed in answering. Now certainly Oedipus seems free to investigate the crime he himself committed—on the other hand he does not know, when he begins his investigation, that it was he who was guilty of the crime. It has been said, rightly I think—each of us can confirm this from his own experience—that we feel most free when we are in fact most determined, so that our feeling that Oedipus, with whom we identify, is free in no sense proves that he is. But what kind of determinism is he subject to?

Not to any kind of natural determinism. But in the Greek world, as Hegel has shown, still another determinism was at work: an individual who acted drastically could not but sin, against either the family or the state. Guilt followed ineluctably on action, and from the very presuppositions of Greek culture. But does not culture have the meaning of freedom from necessity? In Greece, it did have that meaning for the many, not for the few. There are few who act; and action, in Greece, meant exposure to a determinism set in motion by society itself. To be sure, such cultural determinism did not exclude freedom; sin was not inevitable for those who could avoid drastic action, and they are represented in the Greek tragedies by a chorus that does not act. Oedipus, because of his nature and station, had no choice but to act.

It is from Hegel's perspective that *Macbeth* and *Bérénice*—as I suggested before—can be seen as Greek works; here I should like to make this judgment, which some may find odd, more pointed and precise. Let us take *Bérénice* first. In Racine's play, Titus, Emperor of Rome, is subject to a Roman law applying only to emperors; any other Roman but the emperor is free to marry a queen. Titus does not have to submit to this law. He is free to yield up power, to become an ordinary citizen, or to go into exile with Bérénice. As emperor, he remains subject to a law applying only to him.

And Macbeth, in Shakespeare's tragedy, is subject to an atmosphere which could not but envelop anyone who had the ambition to be king. This murky and controlling atmosphere, like the mist in which the Weird Sisters appeared, materializes the belief held at the time that kings rule not by moral, but by metaphysical, right. Duncan's character is unimpeachable; but the Weird Sisters, representing the metaphysical, in their prophecy offer the crown to Macbeth. Moreover the descendants of Duncan are rejected by them: only the descendants of Banquo will have metaphysical support. Now it was under a descendant of Banquo, James I, that Shakespeare staged his tragedy. We may assume that for the playwright and his audience, with James on the throne, the metaphysical was no longer felt to be at odds with the moral.

In any case, it was the atmosphere of moral ambiguity ("Fair is foul and foul is fair") operating with the power of a causal law which excited Macbeth and his wife to their tragic action. Here too, as in *Bérénice*, and in the Greek plays, we have a type of determinism to which only the hero is exposed.

But does the writer of tragedy have to be aware that he is

28

dealing with the presuppositions of his culture? By no means. Shakespeare in writing *Macbeth* need not have reflected directly on the moral significance of the divine right of kings. And Racine in writing *Bérénice* may never even have noticed how perfectly the defeat of reason—for the seventeenth century reason was the regal faculty—could be expressed in the story of an emperor's impotence; Racine may have been led to his subject merely by sympathy for Louis XIV in love with La Vallière. As for the Greeks, may it not be precisely because they did not understand the cultural determinism they were subject to that they were able to represent it as fate in their tragedies? A fatality understood calls for action, for change. Hegel was even of the opinion that the writing of tragedy becomes impossible once the presuppositions of a culture are directly known.

We may pause over this thought, which can lead to a fuller comprehension by us of the power of the presupposed. We have some notion of what that power is from metaphysical analysis, in which the ideas controlling most of our thinking are located somewhere behind, and even hidden by, our thoughts. In social life and action, what we presuppose has power over us by being immediately intimate and yet at the same time remote; and it is the source of whatever piety we are able to bring to the achievement of our goals.

So it is not from his clearly thought out views about life or about action, but from what he along with others of his culture and period presupposes, that the writer of tragedy draws his special and incomparable power. I am referring once again to what I take to be not a notion but a truth (we owe its clarification to Scheler, its revelation to Hegel), that the causality at work in a proper tragedy is one not found in nature. And I wish to stress once again that this type of causality is derived by the writer of tragedy through his felt union with his society. When at one with what controls the action of his fellows, the writer can feel such pathos as is implicit in their aims; he gains, in addition, a special—I almost said a technical—power, the power to be independent of the empirical, and to discern behind some shocking instance of human adversity a subtly spun givenness as its cause. Thus it is that he is able to formalize and lighten analytically a domain which at first sight seems incapable of order and lightness, the domain of human defeat and suffering, of those things which, as Pascal puts it, "take us by the throat."

It should be possible to answer more fully now the

question with which I began: Why is tragedy a problem for us, why do we feel cut off from it? True, we tend to understand our own acts and those of others in the light of psychology, and we lack any independence of the empirical; but what separates us most decisively from tragic thinking—which is something quite different from thinking about tragedy—is that we are lost in a welter of suppositions and countersuppositions, and incapable of ever getting back to the presuppositions governing all these. So divided is society now, that we may well wonder whether there are any presuppositions at all behind the multitude of things, often catastrophic, now being done. Our fate seems to be that we cannot find fate anywhere, in any action, no matter how lofty its motive or grim its consequences. We are, however, able to think about tragedy, and here our very separation from it may work to our advantage. After all, it was in a Greece in which there was no longer a single writer capable of tragedy that Aristotle formulated the conception which has not since been set aside, calling tragedy the imitation of an action so designed as to relieve, by stimulating, the feelings of pity and terror.

Lionel Abel

September, 1966

Recent Literary Opinion.

Bellac and the Theater of Tragedy

JEAN GIRAUDOUX

IT WAS IN Bellac, Haute-Vienne, that I arrived—I shan't apologize for being born there. I'll not apologize, either, for being without experience of any large city up until my maturity: five small towns, of which not one had over 5,000 inhabitants, shared my youth. My probation was not without its advantages. For instance, I never counted for less than one five-thousandth of whatever human agglomeration I happened to be part of, and twice I counted for no less than a thousandth; this surely makes a child feel bigger, giving him a greater confidence in life. Besides, the only way of getting to know how the French live is by making the round of the narrow market towns and the sprawling cantons. Thus, I missed the regularly rewarded itinerary through the prefectures, the Bordeaux-Angoulême-Paris route favored by the Roman legionaries, favored also by civil servants with ambition, and which by some geographers and historians is seen as the sacred road to a knowledge of France though looking rather more, I should say, like a longish stretch of signposts, whether for automobiles or war chariots; I drew, instead, a different lot, moving within a cluster of cantons and subprefectures, the kind of nerve center that affords a quite special perception into the total French character. No Cook's tour could have foreseen my journey: Bellac-Bessines-Pellevoisin-Cérilly-Cusset—inconceivable to accomplish save by submitting to a wonderful diversity of fecund chance attractions. Gold, busily measuring everywhere, drew in and out of this circuit a train of bill-claimants, mortgage holders, tax collectors: there was no other kind of intrusion from civilization outside. Of course the talented boys and girls among us had been sent off to the district prefecture, but then only to be put behind iron gates into the lycée and right off shackled so intimately to antiquity as to be more than ever removed from the world. The world just there, though, was in its own way also ancient, with scant allowance for individuality of character. The fact is these country towns in France have more or less the general compass and population of antique cities, their surface features imaging the kind of moral order within which a man is held answerable for his name, for his virtues or his failings. Each person is known to every other, and to the core; apart from the self-consciousness that remains unexposable, there is not much that may be kept private. With all that, and however listless and undistinguished, each of these same country towns has its turn at glory. Every two or three hundred years, in one of them, by the labors of a sudden harmony among the owners of property, the sellers of goods, the holders of public office, and of a suddenly fervent embrace between practical pursuits and the local dispositions to culture, there is brought to birth a new era, which may last several years. While it lasts, the country town blooms with the moral and physical graces of a capital city. It was this that happened once upon a time to a tiny island of the Aegean, when after 2,000 dullish years it came suddenly ablaze, lit by the fires of Greek civilization. And with the thought in mind that every old French town—two instances were known to me directly—boasts somewhere in its past a Periclean Age, I recently decided I should like to find out when Bellac's was, and to that end began studying some history.

So it was I met with the surprise awaiting anyone who imagines that the place of his happy and pacific youth must always have been a place of harmony and well-being. Explore far enough beneath the superstructure of French union and French felicity, you will more than likely stumble on foundation piles of wretchedness and discord. My own Bellac, a kind of oasis I had thought, seated there upon the oldest rocks of France just where the yellowish grasses of Poitou and Berry become the thick rich English green on which once tumbled the huge frame of Richard the Lionhearted—the mortal wound had been dealt a few leagues distance from there—this Bellac which I took for granted as sheltered against all history's vicissitudes, had not been spared a single one, I found. Bellac: the serene name which I had been taught was from *bella aqua*, "lovely waters," I now learned came from *Belli vicus*: War Town. Its founder, it turned out, had been poisoned by his spouse—a nasty business and a bad omen, surely. In the year one thousand a dragon appeared inside a cloud, and the fires of erysipelas raged. Many from among the highest ranks, then, in the monasteries throughout the Lower Marche of which Bellac was the seat, reduced themselves to monks so death might find them in the garb of that penitence which abbots had to refuse even to emperors. I call to mind the Emperor turned away by the friar at the gate and going dejected back to his throne over the Limousin heath where suddenly as the night came on his melancholy was for a brief moment broken into by the sound of fox teeth stealthily crunching the berries from a juniper bush. Two centuries pass and the plague strikes, followed by famine. And in between all else there is a recurring state of war: the invasions; the Crusades: when, once, Geoffroy of Bellac, near Antioch bemused by the green meadows below that filled his gaze with a vision of home, descended from the barren height he held and got himself and his hundred thousand men massacred. Then there were the wars of the English, of the Jacquerie, of the League; and during the rare intervals of a fragile peace such disquietudes as revolt of the peasants against the tax, or the stubborn feuding with the neighbor town of Le Dorat for primacy in the Marche. At the heart of these dark epochs, though, the bright time of happiness was being prepared; was ready, actually, with the start of the fifteenth century; and then, about to open and irradiate the entire province, encountered a setback. Bellac's resistance to the English had been acknowledged by three fleurs-de-lys for its banners, and now the Bellacons were about to receive the added reward of a visit from Charles VII himself, together with his son, such an honor surely as to introduce their season of abundance, which then only delayed it. For though he came, the fastidious Charles speedily left, fairly in shock from the ugliness of the Bellac women's head-dress which as he went he commanded be changed, and at once. The Dauphin too was unlucky at Bellac, losing the lioness Tanneguy du Chatel had sent him when sometime during the night leaping through a window it strangled. The Bellacon tanners needed only one night to cure his lioness's hide for him; but the Dauphin had conceived for Bellac a most passionate disaffection, and rudely fled. The presence on Bellac soil of Saint Colette once again signalized a flowering, this time nipped in the bud by the plague of 1588. At last, following the Siege of 1591 when the Partisans of the League lay routed before the walls (beneath which even the Bellac women had joined the defense), at last the era of prosperity opened wide: when taxes no longer oppressed; when the notaries saw eye to eye with the magistrates and the military with the religious; when the great of France, mysteriously drawn upon a route they never afterwards took, passed through Bellac: whether it was Henri IV, who there saw an eclipse for the first time; or La Fontaine, who, thanks to an ancestor of mine, at Bellac conceived his fable *The Coach*; or Fénélon, who has insisted, on the evidence of the number of metaphors in the welcoming speech, it was the Limousin pedant right out of Rabelais who received him there; when, also, Bellac had an abundance of local intellect, could send professors to the College of the Louvre, geographers to the King, bishops to Tulle; while at the same time there thronged into the town for the horse-racing at the edge of the Bazine the great nobility from the neighboring heights of the Massif Central.

But I must come to my subject. In what way did the general happiness of this favored region express itself? By a taste for tragedy. Tragic poets and tragic characters invaded the environs of Bellac. As with most other French towns between the end of the Valois and the death of Louis XIII, so Bellac in this exalted period of our literature chose to recapitulate tragically the small fits of its daily life. Now the rivalry with Le Dorat was no longer threshed out through practical jokes and such, but in the tragedies, year in year out, of the honored Pierre Mailhard, a doctor, whose mother, moreover, was by the common gossip rated a sorceress; and also in the tragedies of the lawyer Barroque: he in the common gossip a skinflint and leper. Disputes of family and neighbors found expression, not in legal prose, but, by favor of the poet Jean Prévot, in tragedies bearing such titles as *Oedipus* or *Britannicus* and with some added distinction of their own. And every felicitous turn of daily life brought onto Bellac soil one or another of the Greek heroes—how explain it? Why, for instance, should the long awaited appointment of the local magistrates have convoked Dido and Aeneas too? And as the celebrated Limousin horses rode into town for the special fairs, who had arranged for there to be conspicuously in the procession Juno and Achates? When, in a step forward for the Bellac clergy, the parish priests finally had the curacies they wanted, how did it happen that at the same moment Bellac also had King Saul and the souls from out of Sodom and Gomorrah? The edifices of salthouse and water tower no sooner splendidly rose than in the market place and church porch on feast days up rose the Babylonians and the Athenians. How explain this? In short, how shall we explain that in the time of their own joy my unlettered Limousins liked tragedy best, reserved their warmest welcome for the heroes of tragedy? The paradox of

34

Bellac, set before me, widened suddenly in scope: and reached from the Lower Marche to take in all France.

What is tragedy? Tragedy affirms a horrible link between humanity and a destiny greater than the human destiny. In tragedy, man is pulled away from his quadruped's stance on all fours by a leash which holds him upright, whose rule he is ignorant of, whose tyranny he knows by heart.

What is France? France asserts a human truth; France will not bend the knee before any beyond-of-truth or any super-lie. Tragedy presupposes the existence of horror as such, of an immanent menace and a densely populated stratosphere. France supposes that above her rises an expanse of air good to breathe—the higher one goes, the less dense.

What is the tragic hero like? He is a being peculiarly re-signed to coexistence with the forms and monsters of fatality. Who is the Frenchman, whether or not a Bellacon? A member of the human race who finds it hard to be cordial to strangers, let alone to the strange; and whose language, above all lucid and precise in syntax as in vocabulary, rejects translation into the non-human.

What then can fatality mean to a Frenchman? He admits only one mode of it: fate by family. The Frenchman is a homebody; those embroilments which others insist on having with persons divine or infernal, he can readily find inside his family circle. The entire range of French drama, tragedy as well as comedy, on stage wants only a simple bedroom or dining room for a set. As to the French version of Olympus, it may be seen in the reunion of the family clan, at table for a repast, or seated before the notary who is about to read a last will and testament. The nest of vipers which the Greeks place on the head of the Medusa and the Germans feel as the writhing of instincts and private yearnings, this nest in our country is the ineluctable entanglement of cousins, uncles, aunts—caught by their tenderer sentiments as well: nest of ermine, nest of adders. Consider the affection to solitude that figures in tragedy, you will see that among us its source is not in the need for converse with nature; the Frenchman solitary has turned away not from the human community but simply from family; it may even be from the part of his family which is himself. Most of the plays we count our master-pieces of tragedy are nothing other than familial debate, family rows. What criticism generally presents in Corneille as the conflict between love and honor, turns out to be more often than not the contradiction between love and duty to family.

Siegfried in his encounter with the Rhine maidens, or with the Giants—Water, Earth—Faust confronting Mephistopheles, in our understanding of pathos is expressed by the Cid confronting his father, Polyeucte his wife, Horace his sister; and Cinna will excuse it if we remain a bit cool to his difficulties, inasmuch as he chose to have them only with an uncle. Family, we know too, lay behind that tragedy we had from Racine, which I daresay was the most affecting one of all, the personal tragedy of his silence.

A Frenchman's intellectual realism and discretion hold him from entering any kind of union, licit or illicit, with abstractions; and only with the greatest misgiving might he sometime open his door to a divinity interested in upsetting his daily routine: clearly, a Frenchman's moral world is in little danger of being invaded—by either divinity or abstraction. There do exist, as we know, two categories of Frenchmen; there is the believer and there is the freethinker. Now, French belief presupposes a God of relaxed, benevolent temper, disposed to be human in his dealings with men; and, sharing with our small business, also with our provincial freemasonry, an optimistic preference for what is sensible, French atheism, for its part, presupposes a nothingness of sound composition and proven quality, in short, a loyal nothingness. Obviously neither one, belief nor unbelief, would operate to import into our souls or onto our soil those forms of menace we regard as the substance of tragedy, and for a fact they are nowhere around, not in our landscape and not in our words. The two or three werewolves who still inhabit the provinces are tied up there and will have to stay. Try putting Macbeth on our stage; at the witches' incantations everyone will insist on being reminded of the cigarette girls' chorus from *Carmen* or the singsong give and take of Labiche's heroes. Not to mention the way nature itself among us has undergone dilution of its intenser moments and moods; can anyone doubt that our very night, the one which falls each evening over Orléans or St Jean de-Luz, is only an edulcorated, a disinfected version of that night which at the same hour is brooding over Saxony and Glasgow?

All this notwithstanding, the French theatregoer prefers still to be entertained by the kind of spectacle Bellac once adored. Aside from the bull fights—animal tragedy—the only other diversions that can lure the peaceable mob to the arenas at Nîmes or Saintes are, not comedies and not musicals, but plays entitled *Philoctetes* or *Britannicus*. Blood's the thing: let Andromache be showing in one of our open-air theatres and the house is soon sold out. The world war itself seemed known only as an engagement of the Medes or Carthaginians in the more than sixty tragedies about it that were submitted to the Comédie-Française and the Odéon. The fanaticism with which the typical devotee supports the French theatre is in no small measure due to his having followed all of the actors in their tragic roles, so that he need have no difficulty in viewing any comedy playing, however modern and frivolous, as through a thin veil cast over tragic voices, tragic silhouettes. When Mounet-Sully scored one of his greatest hits playing a jovial character from Alexandre Dumas, this was undoubtedly because his fans saw before them none other than: Oedipus Rex, in the very modest disguise of a domino; their applause was all for Oedipus Rex in high good humor, for an Oedipus unable to resist making puns. The spectacles put on to celebrate directresses' birthdays in our young ladies' boarding schools must always include a Cleopatra or an Antigone, and certainly the immolation of one such, the passionate variety or the pure, is absolutely necessary to the pervading gaiety, as much so as the sacrifice of an Iphigenia was necessary to the schemes of the Greek pantheon. Our greatest poet of the past is a tragic poet as he will be of the future: our greatest actors have always been the actors of tragedy: our great men, from Napoleon to Renan, in their theatre have cared only for tragedy. Should you, inadvertently, as I did not very long ago, open a drawer belonging to the most up-to-date minister of the arts, you would very likely find in it the script of a tragedy, interspersed of course with a memorandum of some official conference at Toulouse. And when a young poet dies untimely, as did Pierre Frayssinet at twenty-five, his brief life through its catholicity of interests and the purity of its lyric gift becoming straightway a symbol for present youth, we find, after his passing, that those of his own works he most admired, the only ones he finished, were three tragedies, *Alcestis, Admetus, Ajax.* . . . I am thinking of the most recent line of verse written in France, the most youthful, the most promising. It is a tragic verse.

So we have this question: how is it that the land for tragedy is not the land of the tragical? How is it that the country of every kind of human freedom is the very country which has assured the survival of a super-human tyranny? A country where trees are trees, where the sky is the sky and not a skyscraper mobbed in its upper reaches, where bulls are bulls and not minotaurs, has found it possible to offer to the most extravagant of legendary fictions a refuge, an arena not inferior to the homeland's where nature stood for something invisible and inaccessible. Indisputably, the Greek gods and heroes have been truly made to feel at home only in the country of Voltaire and Renan, yet not theirs alone, the country also of the bourgeois from Bellac and from the neighborhood of the Bastille. What is the reason?

The reason is that in France—and so it was in Greece—not misfortune and not any sense of fatality is what sends people, either as individuals or in the mass, to the theatre to relish a tragedy; on the contrary, it is a satisfaction in the soul, and ease of circumstance. Finding himself in a bad seat at the theatre, a Frenchman may yet appreciate the play well enough; but not at all, from an uncomfortable situation in life. If he submits to the tragedy's affects, it is not because he chooses to see in it his own destiny unfold through the destinies of more exalted personalities; rather, the anguishment of remorse, the impulses of gratitude, are his to enjoy watching how in the name of Philoctetes, or Samson, or Agamemnon, the ransoms are paid inside the theatre which will redeem his private peace of mind outside it. To talk literature: the extraordinary resemblance of Greek to French thought comes precisely from the distinction made formidably by both between the dramatic character and the living man, though they seem to have arrived at the same point from opposite directions, the Greeks from the structure of Olympus, the French from that of the bourgeois class. France and Greece both introduced into their cultures the notion of the idea which acts, man its spectator or reader—that is to say, they introduced the true notion of what a spectator is, of what reading is.

A Frenchman does not go to the theatre—and no Greek ever did—thinking to absorb from a tragedy some kind of moral good, or discover in it some configuration of his own life. The German at the theatre becomes Siegfried, becomes Werther, whichever the play. No Athenian ever dreamed of identifying himself with Oedipus, no Parisian with Britannicus: there the Frenchman sits, out of some strange egoism, or a curious altruism, impelled to endure sufferings—but only those of others. A sort of diffidence, humility indeed, forbids seeing himself in personages so very exalted, their destiny in hot pursuit of them. At most, he might grant such an identification to a sovereign, as when he chooses to see Louis XIV in Titus or La Vallière in Bérénice. The crowds pressing before our arenas, or inside the Comédie-Française, are very

38

little like the spectators who silently file into the theatres at Bayreuth or Munich, anxious, as if about to undergo an experience that will alter character and destiny. Silent and respectful the French audience will also be, from the moment the opening speech is heard; but up until then, they must laugh, banter, pelt each other with the oranges that have to make do in southern France for snowballs. The first actor appears, and all personal comes to a halt. Attention is now on the stage heroes and heroines, who to the audience are a sort of army of gladiators for letting the wild beasts loose on: certainly not the four-legged kind, but the ferocious enough ones—if I may repeat my metaphor—of the human destiny, the human heart. Does a tragedy by Silvain or Poizat have as much drawing power as one by Racine or Sophocles, it is because the hero alone counts, as only the bull counts, or only the gladiator. How that hero will stand up to yet another incarnation of fate cannot cease to be interesting; and so much is guaranteed, that inside this ring the bulls which are named incest, jealousy, pride, come what may, will be met with the finest of combat from such a lineup of antagonists as Oedipus, Ajax, Athaliah, whose capabilities of endurance and courage are as well known to the aficionados at Saintes, at Orange or the Palais-Royal, as those of the Miura bulls to their Spanish breeders. Thus, in the masses an innocence of the literary plus their natural modesty, and in the elite their sophisticated overpreoccupation with literature plus the rule of expertise, conjoining, have worked toward this singular achievement, setting apart a segment of humanity to specialize in superior sufferings, to receive and endure fate's direst turns: whereby the world divides into a limited number of actors and countless spectators—but right here is the definition of tragedy. Add the love of speech and speechifying which the tragic hero—and the Greek citizen—shares with the Frenchman; add also a preference for verbal décor and the atmosphere of resounding names from history, as against any of those mechanical stage trappings that must only interfere with the process of a sublime digestion which the tragic spectacle exacts—and you have the explanation for the living presence, in France, of tragedy.

Such is the truth of Bellac, and of France. And when toward twilight of an evening in the spring of 1621, the tailor Jacques Rondeau from the town of Montmorillon, the curé Pierre Retonnau, and the woodseller Mathurin Cognac from Chauvigny, arrived at the flatland bordering on the Gartempe and which is dominated by Bellac, and came upon a great crowd where to one side stood a lady, in a long-trained robe of black, broidered in hearts, torches, and teardrops of white satin, surrounded by a bevy of bare-limbed maidens carrying earthenware jugs that emitted smoke; and, to the other side, a goddess crowned with flowers who in her outstretched arms bore a great branch of cypress dangling a multitude of tiny crystals, she flanked by eight fine fellows naked to the waist, brandishing clubs: our countrymen were not, as they thought they were, seeing a sign from heaven in the shape of this procession, but only Proserpine and Ceres, together with all their company, proclaiming there, before the Lower Marche sank into a final decline, the apotheosis of the Periclean Age of Bellac.

Translated by Sherry Abel

The Christian Tragic Hero:

Contrasting Captain Ahab's Doom and Its Classic Greek Prototype

W. H. AUDEN

MOBY DICK is at once an heroic epic like the *Iliad*, an heroic tragedy like the *Oresteia*, an heroic quest like the legend of the *Golden Fleece*, and an allegorical religious quest like *Pilgrim's Progress;* it is also a nineteenth century American novel. Even if it were not the great book it is, it would therefore be of unusual interest to the critic who would compare the values believed in and the attitudes held at different stages in Western civilization. I propose in this article to consider only one of them, the concept of the Tragic Hero in Greece and in Christendom. Most of the characteristics one observes in Melville's hero can also be seen in, say, the heroes of Shakespeare's tragedies, but Melville's choral asides make them more explicit in his own case.

To sum up in advance, the conclusions I shall try to demonstrate are these: first, Greek is the tragedy of necessity; i.e., the feeling aroused in the spectator is "What a pity it had to be this way"; Christian tragedy is the tragedy of possibility, "What a pity it was this way when it might have been otherwise"; secondly, the hubris which is the flaw in the Greek hero's character is the illusion of a man who knows himself strong and believes that nothing can shake that strength, while the corresponding Christian sin of Pride is the illusion of a man who knows himself weak but believes he can by his own efforts transcend that weakness and become strong.

In using the term Christian I am not trying to suggest that Melville or Shakespeare or any other author necessarily believed the Christian dogmas, but that their conception of man's nature is, historically, derived from them.

As an example of Greek tragedy let us take *Oedipus Rex*. As a young man, Oedipus learns from a prophecy that he is fated to murder his father and marry his mother. Believing that his foster parents are his real parents he leaves Corinth. He meets an old man on the road; they quarrel about who shall give way to the other, and Oedipus kills him. He comes to Thebes, saves it from a monster, and is rewarded by the hand of its Queen, Jocasta. Thebes is stricken with plague, and the Oracle declares the cause to be the undetected presence of a criminal. Oedipus undertakes an investigation and discovers that the criminal is himself. In expiation of his crime he puts out his eyes, and Jocasta hangs herself.

A modern reader, accustomed to the tragedy of possibility, instinctively asks, "Where and when did he make the wrong choice?" and as instinctively answers, "He should not have listened to the prophecy in the first place, or, having done so, then he should never have struck the old man or anyone else and should never have married Jocasta or anyone else." But such thoughts would never have occurred to Sophocles or his audience. Macbeth and Captain Ahab are wrong to listen to the prophecies about them, because they are equivocal, and each reads into his a possibility he is wrong to desire; the prophecy Oedipus hears is not only unequivocal but something he is right to wish to avoid. When he kills the old man he feels no guilt, neither is he expected to feel any, and when he marries Jocasta there is nothing the matter with the relation as such. It is only when it turns out that, as a matter of fact, the former was his father and the latter is his mother that guilt begins.

The tragedy is that what had to happen happened, and if one asks what was wrong with Oedipus, that such a terrible fate should be assigned to him, one can only say that it is a punishment for a hubris which was necessarily his before he learnt of the prophecy at all; i.e., had he not had such a character, the prophecy would never have been made.

Other Greek heroes are faced with the tragic choice between two evils: Agamemnon must either sacrifice his daughter or fail in his duty to the Greek Army; Antigone must be false either to her loyalty to her brother or to her loyalty to her city.

The tragic situation, of learning that one is a criminal or of being forced to become one, is not created by the flaw in the hero's character, but is sent him by the gods as a punishment for having such a flaw.

The pessimistic conclusion that underlies Greek tragedy seems to be this: that if one is a hero, i.e., an exceptional individual, one must be guilty of hubris and be punished by a tragic fate; the only alternative and not one a person can choose for himself is to be a member of the chorus, i.e., one of the average mass; to be both exceptional and good is impossible.

How does "Moby Dick" compare with this?

The hero, Captain Ahab, far from being exceptionally fortunate, is at the beginning, what in a Greek tragedy he could only be at the end, exceptionally unfortunate. He is already the victim of what the modern newspaper, which is Greek in this respect, would call a tragedy; a whale has bitten off his leg. What to the Greeks could only have been a punishment for sin is here a temptation to sin, an opportunity to choose; by making the wrong choice and continuing to make it, Ahab punished himself. To say that a character is tempted means that it is confronted by possibility, that it is not a fixed state but a process of becoming; the possibilities are not infinite; i.e., Ahab cannot become Starbuck or Pip or Ishmael or anyone else except Ahab, but the possibilities are eternal; the past is irrevocable but always redeemable now.

Thus we can at every moment answer the question, "What should Ahab do now?" Before the story opens he has suffered and made his first wrong choice. He was not wrong to make Moby Dick into a symbol of all the inexplicable suffering in the world; on the contrary, the capacity to see the universal in the particular is the mark of human greatness, and it is only Flask, the Philistine trimmer, who says, "A whale is only a whale"; he was wrong, however, to insist on his own explanation, that the motive behind the whale's act and behind all suffering is personal malevolence. Once he has done so, he can still be saved, but he has made his salvation a much harder task, for he is now required to forgive the whale personally, in contrast, for instance, to Captain Boomer, who, like Ahab, has been deprived of a limb by Moby Dick, but in his pragmatic English way explains the whale's ferocity as mere clumsiness which is easier to forgive than malice.

In Greek tragedy are two kinds of characters, the exceptional hero and the average chorus, and neither can become the other; in Christian tragedy there is not only an infinite variety of possible characters, varying all the way from Ahab, the captain, who defiantly insists on being absolutely unique, down to Pip, the cabin boy, who is too afraid to claim even his own name, but overshadowing them all is the possibility of each becoming both exceptional and good; this ultimate possibility for hero and chorus alike is stated in Father Mapple's sermon, and it is to become a saint—i.e., the individual who of his own free will surrenders his will to the will of God. In this surrender he does not become a ventriloquist's doll, for the God who acts through him can only do so by his consent; there always remain two wills, and the saint, therefore (unlike the late Greek conception of the undramatic Sage who is good by necessity because he knows), never ceases to be tempted to obey his own desires.

Of this possibility Ahab's career is at every point a negative parody.

The saint does not ask to be one, he is called to become one, and assents to the call. The outward sign that Ahab is so called, is the suffering which is suddenly intruded into his life. What he is called to become, we do not, of course, know for certain—all we know for certain is that he rejected it—but we can guess that he was called to give up hunting whales—i.e., the normal cannibalistic life of this world, a life which is permitted, for instance, to Queequeg (who, though sinless, is not a saint, but the innocent man before the fall) but no longer to Ahab once he has been made uniquely conscious of the suffering it inflicts. Of the others, less is required: of Starbuck that he face evil instead of superstitiously avoiding it, of Stubb that he face his fears instead of whistling in the dark; but of Ahab alone is required, because he alone has the necessary heroic passion, to become a real and not a merely respectable Quaker.

Ahab is not deaf; he hears the call and refuses it with all the passion with which he might have accepted it; like the saint he wills one thing—to kill Moby Dick. For this he leaves his wife and child; for this his first act in the book is to throw away his pipe, his last physical addiction, his last relation with the elements of earth; for this he destroys the ship's quadrant, its relation to the element of air so that the Pequod can only know the universe through compass and line in terms of the dualistic antagonism of fire and water.

The saint, knowing his will to be weak, may express his external resolve by a temporal or bodily ritual act, but his vow and his act concern his own will alone. Ahab attempts to use ritual as a magical means of compelling the wills of others, as when he forces the crew to swear on their harpoons, and finally even to compel lifeless things, as when he baptizes a harpoon itself.

Just as the saint never ceases to be tempted to forsake his calling, so, vice versa, Ahab is never free from the possibility of renouncing his refusal. Divine grace offers itself, now in the nostalgic beauty of fine weather, now as Gabriel, the mad idolater of the whale, an unlovely reflection of himself, and finally, in its strongest and least disguised form, as the cry for help of a friend in distress when the Pequod meets the Rachel, and it is only after he has refused this last offer that his doom becomes necessary. Melville portrays this decisive change with great subtlety. For it is at this point that Ahab places the idiot Pip in his cabin and, in a grotesque parody of the saint as the servant of servants, takes for himself the humble position of lookout on the mast which is the negative image of the martyr's cross. Instead of gaining a martyr's crown, however, his hat, the badge of his authority, is snatched from his head by the Jovian eagle, and from this moment Fedallah, the slave, the projection of Ahab's will, seems suddenly to have taken charge of his creator, or rather his summoner. Fedallah is clearly intended by Melville, I think, to represent the demonic, i.e., that which (unlike Ahab, who is tempted by suffering) tempts itself and denies for the sake of denying, and about which, therefore, nothing historic can be said; we are only told his religion.

So Ahab, refusing life, goes unrepentant, like all of Shakespeare's tragic heroes, to the unnecessary death he has chosen, dragging with him all his companions, and the only survivor is, as in Greek tragedy, the Chorus, the spectator, Ishmael. But Ishmael is not, like the Greek Chorus, the eternal average man, for he isn't a character at all. To be a character one must will and act, and Ishmael has no will, only consciousness; he does not act, he only knows, and what he knows is good *and* evil, i.e., possibility. He cannot die because he has not yet begun to live, and he ends the book as a baby, reborn from the sea in Queequeg's coffin, thrust back into life as an orphan with his first choice still to make.

Andromaque

LUCIEN GOLDMANN

BEFORE STUDYING the play itself, I must say something about Racine's prefaces. For the sociologist, they are, of course, texts of a completely different nature from his plays. The plays represent a world of beings, objects and relationships which must be analysed from the point of view of their structure and meaning; the prefaces, on the other hand, merely express the writer's own ideas and his attitude towards his work. And although they are extremely interesting and cannot in any way be ignored, there is no real reason why what they say should be absolutely correct, or why Racine should have understood the meaning and objective structure of his own works. There is nothing absurd about the idea of a writer or poet who does not understand the objective meaning of his work. Conceptual thought and literary creation are two completely different intellectual activities, which can, of course, be combined in one person, but which by no means are necessarily found together.[1] However, even when this does not happen, the theoretical writings of an author are very important for any study of his work, for even though they may not bring out his objective meaning, they do nevertheless reflect many of the problems which he had to face while he was actually writing. However, in this case we must read them not in order to discover reliable theoretical information, but particular symptoms. We must not only understand them, but also interpret them in the light of the completed work. In doing so, we shall take account of Racine the individual only in so far as he is the author of aesthetically valid plays, for the rest of his personality remains foreign to this type of investigation.

We should note that, adopting Aristotle's opinion, Racine

---

[1] In a letter to the abbé Le Vasseur, Racine himself points out that this difference exists when he writes that: "Poets are like hypocrites in this, that they always defend what they do, but are never left in peace by their own conscience." Letter dating from 1659 or 1660. Cf. *Oeuvres*, Mesnard edition, Vol. VI, p. 372.

maintains in the preface to both *Andromaque* and *Phèdre* that tragic characters, that is to say "those whose misfortune constitutes the tragic catastrophe" are "neither wholly good nor wholly evil". It is a formula which did apply to many Greek tragedies, and which is still partially applicable to *Andromaque*; it is not, however, a valid description either of Junia or Titus, both of whom are wholly good, or of Phaedra, whose only real characteristic is that she is "wholly good and wholly evil at one and the same time". From the point of view of Racinian tragedy, the expression "neither wholly good nor wholly evil" also applies to the majority of the inhabitants of this world; and it is this qualitative distinction between tragic man and the man who lives in this world, a distinction peculiar to modern tragedy, which differentiates it from the tragedy of classical Greece. As far as dramatic technique is concerned, this difference can be seen in the fact that the chorus is as indispensable to a classical tragedy as it is inconceivable in a play by Racine. I shall come back to this point when I discuss *Britannicus,* and it goes without saying that I reserve judgment on the problem of *Esther* and *Athalie*.

In his views on his own characters, Racine contradicts himself in the two prefaces which he wrote for *Andromaque*. Thus, in 1668 he justifies his presentation of Pyrrhus as a violent man by the argument that "violence was a natural part of his character" and that he, Racine, does not want to alter the character of his classical heroes. However, in 1676 he says that he has "respected the idea that we have of that Princess" by making Andromache faithful to Hector. We can conclude from this that he followed the laws of his own universe by expanding the moral grandeur of Andromache in order to emphasise the radical difference between her and Pyrrhus.

In this play only two characters are really present: the world and Andromache. There is, however, one other character who is both absent and present at one and the same time, the God whose two irreconcilable faces are incarnated by Hector and Astyanax, and by the contradictory and therefore impossible demands which they both make.

It is obvious that Hector already foreshadows the God of *Britannicus* and *Phèdre*, but without, however, coinciding with him completely. For *Andromaque* is still a drama, in spite of its great closeness to tragedy.

The world is represented by three psychologically different characters, for Racine creates beings who are alive and vividly individualised, but who are nevertheless morally identical by their absence of awareness and human greatness.

Thus, the differences between Pyrrhus, on the one hand, and Orestes and Hermione, on the other, exist only for the spectator who adopts an attitude of psychological analysis which is external to the work. What characterises tragedy and provides its real perspective is a primacy accorded to ethics, and to an ethical system which does not admit degrees of difference. People either have authentic awareness or else they lack it completely, in exactly the same way as Pascal's God is both present and absent, unreachable and even unapproachable through any spirituality or any paths of gradualness or degree.

The basic pattern of the play is that of any Racinian tragedy. Andromache is faced with a choice between two alternatives—faithfulness to Hector, life for Astyanax—which are both equally essential for her moral and human universe. This is why her final choice can only be death, for only death can save both of these antagonistic but, at the same time, inseparable values.

Yet in spite of the fact that she is the only human character in the play, Andromache is not the central one. She is on the periphery of the real centre of the play, which is the world. Or, in more concrete terms, the world made up of the wild animals inhabiting a universe of love and passion.

It would, however, be wrong to draw a rigorous distinction between the passion which characterises Pyrrhus, Orestes and Hermione, and which is lacking in both greatness and self-awareness, from the other domains of life. Throughout the play, the background of war, barbarism, the murder of the vanquished and the ruins of Troy, all show us that people who are wild animals in the realm of passion are also egotists who, devoid of any genuine ethical norm, thereby fall only too easily into savagery in all life's other domains.[2] This can be seen particularly clearly in the speech where Andromache recalls the horrors of the sack of Troy, the killing of a whole people in a single, interminable night and the figure of Pyrrhus, covered with blood, his eyes gleaming in the light of the burning palaces, cutting a path for himself over her brothers' dead bodies and urging on to further slaughter; where she reminds her *confidente*, Céphise, of the screams of the conquerors and of those choked with flame or put to the edge of

---

[2] It is not a valid objection to this argument to point out that these were normal customs for the Greeks and that our own moral judgments are therefore anachronistic. In the first place the play was written in the seventeenth century, and in the second place these judgments are expressed within the play itself, and therefore do not need to be brought in from the outside.

the sword; where she asks her to try to imagine with what horror she, her mistress Andromache, saw such horror—and then to understand how Pyrrhus must now appear before her[3] (Act III, Scene 8, ll. 997-1006).

The world of Orestes, Hermione and Pyrrhus is already that of *Britannicus*, the play in which Nero is under the power of the same amoral and unreflecting love that we find in these three characters from *Andromaque*. We find the same world in all Racine's plays, each of which differs from its fellows, from this point of view, solely by emphasising a different aspect of it.

It thus becomes an easy and almost an obvious task to analyse the speeches and actions of the characters. Both Orestes and Pyrrhus are confronted with an alternative, but neither of them has a single reaction worthy of a man who has attained authentic awareness. Although to do so would still be inadequate within the Racinian universe, they cannot even openly and deliberately choose one of the two alternatives confronting them. They go constantly from one extreme to the other, impelled not by their own decisions but by external events, and they most frequently contradict both their own statements and their own desires. Ostensibly, Orestes has come to demand Astyanax, the son of Hector whom the Greeks still fear as a possible avenger of his country's defeat; in reality, this mission is merely an unimportant pretext, a lie; the only thing that really matters to him is his love for Hermione, and he tells us so in the very first scene, when he confides to Pylades both his intention to take Hermione away with him and his readiness to sacrifice his official mission to his private desires (Act I, Scene 1, ll. 93-4 and 100).

We are also told, in the same scene, that Pyrrhus is characterised by the complete absence of any conscious and controlling norm, and that he is quite capable of "marrying where he hates and killing where he loves" (l. 122). The same thing is true of Hermione, whom Pylades describes as "constantly ready to leave yet still remaining" (l. 131). Similarly, the dialogue between Pyrrhus and Orestes is also introduced in exactly the same way, with Pylades advising Orestes to "ask insistently for everything in order to obtain nothing" (Act I, Scene 1, l. 140).

Thus, with Hermione, Orestes and Pyrrhus we are in the

[3] Cf. also what Pyrrhus says in Act I, Scene 2, 1. 209. "Everything was just at that time"—i.e. at the moment of the sacking of Troy. All references to the text of Racine's plays are to the *Grands Ecrivains de France* edition (Hachette, 1929).

world of mere words and of false awareness. Words never mean what they say, and, instead of being the means whereby the speaker expresses his inner and authentic essence, they become merely instruments that he uses to deceive others and to deceive himself. This is the false and savage world of inessentiality, the world of the difference between essences and appearances.

But in Scene 4, Andromache appears and the atmosphere changes. Her arrival takes us into the world of absolute truths, the world without compromises of the tragic hero. Pyrrhus derives no advantage from the fact of being her master, the man on whom her own life and that of her son depend, for when he greets her with the hope that, for once, she has come in search of him, her reply is clear and unequivocal, uninfluenced by all the dangers he is facing. "I was going," she tells him, "to the place where my son is kept. Since I am allowed only once a day to see all that remains to me of Hector and of Troy, I was going to weep with him." (Act I, Scene 4, ll. 260-4).

The clash between the two characters could not be more complete, and what follows is quite foreseeable from the very beginning. Pyrrhus—the world—tells her of Orestes's mission, the dangers which it involves for Astyanax, and offers her the possibility of a compromise. He will refuse to hand over Astyanax, but—and in the world of Pyrrhus there is always a "but"—on one condition: that she should look "less severely" upon the man who "defends her son's life at the cost of danger to his own" (ll. 290-4). His initial refusal to Orestes was, for all its appearance of finality, merely a ruse intended to influence Andromache. He now asks for his reward, and it is at this point that the play, which had begun as a tragedy, starts to become a drama. Andromache's reply, although possessing at first sight the absolute veracity which characterises the tragic hero, already contains the seed of her future "sin" or "tragic error." She confronts Pyrrhus with the demands of human greatness and of human morality when she asks him if it is really his intention to defy the enmity of a hundred different peoples solely in order to defend a child, and to give back a son to his mother without demanding that his mother marry him in return. This, indeed, she suggests would be a task worthy of Achilles' son (Act I, Scene 4, ll. 296-300).

Andromache really does believe everything which she says here, and is expressing her own values and her own very essence. This is how she would act if she were in the same position as Pyrrhus. But she neither has nor can have any illusions about the possibility of making him understand what she is saying since the world of absolute truth is one which he cannot even begin to understand. Nevertheless, she pretends to be really talking to him and to be in complete good faith. There is thus, in this speech of hers to Pyrrhus, an element of irony or trickery about her words, for she is talking to a wild animal as if she were speaking to a man.

For the truly tragic character, this is indeed a "moral error," or a "fall from grace," but it remains extremely slight, even in the projected marriage with Pyrrhus later in the play. Andromache foreshadows Phaedra, but only in so far as she herself is not taken in by the illusion of being able to live in the world and be reconciled with it. What she is trying to gain by deceiving Pyrrhus are merely the conditions that would make her refusal of the world not merely morally great but also effective. What she wants to do is triumph materially over the world at the very moment she is crushed by it.

This is why Andromache does not finally enter into the tragic universe to which she comes so very close. The difference is certainly a very small one, but it does exist. And in the world of tragedy the slightest difference weighs as heavily as the greatest. There is not, and there cannot be, any progressive scale of values between appearances and essences or between truth and treachery.

We have, moreover, an indication that Racine himself was aware of these problems: it is the differences between the way the first tragedy ended in the 1668 edition and the ending given to it in all the editions after 1673.

The world of a literary work is a single coherent whole. If *Andromaque* were to remain a tragedy Racine would be obliged to treat Andromache, from the fourth scene of the first act, as a tragic heroine who ends as Phaedra does by recognising her error. Racine was still a long way from such a maturity, and, even if he did consider this way of presenting Andromache, we have no evidence to prove it. What he did do, however, was become aware that a tragic ending to such a situation would destroy the coherence of the rest of the work, and draw logical conclusions from this realisation. In the first, 1668, version he inserted a scene in which Hermione liberated the captive Andromache. Nevertheless, he also probably felt the inconsistency that this introduced between the irreconcilable conflict of the first three acts and the final reconciliation which it would thereby bring about between Andromache and Hermione.

50

This is why he modified his text and replaced this ending by the version which we now have. Although this is not tragic, it does maintain, if not the opposition between Andromache and the world, then at least the difference between her and the three other characters who represent the world in this play.

I will resume my argument: Andromache is tragic in so far as she refuses the alternatives, and confronts the world with her voluntary refusal of life and her freely accepted choice of death. She ceases to be tragic, however, when she decides to accept marriage with Pyrrhus and then kill herself, thus trying to transform her moral victory into a material victory which will live on after her. The play is thus a tragedy which, in the last two acts, suddenly becomes a drama. This is possibly the reason why Racine decided to treat the same theme for a second time in a purely and exclusively tragic perspective in *Britannicus*.

I will now continue the analysis of the text at the point at which I broke off. Naturally, Pyrrhus does not understand what Andromache is saying, and this is quite natural. He sees only that she is refusing his offer and therefore concludes that he has no further reason to protect Astyanax. He even says that this is "just"—by the standards of this world, of course—when he proclaims that in his "righteous indignation" he will use the son to revenge himself for the scorn shown by the mother (Act I, Scene 4, ll. 369-71).

As far as Andromache is concerned, she now rediscovers her own universe. Her reply is quite clear, and she accepts the fact that her son's death will follow naturally from the impossibility of any compromise (l. 372).

But Pyrrhus, who judges Andromache according to the laws of his own world (and he is not entirely wrong to do so), asks her to go and see Astyanax again, hoping that this will induce her to change her mind.

Act II marks the appearance of Hermione, the third character who constitutes the world. Like Pyrrhus and Orestes, she lacks real awareness and human greatness and I shall show this by analysing two aspects of her personality.

She is afraid of the truth, and would like to be deceived in order to be able to deceive herself. Indeed, in the very first scene in which we see her she is telling her *confidente* Cleone that she is "afraid to know herself in her present state," and asking Cleone to "believe nothing of what she sees at the present moment"; to "believe that her love is dead, to proclaim her victory," and "if possible, to make her believe it also" (Act II, Scene 1, ll. 428-32).

The greatness of tragic man lies in his clear and unambiguous awareness of his own condition. Those characters who represent the world, on the other hand, lack greatness precisely because they refuse to become completely aware of their situation, and are afraid to discover the definitive and inexorable nature of the position in which they are placed.

Hermione is also characterised by her desire to run away from reality, and the theme is a particularly important one, since it recurs in *Phèdre*, in the character of Hippolytus. For example, when Cleone proposes in the first scene of Act II that Hermione should reply to Pyrrhus's neglect of her by departing with Orestes, she immediately accepts—at least in principle—but only to hesitate again at the idea that Pyrrhus might come back to her. What in fact she does is to remain, but without becoming fully aware of the danger and of facing up to it. It is, indeed, precisely because she does not understand the real situation and because she allows herself to be deceived by the illusion to which her love for Pyrrhus gives rise that she in fact decides to stay.

We find this same lack of awareness and human greatness in Orestes, Pyrrhus and Hermione through the play.

Orestes gives his own description of himself as a person who always does the opposite of what he means to do when he tells Hermione, in the second scene of Act II, that his destiny is "constantly to return to adore her, while at the time swearing that he will never come back again" (l. 484) and in Act II, Scene 5 we find exactly the same failure on the part of Pyrrhus to understand the universe in which Andromache lives. Similarly, in Act III, Scene 1 we find the same illusions occurring in Orestes, and the same refusal to accord any importance to the diplomatic mission which he had nevertheless accepted, when he tells Pylades that Hermione will still enjoy his misfortune, however much the Greeks may triumph over the death of Astyanax (1. 766).

We also find Hermione lying in the same way to Orestes, and making him think that she might love him, and still keeping the same illusions about the feeling which Pyrrhus has for her (Act III, Scene 3). She shows her cowardice, when she thinks that she has triumphed over Andromache (Act III, Scene 4); and the unchanging attitude of Pyrrhus towards Andromache reaches its highest point when, in Act III, Scene 7, he offers her in its most absolute form the alternative that the world represents for Andromache: either live or die, either live or reign, save Astyanax and save yourself at the same time (l. 960).

Cephise even finds a Pascalian-like phrase to describe Andromache's situation when, discussing the choice before her, she tells her that "too much virtue would lead you to act as a criminal" (Act III, Scene 8, l. 982).

Andromache turns for advice to the supreme authority, to the absent being who judges everything but never replies: finally, she decides to visit Hector's tomb in order to discover what his will might be (Act III, Scene 8, l. 1048).

But the play is not a tragedy, and unlike the God of tragedy, Hector does not remain a silent and passive spectator. He intervenes in the action, as Racine indicates quite clearly when he makes Cephise tell Andromache, in the very first line of Act IV, Scene 1, that her "miraculous" decision to marry Pyrrhus has been inspired by Hector (l. 1049).

Neither is Andromache a genuine tragic heroine. The decision which she takes on Hector's tomb is certainly a great and courageous one, since it will enable her to sacrifice herself in order to save Astyanax's life while at the same time remaining faithful to her husband. There is almost nothing in common between her sacrifice and the self-centred behaviour of Pyrrhus, Orestes and Hermione, but there is nevertheless a common element, and it is this, however slight it may be, which is sufficient to eliminate true tragedy from the play. Andromache will indulge in trickery in order to transform her death into a material victory over the world.

Her decision to do this, which is the decisive turning-point in the play, is announced in two lines, the first of which prepares us for it, while the second expresses it completely, with all the consequences that it involves. We appear, indeed, to be entering into the universe of tragedy when she tells Cephise that she will go to the temple where the wedding is to be held, but that before this she is going to see her son "for the last time." She then explains the solution she has found, the trick which will enable her, by killing herself immediately after becoming Pyrrhus's wife, to do her duty towards "Pyrrhus, my son, my husband and myself" (l. 1096).

This second line would be wholly tragic if, among the people to whom she owes something, there were not Pyrrhus, a being of this world. This distance which separates her from Pyrrhus still exists, and will even continue to do so until the very end of the play; it has, however, become smaller than it was, and is contradicted by the link between her and Pyrrhus that will continue to exist after her own death.

The whole of this distance and drawing together, of this conflict and link, is expressed in a single line. Giving her instructions to Cephise on what is to be done after her death, Andromache tells her that she agrees "if it is necessary" that her name should sometimes be mentioned to her son (l. 1118).

"If it is necessary" represents the distance, the inner opposition which Andromache feels for any contact with Pyrrhus; her "agreement" expresses the rest. For Andromache can kill herself, not because, like Junia, Bérénice and Phaedra, she has refused the world, but because on the contrary, she is counting on the loyalty which Pyrrhus will continue to show to her after her death. In fact, she could just as well continue to live in the world, and it is even her duty to do so, since there is nothing at all in Pyrrhus's character to justify the hope which she places in him. He would be just as capable of avenging himself by handing Astyanax over to the Greeks in a fit of anger at the way Andromache has deceived him. Andromache has used trickery, and this is why she might now be tricked herself. In spite of all her moral greatness, she does, in a way, come to fit into the world. This is probably the real reason why, in order not to contradict the general atmosphere of the play, Racine makes Pyrrhus die and Andromache live on. It also explains why he maintains Andromache's moral and material greatness intact by making Pyrrhus, Hermione and Orestes either die or plunge into madness. On the material plane, Andromache's victory is certain. The last two lines of the play tell us that the only reason why Orestes is still alive is that he has gone mad. In Andromache's world—and Pylades's words at the end of the play, telling us that Andromache is now reigning as queen and observing an absolute fidelity to the memory of Pyrrhus, indicate that it is this world which has quite simply taken over from that of Pyrrhus—there can no longer be any place for a living Pyrrhus or for Hermione; neither could there be any place for an Orestes who was still capable of acting with the same ferocious absence of awareness that characterised him when, theoretically at least, he was still sane.

Was Racine himself aware that this is what happened in his play? Would he have accepted the analysis that I have just given of it? Did he, in his own life, quite simply accept the moral laws which govern the lives of Junia, Bérénice and Phaedra? In fact, we simply do not know. The problem is one which only scholars, and psychologists who accept the idea of retrospective analysis, can hope to discuss. The probability is, however, that he would have rejected it. Nicole and Mother Agnès de Sainte-Thècle were even more justified than they realised in attacking Racine for writing for the theatre. For, in composing his tragedies, Racine—fortunately for posterity— was not only going against the moral principles of Jansenism but was also contradicting his own ideas. He was presenting the world with a universe where true greatness could be found only in a refusal of the world. A psychologist might perhaps conclude that, in order to write these tragedies, Racine would in fact have been obliged to know and understand Andromache, Junia, Bérénice and Phaedra, but without identifying himself with their moral universe; that, in other words, he would need to have been a member of Port-Royal but to have now left it behind him. These questions are not relevant to my purpose, and I am not competent to decide them. My only reason for raising this problem is to insist upon the fact that, in order to create a coherent universe of beings and things, the writer does not need to have a conceptual knowledge of this universe, and, above all, does not need to accept it himself. Literary history is full of examples of writers whose ideas completely contradicted the meaning and structure of their work (Balzac and Goethe, for example). We must therefore conclude that the analysis of a work of art and the study of its author's ideas belong to two different domains. These, it is true, can be treated as complementary, and facts from one can be used to throw light upon facts from the other, but we must not expect our results always and necessarily to agree when we do this.

This is why the analysis which I am putting forward in this book does not claim to make any statements at all about the moral and religious views of Racine himself. It is merely an analysis of the universe of his plays, a universe which is one of the most rigorously coherent to be found in world literature.

Translated by Philip Thody

Character Change and the Drama

HAROLD ROSENBERG

*We have already seen Bernard change; passions
may come that will modify him still more.*
Gide, *The Counterfeiters*

I

AN EGG with an ancestry, developing, changing its form,
maturing—later, degenerating, dying, decaying, again changing its form—all in a slow gradual way, with but few shocks
like birth and death, such in broadest outline is the career
of the personality, the regular ego, which the organic point of
view, expressed most often in those studies of mutation,
biology, history, biography and associated subjects, finally
presents before us. Whatever unity an organism maintains
at the base of its transformations is something mysterious; an
organism may be arranged with reference to other organisms
with which it sustains resemblances, it may be classified, noted
statistically, or subsumed under an imagined archetype, but
its individual unity can only be "felt." From the viewpoint of
the human person himself, his coherence is, as Herbert Read
has put it, "an organic coherence intuitively based on the real
world of sensation."[1]

On the other hand, the concepts of morality or social law,
specializing in the human and ignoring any possible connection with "things," tend to define the individual not as an
enduring historical entity but by what he has done in given
instances. A special sequence of acts provokes a judgment,
and this judgment is an inseparable part of the recognition of
the individual. Here too there is no final comprehension of
individuals; but whereas the historical approach, even when
it reaches mechanistic conclusions, points toward the existence
of individuals, who, however, can be grasped singly only by
a non-rational operation, social legality acts as though it were
unaware of them altogether except as they are completely
defined by their "overt acts." If the law is not always satisfied
with itself, it is not because it has at any time still to discover
something about the nature of individuals, but for the reason
that it realizes all at once that acts are being performed which
it has no means of controlling.

[1] "Personality in Literature," *The Symposium*, July, 1931.

The law pronounces, or should pronounce, its judgments and penalties with regard only to the acts of individuals and without recognition of the individuals as persons; its judgments are applied at the end of a series of acts. Thus the law creates a definite fiction, an individual who is identified by the coherence of his acts with a fact in which they have terminated (a crime or a contract, for example) and by nothing else. The judgment is the resolution of these acts; the law visualizes the individual as a sort of actor with a role, and its judgment relates him finally to the broader, more universal system of the legal code. This assertion that the individual is what we may call an identity in contrast with a personality, that is, one defined solely by the coherence of his action with an adjudged fact and not by the continuity of his being, is entirely contradictory to the biological or historical organism-concept, which visualizes action as serving for a clue to the existence and endurance of a thing *in esse* whose real definition can only be attained by an intuition.

The modern novel, which contains most of what we have today in the way of dramatic literature, has more in common with the historical or biological view of character than with the legal. Consider *Ulysses, The Magic Mountain,* or *Remembrance of Things Past:* in the growing and decaying of their characters, the portrayal of organic texture and change is of the essence of the attempt.

As for the legal definition, it seems at first glance to be far removed from the needs of literary fiction, since it stands ready with its systematic chopping-block to execute come who may on the basis of his most easily definable acts and without consideration of the finer points of his feeling or motive. Only action which is "relevant and material" to the fact to be judged can the party to a suit plead as bearing on his status. The law is forever fixed to that edge of individuality where the particular is caught in the web of the abstract and is shifted against its will into a position where it can only suffer and be tortured by the contradiction between its own direction and the rules of the place in which it finds itself. . . . Yet in the old tragedy, the individual was similarly menaced by an external organization with laws and habits of its own.

Even from this angle, however, there are distinctions to be made; social law is not dramatic law. The persons who appear before the bar of justice are identities, they can be seen to have obeyed and to be completely interpretable by the apparent logic of their crimes, only for the convenience of judicial pronouncement. In fact, however, a man who has committed a murder may not have acted in a manner which we recognize and condemn with all our hearts as murderous until that last moment when he pulled the trigger of his revolver. That he meant to kill at that moment satisfies the law's demand for premeditation and murderous intent; but since all the acts of the criminal person were not of a criminal quality, we are forced more or less to think of extenuating circumstances. All those puny, common details, small gestures in every way resembling our own, which may have preceded the murder, entering an automobile, stepping on the gas, obeying the traffic lights—and further back, receiving certain influences, being molded by certain values—and which go more to form part of the criminal, in the innocence or "alegality" of his mere endurance, than of the relevant *res gestae* of his crime, the law takes into account only for the purpose of filling in the scenic accompaniments of the last act and intent. So that in spite of the fact that social law deals with identities rather than with personalities, it can do so only by arbitrarily converting persons with histories into emblems of unified action of a given quality. In other words, the law, like its victims, suffers from the discrepancy between action and being, the failure of the individual to conform in every respect to his role. If this were not so, law and justice could be synonymous terms.

If, then, the old drama, as contrasted with biography (of actual or of fictitious personalities), succeeded, as has been asserted by ethical critics, in supplying a picture of action in which a kind of justice and a kind of law conform to each other, it must be because the dramatist started with identities. Like the judge he left aside personalities, their growths, and their structural peculiarities; like the judge he established the particularity of a character only on the basis of the coherence of all of his acts with a special fact; like the judge phenomena of character interested him not for themselves merely but only in so far as there were involved in them the means of reaching a decisive termination of the action. But unlike that of the judge, the dramatist's definition of the character was not an arbitrary superimposition which negates the horde of emotional, intellectual and mechanical characteristics of a person whose some one deed concerns the court; it constituted instead the entire reality of the character and, avoiding the ruinous abstractness of the law, determined in advance that his emotions, his thoughts and his gestures should correspond with and earn in every respect his special fate. . . . Of course, it is because the dramatist had created his characters that he could maintain the proportion between their emotions, their thoughts and their destinies; while those who confront the judge on his dais were, unfortunately, born.

This distinction, quietly implied by their modes of approach to the problem of the definition of the individual, between a personality and an identity, and the decision that the identity alone is of importance in the consideration of the status of individuals, is what the dramatic attitude has in common with the legal. The characters of biography and the biographical novel are persons with histories, but in the drama the characters are identities with roles. The distinction also entails a contrast in the purposes of biography and tragedy. Biography presents the picture of a life precisely enlarged and developed with that type of exactitude which is proper to history, to events visualized as successive in time. But drama, as a "poetical picture of life," is composed of events which, though apparently related sequentially and causally, are chosen with reference to a special type of judgment, to the application of specific laws; the conventional coherence of these events, the suggestion to the observer that such things may have happened in actuality and are at least within the range of rational possibility, is superficial, and, far from determining the outcome of a tragedy, serves merely as a link to connect in the mind of the audience the natural world of compulsive cause and accident with the dramatic world of judgment. Those psychological explanations of the motivations of dramatic figures which form so large a part of modern criticism apply to this layer of reasonable causality which is the outer form of dramatic movement; they have no reference to the dramatist's act of judging[2] which constitutes the sub-surface impulsion of the characters. Once the *rationality* of it has been established by psychology, the *sufficiency* of the motivation of a Macbeth or a Lear is to be referred not to the probable, nor even a possible, human equivalent, but to those laws of

[2] Instead of the "dramatist's act of judging" we may refer to the "dramatist's act of seeing judgment as involved in and carried out by action." From the historical or the common-sense point of view, there is no judgment impressed upon action, and the presence of judgment in the drama must therefore be attributed to an act of the dramatist; but from the dramatic viewpoint there is no action that does not effect judgment, and the judgment is therefore projected, in Platonic fashion, into the real formula of the action, is said to be discovered by the dramatist, and not to be the result of an act of judgment. In any case, it is a judgment which is at the basis of the dramatic act and not a psychological cause.

Shakespeare's world which criticism formulates as pivots for the action of his dramatic identities.

It is with respect to these laws, rather than by copying types, that drama is objective, that the dramatist's image has external application, that it comments on the lives of other people. "Natural" individuals may evade any system of justice, or seem to, but a dramatic identity is a creature in whom a judgment is involved at his birth; a judgment which instigates to a pathos and also gives meaning to it. And by this substitution for personalities, who erratically live and grow within the mystery of moral laws not yet discovered, of identities whose motor organs are judgments,[3] dramatic figures are rendered at once particular and general, and drama appears as "more philosophical" than history.

II

Religious experience also interprets the individual as an identity. In contrast with psychology, which concentrates upon his personality, religion looks to the judgment which will establish his external role. And upon the fixed operation of an identity mutations of the personality have no bearing. As in the bloody book and bitter letter of the law, there are in religion stark examples of this division between identity and personality. For instance, in demoniacal possession identities usurped personalities: the demon, in all respects a new being controlled by the facts and laws of a supernatural world, subjected the individual to its own will.[4] The personality of the possessed remained intact. The demon was a character with a name of his own. His voice was heard from the mouth of a man—but he was not that man, any more than Hamlet was Barrymore. And he could be influenced only by special means fundamentally identical in all cases of possession. There was one law for all demons. Exorcism was applied, a contest between powers of a purely religious cosmos. The exorcist addressed the demon directly, and no attempt was made to alter the psychological texture of the possessed. It was irrelevant!

[3] Of course the moral judgments of drama may not seem moral at all in the conventional sense. For example, the dramatist may rather choose to execute a character because he seems strong and is yet destructible than because he is wicked.

[4] The cases reported in the Middle Ages are the best examples. The reader who is not familiar with these may recall Socrates' description of poetical inspiration or possession in the *Ion*.

As we have seen, a character becomes an identity through the integration of his life about a single fact adjudged by the author of the identity, and this fact determines his position and the reconstitution of his existence as a role. It is by fixing his ideas and emotions around the particular fact that the character's limitations and his definition are concretely shown. In law and religion it is easy to isolate the character's identifying fact, the crime, the contract, the spirit or deity. In drama it is often more difficult, and we are led to speak of the theme of the play, which is nothing else than a vague description of the central fact of the protagonist's role (e.g., *Macbeth* —fair and foul Murder).

An identity is a constant thing. From the viewpoints which create them growth is impossible, and psychological mutation occurs above a rigid substratum. Dramatic reversal of situation depends for its effectiveness upon this persistence of identity. The mere possibility of a psychological adjustment to the new position would destroy the tragic irony, disperse the pathos, and render the imitation natural rather than dramatic.

The identity may be revealed more fully as a drama progresses; this is commonly called character development. The character's action rises or declines on the moral plane, without, however, altering the fact by which he is identified. E.g., Prince Henry's—*Henry IV, Part II*—abandoned

> Well, thus we play the fools with the time

belongs to the same "princely" identity as King Henry's— *Henry V*—conscientious

> Our bad neighbour makes us early stirrers,
> Which is both healthful and good husbandry.

This is also true of the sudden reversals of moral direction which appear in the *crises de conscience* episodes of certain dramas; moral reversal being merely a species of character development carried on at quicktime.

Yet characters may change in a drama not through moral or psychological modification but by means of a change of identity. In genuine cases of change of identity a special process causes the central fact which identifies the character to give place to another of a different type and value, and the fact to which the character's action was previously attached becomes powerless to motivate or explain him. His moral situation may remain substantially the same, but the quality of his acts is altered and his movements transpire on another level; he is a different dramatic individual, and acts which before were in his probable range are now no longer even seriously thinkable.

It is especially in the substitution of one identity for another, or for a personality, that the type of coherence which marks the identity is clarified, *since the change of identity takes place,* as we shall see, *all at once, in a leap,* and is not, as in personality, the result of a continual flow.

To begin with the legal instance: the fact of the crime interpreted and limited (by determining their relevance) the acts of the criminal. For the law, he lived by that fact alone. If it were suddenly discovered that no crime had been committed, the coherence of action which had led to the apparent fact would collapse, and the prisoner, having been converted in an instant into the figure (hypothetical) of an innocent man, would no longer exist under the eye of the court. But if thereafter he were charged with a different crime, his legal identity would depend upon this new fact and would be entirely other when established than the former one.

We may next indicate how the idea of identity and change of identity has been treated by religions, and has even, one may say, been made the dominant feature of their most significant and important ceremonies. To use familiar material, this is Professor Guignbert's version of the pagan taurobolium:

> In the Phrygian cult of Cybele and Attis, but not in that alone, for we find it in various other Asiatic cults and in that of Mithra, a singular ceremony, called the *taurobolium,* took place. It formed part of the mysterious initiatory rites exclusively reserved for believers. [*Christianity.*]

Here follows a description of the rites and this explanation:

> The pit signifies the kingdom of the dead, and the mystic, in descending into it, is thought to die; the bull is Attis, and the blood that is shed is the divine life-principle that issues from him; the initiate receives it and, as it were, absorbs it; when he leaves the pit he is said to be "born again" and milk, as in the case of a new-born infant, is given him to drink. But he is not born the mere man again he was before; he has absorbed the very essence of the god and, if we understand the mystery aright, he is in his turn become an Attis and is saluted as one.

Guignbert then draws attention to the resemblance between these rites and the Christian baptism and eucharist.

The change consists, then, in both the legal and religious instances in (1) the dissolution or death of the previous identity—this may involve the death of the individual, as with Ivan Ilych, abandoned by Tolstoy on the threshold of change, or it may be indicated by cancellation of the central fact of the identity,[5] or by a symbolic proximity to death; and (2) a re-identification, wherein the individual is placed in a new status, is "reborn," so to say, and given a new character and perhaps a new name.

Drama is no more religion or law than it is psychology, history or biography. But the fact that the phenomenon of religious conversion is the only one "in life"[6] which effects a change of identity, in which, through the touch of death, a course of action and valuation is completely annulled and another substituted without breaching the duration of the individual, relates religion and drama in a special way. To present the change objectively, to suggest the actual method of identity-replacement, the dramatist must make use of events indicating the character's experience of death. But drama speaks in terms of action alone, and it neither contradicts nor supports any explanation religious or psychological. Dramatic "death and regeneration" is no mystery.[7] There is the death-laden incident; and then occurs a coupling of two different identities under a figure presented as one, a change of the faces behind the mask.

To indicate the similarity and differences in the treatment of this type of change in drama, I have chosen examples from three literatures.

---

[5] That the purpose of the law in executing a criminal is to avenge itself upon him or to offer his fate as a deterrent has been denied by philosophers of the law. The logic of the law's act becomes clear when we understand the execution as an attempt to eliminate the criminal identity, and that the death of the criminal is incidental to this aim. Any means equally certain as death of accomplishing the dissolution of the criminal identity would be satisfactory, at least theoretically, even though it worked no harm to the criminal.

[6] The legal identity is a formal one.

[7] Death in the drama means only cessation of the character's action with the impossibility of taking it up again. In tragedy, when no change is present, death comprehends the destruction of the individual and mirrors natural death; in the "impostor" type of social comedy death applies to the false identity—the individual continues to live but through the exposure he cannot go on with his old act.

A very early account of identity-change is the life-story of the Biblical Jacob. From the moment he begins his career by outwitting his brother in the matter of the pottage his character is consistent with the trait described by his name. A tricky winner, he dreams but once, and his dream is of promised protection and prosperity . . . until the threat of death descends upon him in the form of the avenging Esau, victim of his precocious cunning. Then "greatly afraid and distressed" he calls on God to save him and schemes to be the last of his company to die. But alone behind the encampment he is met by the angel, who wrestles with him until dawn. During this contest he receives the sign of the dislocated thigh and his name is changed to Isra-el (Wrestler-With-God). In the morning he advances to meet his brother, whose fury has been unaccountably—on psychological grounds though not in regard to the symbolism of identity-change—transformed to love.

From that time, the lone adventurer, gatherer of property and wives, disappears; he has become the patriarch, and the interest shifts to his children. In the next episode, the seduction of Dinah, it is his sons who plot the vengeance and perform the treacherous action. The transformed Jacob, Israel, is busy with God and the erection of altars; his practical career is at an end.

This is an extremely simple picture of the process of identity-change as it appears in dramatic literature. There is a minimum of action-detail, only the death-threat and the change by divine contact and renaming.

In the next example a personality is transformed into a dramatic identity; it clarifies the contrast between the action of a personality, which is the expression of a psychological condition, and that of an identity, who always acts with reference to his role, who performs what is required of him by the plot, by the whole in which he is located. The fact that the hero at the outset is the image of a personality means that our example begins as a biography in dramatic form, and the fact that he changes into an identity means that from that point the biography-drama becomes a true drama.

In *Hamlet* there is an interfusion of two forms of interpretation, the psychological and the dramatic. The argumentative, self-analytical, naturalistic Hamlet of "non-action," describing himself in every speech and using speech as a substitute for deed, is very much the figure of a personality, of a being insufficient for, *because irrelevant to,* the dramatic role offered to him.[8]

> I do not know
> Why yet I live to say "This thing's to do,"
> Sith I have cause and will and strength and means
> To do 't.

Despite the views of psychological criticism, Hamlet has all the qualities required for action, the will and the strength; he lacks only the identity structure which would fit him to be a character in a drama, the identity which originates in and responds totally to the laws of his dramatic world. Thus he is contrasted or "paralleled" with Laertes,

> For by the image of my cause, I see
> The portraiture of his,

whose situation is equal to his own but whose identity is dramatic;[9] and he sets himself off in his helplessness against the drama of the visiting players. It is not a weakness of personality that cripples his action but the fact that he is a personality at all. His moves are cut off as by the Revolving Sword at that point where they would force an effective entry into the dramatic cosmos. He lives on a sort of middle ground between the natural world and the dramatic, a world of fantasy somewhat insane, because its laws are contradictory. He is inadequate to carry out the judgment which has been pronounced upon him because he has been permitted to retain a portion of himself. He thinks too much not because he is an intellectual, but because it is impossible for him to do anything else. The mystery which surrounds him consists in that he is neither an identity nor a personality wholly, but a combination of both, a being who has wandered by accident upon a stage.[10]

Clearly then, this character must be changed if the play is to become a tragedy, if it is not to go on like a naturalistic

[8] In the customary psychological criticism, Hamlet's failure to act is laid to the preponderance of one trait or another, usually the reflective one. But interpreting the character in terms of dramatic identity, we relate his incapacity to a structural insufficiency, a defect which no psychological correction could remedy or even affect.

[9] Cf. IV, v: "Save yourself, my lord," etc. The scene belongs in all respects to the role of Hamlet.

[10] "For he was likely, *had he been put on,*
To have proved most royally."

novel peeling him to expose his psychological layers. As he stands, his career can lead to no pathos or dramatic termination. Hamlet must be given an identity before the finish which will alter his status and fit him into the drama. And there is only one way of representing dramatically such a change.

So that until we meet him returned from the voyage to England, where he had been sent to his death and narrowly escaped in the grapple with the pirates, we have to do with the standard figure of Hamlet-criticism. But when we come upon him after this immersion in symbolic death,[11] we encounter a new character, a regenerated man. In his very next appearance on the stage, Hamlet discourses maturely on death. Also he has acquired a certainty with respect to his feelings and a capacity for action. This is I, he announces, as he leaps into the grave of Ophelia, Hamlet the Dane! Having named himself, he is at once fiercely attacked by Laertes, but he proclaims his dramatic equality with unexpected firmness.

> I prithee, take thy fingers from my throat;
> For, though I am not splenetive and rash,
> Yet have I something in me dangerous,
> Which let thy wisdom fear. Hold off thy hand!

This "something dangerous" in him is new and could not have been predicted; it refers directly, of course, to his ability to act. While about the emotion which had so disconcerted him earlier he says:

> Why, I will fight with him upon this theme. . . .
> I loved Ophelia. . . .

To his mother this new self-assured identity is unrecognizable; her comment on his dramatics is a description applicable before the change.

> This is mere madness,
> And thus a while the fit will work on him.
> Anon, as patient as the female dove
> When that her golden couplets are disclosed,
> His silence will sit drooping.

11 "High and mighty," he writes upon his return, "you shall know I am set naked in your kingdom." We need not, however, trace the symbolism of rebirth into the language but only to follow the course of the action. Acts are a firmer foundation than words for the acrobatics of interpretation.

But she is in error. For Hamlet had commenced to act with reference to his role of self-purifying vengeance, had taken up immutably his appropriate dramatic position, at that moment when aboard the ship bound for England he had read his sealed death-warrant. Then for the first time he had known immediately and with certainty what he had to do.

> Being thus be-netted round with villainies—
> Ere I could make a prologue to my brains,
> They had begun the play—

And now, this hero who had looked with such passionate envy upon passion is "constant in his purposes" toward the King. Some experience barely indicated ("Had I but time, O, I could tell you") has released his forces. His action hustles the play to its tragic close, and the apparently accidental character of his revenge serves to emphasize that he is controlled at the end not by the dualities of his ego but by the impulsions of the plot. Transformed from the image of a personality into that of a dramatic identity, he has found at last his place in the play.

The third example is from Dostoevsky's *Brothers Karamazoff*. This author's handling of the subject follows more closely experience of typically religious change of identity than does that of the writers of the Old Testament or of Shakespeare. He tends to relate the phenomenon to Christian belief and emotions. Identity-change in his novel is connected with stimuli of the kind mentioned by religious psychologists.

The "biographical notes" of Father Zossima set out two parallel cases of identity-change. First there is Markel, Zossima's brother, whose conversion is briefly stressed to furnish a ground for Zossima's own conversion which comes later and is developed in greater detail. After his brother's death, Zossima was sent to Petersburg to enter the Imperial Guard. From the house of his childhood, he records, he had brought none but precious memories of a religious import, but these grew dimmer in the cadet school and he became a "cruel, absurd, almost savage creature." . . . A disappointing love affair, an insult, and a challenge to a duel . . . "and then something happened that in very truth was the turning point of my life. . . ." The evening preceding the duel, he flew into a rage and struck his orderly so violently that his face was covered with blood. When Zossima awoke the following morning he went to the window and looked out upon the garden. The sun was rising. "It was warm and beautiful, the birds were singing." At that point the conversion began.

> What's the meaning of it, I thought, I feel in my heart as it were something vile and shameful? Is it because I am going to shed blood? No, I thought, I feel it's not that. Can it be that I am afraid of death, afraid of being killed? No, that's not it, that's not it at all . . . And all at once, I knew what it was; it was because I had beaten Afanasy the evening before!

Then Zossima recalls his converted brother, the deceased Markel. On the field of honor, risking his companions' contempt, he halts the duel after his adversary has fired. A short time later he becomes a monk.

This incident contains the typical antecedent conditions listed by psychologists for cases of religious conversion; and it stages a death-danger, though fear of death is denied. It may be assumed that Dostoevsky had read books on the psychology of conversion. Yet Zossima's change leaves no suspicion that it is a psychological mutation disguising an orthodox conception of the descent of grace rather than a genuine dramatic happening.[12] The change takes place on the dramatic level; the psychological conditions described, while belonging to realistic literature, are equivalent to the legendary and picaresque adventures in transformation of the Bible and of *Hamlet*.

In our three examples, the process underlying the character's change remains the same, although the actions accompanying it vary, and the explanations for its occurrence range from angelic intervention to nostalgia and remorse. Besides the close danger of death common to all three, the same anxiety is present. In the terse account of Jacob's transformation he is "greatly afraid and distressed," Hamlet relates that

> . . . in my heart there was a kind of fighting,
> That would not let me sleep,

while Zossima feels "something vile and shameful."

The so-called psychic states preceding conversion [says

[12] Such as, for example, the *Madame Gervais* of the de Goncourt frères, in which, by means of a sequence of credible psychological episodes, a nominal conversion to Roman Catholicism was effected which, however, resulted in no change of identity manifest in dramatic conduct, but only in a psychopathological regression. Such a naturalistic representation of the degeneration of a personality has no bearing on the problem of identity-change.

Sante de Sanctis] seem all to have this in common, that they dissolve the economy of the individual, and excite the soul, but cannot satisfy it or allay its disturbance. They are psychic states which propound questions, but do not answer them; they initiate, but do not complete. They provoke a suspension of the soul in which they are being experienced. [*Religious Conversion.*]

III

The forms of thought which conceive the individual as an identity have to do with action and with the judgment of actions. The concept of identity suggests that in this realm of action the multiple incidents in the life of an individual may be synthesized, by himself or by others, into a scheme that pivots on a single fact judged to be central to the individual's existence and which, governing his behavior and deciding his fate, becomes part of his definition, though it is external to him. Here unity of being becomes one with unity of the "plot,"[13] and through the fixity of identity change becomes synonymous with revolution.

With this dramatic integration religious conversion of all actual conditions of the human individual supplies the most complete example, though it is only an example. Through conversion the individual gains an identity which revolves upon a fact which is both private in its unifying effect upon him yet extra-personal in its relation to his world. All converts are by no means, of course, converted to the same thing, their identities after the conversion are not identical, and with regard to each the moral question will receive a different answer. But in all there is that integration about some one thing which instigates their action in a coherent line susceptible of judgment which is the mark of the dramatic character. To other individuals such unity may be attributed;[14]

[13] Whether or not the identity exists and what it is are metaphysical questions. From the psychological view, identity may seem a fictitious unity inhibiting personality, just as the personality may seem from the religious view a fiction dissipating identity. This essay has been dealing with those forms of thought which uniformly interpret the individual as an identity. But even from the empirical view, the identity differs from such intellectual-repressive factors as "character." Its coherence is not necessarily the effect of a negation; its function is not inhibition but affirmation of a "new reality"; it has its own sentiments, emotions, sensibility—it may produce lyric poetry.

[14] This is rarely done by biographers who stress the "human" aspects of a character. But see Prince Mirsky's biography of Lenin as a man who had almost no "personal life."

the convert openly asserts it of himself and compels his life to accord with his interpretation.

It is on the basis of identity and character-change that the fundamental connection is established between religious and dramatic thought which often permits the processes leading to the phenomena of religious life to suggest dramatic movement, and the vice versa. The identity which both of these attitudes recognize *as* the individual repeats itself to the satisfaction of an eternal judgment, symbolized by a role, and unaffected by any possibility of organic transformation. In drama the judgment is carried out by reversal of position and by a transposition of roles where the character survives. In religious thought the individual is judged by his situation in a hierarchy according to the consistency of his acts with the god-fact. In both instances he does not obey his own will but the rules of the location in which he finds himself. And in both, change can only be accomplished according to the same law, the dissolution of the identity and the reappearance of the individual in a "reborn state."

Dramatic and religious thought, then, retrace the steps which social legality overleaps; they reconstruct the entire individual to fit him into their schemes of justice. The law court receives the individual as he is and in judging him changes him. But dramatics and religion are creative methods, and they elaborate the means according to which the individual relates himself to law and receives justice from it.

Critique of Corneille's "Horace"

PAUL GOODMAN

BACKGROUND OF THE PLAY

IN THE following analysis of *Horace* I try to show how a structural defect in a play leads us to important considerations outside the play, in our social existence. But this is true, of course, of many "bad" poems. *Horace* is not, however, merely a "bad" poem but a work of extraordinary power that carries us away. Then we are confronted with the question how such a work by such an author can contain such a lapse. And in answering this we find a discrepancy in our social existence. Corneille fails because we fail. Our society, as at present, will not bear a better play than this on this theme.

To a psychologist, war—whatever else it is—is a means that people have of destroying their self-conquering egos and of most strongly affirming the imperial will of those egos. It is a mass (guiltless) suicide and, like any masochism, is a desperate effort to release repressed feeling.[1] And the institutions of authority, the authoritarian family and eminently the state, are the expressions of this self-conquering will, and they therefore tend to nothing but the war that they themselves make necessary. With this orientation we may turn with sharper eyes to tragic poems of war, cries of the outraged spirit. And not only to the works of the Greeks—the *Iliad,* the *Trojan Women*—for the Greeks understood the carnage too clearly for what it was and therefore did not explore under the surface; but to the modern tragedies that concern precisely the moment in the soul where nature resists and the imperial will asserts itself the stronger. And then especially to Pierre Corneille, who lived in the period of the consolidation of the personal-impersonal warring state, when the psychological problem was clearer than now, for the state still seemed, somehow, to be the will of a man; at just this period he saw tragedy in the conflict of "love" and "duty." And Corneille returns again and again to the idea of Rome, the *patria* in the supreme sense, the will that strips the soul of every resource but the collective affirmation of will, proved by the oracles of the gods assigning empire as a destiny. And among the tragedies and the Roman tragedies of Corneille, we must look precisely at *Horace,* the tragedy of the Roman family, whose pivotal character is the paterfamilias subordinating himself in all things to the state and impressing his character on the youth. Here, in the scene of early Rome, we have the psychological elements in their purity and in their connection: affection and natural ties, the honor of the

---

[1] For the psychology see Perls, Hefferline, and Goodman, *Gestalt-Therapy,* Part II, chap. viii, esp. pp. 345 ff.

ego, fatherly authority, and the state—the elements that are divided in *Le Cid* and *Cinna*. The strength of this masterpiece is the severe analysis of the psychology of war, when the gods, the state, and the father impose a single pattern of authority. Its weakness, especially in the conclusion, is the inability of the honest artist to energize the consequences of his plot (and of history); or, conversely, it is the unwillingness of the man, writing, to show the situation truly and to draw the more terrible consequences.

Let us look first at the story in Livy (i. 22-26): It establishes that the war between Rome and Alba was "most like a civil war, almost between parents and children." Therefore, against the inclinations of the Roman king, the Alban dictator suggests that a means be found to decide the issue without general slaughter, for, "if the true rather than the specious reason be told, it is the desire for Empire that spurs the two neighboring and cognate peoples to war." (But how on earth *would* such a desire begin to realize itself except by the murder of the cognate and neighboring?) So two pairs of three brothers, the Roman Horatii and the Alban Curiatii (unless, as Livy says, the names happened to be the other way!), are set to fight as champions of the two armies; and, after his two brothers are slain, the third Horatius by a ruse, feigning flight, slays the separated pursuers. Then,

> Horatius went home, bearing before him the triple spoils; and when his sister, who had been betrothed to one of the Curiatii, came to meet him, recognizing on her brother's shoulders the mantle of her beloved that she herself had made, she loosed her hair and tearfully called on the name of the dead. The sister's grief, in the midst of his victory and the public joy, enraged the fierce youth. With drawn sword he pierced her through, spitting out the words, "Away to your betrothed with your immature love, forgetful of your brothers dead and live, forgetful of your fatherland. So always away with the Roman woman that shall mourn an enemy!" Arrested for this atrocious crime, Horatius was nevertheless not executed, for his father claimed that the girl was justly slain, and the people were moved more by admiration of his valor than the justice of the case.

HANDLING OF THE STORY BY CORNEILLE

To this ancient legend, whose sacrificial meaning is psychoanalytically obvious, Corneille makes numerous additions. The slain sister is his Camille, but to her he adds Sabine, in a parallel situation, the sister of the Curiaces and the wedded wife of Horace. He brings the betrothed Curiace on the stage, and there is a scene between the lovers. Further, he adds Valerius, the rejected suitor for Camille, who prosecutes Horace for her murder; and Julie, a Roman matron, as confidante of Camille and Sabine. Lastly, he makes enter the King, to pardon the murderer. Thus far, these additions seem to be nothing but the seventeenth-century propensity to sentimentalize and subplot a simple stark episode; but, in fact, they are used by Corneille to bring his analysis to a deep inwardness—though not to the extreme of inwardness.

Horace is ordered as a plot of suspense, threats, and temporary reliefs. At first the women grieve because of the civil war and are relieved by the truce; then Horace is chosen and even congratulated by Curiace; then Curiace is chosen, and the horror of the women is made specific, but it is relieved by the mutiny of the people against the unnatural combat and the pause to consult the gods. Then follows the catastrophe.

Curiace is a foil to Horace. Following the hint of Livy that the Albans are less fanatical and more human than the Romans, Corneille divides the will of the youth several ways: he doubts the piety of the conflict; he admires Horace and is proud of him and somewhat desires him not to lose; when he himself is chosen as the Alban champion, he curses his fate; and, when he must meet the imploring of Camille, it seems to be more his desire not to lose personal honor than his patriotic duty that steels him; and he is about to succumb to her tears. (All this, of course, makes probable his defeat.) But to Horace, self-esteem, personal glory, family training, and patriotic zeal are one single drive. "Alba has named you," says Horace, "I know you no longer." "I know you still—" says Curiace, with that marvelous Cornelian flourish. Nevertheless, the character of Curiace, unlike that of Horace, is rather shallow. Something is missing; it is that he does not fear death, not for one moment. For Horace, this fearlessness is inevitable; he suffers an infatuation that includes also his need to die as well as to kill. But it is by a false convention of noble behavior that Corneille takes away from the more human champion this depth of humanity, the fear that Achilles and Hector are not exempt from. But Corneille cannot round out the portrayal of a flexible human character, as Homer could, because then the war would reveal itself as an intolerable waste.

A similar strength and weakness are disclosed in the portrayal of the pair of Camille and Sabine. Camille is handled simply: her motives are love and family love; at no point does

73

she take seriously the authoritative ideals of *patria* and honor; and she is skeptical of the gods—not of their power (that would be idiocy) but of their affection. At the same time her grief for the betrothed is not the natural spontaneous outburst indicated in Livy but a set design to provoke her brother and hasten her own death: "Offend his victory, irritate his wrath, and take pleasure in displeasing him"; "you blame my grief, you call it cowardly; I love it the more the more it angers you." This is not a natural impulse but a will formed precisely on the rebelliousness of nature. Perhaps this raising of the conflict always to the level of the reasoned will—a necessity of the Cornelian theater—seems artificial; yet in this case it seems to me to be probable and beautiful, and it almost carries the bombast of the famous tirade that ends, "May I see the last Roman heave his last sigh, myself alone the cause of it, and die of pleasure!" (How grand!) This is an insight: the rebellion of simple unself-regarding nature against lunatic authority to end in—egomania.

But Sabine is more difficult, and Corneille eventually fails. The wife of Horace and the sister of the Curiaces, she speaks the first words of the play with a heavy heart for the civil war, yet she will not weep: "If I do less than a man, I do more than a woman." On the one hand, except in this one war, she shares the ambition of the Roman conquest; on the other, her natural relation to her brothers is more than a feeling—it is a moral principle. That is, her conflict is already more intense and irreconcilable than Camille's; and from this beginning her first great action follows admirably: when it becomes known that Horace and Curiace are the champions, she rushes between them with the strange conceit that they must kill *her* and so remove the natural bond between them, in order that they may then kill each other without impiety. This is quite mad; it is her maleness—proper to the sister of the more feminine Curiace—and it is a soul busy forming illusions. And when we next see her, when the men are actually engaged in the fight, we have the promise of the creation of one of the greatest figures in literature. She proposes to herself to dismiss the conflict from her mind and to take joy in any outcome whatever, for if Horace wins, it is her husband's glory; if Curiace, her brother's, etc. "Fortune! whatever evils you sternly send, I've found the means to get from them joy; I can see the fight without fear, the dead without despair, the conquerors without horror." At this moment, in brief, we are presented with a madwoman. The conflict that men have invented is in fact irreconcilable; and the will

74

that will not succumb to it and die (as she threatens) can still take leave of reality. Alas! for Corneille this depth of nature is impossible; there are no madmen in this theater (and therefore there is no extreme of truth, as Shakespeare tells the extreme truth); the reasoned will is itself imperial. Sabine descends into rationality and says, "A flattering illusion, etc." From this moment on she is unimpressive; it is agreed by all critics that her last scene, pleading for Horace before the King, is perfectly frigid and almost silly.

Julie is a "Roman matron." She sympathizes with the two other women; having seen two Romans slain in the fight, she comes away, unable to bear the rest. So far so good. Suddenly one is forced to ask: But why does Corneille not dare to bring a mother on the scene (not only in this play!)? Euripides had no such fears. Suppose that the mother of Horace were presented? What then would this Roman tragedy look like? This Roman tragedy would be simply this Roman butchery, for the poet would not falsify the issue by copying off a mother of Coriolanus. But this deep reach of social nature, the bond between mother and child, prior to the formation of the ego, will, and imperial suicidal need, is rigorously excluded from the Cornelian theater and from almost *all* the modern theater of battle and duty—but not from the *Persians* or the *Trojan Women*. (Partly these mothers are excluded because many of the mothers that we see in so-called real life, who could take part in these warlike intrigues, are so unreal, so lacking in *vraisemblance,* beyond belief to a conscientious poet.)

Lastly, the denouement is the entrance of the King as the dispenser of justice. (In the history, we saw, it was the feeling of the "people" that exonerated the murderer.) To me this scene seems tiresome from the very beginning; but one must suppose that to Corneille and his audience of divine-right theorists the royal presence itself had a certain theatrical force: "I love to render justice to all, at every time in every place; it is by justice that a king makes himself a demigod." So. And what is the justice that the demigod renders at this time and in this place? Valerius, the only person with a natural tie to Camille—the tie of a rejected suitor! (for her father has disowned her)—pleads against the murderer: "In this place Rome has seen the first parricide; the sequel is fearful, the hatred of heaven. Save us from its hand, respect the gods." We can recall the similar moment in the *Oresteia,* when Athene herself decides. But the King says—this is his justice and wisdom—

This crime, though great, enormous, inexcusable, comes from the same hand that today has made me master of two states. Without him, I should obey where I give the law; I should be subject where twice I am a king. . . . The art and the power of making strong the crown are gifts that heaven grants to few; such servants are the strength of kings; and such also are above the law. Let the laws then be quiet.

All this is true enough; it is even subtile. But it is not the resolution of a tragic play; it is not the resolution of what has gone before in the tears and the rebellious tirade of Camille, in the portrayal of the fanaticism of the younger and elder Horace, in the death wish of Sabine, in the dubiety of Curiace, in the return of Horace hot from carnage and ready to slay again. But it is precisely the resolution of the weaknesses of the play that consist especially in the *omissions* of the poet (what he does not dare): this weak resolution follows from the fact that he has omitted to show a warrior willing to fight but fearful of death; that he cannot allow Sabine to pass over into madness; that he dares not bring the mother of Horace on the scene. If such things were not omitted, what would the resolution look like except just what it is, no resolution at all but a continuation of the infatuation, a cause of the same tragedy again and again?

There is a remarkable episode in *Horace* that does not appear in Livy. Let me quote it. The fight between the trios is about to begin when suddenly (Julie narrates it),

no sooner did they appear, ready to measure one another, than a murmur arose in the two camps: to see such friends, persons so close, come to mortal combat for their fatherlands. One is moved to pity, another is seized with horror, another wonders at the madness of such zeal; this one lauds to heaven their unequalled virtue, that one ventures to call it sacrilegious and brutal. But the differing opinions all come to one thing: all accuse the chiefs, all condemn their choices; and unable to tolerate so barbarous a fight, they cry out, they advance, at last they separate them.

Nevertheless, the infatuated boys wish to continue, for their honor, and they turn their swords against the people; but

the two camps mutiny; they cry for a general battle or other champions. The presence of the chiefs is hardly respected; their power is doubtful, their voices scarcely heard. The King himself is astonished, and as a last effort he says, "Since all are so hot in discord, let us consult the sacred majesty of the great gods and see if they agree to a change. What impious man would dare rebel against their will when they let us see it in a sacrifice." These words of his cast a spell. . . .

(The scene is lifelike and oh! familiar.) To continue:

> *Sabine:* Sister, I have good news for you.
> *Camille:* I know it, if that is what you call it. But I see nothing in it to allay my trouble. This delay in our evils will make the blows fall all the harder. The only consolation to hope for is that we can wail later what we must wail for.
> *Sabine:* The gods did not inspire this tumult in vain.
> *Camille:* Say rather, sister, that to consult them is vain. These very gods inspired the King in his choice, and the voice of the people is not always their voice. They do not so easily come down to the lower grades as to the souls of kings, their living images, whose independent and sacred authority is a secret ray of their divinity. . . . Heaven acts without us in these events; it does not rule according to our feelings.

Camille proves to be right; the sacrifice turns out adversely. The same gods that have given to Rome the destiny to conquer empire decree that the brother must slay the brothers-in-law and then also his sister. This is simply the nature of things. But how did Pierre Corneille dare to declare that the people might mutiny, if only so far, and even the King be astonished?

Macbeth *and the Metaphysic of Evil*

G. WILSON KNIGHT

MACBETH is Shakespeare's most profound and mature vision of evil. In the ghost and death themes of *Hamlet* we have something of the same quality; in the Brutus-theme of *Julius Caesar* we have an exactly analogous rhythm of spiritual experience; in *Richard III* we have a parallel history of an individual's crime. In *Macbeth* all this, and the many other isolated poetic units of similar quality throughout Shakespeare, receive a final, perfected form. Therefore analysis of *Macbeth* is of profound value: but it is not easy. Much of *Hamlet,* and the *Troilus-Othello-Lear* succession culminating in *Timon of Athens,* can be regarded as representations of the "hate-theme." We are there faced by man's aspiring nature, unsatiated of its desire among the frailties and inconsistencies of its world. They thus point us to good, not evil, and their very gloom of denial is the shadow of a great assertion. They thus lend themselves to interpretation in terms of human thought, and their evil can be regarded as a negation of man's positive longing. In *Macbeth* we find not gloom, but blackness: the evil is not relative, but absolute. In point of imaginative profundity *Macbeth* is comparable alone to *Antony and Cleopatra*. There we have a fiery vision of a paradisal consciousness; here the murk and nightmare torment of a conscious hell. This evil, being absolute and therefore alien to man, is in essence shown as inhuman and supernatural, and is thus most difficult of location in any philosophical scheme. *Macbeth* is fantastical and imaginative beyond other tragedies. Difficulty is increased by that implicit blurring of effects, that palling darkness, that overcasts plot, technique, style. The persons of the play are themselves groping. Yet we are left with an overpowering knowledge of suffocating, conquering evil, and fixed by the basilisk eye of a nameless terror. The nature of this evil will be the subject of my essay.

It is dangerous to abstract the personal history of the protagonist from his environment as a basis for interpretation. The main theme is not primarily differentiated from that of the important subsidiary persons and cannot stand alone. Rather there is a similarity, and the evil in Banquo, Macduff, Malcolm, and the enveloping atmosphere of the play, all forms so many steps by which we may approach and understand the titanic evil which grips the two protagonists. The *Macbeth* universe is woven in a texture of a single pattern. The whole play is one swift act of the poet's mind, and as such must be interpreted, since the technique confronts us not with separated integers of "character" or incident, but with a molten welding of thought with thought, event with event. There is an interpenetrating quality that subdues all to itself. Therefore I shall start by noticing some of the more important elements in this total imaginative effect, and thence I shall pass to the more purely human element. The story and action of the play alone will not carry us far. Here the logic of imaginative correspondence is more significant and more exact than the logic of plot.

Macbeth is a desolate and dark universe where all is befogged, baffled, constricted by the evil. Probably in no play of Shakespeare are so many questions asked. It opens with "When shall we three meet again?" and "Where the place?" (I. i. 1 and 6). The second scene starts with, "What bloody man is that?" (I. ii. 1), and throughout it questions are asked of the Sergeant and Ross. This is followed by:

> *First Witch.* Where hast thou been, sister?
> *Second Witch.* Killing swine.
> *First Witch.* Sister, where thou? (I. iii. 1)

And Banquo's first words on entering are: "How far is't called to Forres? What are these . . .?" (I. iii. 39). Questions succeed each other quickly throughout this scene. Amazement and mystery are in the play from the start, and are reflected in continual questions—there are those of Duncan to Malcolm in I. iv, and of Lady Macbeth to the Messenger and then to her lord in I. v. They continue throughout the play. In I. vii they are tense and powerful:

> *Macbeth.* . . . How now! What news?
> *L. Macbeth.* He has almost supp'd: why have you left the chamber?
> *Macbeth.* Hath he asked for me?
> *L. Macbeth.* Know you not he has? (I. vii. 28)

This scene bristles with them. At the climax of the murder they come again, short stabs of fear: "Didst thou not hear a noise?—Did not you speak?—When?—Now. As I descended? . . ." (II. ii. 16). Some of the finest and most heart-rending passages are in the form of questions: "But wherefore could I not pronounce Amen?" and, "Will all great Neptune's ocean wash this blood clean from my hand?" (II. ii. 32; II. ii. 61). The scene of the murder and that of its discovery form a series of questions. To continue the list in detail would be more tedious than difficult: to quote a few—there are the amazed questions of the guests and Lady Macbeth at the Banquet (III. iii.); Macbeth's continual questioning of the Weird Sisters in the Cauldron scene (IV. i.); those of Macduff's son to Lady Macduff (IV. ii.); of Macduff to Ross who brings him news of his family's slaughter (IV. iii.); of the Doctor to the Gentlewoman (V. i.).

These questions are threads in the fabric of mystery and doubt which haunts us in *Macbeth*. All the persons are in doubt, baffled. Duncan is baffled at the treachery of a man he trusted (I. iv. 2). Newcomers strike amaze:

> What a haste looks through his eyes! So should he look
> That seems to speak things strange. (I. ii. 47)

Surprise is continual. Macbeth does not understand how he can be Thane of Cawdor (I. iii. 108). Lady Macbeth is startled at the news of Duncan's visit (I. v. 32); Duncan at the fact of Macbeth's arrival before himself (I. vi. 20). There is the general amazement at the murder; of Lennox, Ross, and the Old Man at the strange happenings in earth and heaven on the night of the murder (II. iii. 60-7; II. iv. 1-20). Banquo and Fleance are unsure of the hour (II. i. 1-4). No one is sure of Macduff's mysterious movements. Lady Macbeth is baffled by Macbeth's enigmatic hints as to the "deed of dreadful note" (III. ii. 44). The two murderers are not certain as to who has wronged them, Macbeth or Banquo (III. i. 76-9); they do not understand the advent of the "third murderer" (III. iii. 1). Ross and Lady Macduff are at a loss as to Macduff's flight, and warning is brought to Lady Macduff by a mysterious messenger who "is not to her known" (IV. ii. 63). Malcolm suspects Macduff, and there is a long dialogue due to his "doubts" (IV. iii); and in the same scene Malcolm recognizes Ross as his countryman yet strangely "knows him not" (IV. iii. 160). As the atmosphere brightens at the end of the play, the contrast is aptly marked by reference to the stroke of action which will finally dispel the fog of insecurity:

> The time approaches
> That will with due decisiòn make us know
> What we shall say we have and what we owe.
> Thoughts speculative their unsure hopes relate,
> But certain issues strokes must arbitrate.   (v. iv. 17)

This blurring and lack of certainty is increased by the heavy proportion of second-hand or vague knowledge reported during the play's progress. We have the two accounts of the fighting, by the Sergeant and Ross: but the whole matter of the rebellion is vague to us. Later, Ross brings news to Macbeth of his new honours, confessing that he "knows" not the exact crimes of the former Thane of Cawdor (I. iii. III-16). Malcolm has spoken with "one that saw him die" (I. iv. 4). Lady Macbeth hears amazedly of the Weird Sisters' prophecy by letter (I. v.). Macbeth describes the voice that bade him "sleep no more" (II. ii. 36) and the dead body of Duncan (II. iii. 118). People are continually receiving the latest news from each other, the climax being Macduff's hearing of his family's slaughter (II. iv; III. vi; IV. iii. 161-239). Rumours are alive throughout:

Macbeth. How say'st thou that Macduff denies his person
 At our great bidding?

> L. Macbeth.   Did you send to him, Sir?
> Macbeth. I hear it by the way; but I will send.   (III. iv. 128)

We hear more rumours of Macduff in the dialogue between Lennox and the Lord in III. vi. There is the "galloping of horses" with the mysterious "two or three" who bring word of Macduff's flight (IV. i. 141). It is a world of rumours and fears:

> Ross.   I dare not speak much further;
> But cruel are the times, when we are traitors
> And do not know ourselves; when we hold rumor
> From what we fear, yet know not what we fear,
> But float upon a wild and violent sea
> Each way and move.   (IV. ii. 17)

Ross has heard a "rumour" of a rise in Scotland against Macbeth (IV. iii. 182). In a hushed voice the Gentlewoman describes Lady Macbeth's sleep-walking to the Doctor (V. i.); and the Doctor says he has "heard something" of Macbeth's "royal preparation" (V. iii. 57-8). Siward "learns no other" but that Macbeth is defending his castle (V. iv. 9), and Lady Macbeth, "as 'tis thought," commits suicide (V. vii. 99). These are but a few random instances: questions, rumours, startling news, and uncertainties are everywhere. From the time when Banquo asks "How far is't called to Forres?" (I. iii. 39) until Siward's "What wood is this before us?" (V. iv. 3) we are watching persons lost, mazed.[1] They do not understand themselves even:

> Malcolm.   Why do we hold our tongues
> That most may claim this argument for ours?   (II. iii. 126)

The persons of the drama can say truly, with Ross, "we . . . do not know ourselves" (IV. ii. 19). We too who read, are in doubt often. Action here is illogical. Why does Macbeth not know of Cawdor's treachery? Why does Lady Macbeth faint? Why do the King's sons flee to different countries when a whole nation is ready in their support? Why does Macduff move so darkly mysterious in the background and leave his family to certain death? Who is the Third Murderer? And,

---

[1] Cp. Colin Still's *Shakespeare's Mystery Play: A Study of The Tempest* (Cecil Palmer, 1921; revised and reissued as *The Timeless Theme,* Nicholson and Watson, 1936). In his interpretation, the Court Party are related to the maze in ancient ritual; and in my interpretation of *The Tempest*, I roughly equate the Antonio and Sebastian theme with *Macbeth*.

finally, why does Macbeth murder Duncan? All this builds a strong sense of mystery and irrationality within us. We, too, grope in the stifling dark, and suffer from doubt and insecurity.

Darkness permeates the play. The greater part of the action takes place in the murk of night. It is unnecessary to detail more than a few of the numerous references to darkness. Lady Macbeth prays:

> Come, thick night,
> And pall thee in the dunnest smoke of Hell,
> That my keen knife see not the wound it makes,
> Nor Heaven peep through the blanket of the dark
> To cry, Hold! Hold!   (I. v. 51)

And Macbeth:

> Stars, hide your fires.
> Let not light see my black and deep desires;
> The eye wink at the hand; yet let that be,
> Which the eye fears, when it is done, to see.   (I. iv. 50)

During the play "light thickens" (III. ii. 50), the "travelling lamp" is "strangled" (II. iv. 7), there is "husbandry in heaven" (II. i. 4). This is typical:

> Now spurs the lated traveller apace
> To gain the timely inn.   (III. iii. 6)

Now this world of doubts and darkness gives birth to strange and hideous creatures. Vivid animal disorder-symbolism is recurrent in the play and the animals mentioned are for the most part fierce, ugly, or ill-omened significance. We hear of "the Hyrcan tiger" and the "armed rhinoceros" (III. iv. 101), the "rugged Russian bear" (III. iv. 100); the wolf, "whose howl's his watch" (II. i. 54); the raven who croaks the entrance of Duncan under Lady Macbeth's battlements (I. v. 39); the owl, "fatal bellman who gives the stern'st good-night" (II. ii. 4). There are "maggot-pies and choughs and rooks" (III. iv. 125), and

> . . . hounds and greyhounds, mongrels, spaniels, curs,
> Shoughs, water-rugs, and demi-wolves . . .   (III. i 93)

We have the bat and his "cloistered flight," the "shard-borne beetle," the crow making wing to the "rooky wood"; "night's black agents" rouse to their preys; Macbeth has "scotch'd

82

the snake, not killed it"; his mind is full of "scorpions" (III. ii. 13-53). All this suggests life threatening, ill-omened, hideous: and it culminates in the holocaust of filth prepared by the Weird Sisters in the Cauldron scene. But not only are animals, like men, irrational and amazing in their acts. A falcon is attacked and killed by a "mousing owl," and Duncan's horses eat each other (II. iv. 11-18). There is a prodigious and ghastly tempest, with "screams of death"; the owl clamoured through the night; the earth itself shook (II. iii. 60-7). We are thus aware of a hideous abnormality in this world; and again we feel its irrationality and mystery. In proportion as we let ourselves be receptive to the impact of all these suggestions we shall be strongly aware of the essential fearsomeness of this universe.

We are confronted by mystery, darkness, abnormality, hideousness: and therefore by fear. The word "fear" is ubiquitous. All may be unified as symbols of this emotion. Fear is predominant. Everyone is afraid. There is scarcely a person in the play who does not feel and voice at some time a sickening, nameless terror. The impact of the play is thus exactly analogous to nightmare, to which state there are many references:

> Now o'er the one-half world,
> Nature seems dead, and wicked dreams abuse
> The curtain'd sleep . . . (II. i. 49)

Banquo cries:

> Merciful powers,
> Restrain in me the cursed thoughts that nature
> Gives way to in repose! (II. i. 70)

Banquo has dreamed of "the three weird sisters" (II. i. 20), who are thus associated with a nightmare reality. There are those who cried in their sleep, and said their prayers after (II. ii. 24). Macbeth may "sleep no more" (II. ii. 44); sleep, balm of hurt minds, "shall neither night nor day hang upon his pent-house lid" (I. iii. 19)—if we may transfer the reference. He and his wife are condemned to live

> in the affliction of these terrible dreams
> That shake us nightly. (III. ii. 18)

The central act of the play is a hideous murder of sleep. Finally, we have the extreme agony of sleep-consciousness depicted in Lady Macbeth's sleep-walking. Nor are there dreams only: the narrow gulf between nightmare and the abnormal actuality of the *Macbeth* universe—itself of nightmare quality—is bridged by phantasies and ghosts: the dagger of Macbeth's mind, the Ghost of Banquo, the Apparitions, the Vision of Scottish Kings, culminating in the three Weird Sisters. There is no nearer equivalent, in the experience of a normal mind, to the poetic quality of *Macbeth* than the consciousness of nightmare or delirium. That is why life is here a "tale told by an idiot" (v. v. 27), a "fitful fever" after which the dead "sleep well" (III. ii. 23); why the earth itself is "feverous" (II. iii. 67). The Weird Sisters are nightmare actualized; Macbeth's crime nightmare projected into action. Therefore this world is unknowable, hideous, disorderly, and irrational. The very style of the play has a mesmeric, nightmare quality, for in that dream-consciousness, hateful though it be, there is a nervous tension, a vivid sense of profound significance, an exceptionally rich apprehension of reality electrifying the mind: one is in touch with absolute evil, which, being absolute, has a satanic beauty, a hideous, serpent-like grace and attraction, drawing, paralysing. This quality is in the poetic style: the language is tense, nervous, insubstantial, without anything of the visual clarity of *Othello*, or the massive solemnity of *Timon of Athens*. The poetic effect of the whole, though black with an inhuman abysm of darkness, is yet shot through and streaked with vivid colour, with horrors that hold a mesmeric attraction even while they repel; and things of brightness that intensify the enveloping murk. There is constant reference to blood. Macbeth and Banquo "bathe in reeking wounds" (I. ii. 40) in the fight reported by the "bloody" Sergeant; Macbeth's sword "smoked with bloody execution" (I. ii. 18); there is the blood on Macbeth's hands, and on Lady Macbeth's after she has "smeared" the sleeping grooms with it (II. ii). There is the description of Duncan's body, "his silver skin lac'd with his golden blood" (II. iii. 118). There is blood on the face of the Murderer who comes to tell of Banquo's "trenched gashes" (III. iv. 27); the "gory locks" (III. iv. 51) of the "blood-bolter'd" Banquo; the "bloody child" Apparition; the blood-nightmare of Lady Macbeth's sleep-walking. But though blood-imagery is rich, there is no brilliance in it; rather a sickly smear. Yet there is brilliance in the fire-imagery: the thunder and lightning which accompanies the Weird Sisters; the fire of the cauldron; the green glint of the spectral dagger; the glaring eyes which hold "no speculation" of Banquo's Ghost, the insubstantial sheen of the three Apparitions, the ghastly pageant of kings unborn.

Macbeth has the poetry of intensity: intense darkness shot with the varied intensity of pure light or pure colour. In the same way the moral darkness is shot with imagery of bright purity and virtue. There is "the temple-haunting martlet" (I. vi. 4) to contrast with evil creatures. We have the early personation of the sainted Duncan, whose body is "the Lord's anointed temple" (II. iii. 74), the bright limning of his virtues by Macbeth (I. vii. 16-20), and Macduff (IV. iii. 108); the latter's lovely words on Malcolm's mother who, "oftener upon her knees than on her feet, died every day she lived" (IV. iii. 110); the prayer of Lennox for "some holy angel" (III. vi. 45) to fly to England's court for saving help; Macbeth's agonized vision of a starry good, of "Heaven's cherubim" horsed in air, and Pity like a babe; those who pray that God may bless them in their fevered dream; above all, Malcolm's description of England's holy King, health-giver and God-elect who, unlike Macbeth, has power over "the evil," in whose court Malcolm borrows "grace" to combat the nightmare evil of his own land:

Malcolm.　　　Comes the King forth, I pray you?
Doctor. Ay, sir; there are a crew of wretched souls
　　That stay his cure: their malady convinces
　　The great assay of art; but at his touch—
　　Such sanctity hath Heaven given his hand—
　　They presently amend.
Malcolm.　　　　　　　I thank you, doctor.
Macduff. What's the disease he means?
Malcolm.　　　　　　　　　　'Tis call'd the evil.
　　A most miraculous work in this good king;
　　Which often, since my here-remain in England,
　　I have seen him do. How he solicits Heaven,
　　Himself best knows: but strangely visited people,
　　All swoln and ulcerous, pitiful to the eye,
　　The mere despair of surgery, he cures,
　　Hanging a golden stamp about their necks,
　　Put on with holy prayers: and 'tis spoken,
　　To the succeeding royalty he leaves
　　The healing benediction. With this strange virtue,
　　He hath a heavenly gift of prophecy,
　　And sundry blessings hang about his throne,
　　That speak him full of grace.　　　　(IV. iii. 140)

This description is spoken just before Ross enters with the shattering narration of Macbeth's most dastardly and ruinous crime. The contrast at this instant is vivid and pregnant. The King of England is thus full of supernatural "grace." In

Macbeth this supernatural grace is set beside the supernatural evil. Against such grace Macbeth first struck the blow of evil. Duncan was "gracious" (III. i. 66); at his death "renown and grace is dead" (II. iii. 101). By "the grace of Grace" (V. vii. 101) alone Malcolm will restore health[2] to Scotland. The murk, indeed, thins towards the end. Bright daylight dawns and the green leaves of Birnam came against Macbeth. A world climbs out of its darkness, and in the dawn that panorama below is a thing of nightmare delusion. The "sovereign flower" (V. ii. 30) is bright-dewed in the bright dawn, and the murk melts into the mists of morning: the Child is crowned, the Tree of Life in his hand.

I have indicated something of the imaginative atmosphere of this play. It is a world shaken by "fears and scruples" (II. iii. 136). It is a world where "nothing is but what is not" (I. iii. 141), where "fair is foul and foul is fair" (I. i. 11). I have emphasized two complementary elements: (i) the doubts, uncertainties, irrationalities; (ii) the horrors, the dark, the abnormalities. These two elements repel respectively the intellect and the heart of man. And, since the contemplating mind is thus powerfully unified in its immediate antagonism, our reaction holds the positive and tense fear that succeeds nightmare, wherein there is an experience of something at once insubstantial and unreal to the understanding and appallingly horrible to the feelings: this is the evil of *Macbeth*. In this equal repulsion of the dual attributes of the mind a state of singleness and harmony is induced in the recipient, and it is in respect of this that *Macbeth* forces us to a consciousness more exquisitely unified and sensitive than any of the great tragedies but its polar opposite, *Antony and Cleopatra*. This is how the *Macbeth* universe presents to us an experience of absolute evil. Now, these two peculiarities of the whole play will be found also in the purely human element. The two main characteristics of Macbeth's temptation are (i) ignorance of his own motive, and (ii) horror of the deed to which he is being driven. Fear is the primary emotion of the *Macbeth* universe: fear is at the root of Macbeth's crime. I shall next notice the nature of those human events, actions, experiences to which the atmosphere of unreality and terror bears intimate relation.

The action of the play turns on a deed of disorder. Follow-

---

[2] The "evil" of *Macbeth* is symbolized in a nation's sickness. See v. ii. 27-9; v. iii. 49-56. The spiritual evil of *Macbeth* is directly related to the bodily evil of blood-destruction and sickness in the community.

ing the disorderly rebellion which prologues the action we have Macbeth's crime, and the disorder which it creates:

> Confusion now hath made his masterpiece!
> Most sacrilegious murder hath broke ope
> The Lord's anointed temple, and stole thence
> The life o' the building. (II. iii. 72)

The murder of Duncan and its results are essentially things of confusion and disorder, an interruption of the even tenour of human nature, and are thus related to the disorder-symbols and instances of unnatural behaviour in man or animal or element throughout the play. The evil of atmospheric effect thus interpenetrates the evil of individual persons. It has so firm a grip on this world that it fastens not only on the protagonists, but on subsidiary persons too. This point I shall notice before passing to the themes of Macbeth and his wife.

Many minor persons are definitely related to evil: the two —or three—Murderers, the traitors, Cawdor and Macdonald, the drunken porter, doing duty at the gate of Hell. But the major ones too, who are conceived partly as contrasts to Macbeth and his wife, nevertheless succumb to the evil downpressing on the *Macbeth* universe. Banquo is early involved. Returning with Macbeth from a bloody war, he meets the three Weird Sisters. We may imagine that the latter are related to the bloodshed of battle, and that they have waited until after "the hurly-burly's done" (I. i. 3) to instigate a continuance of blood-lust in the two generals. We must observe that the two generals' feats of arms are described as acts of unprecedented ferocity:

> Except they meant to bathe in reeking wounds,
> Or memorize another Golgotha,
> I cannot tell. (I. ii. 40)

This campaign strikes amaze into men. War is here a thing of blood, not ignorance. Ross addresses Macbeth:

> Nothing afeard of what thyself did make,
> Strange images of death. (I. iii. 96)

Macbeth's sword "smoked with bloody execution" (I. ii. 18). The emphasis is important. The late wine of blood-destruction focuses the inward eyes of these two to the reality of the sisters of blood and evil, and they in turn urge Macbeth to add to those "strange images of death" the "great doom's image" (II. iii. 85) of a murdered and sainted king. This knowledge of evil implicit in his meeting with the three Weird Sisters Banquo keeps to himself, and it is a bond of evil between him and Macbeth. It is this that troubles him on the night of the murder, planting a nightmare of unrest in his mind: "the cursed thoughts that nature gives way to in repose." He feels the typical *Macbeth* guilt: "a heavy summons lies like lead" upon him (II. i. 6). He is enmeshed in Macbeth's horror, and, after the coronation, keeps the guilty secret, and lays to his heart a guilty hope. Banquo is thus involved. So also is Macduff. His cruel desertion of his family is emphasized:

> *L. Macduff*. His flight was madness; when our actions do not,
>   Our fears do make us traitors.
> *Ross*.   You know not
>   Whether it was his wisdom or his fear.
> *L. Macduff*. Wisdom! to leave his wife, to leave his babes,
>   His mansion and his titles in a place
>   From whence himself does flee?   (IV. ii. 3)

For this, or for some nameless reason, Macduff knows he bears some responsibility for his dear ones' death:

> Sinful Macduff,
> They were all struck for thee! Naught that I am,
> Not for their own demerits, but for mine,
> Fell slaughter on their souls. Heaven rest them now!
>   (IV. iii. 223)

All the persons seem to share some guilt of the down-pressing enveloping evil. Even Malcolm is forced to repeat crimes on himself. He catalogues every possible sin, and accuses himself of all. Whatever be his reasons, his doing so yet remains part of the integral humanism of this play. The pressure of evil is not relaxed till the end. Not that the persons are "bad characters." They are not "characters" at all, in the proper use of the word. They are but vaguely individualized, and more remarkable for similarity than difference. All the persons are primarily just this: men paralysed by fear and a sense of evil in and outside themselves. They lack will-power: that concept finds no place here. Neither we, nor they, know of what exactly they are guilty: yet they feel guilt.

So, too, with Lady Macbeth. She is not merely a woman of strong will: she is a woman possessed—possessed of evil passion. No "will-power" on earth would account for her dread invocation:

> Come, you spirits
> That tend on mortal thoughts, unsex me here,
> And fill me from the crown to the toe, top-full
> Of direst cruelty!
>
> (I. v. 41)

This speech, addressed to the "murdering ministers" who "in their sightless substances wait on nature's mischief" is demonic in intensity and passion. It is inhuman—as though the woman were controlled by an evil something which masters her, mind and soul. It is mysterious, fearsome, yet fascinating: like all else here, it is a nightmare thing of evil. Whatever it be it leaves her a pure woman, with a woman's frailty, as soon as ever its horrible work is done. She faints at Macbeth's description of Duncan's body. As her husband grows rich in crime, her significance dwindles: she is left shattered, a human wreck who mutters over again in sleep the hideous memories of her former satanic hour of pride. To interpret the figure of Lady Macbeth in terms of "ambition" and "will" is, indeed, a futile commentary. The scope and sweep of her evil passion is a thing tremendous, irresistible, ultimate. She is an embodiment—for one mighty hour—of evil absolute and extreme.[3]

The central human theme—the temptation and crime of Macbeth—is, however, more easy of analysis. The crucial speech runs as follows:

> Why do I yield to that suggestion,
> Whose horrid image doth unfix my hair,
> And makes my seated heart knock at my ribs
> Against the use of nature? Present fears
> Are less than horrible imaginings.
> My thought whose murder yet is but fantastical
> Shakes so my single state of man that function
> Is smother'd in surmise, and nothing is
> But what is not.
>
> (I. iii. 134)

These lines, spoken when Macbeth first feels the impending evil, expresses again all those elements I have noticed in the mass-effect of the play: questioning doubt, horror, fear of some unknown power; horrible imaginings of the supernatural and "fantastical"; an abysm of unreality; disorder on the plane of physical life. This speech is a microcosm of the *Macbeth* vision: it contains the germ of the whole. Like a stone in a pond, this original immediate experience of Mac-

---

[3] Iago is not absolutely evil in this sense. He is too purely intellectual to antagonize our emotions powerfully.

beth sends ripples of itself expanding over the whole play. This is the moment of the birth of evil in *Macbeth*—he may have had ambitious thoughts before, may even have intended the murder, but now for the first time he feels its oncoming reality. This is the mental experience which he projects into action, thereby plunging his land, too, in fear, horror, darkness, and disorder. In this speech we have a swift interpenetration of idea with idea, from fear and disorder, through sickly imaginings, to abysmal darkness, nothingness. "Nothing is but what is not": that is the text of the play. Reality and unreality change places. We must see that Macbeth, like the whole universe of this play, is paralysed, mesmerized, as though in a dream. This is not merely "ambition"—it is fear, a nameless fear which yet fixes itself to a horrid image. He is helpless as a man in a nightmare: and this helplessness is integral to the conception—the will-concept is absent. Macbeth may struggle, but he cannot fight: he can no more resist than a rabbit resists a weasel's teeth fastened in its neck, or a bird the serpent's transfixing eye. Now this evil in Macbeth propels him to an act absolutely evil. For, though no ethical system is ultimate, Macbeth's crime is as near absolute as may be. It is therefore conceived as absolute. Its dastardly nature is emphasized clearly (I. vii. 12-25): Duncan is old, good; he is at once Macbeth's kinsman, king, and guest; he is to be murdered in sleep. No worse act of evil could well be found. So the evil of which Macbeth is at first aware rapidly entraps him in a mesh of events: it makes a tool of Duncan's visit, it dominates Lady Macbeth. It is significant that she, like her husband, is influenced by the Weird Sisters and their prophecy. Eventually Macbeth undertakes the murder, as a grim and hideous duty. He cuts a sorry figure at first, but, once embarked on his allegiant enterprise of evil, his grandeur grows. Throughout he is driven by fear—the fear that paralyses everyone else urges him to an amazing and mysterious action of blood. This action he repeats, again and again.

By his original murder he isolates himself from humanity. He is lonely, endures the uttermost torture of isolation. Yet still a bond unites him to men: that bond he would "cancel and tear to pieces"—the natural bond of human fellowship and love.[4] He further symbolizes his guilty, pariah soul by murdering Banquo. He fears everyone outside himself but

---

[4] Macbeth prays to night to "cancel and tear to pieces that great bond which keeps me pale" (III. ii. 49). This is the bond of *nature,* that which binds man to the good which is in him; the bond of daylight, reality, life. "Cancel his bond of life" occurs in *Richard III,* IV. iv. 77.

his wife, suspects them. Every act of blood is driven by fear of the horrible disharmony existent between himself and his world. He tries to harmonize the relation by murder. He would let "the frame of things disjoint, both the worlds suffer," (II. ii. 16) to win back peace. He is living in an unreal world, a fantastic mockery, a ghoulish dream: he strives to make this single nightmare to rule the outward things of his nation. He would make all Scotland a nightmare thing of dripping blood. He knows he cannot return, so determines to go o'er. He seeks out the Weird Sisters a second time. Now he welcomes disorder and confusion, would let them range wide over the earth, since they range unfettered in his own soul:

> . . . though the treasure
> Of nature's germens tumble all together,
> Even till destruction sicken; answer me
> To what I ask you.   (IV. i. 58)

So he addresses the Weird Sisters. Castles, palaces, and pyramids—let all fall in general confusion, if only Macbeth be satisfied. He is plunging deeper and deeper into unreality, the severance from mankind and all normal forms of life is now abysmal, deep. Now he is shown Apparitions glassing the future. They promise him success in terms of natural law; no man "of woman born" shall hurt him, he shall not be vanquished till Birnam Wood come against him. He, based firmly in the unreal, yet thinks to build his future on the laws of reality. He forgets that he is trafficking with things of nightmare fantasy, whose truth is falsehood, falsehood truth. That success they promise is unreal as they themselves. So, once having cancelled the bond of reality he has no home: the unreal he understands not, the real condemns him. In neither can he exist. He asks if Banquo's issue shall reign in Scotland: most horrible thought to him, since, if that be so, it proves that the future takes its natural course irrespective of human acts—that prophecy need not have been interpreted into crime: that he would in truth have been King of Scotland without his own "stir" (I. iii. 144). Also the very thought of other succeeding and prosperous kings, some of them with "twofold balls and treble sceptres" (IV. i. 121), is a maddening thing to him who is no real king but only monarch of a nightmare realm. The Weird Sisters who were formerly as the three Parcae, or Fates, foretelling Macbeth's future, now, at this later stage of his story, become the Erinyes, avengers of murder, symbols of the tormented soul. They delude and madden him with their apparitions and ghosts. Yet he does not give way, and raises our admiration at his undaunted severance from good. He contends for his own individual soul against the universal reality. Nor is his contest unavailing. He is fighting himself free from the nightmare fear of his life. He goes on "till destruction sicken" (IV. i. 60): he actually does "go o'er," is not lost in the stream of blood he elects to cross. It is true. He wins his battle. He adds crime to crime and emerges at last victorious and fearless:

> I have almost forgot the taste of fears:
> The time has been, my senses would have cool'd
> To hear a night-shriek; and my fell of hair
> Would at a dismal treatise rouse and stir
> As life were in't; I have supp'd full with horrors;
> Direness, familiar to my slaughterous thoughts,
> Cannot once start me.   (V. v. 9)

Again, "Hang those that talk of fear!" (V. iii. 36) he cries, in an ecstasy of courage. He is, at last, "broad and general as the casing air" (III. iv. 23).

This will appear a strange reversal of the usual commentary; it is, however, true and necessary. Whilst Macbeth lives in conflict with himself there is misery, evil, fear: when, at the end, he and others have openly identified himself with evil, he faces the world fearless: nor does he appear evil any longer. The worst element of his suffering has been that secrecy and hypocrisy so often referred to throughout the play (I. iv. 12; I. v. 64; III. ii. 34; V. iii. 27). Dark secrecy and night are in Shakespeare ever the badges of crime. But at the end Macbeth has no need of secrecy. He is no longer "cabin'd, cribb'd, confined, bound in to saucy doubts and fears" (III. iv. 24). He has won through by excessive crime to an harmonious and honest relation with his surroundings. He has successfully symbolized the disorder of his lonely guilt-striken soul by creating disorder in the world, and thus restores balance and harmonious contact. The mighty principle of good planted in the nature of things then asserts itself, condemns him openly, brings him peace. Daylight is brought to Macbeth, as to Scotland, by the accusing armies of Malcolm. He now knows himself to be a tyrant confessed, and wins back that integrity of soul which gives us:

> I have lived long enough: my way of life
> Is fallen into the sere, the yellow leaf . . .   (V. iii. 22)

Here he touches a recognition deeper than fear, more potent than nightmare. The delirious dream is over. A clear daylight now disperses the imaginative dark that has eclipsed Scotland. The change is remarkable. There is now movement, surety and purpose, colour: horses "skirr the country round" (v. iii. 35), banners are hung out on the castle walls (v. v. 1), soldiers hew down the bright leaves of Birnam (v. iv. 5). There is, as it were, a paean of triumph as the *Macbeth* universe, having struggled darkly upward, now climbs into radiance. Though they oppose each other in fight, Macbeth and Malcolm share equally in this relief, this awakening from horror. Of a piece with this change is the fulfilment of the Weird Sisters' prophecies. In bright daylight the nightmare reality to which Macbeth has been subdued is insubstantial and transient as sleep-horrors at dawn. Their unreality is emphasized by the very fact that they are nevertheless related to natural phenomena: they are thus parasitic on reality. To these he has trusted, and they fail. But he himself is, at the last, self-reliant and courageous. The words of the Weird Sisters ring true:

> Though his bark cannot be lost
> Yet it shall be tempest-toss'd.   (i. iii. 24)

Each shattering report he receives with redoubled life-zest; and meets the fate marked out by the daylight consciousness of normal man for the nightmare reality of crime. Malcolm may talk of "this dead butcher and his fiend-like queen" (v. vii. 98). We, who have felt the sickly poise over the abysmal deeps of evil, the hideous reality of the unreal, must couch our judgement in a different phrase.

The consciousness of nightmare is a consciousness of absolute evil, presenting an heightened awareness of positive significance which challenges the goldenest dreams of blissful sleep: it is positive, powerful, autonomous. Whether this be ultimate truth or not, it is what our mental experience knows: and to deny it is to deny the aristocracy of mind. The "sickly weal" of Scotland is in the throes of this delirious dream, which, whilst it lasts, has every attribute of reality. Yet this evil is not a native of man's heart: it comes from without. The Weird Sisters are thus objectively conceived: they are not, as are phantoms and ghosts, the subjective effect of evil in the protagonist's mind. They are, within the *Macbeth* universe, independent entities. The fact that they instigate Macbeth directly and Lady Macbeth indirectly thus tends to assert the objectivity of evil. This, however, is purely a matter of poetic impact: the word "absolute" seems a just interpretation of the imaginative reality, in so far as an immediate interpretation only is involved. Its implications in a wider system might not be satisfactory. But, whatever be the evil here, we can say that we understand something of the psychological state which gives these extraneous things of horror their reality and opportunity. And if we are loth to believe in such evil realities, potentially at least alive and powerful, we might call to mind the words of Lafeu in *All's Well that Ends Well*.

> They say miracles are past; and we have our philosophical persons, to make modern and familiar things supernatural and causeless. Hence is it that we make trifles of terrors, ensconcing ourselves into seeming knowledge, when we should submit ourselves to an unknown fear.   (II. iii. 1)

A profound commentary on *Macbeth*. But, though the ultimate evil remain a mystery, analysis of the play indicates something of its relation to the mind and the actions of men.

Such analysis must be directed not to the story alone, but to the manifold correspondencies of imaginative quality extending throughout the whole play. The *Macbeth* vision is powerfully superlogical. Yet it is the work of interpretation to give some logical coherence to things imaginative. To do this, it is manifestly not enough to abstract the skeleton of logical sequence which is the story of the play: that is to ignore the very quality which justifies our anxious attention. Rather, relinquishing our horizontal sight of the naked rockline which is the story, we should, from above, view the whole work extended, spatialized: and then map out imaginative similarities and differences, hills and vales and streams. Only to such a view does *Macbeth* reveal the full riches of its meaning. Interpretation must thus first receive the quality of the play in the imagination, and then proceed to translate this whole experience into a new logic which will not be confined to those superficialities of cause and effect which we think to trace in our own lives and actions, and try to impose on the persons of literature. In this way, we shall know that *Macbeth* shows us an evil not to be accounted for in terms of "will" and "causality"; that it expresses its vision, not to a critical intellect, but to the responsive imagination; and, working in terms not of "character" or any ethical code, but of the abysmal deeps of a spirit-world untuned to human reality, withdraws the veil from the black streams which mill that consciousness of fear symbolized in actions of blood. *Macbeth* is the apocalypse of evil.

In *Hamlet* and *Macbeth* supernatural figures are first objective; seen later by the hero alone; and, at the conclusion, clearly do not exist; as though some unrest in the outer universe has been satisfactorily projected and dispelled. Does this help to explain the gathering poetic force of Macbeth's speeches, culminating in the supreme pieces of Act V? Note, too, Macbeth's courage in successfully dismissing the air-drawn dagger and, twice, Banquo's Ghost. Macbeth shows throughout a positive drive. For a further development of this reading, see my *Christ and Nietzsche*.

For a study of the more obvious, countering, positives (e.g. effects of social health, nature, Banquo's descendants and child-images rising to the child-apparitions) see my essay 'The Milk of Concord' in *The Imperial Theme;* and also my analysis of the Apparition scene in *The Shakespearian Tempest*. For Hecate see *The Shakespearian Tempest*, App. B.

The Cid
or
Corneille's Cult of the Hero

SERGE DOUBROVSKY

OTHERS have shown how Corneille's scenes of "bravado," while evidently inspired by feudal ideals, were bent to the taste of the public he wrote for. Surely it is not necessary to repeat once again that *The Cid* gave voice to the concerns of an aristocracy for its feudal origins. The military, political, social, and moral aspects of such a return to the knightly past have been well examined; it is a past, by the way, about which modern criticism is quite without illusion. There is in this play not the traditional Epinal image of irreproachable courage, but rather, in the harsh expression of G. Coulton, "a real feudal racism," both upper-class and international in character, from which every mystic trace of God's judgment has been eliminated, and which rests entirely on "the serene cruelty of the law of the strongest." Now in this essay, I shall try to spell out the dialectic which, in all Corneille's work, underlies historical reality.

What is important in the famous scene when the Count de Gormas opposes Don Diego, and important too in the latter's painful monologue, is that something is at stake which is scarcely reducible to a single honor aimed at by rivals of equal stamp. What matters is that the Count, presently without a peer, has seen a man who might have been his rival yesterday favored over him against all expectation; the opposition is not between two men so much as between past and present service to the King. The two rivals agree in recognizing their equality which flows from a fundamental identity: their conflict breaks forth only because a difference between them in age has to be recognized. Besides, it is not hard to understand why the problem of time is the central problem, and so to speak, the stumbling block of the aristocratic project. If a man aims at the total assumption of himself in a heroic test, this test, to be valid, will have to be constantly repeated; in other words, a paragon, living in time, must find his being put in question at every moment. Just as the dazzling force of love is corroded in its very nature by the possibility of "change," so the virtue and weight of human valiance are tainted to the very marrow by time. Suddenly Don Diego discovers with horror and humiliation that his whole past counts for nothing, a truth the Count has brutally expressed. Up against the pitiless present, against annihilation by time, the nobleman, now old, is quite lost, and seems about to drag down with him not only the honor of his individual past, but that of his whole race. One sees the terrible implications of this fall. It is not just that individual heroism has stumbled against the perilous reality of time: even more important is the fact that a door has been opened to some act or exploit which at one brutal stroke can undermine the race—the very structure of aristocratic society is threatened. The nobility, the dominating class, came to power and justified itself at a given moment of history, a moment of collective time. Now an abyss has suddenly opened, showing that the order founded on valiance can be put in question, and in a new test of strength "betrayed," even as Don Diego is betrayed by "hostile old age. . . ." When the vanquished old man cries out,

> Mon bras, qui tant de fois a sauvé cet empire,
> Tant de fois affermi le trône de son roi . . .

he is literally carrying on his now weakened shoulders not only the weight of his own destiny, but the whole burden of his race, of the empire, the throne, in a word, the monarchical order. His cry of anguish defines and underlines for us the very essence of Corneillean tragedy.

But the answer is there already, the solution is given even as the problem is posed: Roderigo appears on the scene. More precisely, the very terms of the problem point to its solution. The body, that tragic source of decadence, is also an endless source of health. This son, who is the continuation of a "blood-line" ("Come my son, come my blood . . ."), miraculously effects the synthesis of individuality and race, as of the past and of the present, opening also at one stroke the dimension of the future which for a moment had been closed. But if identity is established by birth ("Avenge me, avenge yourself") blood is still not transmitted like property or money; the authentic link between father and son can only be established by a test, such as the one spontaneously accepted, or rather proposed, by Roderigo. This is the meaning of the famous exchange.

> —*Rodrigue, as-tu du coeur?*
> > —*Tout autre que mon père*
> *L'éprouverait sur l'heure . . .*

Such a test of courage can only be a test of blood: of noble blood which shows it is noble by its willingness to be shed. This central truth of aristocratic will, unveiled by Don Diego, is, in fact, the main idea behind all of Corneille's heroic constructions:

> *Va contre un arrogant éprouver ton courage:*
> *Ce n'est que dans le sang qu'on lave un tel outrage.*
> *Meurs ou tue.*

There is point, here, in turning to the famous discussion in Hegel's *Phenomenology of Spirit* which deals with the dialectic of Master and Slave[. . . .]* After all, Hegel was the very first philosopher to show the great importance a systematic study of our relations with others can have; he set forth in an exact way the dialectic pitting master against slave, so an analysis of the theme of Mastery, the essential theme of Corneille's theatre, cannot but be aided by Hegel.[. . .]

According to the *Phenomenology of Spirit,* man only becomes conscious of himself when he is able to say "I." Insofar as man has Self-Consciousness, he is distinct from the animal who never goes beyond the level of an obscure sense of selfness. But since humanity is rooted in animality, the human

---

* To meet the requirements of space, some passages of Doubrovsky's essay, considered inessential for this book, have been omitted. Their omission in indicated by brackets.

"I" first reveals itself in relation to the world by what we call desire. It is indeed an animal desire (the desire to eat, to drink, for instance) which reminds me that I am, which defines me as an ego. The desire for natural objects originally sets up a limited and natural ego immersed in immediate life, and which can appear only as a sense of selfness and not as true self-consciousness. For the emergence of real self-consciousness and authentic humanity, there must be a desire directed at another, or, according to the Hegelian expression, the "desire of a desire." Thus, in love, the human desire becomes distinct from animal desire only when one of the lovers desires not merely the other's body but also to be desired by the other, that is, when the lover wants to "loved" by the other, and thus *recognized*. In man, there is an animal ego, but there is also a human ego; and for a human world to arise, human desire must be stronger than animal desire. A human being can only define himself when recognized as such by another human being. . . .

Now, according to Hegel, there is only one way of proving to any other being that one possesses self-consciousness: and this is to elevate oneself precisely above animality by raising oneself up above life. Life, to animal desire, is the supreme value. Human desire, or the desire to be recognized by another or by others, must therefore show itself by a voluntary risk of life, a willed confrontation of death. Now since recognition has to be reciprocal, it requires two persons and a double risk, that is to say, a combat. In a phrase now famous, Hegel sums up the first stage of human relations thus: "Each seeks the other's death."

Out of the dialectic of recognition comes domination, also servitude. For the death of one of the two adversaries could resolve nothing. As Kojève has explained: "The survivor, since he cannot be recognized by the man he has killed, cannot realize and reveal his humanity. For the human reality of one to be recognized as real, both the contenders must survive their fight. This is possible only if they behave differently in fighting. . . . Without being at all predetermined to act that way, one must show fear of the other, yield to the other, and refuse to risk his life for the sake of being recognized. He must give up his own desire, and satisfy the other's desire. He must 'recognize' the other without being 'recognized' by him. But to recognize him thus is to recognize him as a Master and it is also to recognize oneself and cause oneself to be recognized as the Master's slave. In other words, at the birth of the human a man is never simply a man; he is essentially and necessarily

98

either a Master or a Slave." This succinct exposition by Kojève of Hegel's analysis does clarify in an exact and even profound way those fundamental human relations which are defined in Corneille's *The Cid* and also in his general movement of the drama of heroism. While the Hegelian dialectic goes on to speak of the relations between and confrontation of Master and Slave that leads ultimately to the Slave's victory, Corneille, so to speak, immobilizes the dialectic at the moment of Mastery. One might even say that Corneille's whole theatre contributes the moment of Mastery as such. In this sense it is no paradox to say that Corneille develops the analysis of Mastery even further than Hegel, who was more concerned with the relations of Master and Slave. There is a complex *internal* dialectic in the aim of Mastery, which concerns the Master's relation to himself and to others. Philosophically and politically, the theatre of Corneille is nothing less than this double dialectic of the Master, or if you prefer, the hero[. . . .]

The first act of the *The Cid* brilliantly defines both sides of the aristocratic ethic: the aim of an individual to assert himself in and through a combat with another, and also an intersubjective aim, which gives rise to a plurality of heroic Egos. Their co-existence also can be seen in two ways: horizontally, we see different individuals in the same space: (Don Diego, Count Gormas, Don Sancho, etc.) constituted as a *class*; vertically, they are related to each other in time and constituted as a *race* (Don Diego, Don Roderigo, Count Gormas, Chimena). If every tragedy is, as Corneille puts it, the presence of a "peril," this peril from the very start is double. First of all, the individual's aristocratic aim threatens the aristocratic order. The irrepressible impulse towards Mastery splits the class of Masters: this is the meaning of the deadly rivalry which sets Count Gormas against Don Diego. The quest of absolute superiority, satisfied on the battlefield at the expense of other men, thrusts the conquerors in their turn against each other. Thus the dialectic of Mastery leads the Masters to destroy each other (which is explicitly expressed by Richelieu's edict against dueling). But in addition to the class danger, there is also what might be called the race danger. If it is true that the affirmation of a heroic ego is, as in Roderigo's case, a unique act—though related to a tradition—an absolute beginning, and also a rebeginning, then Mastery cannot be just *inherited*. It has to be merited as well: "Show yourself to be the worthy son of a father such as I." The category "worthy of" that goes with the initiation into mastery of young Roderigo is destined to become the pivot of Corneille's ethics. But soon a new danger is discerned: "That son degenerates who lives one moment past his father's honor!" cries the Count. Unless the son at once proves himself, he may indeed degenerate. Time, which we saw destroying the father, can also be fatal, though in a different way, to the son. This is why, in his duel with the Count, in the struggle against the Moors, in his encounter with Don Sancho, Roderigo always responds immediately, whatever be the challenge. Heroism is entirely present, always there, or does not exist at all. The least internal resistance, the slightest disjunction between acting and being, would be a deadly threat to that Mastery which freedom has to wrest from nature. For the class as for the race, in space and in vital time, a double possibility of tragedy, a double threat to stability, is outlined: the social order may disintegrate, the blood deteriorate. When Roderigo promptly responds to his father's plea, one kind of tragedy, that of decadence at least, seems averted. The race is saved, for good blood doesn't lie. Thus a heroic continuity is sustained against time, and a true identity in Mastery is established. However, when we look at it more closely, we see that Roderigo's response does not quite have the assurance of a reflex: before crying out, "On to vengeance!", for an entire scene Roderigo "remains immobile." The repeated plaint of the famous Stanzas reveals to us the dead and frightening moments between stimulus and the response, and that imperceptible fissure between being and willing which a noble pride tries to overlook. According to Hegel's analysis, Mastery defines itself with the victory over the vital ego by the ego of consciousness; however, his analysis is incomplete: "The movement of absolute abstraction, a movement which eliminates from the self all immediate being," can never be reduced to the test of physical force, to the voluntary risk of life. The arena in which man fights against being swallowed up by nature is as often the arena of love as it is the arena of combat. For never is natural spontaneity more adorned, more attractive, never is it endowed with greater force than in the surging of passion, a total movement of the body which, as Descartes well saw, invades and enchains the soul. The most violent fight to the death is to be found perhaps not in the struggles of warriors, but in those of lovers. It is at this point that the aim of Mastery is connected with the world of comedy, in which the Master is interested exclusively in love. The dialectical transcendence of the comic world by the tragic world does have to preserve something of the first.

Don Diego exclaims: "We have but one honor, but many mistresses!" For this kind of feudal lord, the only thing that counts is the principle of Mastery; beings are interchangeable, identical, in the best sense of that term; is not Don Diego himself resuscitated in Roderigo? But love, in its essence, consists, as is said in the admirable verses of Vigny's "The Shepherd's Cottage," in loving "what one will never see twice"; it is love precisely which makes of the heroic ego an irreplaceable individual, caught up in the radical contingency of sensual life, that above which courage tried to raise itself. Thus a brutal conflict appears between two orders of entirely contrary values, which the civilized feudal aristocrat wanted to unite. Hence the vehement response of Roderigo to the advice of Don Diego, and his insistence on a double fidelity!

> L'infamie est pareille, et suit également
> Le guerrier sans courage et le perfide amant.
> A ma fidelité ne faites point injure . . .

The painful hiatus of the Stanzas is there to testify that the synthesis is not easy to achieve. During those dead moments before he reacts, a fissure between being and willing appears, showing the density and strength of the natural and the sensual against which Roderigo has stumbled. There is an inner movement here which people have tried to understand for the last three centuries: many interpretations have been made of Roderigo's internal conflict. One interpretation seems to go back to Corneille himself, and posits a traditional opposition of love to duty, with duty, happily for morals, triumphant, though in a way not weakening to the power of love. As Laprade said in the last century: "In this marvelous fight between passion and duty, nothing we value is wounded; there is no victim." At the end of the nineteenth century, criticism took a new line: Brunetière, Lemaître, and Faguet discovered that Corneille was not the poet of duty, but the apostle of will. What does *The Cid* express? "The triumph of love . . ." Lemaître answers in his *Impressions de Théâtre*. The critics said, too, that the sole aim of the hero was to test his will and to feel strong. More recently, criticism resolved the problem by suppressing it: there is no conflict between love and duty for the simple reason that love and duty tend toward the same end, as Roderigo himself says: "I invite her scorn, if I do not seek revenge." And he repeats this later to Chimena: "A man without honor would not deserve you." So in order to be worthy of Chimena, and indeed out of love for her, Roderigo kills her father.

We must reject this last interpretation. A conflict does in fact exist, one to which Roderigo attests: "What dire conflicts I feel!" Even the psychoanalyst who tells us that there is something "behind" the feelings of his patient will never try to teach the patient what it is he feels. An equally modest criticism must admit that Roderigo has a better idea than we of what is going on inside him.

Corneille referring to *The Cid* speaks of the conflict "of duty and love"; and Roderigo tells us, "Against my honor, my love arms itself." Our problem is not to know better than Corneille and Roderigo what they should say but to understand what they actually said. Certainly there is an absolute, anguishing opposition of two *values* when only one can be chosen: "Reduced to the sad choice of betraying my love or living disgraced . . ." Some have maintained that there was, in reality, no conflict or choice since love, like honor, required the duel, and because it was necessary for Roderigo to confront the Count to remain worthy of Chimena, also of Don Diego. These critics forget what it cost Roderigo in effort and grief to attain to such "love." At the very beginning, in fact, "love" for Corneille is something quite different from the attraction of mutual "worth": we see from the very first lines of *Mélite* that love is essentially *desire,* the attraction of body for body, aiming at total possession of the beloved. It is so for Roderigo also and we must take literally his cry of despair:

Tous mes plaisirs sont morts, ou ma gloire ternie. . . .
The renunciation of a loving enjoyment of Chimena, the "loss" of the beloved, means for Roderigo physical loss. Later, justifying himself to Chimena, he admits the power of her sensual presence.

Et ta beauté sans doute emportait la balance,
A moins que d'opposer à tes plus forts appas . . .

To follow the road of honor and fight the Count in accordance with the inexorable law of "die or kill" is simply to choose not to possess the beloved, and it is in this way that Chimena herself sees the drama. In this sense the Stanzas represent the painful engendering of a new love on the ruins of an earlier one.

In fact, we never see Roderigo deliberating, weighing the pros and the cons, and then rising above himself to arrive at a decision. There is no pro, no con, for the reason that whatever happens, his misfortune is "infinite." From the start it is a case of an absolute alternative excluding any mean term. The admirable development of the Stanzas springs neither from reasoning nor from passion. It is a lucid and pitiless arrival at self-consciousness. One must understand thereby (as in psychoanalytical experience) the disclosure of an inner truth which consciousness tries to hide from itself. For the grief which Roderigo feels is not a mere fact, a psychological datum, which stands in need of no further interpretation: it has both a meaning and a function. Experienced as some sort of paralyzing emotion in the first stanza ("pierced to the bottom of my heart . . ."), that grief *enables* Roderigo precisely not to take immediate action and to delay the moment and movement of self-sacrifice: "I stand transfixed. . . ." But he cannot remain long under the effect of this god-sent anesthesia; in the second stanza, this petrification yields to "dire conflicts. . . ." The impossibility of choosing between honor and love leads immediately to the temptation of suicide:

> *Tout redouble ma peine.*
> *Allons, mon âme; et puisqu'il faut mourir,*
> *Mourons du moins sans offenser Chimène.*

But if suicide is evidently the typical behavior of escape, we must go further and see that Roderigo's very grief serves here to produce a turn-about in him: in fact, the "dire conflicts" he feels are not *caused* by the radical alternative of love against honor, they *create* that alternative. Since he hesitates, since he feels torn apart it means he can still choose in favor of love and that the road to happiness remains, if he so wishes, open. Now, that which he was hiding from himself and which becomes gradually clear, is the very impossibility of that possibility[. . . .]

What comes to light in the course of this remarkable monologue and represents the decisive turn of Corneillean heroism is the need to sacrifice *love-as-an-enjoyment* for the maintenance of the *aristocratic order*. Roderigo feels the irresistible appeal of the flesh, the bedazzling effulgence of beauty; and thus feels his absolute dependence on Another. He begins by utilizing the ruses of bad faith to hide from himself the ineluctability of sacrifice. He prolongs for some moments the painful indecisiveness of being unable to choose in order to mask from himself the real sacrifice he must make if he wants to remain a Master. But then he realizes that if he wants to dominate

Nature in himself instead of being dominated by it, then the real possession of a woman must be the refusal to possess her. Roderigo, against the background of the original project of Mastery, little by little discovers the internal necessity by which the struggle against another is echoed by a fight against oneself. Will is not superadded to knowledge, but is included in the act of awareness, which in the deepest sense is an act of reflection. . . .

For Chimena as for Roderigo, as for all the characters of Corneille, love is first of all desire. Chimena's dilemma will therefore be the same as Roderigo's: "Honor is pitiless to my dearest desires. . . ." The nature of these desires is later made still more precise: "No matter how much desire may blind us . . ." She speaks, too, of "the sweetest hope he may have of enjoying me," and in these lines (later cut by the author) cries out:

> Qu'un même jour commence et finisse
> mon deuil,
> Mette en mon lit Rodrigue et mon père
> en cercueil?

Accustomed as we are now to literary exhibitionism, we might not see that the regular discretion of language in Corneille as in Racine, shows not the absence but the presence of a restrained yet powerful sensuality [. . . .] Alike in their manner of loving, Roderigo and Chimena have "secret sympathies" that inspire each, in the absence of the other, to express at the same moment the very same thoughts. Sharing Roderigo's values, Chimena feels an identical inner torment. In this tragic situation, she forms the same aim Roderigo did in the famous Stanzas:

> —Après tout, que pensez-vous donc faire?
> —Pour conserver ma gloire et finir mon ennui
> Le poursuivre, le perdre, et mourir après lui.

From that passive Mastery which at the beginning of the play characterizes the noblewomen of the comedies, from the free constraint that "waits for a father's command before choosing a husband," Chimena like Roderigo rises by a painful effort to *active* Mastery, and transforms *love* into loving hate.

Setting Roderigo before Chimena in two famous scenes, Corneille at once touches the apex of pure tragedy and at the same time offers heroism a wholly new horizon. What is astonishing—although it can be explained by the sway of a certain "morality" joined to a romantic sensibility—is that in the course of successive generations literally untaught to read *The Cid,* a vague and marvelous "poem of love" or "miracle of youth" has been substituted for the grandiose brutality of these scenes, which, had they merely presented innocent dove-calls in moonlight, would hardly have caused the scandal they did. . . . We have only to read the Academy's hostile judgment of *The Cid* to realize the true nature and implications of the scenes, which made Scudery exclaim that *The Cid* is "a lesson in evil," and Chapelain say that "Here are monstrous truths which must be suppressed for the good of society. . . ." It is clear that in these scenes Corneille touched the very nerve of the contemporary sensibility, and we must restore to these scenes their shock value. Corneille himself invites us to do this by the admission inherent in his retrospective doubts (*Examen de 1660*): "The two visits of Roderigo to his mistress have something offensive to decorum, when one thinks of her who endures them. . . . To be completely candid, Roderigo's offer of his sword, and his willingness to let himself be killed by Don Sancho, do not please me now." We have had to wait for Nadal's analyses to restore their original force and truth to Roderigo's famous visits to his mistress, to see that Roderigo "never stops tormenting her," and that "Roderigo relentlessly hunts Chimena down like a beast of prey, making her cry for mercy, pausing only when she is vanquished and humiliated. She does not emerge without shame from this hounding and closing-in for the kill." Certainly, Roderigo and Chimena are no Romeo and Juliet, and the nocturnal meeting in *The Cid* has nothing in common with Shakespeare's balcony scene. It is even the exact opposite of that scene, and Corneille's lyricism opens not on a duo, but on a duel of lovers. . . .

In Scene IV of Act III, Roderigo, after he has killed the Count in his own house, emerges from the shadows to echo the last words of Chimena:

> *Eh bien! sans vous donner*
> > > *la peine de poursuivre,*
> *Assurez-vous l'honneur de m'empêcher*
> > > *de vivre.*

And then with an astonishing persistence Roderigo again and again offers his sword to Chimena. This scene, written in 1637, made Corneille uneasy in 1660, and not without reason. As Nadal says, "This insistence of the hero on dying wakes in us a strange uneasiness. Can he really be so generous, or is he hiding an aim he refuses to admit. . . ?" It has often been asked just what Roderigo sought in offering his sword to Chimena; our answer is simple: he sought to die. For, given the particular character of the aristocratic ethic, and the complete allegiance of Chimena to that ethic—something Roderigo does not doubt for one moment—we cannot but think that in giving Chimena the chance to kill him, Roderigo is taking the risk that she will, and it is precisely this deadly risk which distinguishes genuine challenge from mere blackmail[. . . .]He shows her his sword still dripping with her father's blood. He brandishes this "hateful object" to Chimena, who exclaims, "It is stained with my blood." Roderigo then points out to her the proper ending: "Plunge it in mine. . . ." If Nadal is right when he says Roderigo never stops "tormenting" Chimena, he is not right when he adds that Roderigo does this "to provoke and consummate her moral ruin." On the contrary, Roderigo does everything possible to lead Chimena towards her own salvation by helping her to realize her own values. Since Chimena is similar in every way to her lover, in her feelings and in the principles by which she lives, she finds herself in the same situation as he has[. . . .] She at once associates death with merit, love with hate: the animal aim of possessing is gone, the human aim of recognition remains. But here reciprocal recognition, as Hegel showed, and as Corneille felt with infallible intuition, meant that only by the death of Roderigo could Chimena prove herself to be his equal, just as Roderigo could only prove himself to be the equal of the Count by killing him. In asking Chimena to kill him Roderigo is simply demanding the highest consummation of their love.

Roderigo has indeed changed his vital "I" into a human "I," risen from the plane of Feeling to that of Consciousness, from the movement affirming Nature to the movement which denies it. Chimena wants to follow his example but finally cannot; in her, the dialectic of heroism is somehow checked; she is unable to disentangle herself from her passion. . . . In theory, she can vaunt the greatness of her love:

> . . . je veux que la voix de la plus noire envie
> Elève au ciel ma gloire et plaigne mes ennuis,
> Sachant que je t'adore et que je te poursuis.

but in fact, on every occasion, she will deny this love, until forced by a ruse of the king to admit it; and if she denies her love, it is because she is ashamed of it. . . . According to Nadal's excellent description, there is a fatality working in her, a force that eludes the powers of will, and which invades her whole consciousness, obscures it. . . . "Roderigo can only be for Chimena a desired object, of which she feels she must be eternally deprived." That is to say, Chimena has been incapable of achieving the catharsis Roderigo came to in the Stanzas. Remaining at the stage of desire, unable to seek a nonsensual satisfaction, she cannot make a sacrifice of her love, she clings to it, unable to transcend the vital:

> La moitié de ma vie, a mis l'autre au tombeau,
> Et m'oblige à venger, après ce coup funeste,
> Celle que je n'ai plus sur celle qui me reste.

This is precisely the definition of heroic self-mutilation, in which the combat against the other means the sacrifice of the self in the first stage of Mastery. . . . At the testing point: "I see what I lose when I see his worth," she becomes fixed in that grief which immobilized Roderigo for a while. In fact all of Chimena's reasons are summed up in a single one, which is to obtain through others what the true Master will require only of himself. Hers, too, is the typical behavior of bad faith, in which the appeal to others is soon degraded into an appeal to objects:

> Vous qui rendez la force à mes ressentiments,
> Voiles, crêpes, habits, lugubres ornements . . .
> Contre ma passion soutenez bien ma gloire.

Such support is merely the last futile hope of impotence. Far from being the virile heroine she is often taken to be, Chimena becomes Corneille's symbol of shameful weakness, and weeps throughout the play; she weeps to the Infante:

> Que tu vas me coûter de pleurs et de soupirs!

to the King:

> Sire, la voix me manque à ce recit funeste;
> Mes pleurs et mes soupirs vous diront mieux le reste.

to Elvira:

> Pleurez, pleurez, mes yeux, et fondez-vous en eau!

to Roderigo:

> Je cherche le silence et la nuit pour pleurer.

She is still weeping in the Fourth Act and in the Fifth, even swears to become a veritable fountain of tears. And in Scene V of the Fourth Act, she even faints away[. . . .]

While Chimena sinks to a pathetic, even comic level, Roderigo rises to a tragic height. The one-mindedness shared by the lovers in the beginning of the play yields to a radical difference in attitude. There is no scorn, as has been suggested, in the ardor with which Roderigo hunts down a woman he loves. His is rather a pitiless love which, going beyond possession and sensual contentment (values he has sacrificed in himself and in others), strives to keep alive the recognition he won in combat, and finds sexual pleasure in a death struggle with minds and bodies—this is in brief the love of a Master, ready to kill as well as to die. Roderigo defeats father and daughter, completing at their expense his apprenticeship in heroism, continuing against Chimena the duel he fought with the Count. This is not cruelty but *violence,* something quite different. Authentic violence is the mark and source of strength; it spurs the conqueror onward. It does not freeze the mind in a fascinated contemplation of suffering, but propels to action. Roderigo seems perhaps insensitive when he cries, "O miracle of love!" just when Chimena sighs "O peak of misery!" In reality, each conquest of Roderigo, instead of making him pause in contentment, makes him rebound like a springboard. What for Chimena, locked in her passion, is the "peak of misery," becomes for Roderigo, who has experienced the catharsis of heroism, a "miracle of love," from which he draws new inspiration. For he too knows the sufferings of passion and its elegiac temptations. But the "deadly griefs" in which Chimena sinks are for him "superfluous regrets," to be overcome by action[. . . .]

The movement of ascension is not yet complete, the birth of the hero not yet achieved. He is unable to prove himself entirely in the drama of love, and will become the Master, the Cid, only when history erupts into his life. Even after having triumphed over the Count and over Chimena, Roderigo is not yet saved. A conqueror, he has however triumphed only in appearance, since his relation to death in his scenes with Chimena can be interpreted as a yielding to the desire for suicide —a temptation he had already expressed in the Stanzas. . . . The heroic act opens on a void and remains useless, insofar as loving energy has not yet been converted into historical energy. In the encounter of Roderigo and Chimena, both would have been vanquished had not Don Diego interposed a new order of reality:

> *Il n'est pas temps encor de chercher le trépas:*
> *Ton prince et ton pays ont besoin de ton bras.*

The trial by duel of a noble, completed by the duel of love, is somehow but the trial of initiation of the knight sworn to a higher destiny. To call this play a "love poem" comparable to *Romeo and Juliet* is to forget its title. Roderigo becomes the Cid only when the Moors arrive.

Their arrival later made Corneille uneasy, and as often happens, the retrospective judgment of the pedant betrayed the original intuition of the creator: "This arrival of the Moors isn't brought off without a flaw: they present themselves, without being summoned in the play, directly or indirectly, by any actor in the first act . . ." (*Examen du Cid*). But it is precisely the fact that no actor in the first act, that is to say no internal necessity of the plot, required this foreign presence which gives meaning to the event. The pure dialectic of individual relations, the pure logic of the heroic gesture, are, so to speak, recovered and snatched up by history, which often breaks the closed circle of private relationships. If, as Corneille says, "This arrival is a surprise," it is because for the subjective person bent on his own ends, the historical event always arrives unexpectedly[. . . .]

Caught unawares by the arrival of the Moors, as he had been surprised by the quarrel of his father with the Count, Roderigo on the plane of action, contrary to what happened on the plane of love, invents no special solution: the event, unexpected by the individual, takes its predestined place in the framework of history. Just as the established code of the aristocratic ethic dictated his confrontation with the Count, Roderigo now finds his ground of action entirely prepared by the feudal order.

> *. . . j'ai trouvé chez moi cinq cents de mes amis,*
> *Qui, sachant mon affront, poussés d'un même zèle,*
> *Se venaient tous offrir à venger ma querelle.*

Roderigo suddenly finds that he has been assigned a role from outside:

> *Va marcher à leur tête où l'honneur te demande:*
> *C'est toi que veut pour chef leur généreuse bande.*

Designated as "leader" and spontaneously accepting the role ("henceforth, under my guidance will this army march. . . .") Roderigo still has to prove himself as a leader. In the presence of history which abruptly jostles and transcends him, the hero suddenly finds himself seized, almost swallowed up, by that new dimension of existence in which he no longer confronts the Other in single combat, but others surging from all sides. . . . The real problem raised for the hero by the arrival of the Moors is to find out whether he can maintain his monadic autonomy in the limitless expansion of existence by history, in a word, whether he can survive.

The famous account Roderigo gives of his victory over the Moors is the answer. The tone, the "style" of the action are given from the outset:

> *J'en cache les deux tiers, aussitôt qu'arrives . . .*
>
> *Et je feins hardiment d'avoir reçu de vous*
> *L'ordre qu'on me voit suivre et que je donne à tous.*

This audacious "I," which at once assumes command and imposes its will without discussion, dominates from the start. The action of Roderigo has recalled the epic, as if Roderigo were Roland; nothing could be more false. The true epic is essentially a collective action, the paean to a race, a religion, a country. The exploits are never individual, and the deeds of individuals of more than natural greatness, from Achilles to Roland, celebrate not them but that Greece or that France which is engaged in singing its past. The epic ego is in fact a disguised "we." The heroic ego, on the contrary, even when it is engaged in collective action, pursues only individual ends. There is solidarity in the epic ego, the heroic ego is solitary. In a sense we must be wary of Roderigo's use of the word "we":

> *Ils abordent sans peur, ils ancrent, ils descendent . . .*
> *Nous nous levons alors, et tous en même temps*
> *Poussons jusques au ciel mille cris éclatants.*

[. . . .] Now we understand the hero's triumphant response to the dangers of history. Instead of allowing himself to be absorbed by history, he absorbs history into himself. The struggle with an indefinite multiplicity of Others is only one particular example of the test of Mastery; a battle becomes a variant of the duel. The historical aggrandizement of the hero, one which leaves his own attitudes unchanged and his nature

110

unaltered, is a transformation, to be sure, but not at all a metamorphosis: Roderigo becomes the Cid. . . . Fully in possession of itself, the ego of valiance has come through the trial of history, attained against it a defensive victory (one has often noted the "defensive" character of the victory over the Moors without seeing its real meaning), and is now going to suddenly take the offensive and attack history on that double terrain where history threatened it. The autarchic ego of the Master is now going to expand continuously in space and in time. For the victory over the Moors cannot be localized. Henceforward all yield—Granada, Toledo, and later many others:

> Paraissez, Navarrais, Mores et Castillans
> Et tout ce que l'Espagne a nourris de vaillants . . .

But Spain itself is too narrow a battlefield:

> Faut-il combattre encor mille et mille rivaux,
> Aux deux bouts de la terre étendre mes travaux?

The irresistible conquest of space would be quite meaningless without a similar conquest of time. The hero's problem is to succeed in a spatial possession of the world and in the control of others in the present, but he also has to perpetuate his role in eternity. Otherwise—as the misadventure of Don Diego has shown—the effort at heroism is so fragile that a single instant may hurl it into nothingness. So it was necessary to give at the end of the play a radical solution to the tragedy of human temporality, or see the work of salvation patiently constructed for five acts fall apart. Now we see Roderigo named "The Cid" by two Moorish kings; the "name" of the hero becomes much more than a title: it is an immortalizing essence. At a certain height of valiance, reached neither by Don Diego nor Count Gormas, the hero is able to exchange his acts for a name, which, like the Divine Name, has an active virtue: "Let all yield to this great name. . . ." The end of the play sees the realization of this wish: "Just to hear of the Cid will be enough to make them tremble." Thanks to the name, a life will be perpetuated, the ego will become immortal, not in another imaginary world but in this one[. . . .]

Thus the heroic project ends ultimately in a theology, that is to say, a theology made incarnate in history. If Corneille did in fact systematically secularize the drama, this secularization is still only apparent. If the Christian God has disappeared from the stage, the latter is not, for all that, empty of a divine presence; God is there, and God is Roderigo.

Carried irresistibly upward, the play could not but end well. So we must now say something about the marriage of Roderigo and Chimena, that marriage which the virtuous saw as scandalous; and which inspired the famous "Sentiments de l'Académie": "After this the critic goes on to examine the morals attributed to Chimena and to condemn them. In which we are entirely on his side. It is impossible to deny that she [Chimena] is too sensitive a lover and too unnatural a daughter, and acts against the decorum proper to her sex. However violent the passion within her, one thing is certain: she ought not to have relented in her pursuit of vengeance for her father's death; even less should she decide to marry the man who killed him. In this, we have to say that her morals are at the very least scandalous, if not in fact depraved." It is interesting to note to what extent the reaction of the "proper" critics of the time is peevish and even in bad faith. On the one hand Chimena is reproached for not being able to dominate her passion: "We blame her for this, that her love blots out her sense of duty." Which means, she is reproached for not being up to the Master's ethic. On the other hand, her marriage is condemned insofar as it is wrongly taken to represent the prolongation and satisfaction of her passion—hence as the supreme defeat of the aristocratic ethic. It is in fact the triumph, and climax, of that ethic. In marrying Roderigo at the end of the play, Chimena does not abase, but redeems herself.

If in killing Count Gormas Roderigo has saved the honor and the life of his own father, thanks to the fundamental identity of their "blood," in crushing the Moors he has redeemed the life and honor of the Count, thanks to their fundamental identity of "rank." From this higher point of view, the two lives become equivalent. The Count, by his own admission, was essentially a function:

> . . . ce bras du royaume est le plus ferme appui . . .
> Mon nom sert de rempart à toute la Castille.

It is exactly in these terms that Roderigo must now be evaluated:

> Rodrigue maintenant est notre unique appui . . .
> Le soutien de Castille, et la terreur du More.

To the extent to which Roderigo takes over the Count's role, he brings him again to life, the particular incarnation of the role being without importance. Chimena implicitly admits this assumption of the Count's identity by Roderigo:

> *Et traites-tu mon père avec tant de rigueur,*
> *Qu'après l'avoir vaincu tu souffres un vainqueur?*

The king comes to this same conclusion when he declares to Chimena:

> *Ta gloire est degagée et ton honneur est quitte;*
> *Ton père est satisfait . . .*

In order that the "satisfaction" of the deceased be complete, Roderigo, after having brought him to life again, must go on to perpetuate him: not pleasure but duty obliges Chimena to marry the conqueror, in terms of the aristocratic law of the best, which is to say the strongest:

> *Rodrigue t'a gagnée et tu dois être à lui.*

The marriage of Chimena (and not love) will reconcile erotic "possession" and patrician "service," which the beginning of the tragedy seemed to have irremediably dissociated[. . . .]

When Roderigo challenged the Count, his cry was also a prophecy: "Your arm is unvanquished but not invincible." But the Cid, at the end of the play, has achieved the blessed state of invincibility, something more than victory: "Your hands alone have the right to vanquish one who is invincible." All the dangers which threaten heroism, thematically unfolded in the progress of the play—the deterioration of the heroic ego affected by time, the tearing force of love, the mutual extermination of the individual selves, leading to the destruction of the state—seem forever conjured away; what threatened to be pure tragedy becomes tragedy overcome, tragi-comedy. And in fact, begun on a comic level, the play ends as comedy . . . with the invincibility of the hero loudly proclaimed, the will to Deity here issues its most enthusiastic challenge. The test of heroic strength with the world and with others opens on a plenitude of salvation: for the earthly ego, sacrificed at one moment, is recaptured; Don Diego is the conqueror of old age and reconciled with the Count as the head of a common line; Chimena finds herself again in marriage after having lost herself in love; and Roderigo assures an infinite future to the realm by his courage, even as by his love he will perpetuate the irresistible race of Masters.

Translated by Lynn Lawner

Bérénice: *The Action and Theater of Reason*

FRANCIS FERGUSSON

Le Cimetière Marin—

> *Zénon! Cruel Zénon! Zénon d' Eléel*
> *M'as-tu percé de cette flèche ailée*
> *Qui vibre, vole, et ne vole pas!*
> *Le son m'enfante et la flèche me tue.*
> *Ah! Le Soleil! . . . Quelle ombre de*
>   *tortue*
> *Pour l'âme, Achille immobile à grands*
>   *pas!* [1]

THE TRAGEDY OF REASON: BÉRÉNICE, ACT I

THIS STANZA by Valéry, at the latter end of that rationalist tradition which had its beginnings in the age of Racine, puts very beautifully the abstract and timeless situation of the soul as reasoning. Zeno's famous paradox of the arrow's flight, though a triumph of the reason viewing itself, nevertheless pierces the soul; the arrow kills, though the music of its winged flight wakes the soul to its own life. It is like the other parable of Zeno's: the very brilliance of the demonstration (in Zeno's rational terms) that Achilles can never overtake the tortoise casts a shadow upon the soul in the act of reason. In the clarity with which the metaphysical tragedy of reason is thus conceived; in the use of illustrative metaphor, and in the musical effects—the plucked string, the vibrant stillness—one may recognize the action and the form of Racinian tragedy.

I have selected *Bérénice* to illustrate the tragedy of reason and the peculiar properties of the Baroque theater. It is true that some of Racine's contemporaries and some subsequent critics[2] deny that this play is really a tragedy at all. The pas-

---

[1] Zeno! Cruel Zeno! Elean Zeno! / You have transfixed me with that wingéd arrow / Which vibrates, flies, and does not fly! / My birth is that sound and my death that arrow. / Ah! The brilliant Sun! . . . What tortoise-shadow / On the soul, Achilles motionless in stride!

[2] Cf. *The Classical Moment,* by Martin Turnell, for example.

sion in it is only that of love; the catastrophe only the separation of Antiochus from Bérénice, whom he loves, and of Bérénice and Titus, who are in love, from each other. But Racine himself thought it one of his most perfect tragedies: "It is not necessary," he writes in his preface, "for there to be blood and corpses in a tragedy: it is enough that its action be great, its actors heroic, that the passions be excited in it; and that the whole give that experience of majestic sadness in which the whole pleasure of tragedy resides." Racine was right: *Bérénice* lacks the complicated intrigue and the off-stage violence which one so often finds in Corneille's tragedies; but this is the sign of its formal and intellectual integrity. It never lapses from the high plane which the idea of Neo-classic tragedy demands; and in it, therefore, one can see this idea very clearly.

The story which Racine used is simple. Antiochus, King of Comagene, is in love with Bérénice, Queen of Palestine. But Bérénice has dismissed Antiochus because she is in love with Titus, as he is in love with her. When the play opens Titus is about to be made Emperor of Rome, and Antiochus and Bérénice (tributary monarchs like nobles at the court of Louis XIV) are in Rome for the coronation ceremonies. It is assumed that Titus will presently marry Bérénice; but there is one possible hitch: the Roman Senate may object on constitutional grounds to his marrying a foreign queen. Thus there is implicit in the situation a conflict between the love and the reasonable duty of each of the three monarchs. Antiochus' duty is to conceal and renounce his love for the Queen, unless her feelings and Titus' have changed. It will be Titus' duty to sacrifice his love for Bérénice to his duty to Rome, unless the Senate relents. And Bérénice will have to stifle her love for Titus, both because of her own regal integrity and because of the regard for Titus' duty which reason demands. When we have learned that Bérénice's feelings are unchanged, and that the Senate is adamant—when all the facts are in hand, and all the possibilities explored—the passionate monarchs part forever, in obedience to their sad and separate duties.

Thus we have, in this play, a tragedy exactly as the textbooks define it: *"Une action héroique, accomplie par des personnages ayant pour idéal le triomphe de la volonté sur l'instinct."* Moreover, the situation of the three monarchs, in which Rome is identified with both reason and duty, is the metaphysical situation of the rational soul which Valéry's stanza presents. This basic situation is clear in advance; and though it is explored with the orderly thoroughness of logic, it never changes: Reason reveals with triumphant clarity its own tragic incommensurability with the merely actual world of the senses and the emotions; the soul realizes its timeless life in reason by the same moral-intellectual act which kills its temporal life. Voltaire marveled that Racine was able to make five acts out of so single a theme and so simple a situation. He concluded that only Racine understood the human heart well enough for such virtuosity; and he might have added that only Racine understood the Baroque theater—the theater of reason—well enough to use it with such perfect consistency.

The art by which Racine makes his story seem to move, though a most difficult technical achievement, is fundamentally very simple. He withholds until the very end, from one or more of his three main characters, some crucial fact of that character's situation, and so forces them all to explore every logical possibility, and ring all the changes upon hope and despair. Neither the basic situation, nor their principles, change; but the available facts are shifted like the pieces on a chessboard. Thus at the beginning of the play Antiochus does not know beyond doubt how Bérénice feels about him now; and neither he nor Bérénice knows that the Senate will forbid Bérénice's marriage to Titus. This is the first situation; and Act I analyzes its uncertainties and tantalizing possibilities. But, in order to show how this works, one must try to get a little closer to the actual play, and to the consistent basis of Racine's peculiar make-believe.

The difficulty we have with Racine seems to be due to the fact that we do not want to accept as "really" tragic the single moment of experience and the single angle of vision upon which the whole drama is based. We instinctively demand the shifting perspectives, comic and tragic in alternation, which Shakespeare's wider stage provides—or else we simply refuse to relinquish the cosier and more slovenly habits of mind of modern naturalism. If we are to perceive Racine's tragedy at all, we must abstract such moral integrity as we possess from all qualifying circumstance and boldly contemplate *it*. In the very beginning of the play Racine directs our attention to this intimate yet abstract moment of experience, this timeless theater of life and action. Antiochus addresses Arsace, his indispensable *confident*:

> *Arrêtons un moment: la pompe de ces lieux,*
> *Je le vois bien, Arsace, est nouvelle à tes yeux.*
> *Souvent ce cabinet, superbe et solitaire,*

Des secrets de Titus est le dépositaire:
C'est ici quelquefois qu'il se cache à sa cour,
Lorsqu'il vient à la Reine expliquer son amour.
De son apartement cette porte est prochaine,
Et cette autre conduit dans celui de la reine.

Let us pause a moment: the pomp of this place,
I plainly see, is new to you, Arsace.
Often this chamber, in its lonely pride,
Receives the secrets which Titus would hide;
Sometimes it is his refuge from the court,
When he shows the queen the feelings in his heart.
His own apartments are beyond that door,
And this one leads to the queen's lodgings here.[3]

The ringing words (in French) establish not only the stage itself, with its two significant doors, its lusters, and its polished floor, but the spiritual locus also: the *pureté* and *clarté* of the enlightened moral consciousness. For all its *pompe,* this region is sad, being shadowed by the mortal peril of love. It is shared (for all its secrecy) by the Emperor Titus, by Queen Bérénice, and by Antiochus, since he now, in wig, breastplate, and ruffles, gravely takes it for his own. We in the audience must pull ourselves together, for it is assumed that we too can live up to these rigors, both in their searching intimacy, and in their visible, ceremonial, full-dress solemnity.

In a sense, this scene is the whole matter of the play: Racine makes a bull's eye at the first shot. But as we shall see, he can play many variations within the one vibrant mode of awareness.

Arsace departs to summon Bérénice, and Antiochus is left to *expliquer* his love for the Queen, in terms of his present situation, as Titus so often does in this very place. His tirade is a firm, light structure of parallels and antitheses. Shall he hope, or despair? Shall he speak, or be silent? Offend the queen, or do an injustice to his own constancy? Every possible formulation of his situation is explored, and every possible result of the forthcoming interview; his strict intelligence follows every subterfuge of his suffering heart, and politely lays it bare for us. Racine says that the passions must be excited; but they are roused only to enter the inimical realm of the mind. The action of the whole tirade occurs on that thin and cutting edge where rationality meets its opposite. For all the

---

[3] I am responsible for this English. Racine is notoriously untranslatable; and yet a literal prose version gives a hopelessly distorted impression.

tremors of his inner being, Antiochus is firmly planted on the very point of hopelessness itself; and so we are never far from the ultimate statement of the tragic split which is the single matter of the play. Antiochus puts it very musically at the highest lyrical point of the tirade, just before we modulate into the more prosaic key of his forthcoming scene with Arsace:

> *Example infortuné d'une longue constance,*
> *Après cinq ans d'amour et d'espoir superflus,*
> *Je pars, fidèle encor quand je n'espère plus.*

An ill-fated instance of long constancy,
After five years of love and hope in vain,
I go, still faithful, with nothing more to gain.

When Arsace returns, after we have learned that Bérénice will see Antiochus presently, the excitement drops for the scene between Arsace and Antiochus. We are farther from the inner being of Antiochus, where the soul-as-reason has its imperiled life; we descend from reason-intuiting-itself to the plane of the discursive reason. Here we develop the corollaries which follow from Antiochus' integrity; the policies to be followed, the machinery of the "intrigue" of the play. The scene is in the dialectical form of question and answer. Arsace does not see Antiochus' integrity itself; but he very shrewdly asks all the practical questions, such as, "Why do you owe the Queen anything?" Thus he gives Antiochus an opportunity to demonstrate the logical impeccability of his tragic position. When Arsace has been silenced, and the mind satisfied, we are back to the crux of reason and passion, just in time for Bérénice's entrance.

The scene with Bérénice reaches greater intensity, with richer musical effects, than Antiochus' tirade. Bérénice is contemplating, in the steady light of reason and duty, but in ignorance of Rome's opposition, the beautiful prospect of her love for Titus, while Antiochus contemplates his renounced but living love for her. Thus the subject of Antiochus' solo is resumed as a duet, and Antiochus (closer to the painful reality than Bérénice, because she lacks one fact) brings it to a close as he had his solo:

> *Surtout ne craigniez point qu'une aveugle douleur*
> *Remplisse l'univers du bruit de mon malheur:*
> *Madame, le seul bruit d'une mort que j'implore*
> *Vous fera souvenir que je vivais encore.*

Above all, have no fear that my blind sorrowing
Could ever make the world hear of my suffering:
Only the rumor of my longed-for death
Will remind you, then, that I once drew breath.

On this perfectly controlled scheme, Racine continues to demonstrate the variety in unity, and the unity always in the variety of his play. He moves majestically from the concentrated intensity of the tirade—which he sometimes develops at more length as a duet or trio—to the more relaxed discursive analysis of the dialogue scenes. But the peculiarity of this dramatic form is that all of the developments may so easily be reduced to the one identical theme. The characters, for instance, have little individual being. Arsace is essentially a voice in Antiochus' conversation with himself; the same is true of Bérénice's and Titus' *confidents*. As for the three monarchs themselves, Bérénice is a woman and a queen, Titus the emperor of Rome, and Antiochus a tributary king, but the tragic life of reason which they share is one, just as the proud and solitary scene where it performs its sad feat of perpetual self-demonstration is one. At the end of the trio which closes the play, Bérénice's single voice can convey their common triumph and lament:

> *Adieu. Servons tous trois d'example à l'univers*
> *De l'amour la plus tendre et la plus malheureuse*
> *Dont il puisse garder l'histoire douleureuse.*

> Good-bye. Let us, all three, be emblems for the world
> Of love, the saddest love and the most tender
> Of all the stories that the world remembers.

If one looks at this play from an alien angle of vision, deviating ever so slightly from the point of view which Racine maintains and demands from the audience, the whole crystalline structure may appear lifeless and absurd. But if one brings the play into focus in the mirror of reason (the underlying idea of the Baroque theater) one sees an intense, inescapable, and intimate moment of human life. By limiting himself so strictly to this moment, or mode of psychic being, and to its resources of expression, Racine defines a histrionic, and thence a verbal, medium almost as abstract as that of musical sound. Like music, it may touch us with surprising depth precisely because it is so purified; and, again like music, it is the abstractness of the medium which makes possible such economi-

119

cal and controlled actualizations of the poet's idea: such literally perfect form: such intellectual and esthetic univocity.

These points may be made a little clearer by considering how the principles of Racine's dramaturgy are derived from his strict and final sense of human life and action.

In the chapter on Sophocles' *Oedipus*, we endeavored to find our way through the words, characters, and changing events of the play to the one action which Sophocles was imitating; and this action was seen as the clue to the coherence of the whole complex structure. It then appeared that one might think of the life, or hidden essence of the tragedy, as having been realized in the poet's successive acts of imitation: in plot, in character, in reasoned exposition and dialogue, and in the choric odes. So Sophocles would have adumbrated the one essence, basing his art upon the primitive and subtle histrionic sensibility and the ceremonial make-believe of the Greek tragic theater.

It is very clear that Racine and Corneille did not understand the art of drama as the imitation of action in just this way, though they thought their plays were tragedies in the Greek sense, and obeyed Aristotle's principles. Corneille's *Trois Discours* and Racine's prefaces frequently mention the imitation of action; but "action" in these contexts does not suggest the notion which I have attributed to Aristotle and used in the analysis of *Oedipus*. As Racine and Corneille use the word, it does not mean action so much as its results: not the movement or focus of the soul which actualizes its essence moment by moment but the overt deeds, chains of events reportable as facts, which action produces. Thus when they say "action" they usually mean the concatenated incidents of the rationalized plot, or "intrigue" as they call it.

One must not conclude from this that Racine and Corneille did not sense action at all. They did not make the distinction between action and deed, nor between the plot as the formal cause or "soul" of tragedy and plot as a rationalized series of incidents, intended to satisfy the discursive reason. But the life of their drama *is* the rational mode of action. When Racine says of his Phèdre, "Her crime is rather a punishment of the gods than a *movement of her will*," he has his eye upon the action of that character, as I understand the word, though

120

only action in the rational mode. They assumed this mode of action as self-evidently the one shape and substance of truly human life. They assumed that the audience assumed it; and so they took the art of drama to be, not that of imitating and celebrating action as a central mystery, in various modes and from various angles of vision, but rather that of demonstrating with the utmost clarity, economy, and harmony, an essence already given and accepted.

Thus if one wishes to study the histrionic basis of the art of Baroque drama, one gets no help from Neoclassic theory, though so much of it is ostensibly an elucidation of the *Poetics*. One must look at the wonderfully single action of the plays themselves; in that light one can understand the rules which the dramatists and the critics thought they had taken from Aristotle.

The action of *Bérénice* (using an infinitive to suggest if not to define it) is "to demonstrate the tragic life of the soul-as-rational in the situation of the three passionate monarchs." It is this demonstration which the audience is invited to see, which the three principal characters perform, and which Racine makes, first in his rational plot, then in his reasonable presentation of character (kings and queens as they logically would be by conventional agreement); and finally and above all, in the logical and musical order of his language.

But I must attempt to make a little clearer what I mean by Racine's art of plotting as rational demonstration. In Book VI of the *Ethics* Aristotle points out that fully conscious choice has the implicit form of the syllogism. The facts of the concrete situation (Rome forbids Titus' marriage to a foreign queen) constitute the minor premise. The general principle to be obeyed (rationality itself; the categorical imperative) is the major premise. I have only to recognize the voice of Rome as that of reason-duty itself, and my action follows by a series of connected syllogisms: i.e., as though by pure logic. If one now endeavors to imagine, not the completed plot, but the author as he makes the plot, one can see that plot-making must itself have appeared to him to be essentially logical, and to have as its purpose the satisfaction of the mind. The essence he wishes to demonstrate is the tragic life of the soul as reasoning. Reason is the sole value: reason is always to be obeyed. From this both the selection, and the arrangements of the facts of the story, follow deductively. Such facts will be chosen as will best illustrate the eternal nature of the reasoning soul: i.e., its life as a conflict with passion.

And they will be arranged in such a way as to demonstrate, again and again, the logical inevitability of its choices. So in his plot-making Racine (like one of his own heroes) seeks the cruelest constraints of passion in order to demonstrate to the mind of the audience that essence, that rational mode of action, which he politely assumes we share.

In Racine's dramaturgy, the situation, static in the eye of the mind, and illustrating the eternal plight of reason, is the basic unit of composition; in Sophocles' the base unit is the tragic rhythm, in which the mysterious human essence, never completely or finally realized, is manifested in successive and varied modes of action. Is there any analogy between the timeless tragedy of reason, and the temporal *change* from one realization of the human essence to another which the tragic rhythm shows?

If you consider the succession of situations in the five acts of *Bérénice,* you can see a shape which has an abstract resemblance to that of the Sophoclean tragic rhythm. In the first three acts the characters are acquiring and ordering the facts of their situation, as these become available: dialogue scenes predominate; and this part of the play corresponds to the moment of "purpose" in the tragic rhythm, represented (in *Oedipus*) by the agon. In Act IV, with all the facts clear to all, the rational soul suffers a more direct intuition of its plight; there are no discursive dialectical analyses, but only the tirades of Bérénice and Titus, and their duet; and this act corresponds to the pathos, which Sophocles represents by means of the chorus. Act V corresponds to the moment of perception which ends the tragic rhythm. The three monarchs accept the outcome of their situation—their eternal separation: the triumph of duty and the sacrifice of love—as the clear, distinct, and final illustration of the tragedy of reason. The action of reason in this situation has its beginning, middle, and end. But the full scope of the tragic rhythm as we find it in Sophocles, which spreads as it were a whole spectrum of modes of action before us by varying acts of imitation—this scope we do not find in Racine's tragedy of purely ethical motivation.

It is revealing to look more closely at the traces which are left, in Racine's plot, of the parts of the Sophoclean plot: the agon, or conflict; the scene of suffering or pathos, with its chorus; and the new perception or epiphany, with its messenger, or its visible stage tableau, and its awe-struck contemplation. The scenes of dialogue correspond to the agons; but the polite exchange between Arsace and Antiochus, in the first act, is far from the terrible conflict between Oedipus and Tiresias, wherein the moral beings of the antagonists are at stake. Arsace is best understood as merely one voice in Antiochus' polite discussion with himself: the moral being is unmistakable and impossible to lose while the stage life continues at all. And this is true also of those more painful discussions between principals: the very possibility of the interchange depends upon the authority of reason, which secures the moral being in any contingency. Even when the Baroque hero is very angry (like Thésée in *Phèdre,* and many of Corneille's heroes) he bases his anger upon the congested sense of outraged rationality, and one is reminded of Aristotle's dictum that anger is the passion which does least violence to reason and is most easily cured thereby. But if the moral being is *ex hypothesi* secure, the very basis of the whole make-believe of the play, there cannot be a *pathos* in the Sophoclean sense at all. The pathos pictured by the Sophoclean chorus is a moment of change in the moral being: it includes the breakdown of one rationalized, moral *persona;* the suffering of feelings and images suggesting a human essence capable of both good and evil, and always underlying the individual with his desperate reasons and his fragile integrity. The Sophoclean pathos can only be conveyed by the chorus, with its less than individual mode of being; its musical and kinesthetic mimicry, and its sensuous dreamlike imagery, precisely because it has to convey a change in the highly realized and rationalized individual moral being. With this in mind, it is easy to see why Corneille and Racine had no idea what to make of the chorus: it is based upon a mode of action (an attitude toward suffering) which the theater of reason cannot mirror. And for the same reason they did not understand, or try to use, the epiphany or new perception with which the Sophoclean tragic rhythm ends.

And yet it is clear that Racinian tragedy as a whole is a kind of epiphany. The direct intuition of the life of reason, upon which all is based, is (though abstracted from experience) like the intuition in which a Sophoclean chorus, or a Sophoclean tragedy, ends. Racine feels that this abstracted moment of action contains by implication all the rest: that this mode of being *is* the human essence. He sees it as so abstracted, so clear and distinct, so final, that he senses no analogies whatever between it and other modes of being: the less definable "conscience of the race" represented by the chorus; or the less formulated perceptions of the young and the naïve; or, at the other end of the scale, the hidden councils of the gods. Because the Racinian hero is assumed to intuit the essence of human life from the first, his tragedy is in every sense absolute. He is as responsible as God; is hero and scapegoat at once; his heroic action (like that of Eliot's Thomas of Canterbury) is the same thing as the martyr's suffering for the truth.

Thus the histrionic basis of Baroque tragedy is extremely narrow; a pin-point on the spectrum of action. It determines an art of plotting which is simply the demonstration of an essence; and it defines a dramatic medium natural to reason: that of word and concept. For this reason, the classic French style of acting, capable of great subtlety within its narrow range, tends to identify acting with recitation. The action Racine is conveying generates, as it were automatically, the Alexandrines in which the tragedy is audible and understandable to us; and through his logical and musical verse Racine controls the actor's performance as completely as Wagner does through the musical score.

The art of Racine's Alexandrines is so identified with the genius of the French language that one cannot get at it by way of English, or even, I suppose, enjoy it to the full unless to the manner born. But one can see its main outlines, and one can see that the verse itself realizes in every detail the action of the whole. The play moves between the intensely felt intuition of the tirades, and the more relaxed and discursive dialogue scenes; but it is all put in Alexandrines, and this basically simple, symmetrical form serves equally well in both cases. In the perfect balance of the rhymed couplet, in the perfect balance of the individual line (regularly though not invariably broken in the middle) one feels the logical form of thesis and antithesis, the tragic split between reason and passion, and the irreconcilable contradiction, in the illustrative situation, between Rome and the loves of the three monarchs. But on this very simple formal basis Racine builds logical and musical arabesques of great variety. In the very first line of the play, *"Arrêtons un moment,/la pompe de ces lieux,"* the two halves of the line are equally good illustrations: the awe-struck pause of Antiochus and Arsace (indicated both in the meaning of the words, and by the caesura) and the pomp of Titus' chamber (which the actual stage shows visibly to the actors and to us) mean equally the one essence: the tragic and enlightened moral consciousness. In the beginning of Antiochus' first tirade we get four balanced ways of saying the same thing:

> *Eh bien! Antiochus/es-tu toujours le même?*
> *Pourrai-je, sans trembler/lui dire: Je vous aime?*

Antiochus, the question of his continued identity, the tremors of his inner being, and the question of his avowal of love, are felt, and presented in the very structure of the verse, as identical. This is what I mean by the vibrant stillness of the *one* moment of action: in the tirade we are close to the life of the soul itself. Near the end of this tirade the tragic contradiction (which the balanced form conveys even when it is used to present an identity) makes the two balanced halves of a single line:

> *Craint autant ce moment/que je l'ai souhaité*

The structure of the line, and the equal and opposite forces of fear and desire, all in twelve syllables, make the tragic crux itself. Of Racine's music—his endlessly resourceful rhythms, and his pure and chiming sounds—I do not attempt to speak; but his music is another means of emphasis and variety on the same formal principle. This principle is to be, at every moment, perfect: always at the end. The throb of the tragic split may rise and fall in intensity but essentially it never changes. The balanced illustrations and formulations of the same point may pile up for emphasis but they always *feel* like the balance of thesis and antithesis. From one point of view the tragic split is never transcended: the form of the Alexandrine looks two ways. From another point of view, this split is always transcended: the formal principle is one, the essence envisaged is one. And, in short, the form of the Alexandrine itself is the final actualization of the paradoxical life of reason which has been put in so many ways from Racine to Valéry, and yet is one.

If one thinks even in very general terms of two other verse forms wherein action has been imitated, Shakespeare's blank verse and Dante's terza rima, both the perfection and the narrowness of the Alexandrine are evident. Blank verse is so close to daily rhythms of speech, so flexible—one might almost say so formless in itself—that it can take the shape of any action, whether pathetic, or ethical, or realized in the endless variety of individual character. By the same token, it does not offer, like the Alexandrines, one standard view of action; its use depends upon the insight of the artist prior to versifying. Dante's terza rima is a verse form as highly elaborated and consciously developed as the Alexandrine, and in the same way the form itself suggests a conception of action. But this conception is not that of the static completely realized essence, but that of the tragic rhythm; and though the tercet may present a momentary image of great clarity and distinctness, the interlocking rhymes point always ahead, and the movement of the verse, which never ceases, suggests a human essence never finally realized yet always present in its changing actuality.

Thus the language of *Bérénice*, like its plot, demonstrates the one unchanging essence. But what of the individual characters? How may an individual being demonstrate so univocal a concept? Aristotle's notion is that characters are imitated "with a view to the action," and we have seen how well this formula applies to *Oedipus:* the action of that play is presented in distinct, but analogous, individual forms; in the various characters and in the various modes of being of the one character. In our experience of the completed play, we see the individuals first, and only later divine, by analogy, the unity of the whole. It is evident that in Racine's dramaturgy the reality of the individual is very differently understood: he is interested in individual characters as illustrations of his abstract idea, insofar as they are required for the concrete situation he uses; and he is interested in them insofar as their life is the one life of reason. He imitates character, not "with a view" to revealing action from various angles and in various modes, but either to illustrate an a priori conception of it, or else (as in the Tirades) to present this essence directly.

Thus he makes his kings and queens of Comagene or Palestine according to a recipe for which he formally invokes the authority of Aristotle. Bérénice has nothing to do with Palestine, and it is impossible to care whether she is a queen or not. She does not inhabit that mortal realm in which racial tradition, geography, social status, and the historical context have their fatal importance. Because Racine is interested only in one moment of psychic life, he replaces all the rest with purely illustrative conventional signs.

But it is astonishing how much life, even individual life, Racine is able to show by sticking so consistently to the one angle of vision, and the one mode of action. A visit to the dentist makes the whole world kin: that small buzzing steel sphere has an intimate meaning for all who have heard it approaching the jawbone. It rouses the passions and induces arabesques of rationalizing without regard to race, color, sex, or religion; yet, in the narrow and searching perspective it provides, one might note individual differences. In the same way the rigid perspective of reasoned duty, once accepted as both inescapable and final, transfixes the whole creature and may serve, if one is interested, to bring out individual variations in attitude. Bérénice, though her life is seen only on the abstract stage of reason, nevertheless feels extremely female; and the great duet she has with Titus in the fourth act is full of the most delicate psychological insight. Moreover, Bérénice is felt as a particular woman, very different from Phèdre, for instance. All the encomiums which have been written on Racine's psychology, and the accuracy and resourcefulness of his "knowledge of the heart" have their justification, especially in his portraits of women. If the perspective he adopts is extremely narrow, it is extremely revealing; and his use of it is due to his austere and ambitious conception of form, and to the theater for which he was writing, rather than to lack of direct insight into the individualized diversity of life.

The fact is, of course, that it takes more than pure reason to make a tragedy. And whenever one studies the life of Racine's play, one sees that, for all its efforts toward universality, it is rooted in the actual life of a particular time and place, and fed with his own direct sense of life. And one encounters the fact that the theater of reason, which once seemed in its perfection to be *the* theater itself, preventing any other notions years after all life had left its beautiful forms, now looks as grotesquely French and Baroque as Louis himself; wig, laces, high heels, and all.

THE THEATER OF REASON IN ITS TIME AND PLACE

Rationalistic philosophy bears a relation to Racine's tragedy like that of Aristotle's philosophy to the tragedy of Sophocles, and one may learn from it a good deal about Racine's notion of action, and also about his principles of composition. When Descartes deduces existence from thought, when he demands, for the proper conduct of the mind, clear and distinct ideas only—the clarity of mathematics—he might be describing the principles of Racine's dramaturgy. And Kant's *Metaphysic of Morals,* based upon the intuition of the soul as reasoning, and deducing an infallible guide to conduct from the notion of rationality itself, may be read as an exposition of the action of *Bérénice.* But the theater of reason, as it actually existed, was an expression of Baroque taste; and it was a public institution, with stage, actors, audience, and general support and comprehension. In short, it was a mirror of human life and action formed at a particular time and place, and enjoying a merely mortal life like that of any other real theater. Its rational principles no longer look self-evident and eternal to us; we see that Racine enjoyed a sanction which we have lost; and we are uncomfortable with the perfection of the mind which he achieved.

Professor Jacques Maritain[4] offers a perspective upon modern rationalism itself; he enables us to see the difference between the deified reason of the Age of Reason, and the realist intelligence of the Greek and Medieval tradition. Bergson, in *Les Deux Sources de la Morale et de la Religion,* offers another perspective on modern rationalism, derived from his studies of the role of reason in society. Taking direct issue with Kant, he says that the nation of the absolute constraint of reasonable duty (the basis of Racinian tragedy) is in fact always derived from a concrete and fixed social order. Only after such a social order is (more or less tacitly) accepted as final, can it be rationalized; and only then can one identify duty and reason as Racine and Kant do. The historic moment when ethics is based solely upon reason, would be the moment when society is not too visibly changing, and its order may therefore be regarded as both right and timeless. Such a society Bergson calls "closed": to the possibility of any change except mere destruction; to the sense of analogy between its form and that of different societies, past, present, or imagined; and to the possibility of a different relation between the human community and the surrounding world.

I do not know how accurately Bergson's description would apply to the historic France of Louis XIV; but it certainly describes the idealized society of Racine's theater, the official mirror of the times. The literal detail—the curls, the ruffles, the protocol, the manners—are frozen into immobiliity and fixed with extraordinary clarity by the eye of the mind; yet they are supposed to illustrate a social order which is univocally the same as that of Rome, Palestine, or Comagene. The people, whether "adorateur" or "volage," is kept off-stage; and upon the narrow platform of the eternal elite the reason focuses, with a passion for both literal and abstract perfection.

If one looks at Racine's theater from this alien point of view—not as truth itself, but as reflecting an image formed at a moment of history—it appears that this theater had its own kind of ceremonial significance: not the religious and natural ritual meaning of the Greek tragic theater, but the more limited and artificial significance of the *game.* M. Denis de Rougemont shows in *Love in the Western World* that during the period of the Enlightenment when society felt righteous

[4] For example in *Trois Réformateurs* ("Descartes"), *Réflexions sur l'Intelligence,* and *Distinguer pour Unir.*

and secure in itself, many social functions could be limited and defined, like games, by rules agreed on in advance. Even war, he says, was not our total conflict, but a limited contest for limited stakes, like chess. Strategy was prior to slaughter; form to content. Provinces might change hands, fines be paid, individuals lose their lives—but the basis of civilized life was not at stake. This account throws a good deal of light upon the sacrifice and the ceremonial game of Baroque tragedy. The "sacrifice" was the price of admission to the game: the acceptance of the authority of reason. Only the elite—only monarchs—were eligible; but by convention their ceremonious agony stood for human life itself, as the nuptial combats of queen bees, larger and gaudier than the workers, focus the life of their perfect societies. It is a grave, high, and civilized conception; yet it suffers from its too proud and drastic limitations. And (thinking of the wigs, the glitter, and the stink) one may be reminded of Cocteau's description of the style of his Antigone: *"L'ensemble évoquant un carnaval sordide et royale, une famille d'insectes."*

M. de Rougemont has very interesting things to say about Racine's *Phèdre*, which interests him as one version of the myth of passion which his book traces. He shows how much passionate life was poured into the reasoned form of the play, and caught in the eye of the mind. He says that Racine is more or less consciously continuing the heretical tradition of *Cortezia,* with its Courts of Love, and its knightly ordeals and game-like tourneys, games of passion. Racine is of course often described as celebrating not reason, but passion; he often thought of himself in this way, but saw no contradiction between *picturing* passion and adhering to his principles of reason and decorum. M. de Rougemont does see this contradiction, and emphasizes it, I think, to the point where the nature of Racine's art is obscured. Nevertheless, it is true that Racine's plays, and indeed Baroque art in general, show signs of strain, as though the rigid forms could not quite contain the life which they were supposed to. The universal terms in which the Neoclassic protagonist puts his plight— Rome frowns or trembles; the universe weeps or applauds— sound a little hysterical to us. The sculptured saints, writhing and weeping in their demand for Grace, seem impotent; the highly evolved dress in which the monarch expresses his reasoned responsibility looks like a sly vengeance of the creature upon his hard strait-jacket.

Bérénice is a convenient instance of this theater precisely because its highly conscious ethical theme is so largely the official theme of the period. But the Baroque dramatists sometimes tried to show moral change in their motionless mirror; and some of these efforts are very interesting, both when they succeed, and when their partial failures show the limitations of the theater of reason itself. Racine's *Phèdre* seems to me to be one of the successes, though it represents only the first step in moral change: dissolution of the rationalized moral being in passion or suffering. The play succeeds because Racine has shown this dissolution strictly from the point of view of the challenged reason. Phèdre appears, she even exists, only in its light; and when she can no longer obey reason she vanishes from the scene:

> Et la mort, à mes yeux dérobant la clarté
> Rend au jour qu'ils souillaient toute sa pureté.

> And death, taking the light of my eyes away
> Restores to the day they soiled its purity.

Corneille's *Polyeucte* is more interesting in this connection, because it is designed to show change, of exactly the complete kind upon which the tragic rhythm of Dante and Sophocles is based: from one rational form of human life to another analogous one based upon a wider vision. *Polyeucte, Martyr* is supposed to show the transformation of a pagan gentleman into a Christian saint. But few readers, I think, can believe that a change of heart is really the material of this play. When we first see Polyeucte his Christian friend Néarque is urging him to be baptized, and Polyeucte (taking at this moment a role like that of the *confidents* in *Bérénice*) is presenting all the practical objections—his baptism for instance would alienate his lawful and beloved wife Pauline. When we next see Néarque and Polyeucte, the latter has received the impact of Grace off-stage and been shifted in a twinkling to the level of the martyr: he wants to court death itself by smashing the statues of the pagan gods. Now it is Néarque who plays the *confident,* and presents the practical drawbacks to martyrdom, and Polyeucte who sets forth the logical consistency of his position as saint. In the last part of the play Corneille wishes to contrast the impeccable Christian Polyeucte with the impeccably pagan Roman gentleman Sévère, who is hopelessly in love *à la* Antiochus with Polyeucte's wife Pauline. But Polyeucte's Christian-tragic renunciation of Pauline seems to be the same action as Sévère's heroic-rational renunciation. Polyeucte's Christian postulate contradicts Sévère's pagan one, but both are based equally upon the integrity of the reasoning soul; and both gentlemen aspire to increase their "gloire" by renouncing the unfortunate Pauline. Polyeucte is proved to be a saint; everything he does, and everything he explains about his feelings, follow with the inevitability of logic from this reasoned position. But the divine irruption of Grace has broken neither the glittering surface of the salon, the politeness of the characters, nor the motionless mirror of reason. In a detailed study of *Polyeucte* one would try to distinguish the piety and the sense of purgatorial change, which Corneille may himself have had, from the picture he presents in the rationalistic terms of his theater. And one would point to moments (like Polyeucte's beautiful lyric, an anomaly in this theater) when Corneille seems to be feeling for a wider stage and a more flexible medium. But the general point would, I think, be substantiated: the change from one level of awareness to another cannot be shown in the rigidly "ideal" theater of the time.

The Baroque notion of "gloire" as we find it throughout *Bérénice*, *Phèdre*, and *Polyeucte*, indicates both the ideal social hierarchy and the ideal, timeless moment of action of the theater of reason. It would seem on this evidence that when the elite of the age of Louis XIV felt rationality histrionically, whether in the salon or the theater, they called it "gloire." In these three plays the word refers to all the ways in which the individual, in his obedience to reason, could shine forth to his audience. At one extreme, "gloire" is only reputation, as in the scene between Phèdre and Oenone, when they are afraid Thésée will discover what Phèdre has said to Hyppolite. At the other extreme is the "gloire" which Polyeucte seeks in martyrdom. In every instance "gloire" means obedience to reason and duty through the rejection of passion. These uses of the word seem to us to be different; but in the ideal scheme of the theater of reason they were one. The inner light and the glare of publicity, the eye of God and the salon of the Roi Soleil, were all identified, as "gloire," with the unchanging light of reason. So Polyeucte the martyr is as heroic as Sévère the gentleman; and though he stands upon another platform, it is still the platform of reason, bright with the same unchanging "gloire."

If one compares the Baroque theater with the tragic theater of the Greeks, it is evident that the Baroque theater is closed in every way in which Sophocles' theater is open. The scene of *Oedipus* is open to daylight, to common sense, to popular tradition conveyed in myth and ritual; it is sacred, but accessible to all: the old shepherd, with his wilderness taciturnity, has his view of the common mystery of human life, and it is as valid in its way as Creon's or Tiresias'. Behind the human scene we feel the wider scene, dim to us, which only the gods, in the surrounding hills or under the earth, fully understand. That is why the rhythm of human life can be presented here in its shifting forms, and in the varied perspectives of reason and pathos. If the action of Oedipus could be lifted out of the endless rhythm of the play at the moment when he first meets Tiresias' opposition, and repeated again and again without change, he would look like a Baroque hero. If we could see only through his eyes at this timeless moment, we should see a scene like that of the theater of reason. Oedipus' rationalization of his moral being, and of his duty as monarch, would be fixed at the brink of his perpetually rejected passion of fear and anger. The order of Oedipus' regime in Thebes would look reasonable, literally perfect, and "closed," both to the potentialities of change represented by the chorus, and to the hidden knowledge of the gods represented by Tiresias. But though Sophocles shows the rational action of the soul, he does not accept it as final, nor close his view of the human situation within the scene which reason reveals.

The *Purgatorio*, as I have pointed out, is the most highly developed presentation of the tragic rhythm of human action which we possess; and in it also the moment of reason and moral responsibility recurs in many figures. In Canto XVIII of the *Purgatorio*, Dante the pilgrim, growing up, growing sadder, wiser, and more responsible, is told by Virgil of the rational will which he has experienced and may now hear majestically named:

> *Coloro che ragionando andaro al fondo*
> *s'accorser d'esta innata libertate,*
> *però moralità lasciaro al mondo.*

> Those who in their reasoning went to
> the foundation, perceived this innate
> freedom, wherefore they left ethics to
> the world.

The rational-moral action of the soul, in its opposition to sensation and emotion, is material of the daylight scenes in the central cantos of the *Purgatorio*. The pilgrim, in his climb, is under the sign of "reason," and must endeavor to reduce the world he sees to its facts and univocal concepts. Sometimes he sees things with photographic but meaningless clarity, like the black, the white, and the red stair in the brilliant morning light. Sometimes his rationalization makes him reject the world *in toto,* as all black, for which he is scolded: *Lo mondo è cieco, e tu vien ben da lui* ("the world is blind, and you come from the world indeed"). If he attempts to conceive God, it is in the abstractions of rationalistic Deism. But this action of reason, which is presented in so many ways, is taken as part of a wider and longer action, and placed in a scene or "theater" which, like the real world, is wider than reason itself. Thus the pilgrim's reasoned concepts never quite fit, and he is troubled, even in his rationalizing, by sensuous images of undecipherable significance; by sympathetic awareness of other persons, by a vague desire for light and freedom of another order, and by memories of his unregenerate state when his soul, in the innocence of childhood and with an animal-like unity of thought and feeling, moved simply "toward what delights it." Dante shows the Baroque split between passion and reason in a thousand forms; but because he has his eye always upon "the whole psyche in its total situation" he never senses this split as final, and never makes a fetish and a static scene out of purely rational modes of understanding.

The action of reason which makes Baroque drama, corresponds to these moments in the tragic rhythm of Sophocles and Dante; and the theater of reason represents the human condition as it appears at that abstracted, timeless moment: clear, known, and unchanging. It is a much more limited view of the human than that of Sophocles or Dante; but, with its precision and integrity, it is both deep and inescapable. Moreover the very limitation of this view permits a kind of artistic perfection or absoluteness, which Sophocles did not even seek. The Baroque drama itself, as we look back on it, betrays its mortality: it obviously depends upon the sanctions and the fetishes of its time and place, like other forms which make less absolute pretensions. But it offers one of the few great images of human life and action, and its principles and habits of mind are still with us in a thousand forms.

THE DIMINISHED SCENE OF MODERN RATIONALISM

It has been necessary to study the notion of the Baroque theater from several points of view (perhaps at the cost of repetitiousness) because of its crucial importance in our tradition. In the age of Racine, many enduring foundations were laid down, which still determine our efforts to understand both our own times and the more remote past. We still have a habitual tendency to look at the Greeks rationalistically,

133

and to lump Racine and Sophocles together as simply "classic." And though Baroque drama makes a first impression of old-fashioned stiffness, many of its principles still govern the writing of plays, especially those which are supposed to be the most up-to-date and enlightened.

If we have lost the tradition represented by Sophocles, Dante, and Shakespeare beyond all recovery, it is hard to see how we can escape the heroic principles of the Age of Reason. It is natural and courageous to try (as Racine did) to face the human scene as we see it literally before us; fix it in the light of reason, and present a logically coherent picture of it. It is natural to demand that the past measure up (or down) to our reasoned views, and to reject all other modes of understanding as primitive, vague, and childish. There is a close and self-conscious kinship between Valéry's version of the plight of reason, and Racine's, as I indicated at the beginning of this chapter. Joyce's one play, *Exiles,* presents a reasoned moral effort of an almost Racinian strictness—which seems all the more strict because it is incongruously placed in a contemporary naturalistic setting. Eliot's *Murder in the Cathedral* and Cocteau's *The Infernal Machine* both employ versions of Neoclassic dramaturgy. I propose to return to these plays below apropos of the modern poetic theater.

These writers provide a bridge to Racine; but they show also how far we are from the Baroque theater as a living institution at the center of society, and of society's awareness of itself. In spite of the intellectual and artistic triumphs of the modern writers, we cannot say what relation they have to the modern world. What relation is possible to a society with no actual focus of understanding, responsible power, common values?

The full life of the Baroque theater lasted only about two generations. It is true that the Comédie Française still preserves it as a precious heirloom. But by the early nineteenth century (certainly by the time Sardon wrote *The Black Pearl*) another, far cruder but more generally useful, notion of dramatic form had developed, which came to be known as that of the "well-made play." This recipe for play-making has enabled countless dramatists to present the uncentered busyness of our times in entertaining forms. It is taught in innumerable courses in playwriting, and it is the machinery both of the erotic intrigues of the entertainment industry, and of the thesis-plays of Marxians and other social reformers. It is essentially a rationalized art of plot-making, with a very narrow purpose; and it is derived from one aspect of the

134

Baroque plot. In it one may see how a reduced version of drama as rational survives into our day.

In studying the form of Racinian tragedy, I showed that the plot (or formal cause) was best understood as "the demonstration of an essence": i.e., the tragic life of the soul as reasoning. In this view, Racine's plot answers to Aristotle's definition: it is the soul of tragedy, as the soul is said to be the form of the body—it realizes that mode of action which is the matter of the play. But since Racine assumed this mode of action, he never talked about it, and when he says *plot* he usually means simply the intrigue—plot in Aristotle's second sense—the facts of the situation and their logical concatenation. By means of the intrigue he could hold the interest of the audience, and build it to a point of high excitement, whether that audience was interested in the life of reason or not. In *Bérénice* these two aspects of the rational plot are easy to distinguish. At every moment the tragic plight of reason is made clear, if we care to look at it; hence the crystalline intellectual consistency and the beauty of form. But the incidents are also so arranged as to pique our curiosity about the literal facts of the story. Will Bérénice relent, and accept Antiochus? Will the Roman Senate change its mind? Which of the men will Bérénice marry? Every act ends with such a question, and by this means "suspense" is built up, and we are held by the machinery of the intrigue until the denouement. This aspect of the art of plot-making follows quite naturally from the rational basis of Racine's art; and he and Corneille were very proud of it. They rightly saw that the whole notion of suspense, to be gained through alternately piquing and thwarting our curiosity about the literal facts of the situation, was a discovery of theirs: Sophocles, with his ritual basis, does not primarily seek suspense of this kind.

The art of the well-made play is plot-making in the second sense (of arranging the intrigue to pique the curiosity) but not in the first: blind to the formal cause of tragedy, it does not envisage the art of the drama as the imitation of action at all, but as a means of gripping the audience in abstraction from all content whatever. Its purpose is solely to catch the mind of the audience, and to hold it by alternately satisfying and thwarting the needs of the discursive reason. That is why, like engineering, it is so generally useful. The great Sarcey said that the art of drama can only be understood as that of holding an audience in a theater; beyond that it is merely a subjective matter of taste. The art of the well-made plot is based on this rational-empirical notion, and it is a device which works infallibly. It is pernicious only because it does work so well. In the nineteenth century its "objective facts" and its logical machinery seemed to define the scene and the shape of human life itself. Even an Ibsen could hardly see that his direct and subtle vision of life would demand a different version of dramatic form for its complete realization on the stage, and some of his best plays are marred by the meretricious effectiveness of the well-made plot, which he understood and handled so well.

The well-made plot has in common with Racinian tragedy the "scene" of the discursive reason. In *Bérénice*, the intrigue is logically analyzed by Antiochus and Arsace; in *Phèdre*, by Phèdre and her *confidente* Oenone. The *confidents* (looking as it were outward, at the situation) are very alert to the facts, and very logical, and they ask all the questions which a shrewd audience, that wanted to know how the story turned out, would ask. But they are free from all sense of the peril, the responsibility, and the limitations of reason itself, which makes the tragic life of the protagonist—and fixes, as "facts," the situation and the scene in which they are so agile. As the life gradually left the Baroque theater—when the society of Louis XIV ceased to seem eternal, and the strictness of reason itself no longer could be accepted as the one infallible guide to conduct—the protagonist (Phèdre, or Bérénice, or the life of reason which they illustrate) disappeared, and the cynical Oenones and practical Arsaces took the stage. After the "categorical imperative," the "felicific calculus": reason itself no longer appears, but the stage is still the static "scene" which reason has fixed, the movement of the intrigue is still the mechanical one of the rationalized plot.

If one could understand the properties of the well-made plot, one could understand a great deal about the whole modern theater. Because it is so abstract, and so limited in purpose, it can use the facts of any situation and confer upon their presentation the same cachet of professional competence. But because it assumes so narrow and static a scene, so impoverished a human life and action, the ostensible variety it presents—from the ancient Rome of Robert Sherwood to the Alabama of Lillian Hellman—is illusory: its agile little life is actually unchanging and meaningless. I shall return to this point below, when I study the attempts of Ibsen and of Shaw to work out forms which would be truer to their real sense of life.

But the stultifying limitations of the rationalized scene were felt as soon as it took over the public theater of Europe;

and the romanticists sought in many ways to break or to escape its shackles. By the time of Wagner a form of drama which rejects not only the static scene of rationalism, but reason itself, was fully developed. Wagnerian music drama, as we see it in *Tristan und Isolde,* is the diametric opposite of Racine's tragedy of reason, though in its artistic absoluteness it is the same.

The Euripidean Tragedy

H. D. F. KIDDO

1. INTRODUCTION The course of literary analysis does not run smooth. From the point we have now reached there are two distinct developments, one of which we may regard as natural, the other as the creation of an individual genius. (i) The natural development is that from plays like the *Tyrannus* and *Electra,* plays in which tragedy "fulfilled its natural form," drama should turn to something a shade less strenuous; that it should renounce the task of using at once every element of drama in the expression of a tragic idea, and should develop certain of the possibilities of drama for their own sake—an interest to which Aeschylus had already pointed the way. Poetry, creative imagination, belongs to youth and early prime; to maturity, analysis and intellectual imagination; while if the artist returns to poetry in his old age it is often—as in the *Coloneus,* the late Rembrandt, the late Beethoven, the late Shakespeare—in an almost apocalyptic manner that quite transcends the hardly-won perfection of an earlier period. It seems natural that Sophocles' tragic period—we may think of what followed Shakespeare's tragic period—should be followed by plays like the *Trachiniae*[1] and the *Philoctetes,* and that in the development of the art as a whole the intensity of tragedy should be followed by the more purely intellectual pleasures of character-study, tragi-comedy, melodrama, and the use of drama for what we may not unfairly call propaganda.

[1] I am unable to believe that the *Trachiniae* is an early play. The metrical arguments used to prove an early date prove nothing of the sort. See my article in *A.J.P.* 1939, pp. 178 ff.

Our term New Tragedy is meant to indicate this later stage of Greek drama, a stage represented by plays like the *Philoctetes, Ion, Helen, I.T.*; plays which, if they are serious, no longer embody a specifically tragic idea; if not serious, exploit one or more of the elements of complete tragedy—plot, or "intellect" (*dianoia*), or scenic effect or pathos—for its own sake. The justification for using a term like New Tragedy is that it does represent something independent of any one poet's development, a stage in which both Euripides and Sophocles participated (and apparently Agathon too, whose *Antheus* seems to have been a romantic drama) after working through a tragic period. Further, this is a stage of drama which demanded a different technique. It implies prologues, epilogues, decorative lyrics, and half a dozen other new features; and it cannot be criticized by the canons which Aristotle derived from a different stage of Tragedy without some injustice to Aristotle, a great deal to the poet, and embarrassment to the critic.

(ii) But before we can deal with this stage of Tragedy we must consider that development which took its origin not in a general change coming over the art, but in the individual outlook of Euripides. He, like Sophocles, had his great tragic period; it survives to us in the *Medea, Hippolytus, Heracleidae, Heracles, Andromache, Hecuba, Suppliant Women* and *Troades*. These plays are all tragic, all but the *Hippolytus* badly constructed, by Aristotelian standards; they have certain features in common, such as the prologue and "episodic" plots, and in some respects, notably characterization and construction, they are as unlike the rest of Euripides' work as the *Tyrannus* itself. Yet the *I.T.*, even to Aristotle, was a model of construction, and the *Ion, Electra, Orestes, Helen* are at the lowest estimate well-made. Why is it that in the tragic group there is hardly a single play which has not provoked the most serious complaints and the most desperate apologies?

The thesis of the following pages will be that as we were able to trace the characteristic features of the Aeschylean and Sophoclean tragedy to the nature of the tragic idea that possessed these poets, so all the new features in these plays can be seen to be the logical result of Euripides' tragic idea. We shall see him moving from a drama which he made as much like Middle Tragedy as possible to one which, however un-Aristotelian, was at least the powerful expression of what he wanted to say.

Our first task, once more, must be to try to catch that tragic idea, that tragic way of thinking about life which made these plays what they are; for we will not suppose, if we can help it, that a poet of Euripides' calibre made plots like those of the *Troades* and *Heracles* by mere inadvertence, or committed the structural sins which Aristotle censured in the *Medea* from simple inability to do better. In fact we shall find, time after time, that Euripides does very much less than he might have done if Aristotelian perfection of form had been his aim, and intellectual loyalty to his idea of no importance to him. In the dramatic methods which we see developing from the *Medea* onwards there is a purposefulness, or at any rate a positiveness, which is not to be explained by a mere absence of something, a mere lack of harmony between the poet and his form.

We have, to mislead us, important aspects of Euripides' thought—his scepticism, his impatience with traditional religion (as if Pindar and Aeschylus had not been impatient and sceptical), the misogyny which ancient critics regretted in him, the feminism of which some moderns accuse him, his liberalism, his pacifism. These things are important. Politics and religion are more significant in drama than in painting, for instance, because the raw material of drama is drawn from the sphere of social and moral ideas; but if we want to understand the art either of a dramatist or of a painter we have to go deeper. Sophocles' religious tenets and political beliefs do little to explain his drama, and these doctrines of Euripides' do not help us in the least; for they colour all his work, while we are faced with this cleavage between the tragedies and the other plays. The *I.T.* and *Electra* contain more religious scepticism, more realism, more satirical handling of traditional legend than the *Hecuba* or *Troades*, yet they are in the conventional sense infinitely better constructed and contain much more normal characterization. There is some force in the common statement that there was a deep disharmony between his thought and the traditional form of state tragedy, though Euripides did not handle this traditional form, whatever it was, much more freely than Aeschylus had done; yet the *Suppliant Women*, an "encomium of Athens" as it is called by critics ancient and modern, shows little sign that the dramatist for once felt comfortable in his civic bed.

Is there one general explanation of Euripides' strange methods, or must we either resort to a kind of Secret Service like Verrall's or take undignified refuge in phrases like "unevenness," "lack of unity," and "carelessness"?

Let us state the problem more fully. The *Medea* is twice

censured by Aristotle: the Aegeus scene is illogical and is not even used properly, and the end is artificial and therefore wrong. Moreover, by implication he condemns the murder of the children as "revolting" (*miaron*), and the catastrophe, the escape of Medea and the death of the innocent, is hardly what he approved. Both the *Hecuba* and the *Andromache* have a sharply marked duplicity of action; the *Heracles* contains three actions (though with a more obvious connexion) and a character, Lycus, who seems to belong more to melodrama than to tragedy; the *Suppliant Women* offers one scene, Evadne-Iphis, about which a recent editor conjectures that it was put in to interest those spectators who were bored with the rest of the play; while the *Troades* is one episode after another, held together, we are told, by the passive figure of Hecuba—as if Euripides needed Aristotle to tell him that what befalls one person is not necessarily a unity.

In the later[2] series of plays none of these major faults is to be found. Euripides satirizes Apollo, he argues, he ridicules or condemns heroes of legend, he uses the realism and the modern music that Aristophanes disliked, he expresses "advanced" views in religion, philosophy, and sociology, he commits all sorts of anachronisms, he does a dozen other things to which this critic or that may object, but at least he never commits again any of those elementary blunders in construction.[3] When we add that all of the plays in the first series are tragic and none of the second, or, if the *Electra* and the *Orestes* are to be called tragic, they are tragic in an entirely different spirit—then we are justified in asking if these peculiar features in the first series are not intimately connected with the nature of the tragic idea expressed in them.[4]

2. THE MEDEA   There is no need to make phrases about the terrific power of the *Medea*. In important respects it diverges from what we think normal construction, at least normal construction as understood by Aristotle, and yet it is one of the greatest of Greek tragedies.—So one writes, almost automatically, but most of the implications of that "and yet" are wrong; for had Euripides managed to put the stuff of the play into a beautiful Sophoclean mould, making a "better"

[2] It is convenient so to describe them, though the two series overlap.

[3] The prologue to the *Ion* is a special case.

[4] From the discussion that follows I have omitted all but the briefest reference to the *Heracleidae*. In the present state of the text it is a play to be argued to, not from, and to do this would contribute nothing to my theme.

play of it, it would not have been a better play but a ridiculous one. The *Medea* diverges from the Sophoclean pattern because Euripides' way of thinking was different.

Aristotle expressly cites the appearance of Aegeus and the sending of the magic chariot as being "irrational," not the necessary or probable result of what has gone before; but, lest we be tempted to think that these are only casual licences taken by the poet which can, with luck, be explained away, we ought to observe how fundamental is the divergence between the poet and the philosopher here. How, for example, does Medea fit Aristotle's definition of a tragic hero? Not at all. Aristotle's tragic hero is "like" us, for we should not feel pity and fear for one unlike us. He must not be a saint, or his downfall would be revolting, nor a villain, whose downfall might be edifying but would not be tragic. He must therefore be intermediate, better rather than worse, and find his ruin through some hamartia. Medea is not like this; it would indeed be difficult to find a Euripidean hero who is, until we come to Pentheus. Medea is no character compounded of good and bad, in whom what is bad tragically brings down in ruin what is good, and we certainly cannot fear for her as for one of ourselves. In fact, treated as a genuinely tragic heroine she will not work; she causes at least one of her admirers to fall into a grave inconsistency. Professor Bates says (*Euripides,* p. 37), "In the character of Medea . . . the tragic genius of Euripides reaches its highest pinnacle. In none of the other plays is there a character which can approach Medea as a tragic figure." This is a possible view, but it is inconsistent with the judgment (p. 44), that all our sympathy is concentrated on the unfortunate children, "for we have little sympathy with the cruel, savage Medea." Then she is not tragic after all, only melodramatic? The poor children, the wicked mother, the heartless father—surely this will not do?

A comparison with Macbeth is interesting. He is the romantic extreme of the Sophoclean-Aristotelian hero. He is presented at first in a favourable light: "For brave Macbeth— well he deserves the name." "O valiant cousin! worthy gentleman!" He is better rather than worse; but he has the hamartia of ambition, and circumstances, as is their way with tragic heroes, play upon it—first through his very virtues:

DUNCAN. No more that Thane of Cawdor shall deceive
         Our bosom interest. Go pronounce his present death,
         And with his former title greet Macbeth.
ROSS.   I'll see it done.
DUNCAN. What he hath lost, noble Macbeth hath won.

It may be hazardous to claim Glamis Castle for a stronghold of Aristotelianism, but this ironic touch is very like Sophocles, and certainly it is an essential part of the tragedy of Macbeth that he has been noble, loyal, and gallant.

Medea on the other hand is certainly not all villainy; she loves her children, loved Jason (if that is a merit), and was popular in Corinth; but it is the essential part of this tragedy that she was never really different from what we see her to be. Euripides could easily have represented her as a good but passionate woman who plunges into horrors only when stung by deadly insult and injury. There was no need for him to rake up her past as he does—except that this is his whole point. She never was different; she has no contact with Aristotle.[5]

Neither has Jason. In him it is impossible to find anything that is not mean; not because Euripides is satirizing anyone through him, though he does use his Jason to mock the complacency of his countrymen, but for the same reason, whatever it is, that makes his Medea so extreme a character. We may notice here how little the other characters count—naturally, when the chief characters are drawn in such simple colours. The Nurse is this, the Paedagogus that, and Aegeus the other thing, but were they different nobody would be much the wiser. This is not characterization as Sophocles understood it; we have nearly returned to Eteocles' Spy. Sophocles drew his minor characters vividly because he needed them, not because he was good at it; Euripides refrains because he does need it.

From characterization we may pass to the general tone of the play. Aristotle, in a dry little analysis, examines the ways in which *to phthartikon*, the deed of violence, can be brought about: the worst but one is for kinsman to slay kinsman knowing who it is that he is slaying. This is "revolting," and the *Medea* is full of it. The unrelieved baseness of Jason is revolting; revolting in the highest degree is Medea's great crime; and what of the Messenger-speech? The horrible death of Glauce and Creon is described exhaustively in the terrible style of which Euripides was such a master. It is sheer Grand Guignol. We have yet seen nothing like it in Greek Tragedy. We have had before scenes, described or suggested, of horror

---

[5] Neither had Agamemnon. Both he and Medea are tragic figures rather than tragic characters.

—the self-blinding of Oedipus, the murder of Clytemnestra—but always the horror has been enveloped in the greater emotion of tragic pity. It has brought with it its own catharsis. Where is the tragic pity here? In the destruction of an innocent girl and her father there is no possibility of tragic relief. We pity them, as later we pity the children, but as they have done nothing which in reason should have involved them in this suffering, as no flaw of character, no tragic miscalculation, no iron law of life has brought them to this pass, but simply the rage of Medea, our pity has no outlet; we are impotent and angry—or would be, if this assault on our nerves left room for such feelings. From these things we can turn to no grim but majestic universal principle, only back again to that terrifying murderess.

Supposing that Sophocles had given us a comparable description of Antigone's death agonies? It is unthinkable; but is this only to say that Sophocles was Attic, Euripides already Hellenistic? And supposing that Aristotle had had his way, and that Medea, having committed these crimes, had made her way under her own steam to Athens? Or if the dramatic law of the necessary or probable had asserted itself, and Medea had been stoned by an outraged populace? The play would have been no tragedy at all, but the emptiest of melodrama; after this terrific preparation the story would suddenly have relapsed into insignificance, a mere exciting tale about Medea of Corinth. In the matter of the ending Euripides is un-Aristotelian by inspiration, not by mischance, as we shall see in a moment; but before considering this fully we may complete our survey by noting how his use of the chorus and his dramatic style differ from Sophocles.'

The Chorus, Aristotle lays down, should participate in the action, as in Sophocles, not in Euripides. The chorus in the *Medea* finds itself in a famous difficulty at the murder of the children; it ought to participate in the action and may not. Fifteen women of Corinth stand by doing nothing while Medea murders her children indoors—or rather they stand by deliberating whether to do anything or not. In meeting this improbability nothing is gained by saying that the Chorus was a body of Ideal Spectators and that a Greek audience would not expect them to interfere. They have in fact always taken part in the action when circumstances suggested it—in the *Eumenides*, the *Ajax*, the *Antigone*, later in the *Philoctetes*, to mention only a few cases—and Aristotle feels that so it is best. Moreover, Euripides himself feels that they should naturally interfere now, for if no thought of the possible intervention of Ideal Spectators could have arisen in the mind of the audience, why does he go out of his way to suggest that thought?

The question of Euripides' use of the Chorus will recur several times; he did, in the later tragedies, make it a body of Ideal Spectators. Here it is the solid, flesh-and-blood chorus of Middle Tragedy, women of Corinth who come to inquire about Medea and not to sing philosophy; and such a chorus, natural enough when the theme of the play is one which involves the city, as in the *Antigone* and *Tyrannus*, becomes more difficult to manage when the theme is private and psychological, as in Sophocles' *Electra,* and becomes a nuisance when private intrigue has to be represented on the stage. In this respect the *Medea* is half-way between two conventions, and a certain uneasiness is inevitable.

This chorus is a little surprising too in the ode that it sings at one of the most poignant moments of the play, when Medea has finally resolved that her children must die, and just before we hear the horrible story of Glauce's death. If we have in mind the tremendous effects that Sophocles produced with his chorus at moments like these, it is a little chilling to find Euripides going off into his study, as it were, and writing, in anapaests too, on the advantages of being childless.

Such indifference in the orchestra to what was happening on the stage later became a powerful weapon in Euripides' armoury; here it is a little puzzling. The subject is germane to the context, but the treatment is not; such generalized reflection breaks the emotional rhythm of the play. When such desperate deeds are afoot, why does Euripides insert this pleasant little essay? It may be tentatively suggested that it is Euripides' method of preparing for the messenger's narrative, that he deliberately lulls our minds with this inconspicuous piece of pavement-philosophy in order to give the messenger's onslaught a fairer field. But whether this or something else be the true explanation of the passage, we can draw one deduction from it, and that is that Euripides' attitude to his tragic heroine is quite different from Sophocles'. To Antigone or Oedipus it would have been an unthinkable dramatic impoliteness to break off like this to say something interesting; not because Sophocles was a better poet and dramatist in this respect, but because he was writing a different tragedy. For all the sympathy and the tragic power with which Euripides draws his characters, and although he is "the most tragic of the poets," it seems clear that fundamentally he is detached from them. He can, as Sophocles cannot, retire for a moment and invite us to think of something else.[6]

Wherever we look therefore in the *Medea* we find that Euripides differs from Aristotle's theory and Sophocles' practice, and that not merely on the surface but radically; and the more he works his tragic vein the greater does this divergence grow, until in the *Troades* we have a play in which no single incident is the "necessary or probable" result of the preceding one, the characterization is slight and inconsistent, the chorus, far from being a co-actor, takes no notice at all of the action —and yet the *Troades* is magnificent tragedy. The method then must be a logical one, and the logic we must now try to find, so far as it is to be seen in the *Medea*.

Medea is a tragic figure, but we have seen that she is no Aristotelian tragic heroine. She is indeed possessed of a passionate nature, quite uncontrolled in love and hate; this makes her dramatic, but it is not hamartia: it is the whole woman. That certain virtues may plausibly be attributed to her is dramatically of little moment. As she betrayed her father and murdered her brother in her first love for Jason, as in Iolcus to serve Jason she contrived a horrible end for Pelias (exploits which are mentioned by Euripides and are therefore evidence), so in Corinth, when betrayed and insulted by Jason, she thinks first of revenge, not the comparatively honest revenge of killing Jason, but one that shall bring down in ruin Jason, his new bride, his children, his whole house. That they are her children too is unfortunate, but not enough to deter her from her plan; she has her struggle with her maternal feelings—a theatrical struggle rather than a psychologically convincing one—but the decisive thought is that to be laughed at by enemies is not to be borne. She is tragic in that her passions are stronger than her reason (1079); she is drawn with such vigor and directness, everything that she says and does springs so immediately from her dominant motive that she is eminently dramatic; nevertheless she is no tragic heroine as we have hitherto understood the term; she is too extreme, too simple. This is not character-study as the picture of Neoptolemus in the *Philoctetes* is, for in every possible way the characterization is concentrated in the one over-mastering passion, and the situation is manipulated to stimulate this to the uttermost. It is not melodrama, for

---

[6] This same detachment is displayed in Euripides' characterization and in his proneness to argument: the little essay on music (*Medea*, 190 ff.) is typical. Euripides is not absorbed in his *Medea* and does not pretend to be.

Medea, though extreme, is true, and her character and deeds leave us with something more than the mere excitement of a strong story. It is tragic, but we must be careful to see what we mean by tragic.

The tragedy of the Sophoclean hero is that such strength is nullified by such weakness; of Medea, that such a character should exist at all. She is bound to be a torment to herself and to others; that is why Euripides shows her blazing her way through life leaving wreckage behind her; that is why the sufferings of others, of Glauce and of Creon, are not to be glozed over. That she suffers herself is a great and no doubt a necessary part of the drama, but it is not the point of the tragedy, which is that passion can be stronger than reason, and so can be a most destructive agent. Destructive to whom? Here, to the children, Glauce, Creon, Jason, and to Medea's peace—but not to her life; in short, destructive to society at large.

It follows that Euripides had either to describe Glauce's death horribly or to enfeeble his theme; the sufferings of Medea's victims are as much part of the tragedy as those of Medea herself, possibly a greater part. Hence the contrast with Sophocles. The logical climax of the Sophoclean tragedy is that the hero is ruined; others may be involved, as are Haemon and Eurydice in the *Antigone*, but only as they intensify the hero's downfall or are subordinate to it. Even if Greek taste had allowed a detailed picture of Antigone's death agonies, Greek logic would have forbidden it—and Greek taste and Greek logic were the same thing. Antigone's loyalty to her duty leads to her own death; Creon's short-sightedness and obstinacy leads through her death to his own ruin. Horror would have spoiled the first theme and mis-directed the second; we are to watch his error recoiling upon him, not to be made feel that he is a monster of cruelty. There is no contrast here between Attic and Hellenistic; both poets are Hellenic, doing exactly what the theme demands.

The catharsis of Glauce's horror comes when we feel that she, and all the others, are the victims of an almost external force. "Love," the chorus sings, "when it comes in too great strength, has never brought good renown or virtue to mortals." Medea is drawn stark as the strongest possible impersonation of this force; balance of character is necessarily denied her, and this means that we cannot lose ourselves in sympathy with her as we do with Oedipus. Euripides is not asking us to sympathize with her in this way, but to understand her, to understand that such things are, that Medeas, and Jasons, exist, poetically if not actually. He asks us to feel terror when we hear of what her passion leads her to do, pity for all who are broken, tragic enlightenment when we see that all are the victims of a primitive force. So we do feel pity "for the savage and cruel Medea," but only when we regard her in the same objective way as Euripides.

It is perhaps possible to bring all this into relation with Aristotle's theory of hamartia, and it is worth while to make the attempt for the sake of generalizing the Euripidean method. Euripides, like most Greeks, is a rationalist in that he believes reason, not belief or formula or magic, to be the guide to life; but he sees too that we have in us, besides reason, non-rational emotions which are necessary but may run wild,[7] thwarting our reason and bringing calamity. In the last analysis Euripides' tragic hero is mankind. Some natural passion breaks its bounds, and the penalty has to be paid, either by the sinner or by those around him or by both. Within this dramatic cosmos the hamartia is concentrated in one or two people; they, Medea and Jason, are hamartia and not necessarily anything else at all; that is why they are so extreme and so unrelieved. The results of the hamartia fall on the group; perhaps on the sinners, perhaps not; for though Medea suffers here, Menelaus and Orestes in the *Andromache* get off scot-free.

The great difference between Euripides' and Sophocles' approach to tragedy is that Sophocles concentrates into one hero what Euripides splits up, prismatically, among a group. In Sophocles it is the hero himself who prefigures Man; he is strong and weak; he, and no one else (except incidentally), pays for his weakness. It is from this concentration of the tragic idea into the one hero that the Sophoclean drama get its Aristotelian virtues; it is because Euripides analyses his tragedy into the tragedy of society instead of synthesizing it in the tragedy of a representative hero, "like us," that he does not need these virtues, and will use them less and less.

This approach to tragedy, which becomes clear later, is in the *Medea* only partly worked out. It may seem absurd to say that Medea, with her tremendous driving-force and sharply accentuated character, is essentially or theoretically a heroine of the same kind as Hecuba, a purely passive figure. It is not absurd. Hecuba and those around her are regarded as the helpless victims of villainy or cruelty, Medea and those around her as the victims of Medea's disastrous temperament.

---

[7] This point has been well treated by E. R. Dodds, *Euripides the Irrationalist, C.R.,* 1929, pp. 97 ff.

Unless we feel Medea in this way, a tragic victim rather than a tragic agent, we shall try to sympathize with her in the wrong way, and waste valuable time working up emotions about the poor children.

But even if this analysis is correct, is it necessary to our appreciation of the play? Not in the least, the play makes its effect directly, without the help of theory. But the analysis is necessary if we are going to criticize the play. Let us begin with the Aegeus scene, which so glaringly offends against the reasonable Aristotelian law of necessary or probable sequence. How far is this law valid?

In the Sophoclean tragedy of character its validity is absolute. The formula there is that a hero of a certain kind is placed in circumstances such that the play between character and circumstances is bound to result in disaster for the hero. Evidently the whole point of such drama depends on this, that the character shall be a convincing one and that the circumstances, though they may be exceptional, shall develop normally, and always in significant relation with the character of the hero. It would be stultification if the dramatist had to produce a railway-accident without which the hero's doom would not be achieved. But Aegeus comes out of the blue, like a railway-accident. If the *Medea* were really a tragedy of character, if, that is, we were being invited to see how she, a woman of a certain character, was placed in a situation in which her character was inevitably her ruin, and if an Aegeus had to be introduced after all in order to bring this to pass, then the play would be meaningless, as meaningless as if Eteocles had gone to the seventh gate because the champion already chosen had broken his leg on the way. But Euripides is not doing this at all. He is presenting to us his tragic conception that the passions and unreason to which humanity is subject are its greatest scourge. This implies no tragic interlock between character and situation; the situation is nothing but the setting for the outburst of unreason, the channel along which it rushes. What matters now is not that the situation must be convincing and illuminating, not even that the heroine must be convincing as a person; but that her passion must be, in however extreme a form, a fundamental and familiar one. If Medea is in this sense true, we shall not stay to object that she is not likely.

The situation then being only a setting, Euripides is philosophically justified in manipulating it in order to present his tragic thesis in its strongest colours. Sophocles cannot say, "For the sake of working out my tragic clash between character and circumstances we will here assume that a quite unexpected and unrelated thing materially alters the situation, or that my hero will here do something out of character." But Euripides can say, without destroying his whole point, "Excuse me; here is a partial impediment in Medea's course. Let me remove it; you will then have a far finer view of what I mean." Medea was in any case certain to work some ruin; Aegeus only allows her, and Euripides, to go to the logical extreme.

This, incidentally, is the reason also why Jason can be so unrelieved a villain and yet not undramatic. If he stood to Medea as Creon does to Antigone, one whose character fatally interlocks with hers, he would be impossible; being so extreme, he would as it were prove nothing. If the dramatist simplifies his characters far enough, he can demonstrate anything. As it is, Jason is not intended to prove anything. He is a ready-made villain, easily assumed as part of the setting, and if, regarded as a dramatic character, he is a "possible improbability" that matters nothing.

In fact, Aristotle's law is concerned really with two separate things, philosophical cogency and artistic effect. The former is not affected in the least by the "irrationality" of Aegeus; the latter undoubtedly is. In the later tragedies the artistic unity of the plot is not so obviously impaired by such intrusions (as of Evadne and Iphis in the Suppliant Women) because plot there has become frankly diagrammatic instead of organic. Here the plot is made to depend on Medea's will, in the manner of Middle Tragedy, and has that kind of unity and organic growth that comes from this, so that Aegeus, who is quite independent of that will and of the crisis of Medea in Corinth, is felt to be a blemish. Nevertheless, as this is not strictly a play of character, Euripides is logically justified in not making his plot depend on his characters. He may, logically, manipulate the plot himself, or, if you like, arbitrarily interfere, in order that his creations may work out his tragic idea to the end. Our analysis may have seemed farfetched, but it was correct. The difficulty with Aegeus is that Medea is so nearly an Oedipus and the play so nearly Middle Tragedy that we may reasonably take offence. We are in the middle of a transition from one kind of tragedy to another.

As to the end of the play Aristotle's words are:

"In the characters as in the composition of the plot one must always aim at an inevitable or a probable order of events, so that it will be either inevitable or probable that such a person should say or do such a thing, and inevitable or probable that this thing should happen after that. It is obvious therefore that the ending too of the plot must arise naturally out of the plot itself, and not, as in the *Medea,* by external contrivance."

This is not an objection to the *Deus ex machina* as such, only to such employments of it as we have here. The *Philoctetes* ends with a Deus, but the appearance of Heracles there is to some extent[8] a natural result of the action of the play; it has at least been prepared for by the importance in the play of his magic bows and arrows. In the *Medea,* there has been nothing of this magic background; on the contrary, the background has been at times painfully prosaic. We have had a scene of bitter domestic strife in a setting of ordinary social life—children, nurses, curious neighbours, old men gossiping around the spring. Medea may be the granddaughter of Helios, but for all that we are dealing with ordinary life and never feel that the gods are within call. Medea quite rationally, and to the detriment of the play, provides herself with a refuge; why then is an unnatural means of escape provided for her at the end?

It is of course some answer to say that Medea is a barbarian princess and a magician; she is descended from Helios, and she is in possession of certain mysterious powers, or more strictly poisons, which ordinary women know nothing about. We are the less surprised therefore at her miraculous escape; less than if a magic chariot should come for the Second Mrs. Tanqueray. This may be true, but at the most it is only a palliation; it made Euripides' error possible.

But if we look carefully into the last scene we shall see more than dramatic convenience in the chariot. Medea has done things which appal even the chorus, those sympathetic neighbours who had said, earlier in the play, "Now is honour coming to womankind." Their prayer now is "O Earth, O thou blazing light of the Sun, look upon this accursed woman before she slays her own children. . . . O god-given light, stay her hand, frustrate her . . ." (1251 ff.). In the same vein Jason says, when he has learnt the worst, "After doing this, of all things most unholy, dost thou show thy face to the Sun and the Earth?" (1327). Sun and Earth, the most elemental things in the universe, have been outraged by these terrible crimes; what will they do? how will they avenge their sullied purity? What Earth will do we shall not be told, but we are told what the Sun does: he sends a chariot to rescue the murderess.

8 This is of course not the whole explanation.

Is this illogical? Could anything be finer, more imaginative? We [might then] see, in the *Hippolytus*, that although reason must be our guide, the primitive things in the universe —Aphrodite and Artemis there—are not reasonable. The servant of Hippolytus (v. 120) thinks what Jason and the chorus think, that "Gods should be wiser than men". Perhaps so, but these gods are not. They exist; as well deny the weather as deny Aphrodite; but they are not reasonable and can make short work of us. Zeus, "whoever he is," is another matter. There may be a *Novs*, a Mind, in the universe; but there are other powers too, and these we may worship in vain. The magic chariot is a frightening glimpse of something that we shall see in full force in the *Bacchae*, the existence in the universe of forces that we can neither understand nor control—only participate in.

The end of the *Medea* does not come out of the logic of the action by the law of necessity and probability, but is contrived by Euripides, deliberately, as the final revelation of his thought. When we begin to see Medea not merely as the betrayed and vindictive wife but as the impersonation of one of the blind and irrational forces in human nature, we begin to find that catharsis for which we looked in vain in the messenger-speech. It is this transformation that finally explains the "revolting" and deepens a dramatic story into tragedy. Had Euripides been content with a "logical" ending, with the play remaining on the mundane, Corinthian level, the "revolting" would indeed have needed justification. This makes demands on our tolerance which cannot be met if the only profit is the news that barbarian magicians who are passionate and are villainously treated do villainous things. There is in the *Medea* more than this, and to express that Euripides resorts to a manipulation of the plot, an artificial ending which, like Aegeus, would have been ruinous to Sophocles. This imaginative and necessary climax is not the logical ending to the story of Medea the ill-used wife of Corinth, but it is the climax to Euripides' underlying tragic conception.

This is a conception which does indeed call for and receive purely dramatic imagery; we need not be silly and call the *Medea* an illustration of a theme. Nevertheless the conception is not so immediately and completely transfused into drama as is Sophocles' tragic conception; Medea is not quite to Euripides what Oedipus is to Sophocles, completely and utterly the focus and vehicle of his tragic thinking. Euripides remains a little detached. We can go beneath his Medea— for criticism we must, in appreciation we do unconsciously

—to the greater conception underlying her; and in the last resort it is this, not the imagined character of Medea in these imagined circumstances, that moulds the play.

As Euripides develops his method, in particular as the war forced his thoughts more on the social aspects of tragedy, we shall find this gap between the stage-drama and the tragic conception, non-existent in Sophocles but perceptible in the *Medea,* growing much wider. Already the strict logic of plot, the Aristotelian doctrines of the tragic hero, the Sophoclean tradition of characterization and the use of the chorus are receding, and they will recede much farther. Unity of interest, that is of tragic conception, remains; but how far that conception is to be presented through one hero and one action, how far through a diversity of heroes and a multiplicity of actions, is a matter to be decided privately between Euripides the tragic poet and Euripides the playwright.

Bacchae *and* Ion: *Tragedy and Religion*

THOMAS G. ROSENMEYER

THE *Bacchae,* like the *Ion,* is a tale about a god, but that is all they have in common. The *Ion* I called, perhaps for want of a better term, a theological romance. What, then, can we say about the *Bacchae?* Earlier I suggested that it is not intrinsically a religious drama. This flies in the face of certain critical assumptions which have recently gained currency. It has been suggested that Euripides' chief object in writing the drama was to give a clinical portrayal of what Dionysiac religion, hence Dionysus, does to men. According to this view, the *Bacchae* is a more or less realistic document, perhaps an anthropological account of an outburst of manic behavior, of a psychosis analogous to certain phenomena reported from the Middle Ages and not unknown in our own troubled times. The play has even been compared with a modern imaginative treatment of mass psychosis, Van Wyck Brooks' *Oxbow Incident.* I feel that this is mistaken, and for a very simple and obvious reason. Whatever one may say about the ancient tragedians, about the extravagant character of many of the plots, about the implausibility of much

152

that is said and done, the fact remains that the writers are interested in what is typical, in the generic, or, as Aristotle has it, in the universal. To attribute to Euripides a study in abnormality is to indulge in an anachronism. Euripides is not the kind of dramatist, like Sartre, whose poetic urge is stimulated by small grievances rather than catholic insight. Nor is Euripides a scientific observer of sickness; he does not record, he creates. His material is ritual and mythical, and some of it clinical; but the product is something entirely different.

Pindar once uses the tale of Perseus cutting off the head of the Medusa as an image symbolizing the act of poetic creation: living ugliness is violently refashioned into sculptured beauty. The ferocity of the *Bacchae* is to be seen in the same light. By an act of literary exorcism the cruelty and the ugliness of a living experience are transmuted into the beauty of a large vision, a vision which is not without its own horror, but a horror entirely unlike that felt at the approach of the god. It is the kind of horror which Plato touches on in the *Symposium* and the *Theaetetus,* the sudden weakness and awe which get hold of the philosophic soul at the moment when she comes face to face with a like-minded soul and jointly ventures to explore the ultimate. Dionysus is only a means to an end; Euripides exploits the Dionysiac revels to produce a dramatic action which helps the spectators to consider the mystery and the precariousness of their own existence.

Aeschylus, notably in his *Agamemnon* but also in some of his other extant plays, appeals to the audience with an interplay of sounds and sights. With Aeschylus, language is not an instrument but an entity, a vibrant self-sufficient thing, working in close harmony with the brilliant objects filling the stage of the *Oresteia.* The word textures pronounced by the chorus, like the sentence patterns of the actors' speeches, stir the audience as violently as the sight of a crimson tapestry or the vision of evil Furies on the roof. Behind this sumptuous drapery of color and sound, personality takes second place. The characters are largely the carriers of images and speech. Sophocles introduces the personal life, the *bios,* into drama. Now a man is no longer largely the pronouncer of words, the proposer of ideas and emotions, but an independent structure involving a past and a future, a point of intersection for ominous antecedents and awful prospects. This emergence of the organic character, of the heroic life as the nucleus of drama, was a fateful step in the history of literature. Aeschylus also, in some of his later plays, adopted the new structuring for his own purposes.

Euripides goes further. He rejects the autonomy of speech as he rejects the autonomy of the personal life; instead he attempts to combine the two in an organic mixture of his own. In the *Ion* he gives us a parody of the pure *bios* form; mythology is squeezed into a biographical mold, with unexpectedly humiliating consequences for the great hero. In the *Bacchae*, on the other hand, it is in the end not the persons who count, nor the words or sound patterns though the play may well be the most lyrical of all Euripidean works, but the ideas. The *Bacchae*, in spite of its contrived brutality and its lyricism, is a forerunner of the Platonic dialogues. The smiling god is another Socrates, bullying his listeners into a painful reconsideration of their thinking and their values. That is not to say that we have here an intellectual argument, an academic inquiry into logical relations. That would fit the *Ion* better than the *Bacchae*. Rather, the *Bacchae* constitutes a poet's attempt to give shape to a question, to a complex of uncertainties and puzzles which do not lend themselves to discursive treatment. There is no clear separation of thesis and antithesis, of initial delusion and liberating doubt, nor is there anything like a final statement or a solution. Nevertheless the poem is cast in the philosophical mode. Sophocles, in the *Oedipus Rex* or the *Ajax*, takes a heroic life and fashions its tragic nexus to the world around it or to itself. Euripides, in the *Bacchae*, takes an abstract issue and constructs a system of personal relations and responses to activate the issue. He builds his lives into the issue, instead of letting the life speak for itself as Sophocles does.

The issue derives from a question which is simple and raw: What is man? As Dionysus remarks to Pentheus (506),

> Your life, your deeds, your Being are unknown
> to you.

For Plato, the human soul is a compound of the divine and the perishable, a meeting place of the eternal beyond and the passionate here. In the *Phaedrus* he puts the question more concretely. Socrates suggests that it is idle to criticize or allegorize mythology if one has not yet, as he himself has not, come to a satisfactory conclusion about his own nature and being (230A):

> I try to analyze myself, wondering whether I am some kind

154

of beast more heterogeneous and protean and furious than Typhon, or whether I am a gentler and simpler sort of creature, blessed with a heavenly unfurious nature.

The word that I have translated as "creature" is the same that appears in Aristotle's famous definition of man as a "political creature," or rather, as "a creature that lives in a *polis*." "Political animal," the usual translation, is unfortunate, for in his definition Aristotle clearly throws the weight of his authority behind the second alternative of Plato's question. Man is not a ravaging beast, but a gentler being. But perhaps Aristotle is not as fully sensitive as Plato to the difficulty posed by the alternative. Is man closer to the gods or to the beasts?

Another question which is linked to the uncertainty about the status of the human soul is: What is knowledge? Or, to put it differently: How much in this world is subject to man's insight and control? Greek philosophical realism, beginning with the Eleatics and reaching its greatest heights with Plato, taught that reality is unchanging, static, difficult of access, and that in general men come to experience it only through the veil of ever-changing patterns of sensory impulses. There is an inexorable friction between total Being and partial Appearance. Man is constrained to deal with the appearances, but at his best he comes to sense—or, according to Plato, to know—the reality behind the phenomena. The break-through to the reality is a painful process; it can be achieved only at the cost of injuring and mutilating the ordinary cognitive faculties. The perfectionists, including Plato in the *Phaedo,* submit that the break-through becomes complete only with the complete surrender of the senses whose activity stands in the way of the vision of reality. That is to say, the perceptual blindness and the phenomenal friction cannot be resolved except by disembodiment and death.

Now if this, or something like it, is the philosophical issue which Euripides is trying to dramatize, he is at once faced with a grave artistic difficulty. How is he, as a dramatist, to convey the universal scope of reality and the beguiling contradictoriness of Appearance, without rendering the formulation banal or bloodless or both? The statement "Dionysus is all" would be worse than meaningless. It should be emphasized again that Euripides is not trying to say poetically what could also, and better, be said discursively. What does a poet-metaphysician do to clothe the range of abstract issues in the living and self-authenticating flesh of poetry? Is it possible for a dramatist to convey ideas without having his characters preach them ex cathedra, which is by and large the situation we find in the *Prometheus Bound*? Can a philosophical idea which is refracted by a process of poetic mutation continue to score as a factor in a metaphysical argument?

To begin with, the Greek writer has an advantage over his modern colleagues. The ancient conventions of tragedy stipulate that the dramatic nucleus be essayed from a spectrum of approaches. From Prologue to chorus to characters to Epilogue, each constitutive part of the drama contributes its specific orientation. In the end the various perspectives coalesce into one and invite a unified though never simple audience response. This is the desired effect; sometimes the merging of the lines of coordination is not complete, and the spectators are left without a certain key to gauge their participation. Goethe's *Faust* is, perhaps, once again a fair example of such a case on the modern stage. The author is saying something profound about man and reality, but for various reasons the play leaves us with the impression of partial statements instead of a total imaging, because of the vast scope of the action, because Goethe has inserted certain curious elements of diffusion and fragmentation, and because he tries to play off one culture against another in an attempt to universalize the compass of the theme. Any Greek play is likely to be more successful on this score. The traditional spectrum of perspectives is offset by an extreme succinctness of speech and thought, by a narrow conformity to Greek ways, by an economy of character, and, last but not least, by the condensatory effect of hereditary myth. Myth is itself a condensation of many experiences of different degrees of concreteness. Greek drama simply carries forward the business begun by myth.

Dionysus, who is Euripides' embodiment of universal vitality, is described variously by chorus, herdsman, commoners, and princes. The descriptions do not tally, for the god cannot be defined. He can perhaps be totaled but the sum is never definitive; further inspection adds new features to the old. If a definition is at all possible it is a definition by negation or cancellation. For one thing, Dionysus appears to be neither woman nor man; or better, he presents himself as woman-in-man, or man-in-woman, the unlimited personality (235):

> With perfumes wafted from his flaxen locks
> and Aphrodite's wine-flushed graces in
> his eyes . . .

No wonder Pentheus calls him (353) "the woman-shaped stranger," and scoffs at the unmanly whiteness of his complexion (457). In the person of the god strength mingles with softness, majestic terror with coquettish glances. To follow him or to comprehend him we must ourselves give up our precariously controlled, socially desirable sexual limitations. The being of the god transcends the protective fixtures of decency and sexual pride.

Again, Dionysus is both a citizen, born of Semele, and a Greek from another state, for he was raised in Crete, like the Zeus of the mysteries—surely this is the implication of lines 120 ff.—*and* a barbarian from Phrygia or Lydia or Syria or India, at any rate from beyond the pale of Greek society. It is not as if the conflicting pieces of information had to be gathered laboriously from various widely separated passages in the play. All of them are to be found in the entrance song of the chorus. After the introductory epiphany of the god himself, the women of the chorus begin to assemble their picture of Dionysus, and it is indicative of what Euripides means him to be that even these first few pointers should cancel out one another. It happens to be true historically that Dionysus is both Greek and non-Greek; recently discovered Mycenean texts have shown that the god's name was known to the Greeks of the Mycenean period. It now appears that the foreign extraction of Dionysus may have been a pious fiction of Apollinian partisans. Dionysus the popular god, the god of mysteries, the emblem of surging life in its crudest form, of regeneration and animal passion and sex, was endangering the vested interests of Apollo, grown refined and squeamish in the hands of the gentry and the intellectual elite. One of the defense measures, and there were many, was to declare Dionysus a foreigner, a divinity whose ways, so the propaganda went, offended the true instincts of the Greek. There was some apparent justification for this. The genuinely foreign deities who were being imported into Greece often were kindred in spirit to Dionysus. At any rate the propaganda took hold. At the end of the fifth century all Greeks tended to believe that Dionysus came from abroad; and yet they considered him one of their own, a powerful member of the Olympian pantheon. Euripides exploits the discrepancy to the advantage of his purpose; he uses it to emphasize the unbounded, the unfragmented nature of the ultimate substance. But the arrival from foreign lands signifies a special truth; it highlights the violently intrusive character of the Dionysiac life, of the unlimited thrusting itself into the limited and exploding its stale equilibrium, which is a favorite theme of Pythagorean and Greek popular thought.

But all this would be bloodless metaphysics, dry-as-dust allegory, were it not for Euripides' grasp of the essential irony enunciated in the passage of the *Phaedrus* and skirted in Aristotle's aphorism. Man is both beast and god, both savage and civilized, and ultimate knowledge may come to him on either plane, depending on the manner in which the totality communicates itself. It is as an animal, as a beast close to the soil and free of the restrictions of culture and city life, that man must know Dionysus. But that means that in embracing Dionysus man surrenders that other half of himself, the spark of the gentle and celestial nature which, the philosophers hope, constitutes the salvageable part of man's equipment. The incongruity of the two planes, the political and the animal, becomes the engrossing puzzle and the energizing thesis of the play. The double nature of man is what the play is really about; the ambivalence of Dionysus is pressed into service largely in order to illumine the ambivalence of human cognition reaching out for its object, for the elusive pageant of truth.

How does Euripides use the animal in his art? In the *Ion* the relation between men and animals is simple and candid, though not devoid of some humor. At the beginning Ion wages a mock battle against the birds because they interfere with his daily cleaning operations. The kindly gruffness with which he rebukes them deceives no one. Once he threatens death to a swan that approaches too closely to the altar (161 ff.), but he does not take the threat seriously himself (179):

> To think I would murder you,
> messengers of the words of gods
> to men!

Ion is not so cynical as to remember that the swan is said to sing his truest song when he is about to die. Later Ion's life is saved when a dove consumes the poison meant for him (1202 ff.); he accepts the sacrifice gratefully but without comment. Near the beginning of the exodus Ion calls Creusa (1261) a "serpent . . . or a dragon"

> with murderous fire blazing from his eyes,

but this is a metaphor induced by rage, and in any case Ion

158

is mistaken about her, as he acknowledges in the next scene. The history of Athens may have been crowded with serpents and half-serpents; the decoration of the tent features many beings half-man half-beast, including Cecrops himself with his serpent's coils. But the somber tent, as suggested earlier, is the exception. Through most of the action, and certainly at the end of the play when the causes of ignorance have been removed, men know their distance from the animals. Their humaneness entails this; the gentleness which characterizes the true inclinations of Io and Creusa and Xuthus takes us far away from the murky borderland where human nature and animal nature merge and where satyrs and centaurs ply their brutal trade.

In the *Bacchae* this borderland is always present. Men are identified with animals, not as in Aesop where the beasts aspire to be men and become moral agents, but as in a Gothic tale where intelligence and social grace and responsibility are renounced and the irrational, the instinct of blood and steaming compulsion, take their place. Characteristically this way of looking at life paralyzes value judgment. The gulf between men and animals is erased, but whether this is a good thing or not is by no means clear. When the women of the chorus, for example, call Pentheus a beast they do not mean to flatter him. He is the son of Echion, who was sprung from dragon's teeth, and there is dragon blood in his veins (1155). He is said to be a fierce monster (542) whose acts make one suspect that he was born of a lioness or a Libyan Gorgon. His mother also in her moment of visionary bliss sees him as a lion rather than as a man. For her, however, this is not a matter of disparagement; if anything, embracing a lion seems to her to offer a glimpse of perfection. Not so the chorus; in the passages cited they show an incongruous pride in human shape and human achievement. But in the fourth choral ode, as they reach their highest pitch of passion and frenzied insight, they issue the call which is quoted at the beginning of our chapter (1017):

> Appear, in the shape of a bull or a many-headed
> serpent, or a lion breathing fire!

In their first ode also they refer to Dionysus as the bull-horned god wreathed in snakes (100 f.). The god Dionysus, the stranger-citizen, the hermaphrodite, at once superman and subman, is a beast, for which the chorus praise him.

This is the sacred dogma. Even Pentheus, once he has fallen under the spell of the god, acknowledges him as a bull (920):

> And now, leading me on, I see you as
> a bull, with horns impacted in your head.
> Were you a beast before? I should not wonder.

And Dionysus answers:

> Yes, now you see what is for you to see.

But what of Pentheus' own beast-likeness? Are the women suggesting that human beastliness is a mere parody of divine beastliness, and therefore to be condemned? Or have the ladies of the chorus not yet travelled the full length of the Dionysiac conversion, and retain a vestige of civilized values? Their abuse of Pentheus is couched in terms which expose them as imperfect Maenads. Contrast that other chorus, the band of Bacchantes hidden from our sight, whose mysterious acts of strength are reported to us in the messenger speeches. From them rather than from their more civilized sisters on the stage we expect the pure lesson of the new faith. And in fact they preserve no trace of false pride in human separateness. They carry the tokens of animal life on their backs and entertain the beasts as equal partners (695):

> And first they shook their hair free to their shoulders
> and tucked up their fawnskins . . .
>   . . . their spotted pelts
> they girt with serpents licking at their cheeks.
> And some clasped in their arms a doe or wild
> wolf cubs and gave them milk . . .

Under the aegis of Dionysus, men and animals are as one, with no questions asked. The philosophical message is tolerably clear. But the vestigial bias of the pseudo-Maenads on stage is more than a temporary deviation from the orthodox Bacchic faith. In the interest of the message it would have been wiser to abuse Pentheus as a man, incapable of going beyond the limitations of his anthropomorphism. The beast imagery in the choral condemnation of Pentheus is cumulative and emphatic. The praise of Dionysus does not blot it from our memory. It is, in fact, intended to serve as a counterpoint. The animal shape rules supreme; but when all parties have been heard it is not at all clear whether one ought to approve or not. The judgment is suspended, and values are held in abeyance.

It is a mistake to consider the Dionysiac ecstasy a perversion of social life, an impasse, a negative situation. The *Bacchae* does not tell a story of maladjustment or aberration. It is a portrayal of life exploding beyond its narrow everyday confines, of reality bursting into the artificiality of social conventions and genteel restrictions. Waking and sleeping are deprived of their ordinary cognitive connotations; who is to say that sleeping, the drunken stupor which succeeds the rite, does not expand one's vision beyond its commonplace scope? In the *Ion* the premium is on wakefulness; in the *Bacchae* we are invited to rest in a gray no man's land which is halfway between waking and sleep, where man shelves the tools of reason and social compact and abandons himself to instinct and natural law (862 ff., tr. Phillip Vellacott):

> O for long nights of worship, gay
> With the pale gleam of dancing feet,
> With head tossed high to the dewy air—
> Pleasure mysterious and sweet!
> O for the joy of a fawn at play
> In the fragrant meadow's green delight,
> Who has leapt out free from the woven snare,
> Away from the terror of chase and flight,
> And the huntsman's shout, and the straining pack,
> And skims the sand by the river's brim
> With the speed of wind in each aching limb,
> To the blessed lonely forest where
> The soil's unmarked by a human track,
> And leaves hang thick and the shades are dim.

This is the strophe of a choral ode; in the antistrophe the chorus invoke the divine order of things—*physis*, nature—which will assert itself eventually in spite of men (884)

> who honor ignorance and refuse
> to enthrone divinity . . .

The verses cited picture the pleasure and the awe of identification with nonhuman nature, with the life of the fawn bounding free of the snare but never quite eluding the hunter, a life of liberty which is yet not free. The animal senses the sway of natural law even more strongly than the man. Strophe and antistrophe, the vision of animal escape and the address to natural compulsion, are part of the same complex. But in the text they do not follow one upon the other; they are separated by that rare thing in Greek poetry, a refrain which is repeated once more identically, at the end of the antistrophe. Refrains in Greek tragedy always have a solemn ring; they are felt to be echoes of ritual hymns. The fixed severity of the repetition is something foreign within the headlong flow of the dramatic current. The mind accustomed to pressing on after the determined advance of ideas and plot is abruptly stopped in its tracks; time ceases for a while and the cold chill of monotony reveals a glimpse of Being beyond the Becoming of the human scene.

Here is an attempt to translate the refrain as literally as the sense allows (877, 897):

> What is wisdom? Or what is more beautiful,
> a finer gift from the gods among men,
> than to extend a hand victorious
> over the enemy's crown? But beauty
> is every man's personal claim.

Wisdom equals tyranny, beauty equals vengeance. The hunted and the hunter have their own jealous notions of wisdom and beauty, but their pretensions are drowned in the vast offering of the gods, the dispensation of natural law and the survival of the strongest. This is what the refrain seems to say; the message agrees well with the propositions of strophe and antistrophe. But note the didactic quality of the speech, the question and answer, and particularly the academic formulation of the last line which in the Greek consists of only four words: "Whatever beautiful, always personal." It is a line which might have come straight from the pages of Aristotle; better yet, it reminds us of a similarly scholastic passage in a poem by Sappho in which she contemplates various standards of beauty and preference and concludes: "I [think that the most beautiful thing is] that with which a person is in love." The poetess speaks of a "thing," using the neuter gender, and of "a person," any person, desiring the thing. Like a good teacher she starts her discussion with a universal premise. Then, as the poem draws to its conclusion, she discards the generality and focuses on the living girl and on the I, the specific poles of her love whose reality constitutes the authority for the writing of the poem. But the philosophic mode of the earlier formulation remains important; it reminds us that the specific poles of her present love are at the same time representatives of a universal rhythm. In Euripides' ode, also, it is this universal rhythm which comes into view through the hieratic stillness of the refrain and particularly through its last line. The words are almost the same as those of Sappho; the difference is that between a vision intent upon the small joys and sufferings of love, and a vision which comprehends man in the sum total of his powers and feebleness. The refrain may well be the closest approach to poetry shedding its disguise and showing itself as metaphysics pure and simple.

But the glimpse is short-lived, and the clarity immediately obscured. Again it is the chorus itself which is the chief agent of confounding the analysis. It does so by combining in the Dionysiac prospects of its songs the two sides, the real and the ideal, which are inevitably connected in the experience. Both ritual and hope, slaughter and bliss, dance and dream, the cruelty of the present and the calm of the release, are joined together as one. The paradise of milk and honey and the orgy of bloody dismemberment merge in a poetic synthesis which defies rational classification. Of this creative insight into the contradictoriness of things I have already spoken. To complicate the picture even further, Bacchic sentiments are superimposed on traditional choric maxims. In an earlier ode which begins with a condemnation of Pentheus' words and an appeal to the goddess Piety, the women sing (386, 397):

> Of unbridled mouths
> and of lawless extravagance
> the end is disaster . . .
> . . . .
> Life is brief; if a man,
> not heeding this, pursues vast things
> his gain slips from his hands.
> These are the ways, I believe,
> of madmen, or of
> injudicious fools.

We recognize the familiar adage of "nothing in excess," the motto of bourgeois timidity and sane moderation, at opposite poles from the Dionysiac moral of vengeance and expansiveness and the bestialization of man. The injunctions of moderation and knowing one's limits run counter to the hopes of those who worship Dionysus. The two people who live up to the injunctions, Tiresias and Cadmus, come very close to being comic characters, as we shall see directly. Why, then, does Euripides put the pious precept into the mouth of a chorus whose primary artistic function is to communicate precisely what it is condemning, the spirit of unbridled mouths and lawless extravagance? It may be noted that such injunc-

163

tions in Greek tragedy are often illusory. Setting off as they do a heroic imbalance or a cosmic disturbance, they underscore the poignancy of the action. But in this particular instance the use of the Delphic motto is even more startling than usual. The direction of the metaphysical impact is rudely deflected and the opacity of the poem enhanced by this conventional reminder of irrelevant quietist values.

While the Theban women are away celebrating, the foreign votaries are in Thebes. This is a mechanical displacement necessitated by what Greek tragedy permits; for the Dionysiac revels must be reported rather than seen, and so the true Maenads are off stage. But that puts the chorus in an anomalous position. They are worshippers of Dionysus, but they must not behave like worshippers. Few Euripidean choruses are less intimately engaged in the action and in fact less necessary to the action. It is the chorus off stage that counts. Hence the curious mixture of halfhearted participation and distant moralizing, as if the poet were not entirely comfortable with the choral requirements. This may account for the perplexing admixture of Apollonian preaching which I have just mentioned. It may account also for the remarkable poetic color of many of the choral utterances. The poet, making a virtue of the necessity, calls attention to the detachment of the chorus from the heart of the plot—though not from the heart of the philosophical issue—by giving it some of the finest lyrics ever sounded in the Attic theater. This is not the place for a close appreciation of the poetry; that can be done only in the original. The analysis of ancient poetry is a difficult thing; there are few men who combine the necessary scholarly equipment with an understanding of what poetry is about. Further, some of the clues to such an understanding which in modern poetry are furnished by the experience of living speech are missing for the Greek. Nevertheless few readers can expose themselves to the choral odes of the *Bacchae* without realizing that this is poetry of the highest order. Imagery has little to do with it; in this as in most Euripidean plays the choral poetry is even less dependent on metaphor and simile than the dialogue. There is some pondering of myth, to be sure. But perhaps the most important thing about the odes is the wonderful mixture of simplicity and excitement. The women do not beat around the bush; their interest in life is single-minded, and they declare themselves with all the fervor of a unitary vision. This does not, of course, say anything about the poetry as poetry, but it may explain why the lyrics of the *Bacchae* touch us so powerfully.

There is one image, however, or rather a class of images, which ought to be mentioned: the container filled to the bursting point. In their first ode the chorus use the trope three times. They sing of Dionysus stuffed into the thigh of Zeus, golden clasps blocking the exit until such time as the young man may be born (94 ff.). They call on Thebes, nurse of Semele, to (107)

> teem, teem with verdant
> bryony, bright-berried;

the city is to be filled to the rooftops with vegetation, as a sign of the presence of the god. For illustration we should compare the famous vase painting of Exekias in which Dionysus reveals himself in his ship to the accompaniment of a burst of vegetation. Finally the women caution each other to be careful in their handling of the thyrsus, the staff of the god (113):

> Handle the staffs respectfully;
> there is *hubris* in them.

In all three instances it is the fullness of the container which is stressed, not the spilling over. But as the play advances, containment proves inadequate. At the precise moment when the stranger is apprehended by Pentheus' men, the Maenads who had been imprisoned earlier are set free (447):

> All by themselves the bonds dropped off their feet;
> keys unlocked doors, without a man's hand to turn them.

Their liberation is as real as the binding of the stranger is false.

The most striking *mise en scène* of the inadequacy of the container is the so-called palace miracle. Like that of the other passages, its function is symbolic rather than dramaturgical; after it has happened it is never mentioned again. It is not necessary to the progress of the plot, only to the effect and the meaning of the poem. We need not worry much whether the stage director engineered the collapse of a column or a pediment, or whether the spectators were challenged to use their own creative imagination, though I am inclined to assume the latter. At any rate, the vision of the palace shaking and tumbling is the most explicit and the most extended of a series of images pointing to the explosion of a force idly and wrongfully compressed. Eventually this concept converges on what I have called the friction between total Being and fragmentary Appearance, the friction which is worked out also through a series of antinomies: the brute wildness of the thyrsus versus the spindles abandoned in the hall, the fawn-skins versus the royal armor, the civic proclamation versus the bleating shout, the beating of tambourines versus the steady clicking of the loom. Dionysus disrupts the settled life, he cracks the shell of civic contentment and isolation. Probably the most important word in the play, as a recent critic has well pointed out, is *"hubris."* It occurs throughout, and always in a key position. But it is not the *hubris* of which the tragic poets usually speak, the *hubris* which figures also in the legal documents, the thoughtless insolence which comes from too much social or political power. In the *Bacchae, hubris* is quite literally the "going beyond," the explosion of the unlimited across the barricades which a blind civilization has erected in the vain hope of keeping shut out what it does not wish to understand. That is not to say that the word is not used also in its more conventional sense, especially with reference to the campaign of Pentheus. As a result, the efforts of Pentheus take on the aspect of a parody of Dionysiac impulsiveness.

Similarly the hunt is a principal symbol because it catches the futility of organized, circumscribed life. From the van-tage point of the larger reality, all wordly activity appears both hunt and escape. Hunting and being hunted are the physical and psychological manifestations of Appearance, the monoto-nous jolts of the process of generation and decay. Agave cries when approached by the herdsman (731):

> Run to it, my hounds!
> Behold the men who hunt us! Follow me,
> brandish your thyrsus and pursue them!

The Maenads are resting; they are communing with the god and sloughing off the sense of separateness when they are violently pulled back into the world of Appearance and re-sume their game of hunting and being hunted. In this case it is Appearance which causes the disruption; Being and Appearance are so related that one as well as the other may be the cause of disturbance and dislocation. There is a per-petual pull between them which never allows either to win a lasting victory. Without the constant friction there would be no tragedy; without the violent disruption of one by the other there would be no dismemberment. *Sparagmos,* the sacred dismemberment of the Dionysiac rites, is both a means to an end and an autonomous fact. As a means to an end it supplies the frenzied exercise which terminates in the drugged sleep. The explosion of energy, the tearing and mutilation of a once living body, leaves the worshipper exhausted and readies the soul, through a numb tranquility, for the mystic union with the god. But the dismemberment operates also as a self-validating event. Through it, symbolically, the world of Appearance with its contradictions and insufficiencies is made to show itself as it really is. The destruction of Pentheus, then, is not simply a sardonic twist of an unspeakable bloody rite, but a fitting summation of the lesson of the play. The limited vessel is made to burst asunder, refuting the pretensions of those who oppose Dionysus, of the partisans of unreality.

Who is Pentheus, and why is it he who dies rather than one of the other Thebans? When the stranger raises the question whether the King knows who he really is, he answers (507):

> Pentheus, the son of Agave and of Echion.

Thus Pentheus identifies himself as a member of the ruling house, as an officer of the State. He bears a name which establishes his position within the hereditary political structure of his city. Even at the moment of death he throws off the leveling disguise of the ministrant and cries (1118):

> Mother, it is I, your son
> Pentheus, the child you bore in Echion's house.

In the judgment of Dionysus this pride in the house, the emphasis on the limited life, is ignorance. But is it commensurate with the punishment which Pentheus receives? Is there not something about him as a person which is more likely to justify the violence of his undoing? To ask the obvious question: Does Pentheus not exhibit an arrogance which cries out for retribution?

Here we must step gingerly. It is to be remembered that the action of the *Bacchae* is not primarily borne or promoted by the characters. Euripides does not in this play operate with idiosyncrasies but with lives. Suffering is constructed as the measurable content of a life, not as the unique

167

unquantifiable experience of a specific irrational soul. And the lives, also, are largely catalysts for the release of social complications. These complications have nothing to do with the arbitrary contours of individual dispositions, but answer directly to the needs of the author's metaphysical purpose. The personal relations brought into play are devised chiefly as one of the means for the author to invoke his philosophical riddle. In the *Alcestis,* as we shall see in the essay on that play, character is all; in the *Bacchae* it counts for very little. It is sometimes said that the tragedy of Pentheus is not that he tried to do what was wrong but that he was the wrong man to do it—that he was, in fact, not a political strongman but precisely the unbalanced, excitable type of person who most easily falls a victim to the allurements of the Dionsysiac indulgence. In other words, the character of Pentheus is too Dionysiac to allow him to oppose Dionysus successfully. But this argument will not stand up. Pentheus is no more and no less excitable or unstable than most of the heroes of Greek tragedy. An Odysseus, or a Socrates, is no more fit to stand at the center of a high tragedy than a Pecksniff or a Tanner. Odysseus is not a whole man, as Helen is not a whole woman; they are exponents of a partial aspect of the human range: intelligence in the case of Odysseus, love in the case of Helen. But Pentheus is a whole man, precisely as Oedipus is, or as Antigone is a whole woman. And because he is whole he is vulnerable, more vulnerable than the men and women who are weighted in one direction or another.

Of course he is not a moderate. His order to smash the workshop of Tiresias (346 ff.) is not well considered. He happens to be right; Tiresias appears to have turned disloyal to Apollo, and so will no longer need his oracle seat. Under the democratic spell of Dionysus, everybody will do his own prophesying. But even if Pentheus were unjustified in his harshness toward Tiresias, his lack of moderation, or, to put it more fairly, his capacity for anger, does not necessarily discredit him. Stability, self-control, discretion smack too much of asceticism and puritan artifice to provide a solid basis for tragic action. Pentheus is a whole man, with none of his vitality curtailed or held in check. But he is also a king, a perfect representative of the humanistic Greek ideal of the ordered life, a political being rather than a lawless beast. Being Aristotle's "creature living in a *polis,*" he is destined to ask the wrong sort of question, a political question, when faced with the reality of religion. His query (473), shows the political or educational frame of his thinking. The twentieth century, unlike the eighteenth, is once more inclined to the view that the question of usefulness when applied to religion misses the point, that religion cannot be adjusted to a system of utilitarian relations. But where did Euripides and his contemporaries stand on this issue? In all probability Pentheus' question did not strike the audience as irrelevant; it may, in fact, have impressed them as noble and responsible. At the end of the fifth century, as we can see in the *History* of Thucydides, the preservation of social and political institutions and traditions had become the overriding topic of discussion to which all other values tended to be subordinated. The *Bacchae* demonstrates that this sort of nobility, the exaltation of the political and educational thesis, is as nothing before the primary currents of life. But a nobility which goes under is not the less noble for its defeat. Pentheus dies, and the nature of his death, particularly of the preparations which lead to his death, is deplorable. But the fact remains that his stand, and only his, can be measured in positive moral terms. Clearly the force which kills him eludes ethical analysis.

Because Pentheus is a king he offers a larger area to be affected by the deity. His responses differ from those of other men less in their specific quality than in their intensity. As a king he suffers for the group; his name, as Dionysus reminds him (508), means "man of sorrow." But there is nothing Christ-like about him. He proposes to live as a rational man, to leave everything nonrational, everything that might remind us of man's original condition, behind him. Love and faith, the Christian antidotes of the dispassionate intellect, have not yet been formulated. In Plato, characteristically, it is love and reason together, or love-in-reason, which refines man and weakens the animal in him. Nonreason, in the fifth century B.C., is neither love nor hatred but religious ecstasy. This Pentheus means to fight, for he knows it is wrong. Pentheus is not a romantic hero, he does not search for a hidden truth. The same thing is true of the others; both the characters and the chorus are, each of them, convinced that they know best and that their way of life is best. For Pentheus the best is Form, the tested and stable limits of responsibility, law, and control. Against the chorus, which espouses the cause of excitement, of formlessness and instability, Pentheus is the champion of permanence and stability. Neither his anger nor his defeat are valid arguments against the merits of this championship. Like Ajax, as we shall see in the following essay, Pentheus is identified with armor (781, 809); like Ajax, the armed Pentheus, confined in the panoply of embattled civic life, turns against the forces which are wrecking his fragile cause. As a functionary he represents order and limit; as a man he is whole and robust and fully alive.

This cannot be said about Cadmus and Tiresias. For one thing, they are old men, their life force is diminished and stunted. This means that they cannot suffer as Pentheus can. It also means that they have come to terms with the world; there are no issues left for them to battle out, no difficulties over which to fret. Cadmus is a fine specimen of the *arriviste,* proud of the achievements of his grandson, but even prouder of the inclusion of a genuine god in the family. The god must at all costs be kept in the family, even if it becomes necessary to mince the truth a little. Here is Cadmus' humble plea to Pentheus (333):

> And if, as you say, the god does not exist,
> keep this to yourself, and share in the fine fiction
> that he does; so we may say that Semele bore
> a god, for the greater glory of our clan.

The distinction between truth and falsity, between order and disorder, is of no importance to him. At this time of life, a good reputation is a finer prize than a noble life, no matter whether the reputation is deserved or not. Tiresias likewise is not concerned with essentials. This Tiresias is not the Sophoclean man of truth, the terrible mouthpiece of mystery and damnation, but, of all things, a clever sophist, a pseudo-philosopher who strips away the mystery and the strangeness of the superhuman world and is content to worship a denatured, an ungodded god. A squeamish deist, he does not hold with the miracles and the barbarisms of popular faith. In his lecture to Pentheus he pares down the stature of Dionysus to render him manageable and unoffending (272 ff.). Point one: he is the god of wine (280)

> which liberates suffering mortals from
> their pain.

This is to say, he *is* wine (284), precisely as Demeter *is* grain. By allegorizing the old stories and identifying the gods with palpable substances, we can dispense with whatever is

170

not concrete and intelligible in the traditions about Dionysus. Point two: he is a perfectly natural god. The distasteful tale about Zeus sewing him up in his thigh produces a quite satisfactory meaning once it is understood that the grating feature is due to a pun. Like Max Mueller in a subsequent era of facile enlightenment, Tiresias believes that the mystery of myth is caused by a linguistic aberration; with the discovery of the cause, the mystery disappears.

Finally, in the third part of his lecture, Tiresias does pay some attention to the irrational virtues of the god, to his mantic powers and his ability to inspire panic in strong men. But this part of the assessment is underplayed; it is briefer than the other two, and one feels that Tiresias adds it only in order to have a weapon with which to frighten Pentheus. The reference to soldiers strangely routed and to Dionysiac torches at home in the sanctuary of Delphi is not a confession but a threat, calculated to appeal to Pentheus in the only language he understands: the language of military and political authority. Tiresias' heart is not in the threat; what interests him is the theological and philological sterilization of the god. Neither he nor Cadmus really understands or even wants to understand what the god has to offer. But they know that his triumph is inevitable, and so they try to accept him within their lights. They are fellow travellers, with a good nose for changes of fashion and faith. To take them seriously would be absurd; a Tartuffe has no claim on our sympathy.

They do not understand; hence nothing happens to them.[1] Pentheus, on the other hand, is fully engaged, and he is a big enough man to perceive the truth beyond his own self-interest. He is capable of appreciating the real meaning of Dionysus; though he does not approve, he understands. But understanding, in a man of his power of commitment, is tantamount to weakening, and in the end, to destruction. This is what Euripides dramatizes with the sudden break-up of Pentheus' royal substance. Abruptly the officer of the State turns into a Peeping Tom. One shout of the god (810) and the manly general becomes a slavish, prurient, reptilian thing, intent on watching from a safe distance what he hopes will be a spectacle to titillate his voyeur's itch. The civilized

[1] The metamorphosis which Dionysus inflicts upon Cadmus in the Epilogue is a datum from mythology. Because of the bad state of preservation of the final portion of the play we do not know how Euripides motivated the metamorphosis, and what the punishment—for such it is said to be (1340 ff.)—is for.

man of reason is gone, and in his place we find an animal, living only for the satisfaction of his instinctual drives.

Is the rapid change psychologically plausible? Once more, the question is not pertinent. There is no character in the first place, only a comprehensive life-image to symbolize one side of a conflict which transcends the terms of a uniquely experienced situation. Whether it is possible for such a man as Pentheus is shown to be in the first half of the play, to turn into the creature he becomes after his conversion by Dionysus, is a question on which psychoanalysts may have an opinion but which does not arise in considering Euripides' purpose. The truth is that the change is not a transition from one phase of life to another, much less a lapse into sickness or perversion, but quite simply death. When a tragic hero in the great tradition is made to reverse his former confident choice, especially if this happens at the instigation of the archenemy, the role of the hero has come to an end. We remember Agamemnon stepping on the crimson carpet, after Clytemnestra has broken down his reluctance. The blood-colored tapestry is a visual anticipation of the murder. Instead of the corporeal death which will be set off stage, the audience watch the death of the soul. With Agamemnon slowly moving through the sea of red the contours are blurred and the king of all the Greeks is annihilated before our eyes. Aeschylus uses a splash; Euripides, less concretely but no less effectively, uses a change of personality.

That the hero has died in his scene with Dionysus becomes even clearer when the god, with a Thucydidean terseness, announces the physical death (857):

> Now I shall go and dress him in the robes
> he'll wear to Hades once his mother's hands
> have slaughtered him . . .

His death, then, is an agreed fact both while the chorus sing their ode to Natural Necessity and also during the terrible scene which follows in which Pentheus arranges his woman's clothes about him. The King joins the Maenads, but he goes further than they, for he adopts the bisexuality of the god. All this is meaningful as a picture of the complete and devastating victory of reality over unreality, of the natural over the institutional life. But it is not without its psychological aspect; and here, curiously, we may see an ironic parallel to one of Plato's most troublesome concerns. In his discussions of dramatic poetry, Plato takes it for granted that the spectacle affects the soul of the spectator, even to the extent of transforming it in its own likeness. This is what drama demands; the audience must allow what they see to shape their souls, without struggling against the impact. Plato recognizes the legitimacy of the demand, and decides that therefore drama is too dangerous to have around in a healthy body politic, except the kind of drama whose effect is beneficial. Pentheus also is about to see a spectacle, a Dionysiac drama of the type which as a responsible man of the city he had condemned. Euripides knows that Plato's act of censorship is in a hopeless cause. A life which does not reach out to embrace the sight of a greater reality which tragedy affords is incomplete. Watching a play may mean a partial sacrifice of the soul, a surrender to the unlimited and the irrational, but we cannot do without it. Pentheus holds out against it for some time, but in the end he throws down his arms, with such finality that his soul comes to be transformed and enriched even before he goes off to spy on the mysteries.

Pentheus is drunk, without the physical satisfaction of strong drink (918):

> Ho, what is this? I think I see two suns,
> two cities of Thebes each with its seven gates!

This is one way of formulating his conquest at the hand of Dionysus. Drunk he sees more keenly, or at any rate more completely:

> And now, leading me on, I see you as
> a bull . . .

And Dionysus replies:

> Yes, now you see what is for you to see.

For the first time Pentheus' eyes are sufficiently opened to see the god in his animal shape. His vision is broadened; but his role as Pentheus is finished. The disintegration of the king is made particularly painful by the emphasis on the feminine clothing. With Dionysus assisting as his valet (928) the one-time upholder of the *vita activa* becomes fussy and vain about the details of his toilette. Does the cloak hang properly? Is he to carry the thyrsus in his right or in his left hand? The energies which had once been directed toward the mustering of armies and the implementation of public decisions are now bestowed on the arrangement of his Bacchic vestments. Along with this attention to the correct fashion—behold, another Tiresias—to the external signs of his new-found anonymity, there goes an internal change which is equally preposterous. The blocked doer turns into an uninhibited dreamer (945):

> I wonder if my shoulders would support
> Cithaeron and its glens, complete with Maenads?

His speech, formerly royal and violent and ringing, has become pretty and lyrical; he pictures the women (957)

> like birds in the thickets,
> contained in the fond coils of love's embrace.

Compare this with his earlier comment (222) that the women

> slink off by devious ways into
> the wild and cater to the lusts of males.

His imagination has been fired, his surly prejudices are gone. The vision which neither Cadmus nor Tiresias was able to entertain has come to Pentheus and is inspiring him. The Bacchianized Pentheus is a visionary and poet. But it is a poetry which lacks the saving grace of choice. He contemplates the prospect of his mother carrying him home from the mountains, and the prospect pleases him. The political man has become woman *and* child. Having rid himself of the social restrictions and classifications, he savors infancy, a sentient creature for whom the mother's cradled arms offer escape and bliss. He is woman and child and beast, an amorphous organism susceptible to all influences and realizing itself in a life of instinct and unthinking sense. The victory of Dionysus is complete; the king is dead, and the man has been found out, in the god's image.

Is There a Tragic Sense of Life?

LIONEL ABEL

For Merry Abel, 1940-1964, In Memoriam

Our Estimate of Writers with the "Tragic Sense"

WE SET a particular value on those writers of plays—sometimes of novels—who give expression to what has been called the "tragic sense of life." Do we overvalue them? The truth is, I think, that we value them in a very special way, for we see demonstrated in their works the possibility of viewing life other than with optimism or pessimism. And for ourselves, when we reflect, the only possible choice lies with one or the other of these extremes, so that it is not only the art of the writer of tragedy we admire, but some special insight, which we feel that we can achieve only through his intervention, and which he—for that is our assumption—enjoys by some peculiar privilege of rare wisdom, or intelligence, or some yet more mysterious endowment. He seems more *philosophic* than other writers of equal art or scope, so that by a kind of tacit consent philosophers have honored authors of tragedy as the most *philosophical* of writers. In this estimate of the writer of tragedy I think there is a misunderstanding of his very special achievement, hence also a misunderstanding of what he achieves, namely, tragedy. If we can correctly think out what we are right to admire the author of tragedy for, we may correct some wrong notions of what tragedy is.

Our Dissatisfaction with Optimism and Pessimism

Now it should be clear why optimism as an attitude toward life cannot satisfy us. It should be clear, too, that our dissatisfaction with it is mainly *intellectual*. For we are quite naturally optimistic insofar as we are active beings, living in time and planning the future which our very life structure requires us to think of as being capable of yielding to our purposes. But when we reflect, when we remember "things said and done long years ago," and also the things we did not say or do, as well as those said and done by others, we realize—we have to—that there are a great many negative facts. Only a few of these, and there are a great many of them, would be enough to invalidate any optimistic hypothesis that the world as it is can be truthfully described as *good*. Instances of such negative facts may be remote or local: the unjust sentence passed on Socrates, or the fact raised by André Malraux at a congress of Soviet writers during the thirties of a man run over by a trolley car.[1] Such negative facts are able to render void all optimistic *generalizations* about the world, just as a few tiny facts which remain obdurate to explanation are sufficient to refute a whole scientific theory accounting for a multitude of others. So those who live by optimistic beliefs are like bad scientists, clinging, despite the evidence, to refuted theories.

But what about the negative facts? Do they at least justify pessimism? Not as a hypothesis, not as a generalized view. For the negative facts comprise merely one set of facts, and the world is such that no one set of facts is able to speak for it. We know that having heard one set out, we must listen to very different facts. Alas for the heartbreak of the defeated and the dead: if we do not straightway share their fate, we are forced to think of something else.

The Russian thinker Chestov—I will not call him a philosopher—repeated again and again in his writings that the injustice done to Socrates was a fact he could not endure. He thought, too, that a fact of this sort should make us suspicious of any facts we ordinarily think of as positive. But even if the positive facts were far fewer than the negative, they could still not justify our electing for pessimism. (For Schopenhauer a preponderance of negative facts did justify pessimism; his argument lacks subtlety.) The positive facts remain, and they prevent us from resolving without artificiality in favor of a pessimistic view. A very few positive facts can make pessimism unacceptable. This is illustrated, I think, in the biblical story of Abraham's debate with God when the Lord was intent on destroying the wicked cities of Sodom and Gomorrah. Abraham argued that if there were even ten good men in those cities, the Lord's proposed action would be unjust. And God finally conceded Abraham to be

[1] The reply made to Malraux was that the Soviet authorities would see to it that accidents of that sort decreased annually. The argument of the Soviet writers was for optimism, to them obligatory; the greater relative safety of future generations would more than make up for the absolute harm which had befallen one individual.

the better philosopher, admitting that if there were even fewer than ten good men in Sodom and Gomorrah, His pessimism about the two cities would be unjustified, notwithstanding all the wicked in them.

That the positive facts stand in the way of a resolve for pessimism is not in any sense an argument for being optimistic. Far from it! It is a sad fact indeed that sadness will bring us no closer than lightness of spirit to the heart of things.

What argues for optimism is that it is required by our life structure. If we plan to be optimistic, then at least we are not contradicting ourselves; but if we plan to be pessimistic— and since we live in time, to be pessimistic means to plan to be pessimistic—then we are contradicting ourselves; we are placing our trust in the view that things will be untrustworthy; we are reasoning that Failure cannot fail, and so, in a sense, can be depended on. Then too, except in cases of present or permanent distress, optimism is natural and spontaneous, while pessimism is inevitably theatrical. Life requires optimism; but optimism leaves out of account and quite disregards pain, frustration and death; such disregard is, of course, intellectually shallow. So we are back with our dilemma: we can be optimists or pessimists; but can we *want* to be either?

The Tragic Sense

The remedy is a fantastic one: it is a vision of the irremediable. We go to the theatre to see a tragedy. We see human action in the clearest light the mind can cast on it, and behold, we see the human person at his best. We do not disregard pain or frustration or death; in fact we give them our whole attention, and they do not make us pessimistic, they give us joy. As Aristotle said, we are relieved of pity and terror, the very emotions pessimism would yield to and optimism would avoid. We see life tragically; we have for the duration of the play at least and perhaps for some time afterward the tragic sense. Would that it were more lasting!

Can we make it so? Can we not make permanent the view of life we enjoyed in the theatre and in recollection afterward for however short a time? Can we not acquire or develop a sense of life such as the playwright himself must have had? Of course, we cannot be Sophocles, Shakespeare, or Racine. The question then is: can the tragic sense be acquired without the special genius of the writer of tragedy, and if so, how?

Why We Cannot Acquire the Tragic Sense

Suppose, though, for I think this true, that what we call the tragic sense does not form part of the playwright's genius and does not involve superior capacities of mind; then it must be the result of experience. Of what experience? The answer to this question is obvious; we should have thought of it immediately: the experience which leads to the tragic sense of life is the experience of tragedy; it is by undergoing tragedy that one arrives at the tragic sense. Or rather, the word "arrives" is misleading here, for one does not acquire or develop the tragic sense; it is not realized but imposed; one never possesses it, one has to be possessed by it.

We cannot add the tragic sense to our present sense of life, be that present sense optimistic or pessimistic. And without our present sense we have neither terms nor criteria with which to decide whether the tragic sense is worth what it will cost us. And from this it follows that no reason can ever be given for recommending the tragic sense, however good or great a thing the tragic sense may be.

Herbert J. Muller, in a recent book, *The Spirit of Tragedy*, has had the temerity to urge on us the acquisition of the tragic sense for reasons which he himself does not deny are frankly utilitarian. He writes: "We might not continue to get along as a free, open society without more of the tragic sense of life." I think the error he has fallen into is expressed in his use of the word "more." If we had *some* of the tragic sense of life then perhaps we could get still *more* of it, but it would not be the drastic thing it is if that were the way it could be come by. The prospect we would face, if we had not just "more" of the tragic sense but enough of it to have it, would be one of all or nothing.

So we cannot urge the tragic sense on ourselves or on others. To try to attain it or to recommend it is comical and self-refuting, tragedy being real only when unavoidable. There would be no such things as tragedy if a tragic fate could be rationally chosen.

The Writer of Tragedy and the Philosopher

But what about the writer of tragedy? Must he not possess the tragic sense of life since he is able to make it available to us at least for the time we spend under his spell? Is there not reason for thinking that the writer of tragedy must have a more permanent relation to the tragic view than those who receive it from him? Does he have a special philosophy, a tragic philosophy if you please, permanently his, and which through his art he is able to share with us in some small measure? Now I do not think the writer of tragedy has to have any view of life drastically different from our own.

Supposing he were a philosopher, what difference would that make? He could not by means of philosophy resolve the question of optimism or pessimism, which we who are not philosophers face. For philosophers are also either optimistic or pessimistic. (Some philosophies are neutral, but this last attitude is finally comprised under pessimism. Neutrality to life really means pessimism about it.)

When the vision of a writer of tragedy is stated philosophically, it is always converted (I submit, necessarily) into a form of optimism or of pessimism. I shall give two examples. The first is taken from Matthew Arnold's famous poem *Dover Beach*. Arnold, looking out at the sea from Dover Beach and hearing in the cadence of the waves the "eternal note of sadness," thinks of Sophocles:

> Sophocles long ago
> Heard it on the Aegean, and it brought
> Into his mind the turbid ebb and flow
> Of human misery;

And the image of Sophocles hearing the note of "human misery" leads Arnold to this pessimistic declaration:

> Ah, love, let us be true
> To one another! for the world, which seems
> To lie before us like a land of dreams,
>
> So various, so beautiful, so new,
> Hath really neither joy, nor love, nor light,
> Nor certitude, nor peace, nor help for pain;

The view of life expressed here is not one that I, or any one else, could derive from seeing a performance of *Oedipus Rex, Oedipus at Colonus,* or *Antigone.* Perhaps Sophocles had such thoughts when he looked at the Aegean, but these are not the thoughts we think when witnessing his tragedies. And from the reports about Sophocles by his contemporaries, we are scarcely justified in calling to mind an individual contemplating human misery. The tragic poet was said to have been charming, gracious, genial, and with no better opinions about politics or life than other cultivated Athenians.

The wonderful Spanish writer and thinker Miguel de Unamuno, who is actually responsible for the phrase "the tragic sense of life," trying to state this "tragic sense" as a philosophical attitude, converts it, I think, into a refined and pleasing, though somber, form of optimism. Unamuno's tragic sense is even a misnomer; there is little tragic about it, for he is not urging us to set something above life; rather what he does urge us to set above life is nothing other than life, immortal life, the immortality of the soul, on which immortality he asks us to gamble the existence we are certain of. That this violently optimistic Christianity should attract us with its death-splashed Spanish cloak is due, of course, to our obscure recognition, even if we have not thought the matter through, that optimism presented simply as optimism would offer us only what we are well acquainted and dissatisfied with.

A novel and, I think, quite wrong view that thought, even philosophic thought, can have and has had a tragic cast is presented by Lucien Goldmann in his much-praised book on Pascal and Racine, *Le Dieu Cadré*. According to Goldmann there are certain philosophers whose thought can be characterized as tragic. He cites as instances Pascal and Kant. Why is their thought tragic? Because, says Goldmann, it expresses the conflict in them between alternatives and exclusive world views, the world view of mathematical science and the world view of revealed religion. But surely no character on the stage would be convincing in the tragic hero's part if his torment were due to nothing more drastic than his inability to choose between or mediate conflicting views. In fact, Kant and Pascal did both. What I mean is this: Kant opted for religion in his metaphysics and for science in his epistemology. And I think Pascal did the same in his distinction between *l'esprit géométrique* and *l'esprit de finesse*.

I submit that it is not through any particular philosophy that the tragic writer is able to give expression to his tragic sense of life, although this tragic sense does have for us, the audience, a virtue which has been called philosophic. Then is it by art alone that the writer of tragedy affects as he does?

The very great probability is, I suggest, that the writer of tragedy is no more endowed with a tragic sense of life than are we to whom he makes it available. By which I mean that he, too, in his regular experience of life, is condemned to the same unsatisfactory choice between optimism and pessimism that we are, and that only in the act of writing a tragedy, only by making the tragic view available to us, is he himself enabled to envisage life in such terms. His creation then is a communion with us, in the experiencing of a view of things which we could not have without him, but which he in turn can only have insofar as he is capable of extending it to us.

Why could we not have the tragic sense without the *written* tragedy? Let us consider this point from a somewhat different angle. There is something we could have without the help of art, and which many people may confuse with the tragic sense, namely the feeling of a *pessimism that is justified*. This is all we can get from the lesser masters of the art of tragedy, from Euripides, Webster, and Tourneur at their best, and from Shakespeare in his unsuccessful tragedies such as *Troilus and Cressida, Coriolanus, Timon of Athens* and *King Lear*. Moreover, this justified pessimism appears at times even in the greatest works but it is not this which makes them tragic. When Richard in Shakespeare's *Richard II* complains of the vulnerability of kings,

> . . . for within the hollow crown
> That rounds the mortal temples of a king
> Keeps Death his court; and there the antic sits . . .
> Allowing him a breath, a little scene . . .
> . . . and humour'd thus,
> Comes at the last, and with a little pin
> Bores through his castle wall, and farewell king!

he gives expression to a pessimism which in view of his situation he is certainly justified in feeling. And the greatness of the verse penetrates Richard's feeling completely; what he says seems all the more inevitable because said in lines of such power. Who can be secure if the best protected of men, the king, is not? It is to be noted that a negative fact, in this instance death, armed with so mean and trivial an instrument as a pin, is seen as rendering meaningless the highest state a man can aspire to, that of a kingliness. Later in the play Richard will say:

> ... nor any man that but man is
> With nothing shall be pleas'd till he be eas'd
> With being nothing.

The feeling expressed here of life's meaninglessness we may all have felt, indeed must have felt, at some time or other and with some measure of poetry, too, for such feelings provide a verbal talent all by themselves. We would not need the art of tragedy to acquaint us with such a judgment of life nor even with the necessity to pronounce it consummately.

A judgment of life similar in its pessimism to Richard's and equally justified is uttered by Macbeth:

> Life's but a walking shadow, a poor player,
> That struts and frets his hour upon the stage
> And then is heard no more. It is a tale
> Told by an idiot, full of sound and fury,
> Signifying nothing.

This judgment, too, we could form for ourselves without either the experience of tragedy or Shakespeare's art. But what we could not get without actual or invented tragedy is the experience of resolution when nothing can follow from resolve, a resolution beyond optimism or pessimism, hope or despair. This we get from Macbeth's great words:

> Though Birnam Wood be come to Dunsinane,
> And thou opposed, being of no woman born,
> Yet will I try the last.

Richard's speech about the death of kings is a protest against the weakness and impotence of the most highly placed. Macbeth's lines of resolution express a much more complicated feeling, one in which are allied, to use Heidegger's phrase, "utter impotence and super power." Richard's lines about the death of kings, justifying pessimism, point to the negative fact of death which renders optimistic notions of life invalid even for a king. Macbeth's lines of resolution refer to no negative facts at all, not to anything common in human experience, not even to the common experience of kings, but exclusively to the withdrawal of their aid from him by those metaphysical beings, the witches, who had for a time supported him. Macbeth's lines are thrilling; Richard's are merely sad. What has to be explained is why Macbeth's lines thrill us, and why he had to pass through the experience of tragedy in order to be able to utter them. The weakness of Richard is evident, so is Macbeth's. But whence comes Macbeth's power?

What Is Tragedy?

In tragedy it is not the negative facts, rendering optimism invalid, which finally cause misfortune. Such negative facts as commonly threaten all of us are even converted by the mechanism of tragedy into positive goods. Blindness is an evil; yet Oedipus deliberately blinds himself; death we would think is to be avoided at all costs; yet Antigone elects to die and denies her sister, Ismene, the same privilege. Ajax, when told that if he spends the day in his tent he will be allowed to live, deliberately leaves his tent and falls on his sword. In the tragic universe the negative facts of experience are finally unimportant. What might lead us in ordinary life to be pessimistic is never the cause of tragedy.

What is the cause then of tragedy? It is the opposition, as Hegel affirmed, of two conflicting goods. Tragedy is never caused by what is unambiguously evil. It is the sheerly positive in conflict with the sheerly positive that destroys the tragic protagonist. In the Greek world it was the collision of the values of the family with those of the state. Those contrary values, as Aeschylus and Sophocles understood them, could not be held to with equal fidelity in any superior experience of life. The superior man would inevitably violate the one or the other.[2] Perhaps it may be said that while this may have been true of the ancient Greek world, it was not true of the Shakespearean world. For in what sense can the witches who incite Macbeth to kill Duncan be called sheerly positive? In what sense can they be called representatives of the good? Are they not the expression of unmitigated evil?

If they were, *Macbeth* would not be a tragedy. It would be a melodrama, and Macbeth's story would merely be that of a villain defeated. But once again, in what sense can the

[2] It may be asked: why is a collision of values different from a collision of world views? But a collision of views, even if we call them world views, takes place within *consciousness* and not within the *world*. Values such as the family and the state are not merely values; they are valued realities. I should like to point out here that one of the most interesting insights of Martin Heidegger—much more interesting than his remarks about anguish and guilt, which have become part of current twaddle—is his judgment that world views imply the absence of a world rather than a world's enduring presence. Tragedy takes place in a world, not in a consciousness which is uncertain as to what the world is.

witches be said to represent the good? In this sense: the witches in *Macbeth* are the only dramatic expression of the metaphysical. Duncan, the reigning king, is presented as kingly, just, morally right. But Macbeth and Banquo are the characters in the play who have direct contact with the representatives of the metaphysical, that is to say, the witches. Now in *Macbeth* the metaphysical does not coincide with the moral, but is at odds with it; yet both are to be valued. Since the justification for kingship was finally metaphysical—the Elizabethans believed in the divine right of kings as opposed to any merely moral right to kingship—how could an immoral deed of murder to attain kingship, when metaphysical forces, in this case, the witches, seemed to support that deed, be thought of as evil? And, in fact, we never feel Macbeth is evil. We think of him as suffering, suffering because he has violated moral values he cannot deny, in support of values neither he nor Shakespeare's age thought criticizable in moral terms. As in the Greek tragedies, we have in *Macbeth* good pitted against good, and the protagonist is the victim of their collision. What is dreadful then is never the mere negative facts ordinary experience fears. It is the good which is dreaded and has to be dreaded. Soren Kierkegaard, peculiarly sensitive to these matters, summed up what, I think, can be called the experience of tragedy when he said in his acute analysis of dread that it is fundamentally dread of the good.

What Has the Writer of Tragedy Seen?

So the tragic writer has to have seen some collision of good with good in order to have been able to arrange the events he describes into a tragedy. Was he predisposed to see some such collision of good with good? Not, I should say, if it were not there to be seen, even if only he saw it. For can we want to see what it is undesirable to see? Some of us may out of ambition or perversity, but not the writer of a proper tragedy. He sees what it is undesirable to see without desiring to see it. This is one of the things we admire him for. To be sure, there are others. But in any case, what must be understood here is that the object of his vision was given by his age or epoch and not created by him alone. The collision of good with good which he witnessed had then to be given him along with others to see; his part was to take what he saw, and what others may have seen, and fashion it into art.

Thus the tragic view, properly understood, means to have seen the necessity for tragedy, to have recognized it rather than to have created it. That the tragic vision results from a direct act of seeing, and not from the holding of any particular view, or from any predilection for interpreting reality tragically, is something we must understand in order to evaluate that vision and judge it for its true worth. Just as in the tragedy he is going to write, the dramatist will set forth a sequence of events whose connections are necessary, so he himself can only be stirred to set forth such a sequence of events by the sight of a fatality that was thrust upon his view and which was necessarily, not accidentally, there before him.

Once again: what did he see? A collision of good with good. Is it desirable that such a collision come within our view? Not in life. No. Nobody can genuinely say that he wants to see a tragedy enacted anywhere but on the stage. For it is a misfortune to a society or to a culture if its main values contradict one another. On the other hand, tragedy, that art which expresses the collision and not the harmony of such values, is in itself a positive aesthetic good. But this good, this aesthetic good, is achieved through an appropriate description of the ultimate in human misfortune: that man's values should contradict rather than support one another.

Once Again "The Tragic Thinker"

Perhaps it is right to say of the writer of tragedy that his thought, since it had to be equal to what he saw—what he saw was tragedy—is a kind of "tragic thinking." But this can only mean that the writer of tragedy has not permitted any philosophy or ideology to impede or obstruct his vision. But what about those thinkers who have been called "tragic," as for instance Pascal? As I indicated before, I think the term "tragic" when used to designate the thought of anyone not the writer of a tragedy is always wrongly used. Nonetheless, there are in Pascal's *Pensées* many dramatic characterizations of experience which give us a kind of thrill comparable to the kind we get from tragedy. My contention is that in the case of such *Pensées*, Pascal has merely created an abstract replica of the kind of collision of values we find embodied with ever so much more concreteness in tragic poetry. Here is one of the most famous of Pascal's thoughts:

Man is but a reed, the feeblest of Nature's growths, but he is a thinking reed. There is no need for the whole universe to take up arms to crush him; a breath, a drop of water, may prove fatal. But were the universe to kill him, he would still be more noble than his slayers; for man knows that he is crushed, but the universe does not know that it crushes him.

I think what we have here is an imitation in conceptual terms of the kind of event set forth in a real tragedy. It is to be noted that Pascal begins by saying men can be destroyed by a drop of water or a breath; but he chooses not to continue the thought that men can be destroyed by such small means. The drop of water, the breath, are tiny facts: acting negatively, they would be of no interest in tragedy. So in Pascal's thought they are expanded—in possibility, of course —into the universe. From the breath, the drop of water, Pascal goes to the whole universe, which he imagines in the act of overwhelming a man. Even then, says Pascal, the man would be nobler than his slayer. But, in any case, the slayer would be noble, being the universe. Insofar as Pascal's thought here may strike one as tragic, I should say that the event he has described was modeled on that structure of events always present in a true tragedy. For he who is destroyed in a true tragedy is always destroyed by something of worth. The drop of water, the breath, may be thought of, as I said before, as tiny facts behaving negatively but which Pascal had finally to forget about and obscure from his view in order to make a true judgment of man's nobility in misfortune.

What We Should Admire the Writer of Tragedy For

Let us turn from the "tragic thinker" to the writer of tragedy. Why do we admire him? Not for his philosophy, for he has none. If he does hold to one in his personal life, this is not pertinent to his achievement or to our judgment of it. Nor are we required to think of him as a master of experience, as wiser or more deeply human than ourselves. Let us admire him for his art; we should recognize, though, that what he gives us goes far beyond what art generally or regularly gives. And let us admire him for his luck, too, at having been given by his age the opportunity to see in his mind's eye certain paradigm instances of human adversity. Does not Pushkin say that the day after the flooding of Petrograd, "Khostov, poet, favorite of the heavens, already sang in verses never to die the griefs of Neva's shores"?[3]

Moreover, the effort the writer of tragedy makes has to be

[3] From Pushkin's poem *The Bronze Horseman* in Edmund Wilson's translation.

immense. He has seen the collision of the main values of his age or culture; he has seen the nonmeaning of meanings. Now the mind naturally seeks for meanings; the writer of tragedy has to deny and reverse this process in the very movement with which he yields to it.

His interest is, of course, an aesthetic one. May I speak for just one moment from a professional point of view? When you have written a play you are faced with this problem: what does this play mean? If it is meaningless, it is uninteresting. Suppose it does have a meaning, though. This is scarcely better. Have you not then reduced the action in your play to the illustration of an idea? Now illustrative art is scarcely better for many of us today than is meaningless art. Here the idea of tragedy exerts its fascination. For it is the kind of idea that attains to its truth only when represented in the work itself: the play, the tragedy. We are much more clear about what tragedy is when we see a tragedy enacted than when we try to reason about tragedy.

And let us not forget that what the writer of tragedy gives, he himself gets in the very act of giving: communion with us in a privileged view of human adversity. We admire him then for what he makes us see, a world where the highest values collide and in which we know we could not live. We recognize this when the curtain comes down and we do not know where to go. We have to become optimists or pessimists again in order to think of going home.

Oedipus Tyrannus

KARL J. REINHARDT

AS OPPOSED to the static scenes of Sophocles' earlier dramas, almost every scene of the *Antigone*, by a development of the situation into its opposite, entails a reversal. *Oedipus Rex* is from beginning to end a reversal of this kind, one writ large, a reversal running through a whole drama. The fall of kings from their power and glory was, to be sure, nothing unusual for the Athenian stage. But how differently the kings fell in the *Agamemnon* and in *The Persians* of Aeschylus! In these plays the future is prepared from the beginning: dread amidst hope, presentiments, entreaties by the chorus, forebodings in the dialogue; from the very outset, the fall lurks behind every word. Even in Sophocles' earlier *Women of Trachis*, downfall was prefigured and prophesied by a certain mood, introduced with the first word, and furthered by the tone of gloom. How different is the *Oedipus Rex*, what a contrast between its beginning and end, both of equal power and scope! The end reverses the beginning. What the beginning reveals is countered by the revelation at the end. In the beginning Oedipus is the refuge and the shield of all; at the end, he is expelled by all and from all, even from his right to see. Between beginning and end, this play of shifting demonic centers does not develop as did the *Antigone,* through discrete, clearly separated, independent parts, but rather through a single whirling movement beginning slowly and growing ever more torrential.

We know very little about Aeschylus' *Oedipus*, but we may still conclude that it did not rely on this type of reversal. For in the trilogy of Aeschylus performed in 467 B.C., the *Oedipus* stood between the *Laius* and the *Seven Against Thebes*, which last has been preserved. Now the tone and thrust of Aeschylus' *Oedipus* must have been different from that of the *Seven Against Thebes* since doom in his *Oedipus* could not possibly have come to the grandson from a curse on his grandfather and father. It is also to be noted that in the *Seven* there is not a trace of that peculiarly *dramatic development* which makes Sophocles' *Oedipus* what it is.

In order to heighten the contrast between end and beginning, and show the roots and soil from which the royal house is finally uprooted—roots so deep their tearing out is like the removal of all human security—Oedipus in the beginning is not presented as he appears in the legend, which shows him a child of fortune, Tyche, served by chance, he who comes from afar and wins a kingdom. Sophocles' *Oedipus* is the blessed man, the leader, helper, savior; the royal man upheld by the favor of the gods, the man who representing himself represents all men, and whose words are a benefit to all. To enlarge his scope and raise his stature, he is surrounded—like a god—by a procession of pious supplicants, aged priests, and a group of boys; thus the speech he directs to them begins like that of a father:

Oedipus
    Children, young sons and daughters of old Cadmus, why do you sit here with your suppliant crowns?

188

> What do you fear or want, that you sit here
> suppliant? Indeed I'm willing to give all
> that you may need; I would be very hard
> should I not pity suppliants like these.

The solemn speech of supplication by the priest of Zeus,
like an echoing wave, takes up and carries further the tone
and tactic of this introduction:

Priest:
> you see our company around the altar;
> you see our ages; some of us, like these,
> who cannot yet fly far, and some of us
> heavy with age;

> * * *

> We have not come as suppliants to this altar
> because we thought of you as of a God,
> but rather judging you the first of men
> in all the chances of this life and when
> we mortals have to do with more than man.
> You came and by your coming saved our city,
> freed us from tribute which we paid of old
> to the Sphinx, cruel singer. This you did
> in virtue of no knowledge we could give you,
> in virtue of no teaching; it was God
> that aided you, men say, and you are held
> with God's assistance to have saved our lives.

The regal note sounded here is equalled only by Aeschylus
in his *Agamemnon*—there in the tone of the royal speech of
sublime knowledge about the powers of fate; in Sophocles'
play, through the words of a man destined to serve, and by
birthright bound and obligated:

> I know you are all sick,
> yet there is not one of you, sick though you are,
> that is as sick as I myself.
> Your several sorrows each have single scope
> and touch but one of you. My spirit groans
> for city and myself and you at once.

The first shock to Oedipus' sense of power does not, as the
legend might lead one to expect, spring from a memory of
what was said by the Delphic oracle to the departing fugitive,
namely, that he would murder his father and bring shame to
his mother. In sharp contrast to the *Women of Trachis*, where
an ancient prophecy is referred to in the very first scene, the

words of the oracle in the *Oedipus Rex* are not mentioned until secure power has been shaken and real trust broken, that is, not until after the quarrels of Oedipus with Teiresias and Creon. It is a new pronouncement from the Delphic god indicating how the land polluted by the unpunished murder of Laius would have to be purified which first startles Oedipus. His concern is thus stimulated not by what the oracle had said to him in person (as in the legend) but by one of those orders which the Delphic god was wont to give at critical moments of history, in this case imposing on Oedipus the task of discovering himself. The order finds its way immediately to the heart of the protagonist, it soon begins to transform him; it enchants him like a magic potion, and becomes for him a test of his very being. He is seized by a mighty urge to pledge himself and to uncover all—even before the emissary from the oracle, Creon, arrives:

> But when he comes, then, may I prove a villain,
>   if I shall not do all the God commands.

Oedipus
> . . . what is the word you bring us from the God?

Creon
> A good word,—for things hard to bear themselves
> if in the final issue all is well
> I count complete good fortune.

Oedipus
>   What do you mean?
> What you have said so far
> leaves me uncertain whether to trust or fear.

Creon
> If you will hear my news before these others
> I am ready to speak, or else to go within.

Oedipus
> Speak it to all;
> the grief I bear, I bear it more for these
> than for my own heart.

Thus already in the beginning he is forecast as the mighty unveiler; by his every gesture, by his every word, he prefigures the man who at the end calls for the portals to be opened so that all can see him.

But what makes for the suspense, frequently noted, of this drama is not at all the breathlessness with which we wait the unfolding of a fated discovery; this is not just a cat-and-mouse game between a settled fate and an unsuspecting victim; nor is suspense due to false leads like those that turn up regularly in the investigation of crime. In short, the suspense here is not what dramas have since made of suspense. When Schiller —in a passage that has been quoted much too often—characterized the *Oedipus* as a "tragic analysis. . . . Everything is already present and is merely developed. . . . Added to this is the fact that an event, when it is unalterable, is by nature much more terrible. . . ." (Letter to Goethe, October 2, 1797), was he not too attentive to what he himself had done in writing his *Wallenstein*, thinking about the economy of the play, and very little about its real meaning? For Sophocles, as for the Greeks of more ancient times, fate, even when foretold, even when recurring with the strictness of law, never had the meaning of determinism, and was seen as a spontaneous unfolding of the demonic. There is no fatal determinism before the time of the Stoics and the triumph of astrology. The meaning of the *Oedipus* is not to be seen in the unalterability of the hero's past once uncovered, but rather in the hero's active struggle to defend against great threat to it the apparent or "seeming" order of his life. Such a struggle is imposed by the hero's very humanity, calling on him, in the name of truth, to reverse the values of seeming and being. Less than any other Greek tragedy is the *Oedipus* a tragedy of fate, for which it has for so long been taken to be the model. As German classicism well understood, to posit fate is to posit "freedom," and the noblest kind of freedom at that. Distinct from all other tragedies, the *Oedipus* is uniquely the tragedy of appearances, that tragedy of seeming which results from the human need to think of seeming as being, even as Parmenides thought of belief as discovery. It is to be noted that none of the choruses of the *Oedipus* invokes fate, as is common in other plays; what has not been noted is that one of the choruses makes a dramatic point of the idea of "seeming":

> What man, what man on earth wins more
> of happiness than a seeming
> and after that turning away?

The play's attack on and defense of seeming, not noticeable at first, has in fact begun with the command of the god that an inquiry be undertaken. The question about seeming is expressed early in the play by a strange twist, rightly noted by Voltaire the logician, but wrongly judged by Voltaire the critic. After an inquiry into the case seems in order, after the question has been raised: "Is there a witness?" and after a witness has been discovered, "robbers" are mentioned in such a way as to make any investigation suspect. For how could robbers there have dared do what they did, had they not been bribed "from here"? "From here" refers to Thebes. This question, raised by a king, is unavoidable since it concerns the murder of a king. The question is directed to Creon. Creon seems to evade it: the suspicion that was bound to arise could not be pursued, after the deed. Why? The sphinx was the reason. After her coming, doubt seems to have been laid to rest. It was no longer a question of where the deed took place, or of its circumstances and instruments, but of its originators, who may have been bandits. The suspicion comes back in Sophocles' play after Oedipus' quarrel with the re-fractory and clearly malicious seer; and then suspicion is further strengthened, the alliance between Creon and Teiresias is established, and a whole web of hostility is spun.

Luckily there has been preserved from Aeschylus' *Oedipus* a single fragment, in which a witness, the only survivor be-sides the protagonist, tells us of the place where "three roads cross." The discovery of the true facts, or something leading to their discovery, must have followed his testimony. In Sophocles, no such account is given. But the value of the Aeschylean fragment is that it enables us to see what Sopho-cles was ready to set aside for the sake of another effect.

In ignoring the Aeschylean witness, Sophocles added to the original, inescapable, and objective seeming a new kind of seeming, subjective seeming, that is to say, illusion. And in the manner in which this new seeming enters—as suspicion of bribery, of a secret conspiracy in the court, and one that must be countered—the *Oedipus* goes beyond the dramatic formal structure of the *Antigone,* where "seeming" over-powers Creon. Just as in the *Antigone* the suspicion of bribery is first only hinted at by a single word, *kérdos,* and then, after being dropped for a while, is again brought forth and devel-oped in the scene with the seer, so it is in the *Oedipus.* But in the *Antigone,* even the external situation inherited by the ruler Creon suggested something suspicious. The two heirs to the throne were dead after the defeat of the invading army. So suspicion was already present in Creon's first decree, in the prohibition against burying that heir to the throne who had been the country's foe. In the *Oedipus,* since the ruler steps before the community at a moment when he is honored by all, ardently importuned by all, and not proclaiming, like Creon, his seizure of power, there seems to be no basis for any suspiciousness. And yet here too a rather similar doubt seems to haunt the scene, first vaguely; then the doubt, suggested by Teiresias, is strongly taken up by Creon. For in the *Oedipus,* the threat of illusion or "seeming" comes much more from the human subject and emanates much more from the soul itself; "seeming" here is not deducible from outward circumstances but arises from the demonic incomprehensibility of some task which the soul cannot altogether comprehend. Error springs here from the necessity to have a foe at which one can strike, in order not to lose one's own certainty. For Creon in the *Antigone,* the violation of his decree against burying Polynices did not as such signify a threat to his own existence; for Oedipus, everything is at stake even before he suspects what the stakes are. "Seeming," in his case, is threatened at the start not by the truth, its real opposite, but rather by other appearances, other seemings:

Oedipus:
  For when I drive pollution from the land
  I will not serve a distant friend's advantage,
  but act in my own interest. Whoever
  he was that killed the king may readily
  wish to dispatch me with the murderous hand:

The irruption of truth—here one should not speak of reality, since at first Oedipus does not live in illusion but in an objective untruth and order of seeming or semblance—the irruption of truth within the structure of appearance follows successively from two breaches, the first a breach at the periphery and the second at the center. First, there is the question: What is hidden before me which it is my duty to bring to light? Then there is the question: What am I, and what is my true being? The second question conceals itself behind the first; then they operate in secret complicity; finally they become as one. The power of appearance persists, fights back, and shores up whatever of its positions are threatened.

The first defense against the as yet unknown murderer is banishment, and, along with it, a curse. Oedipus knows how to curse: in his curse, he is authentic. Cursing, he pronounces the sentence that will require fulfillment, the sentence both public and personal; he curses with priestly dedication, and at the same time with marked feeling. Consider the curses in the plays of Euripides—a typical one is that of Theseus in the *Hippolytus;* how different is the curse of Sophocles' Oedipus. And just compare the *Oedipus* with the fragment—preserved by chance—of the old epic the *Thebaid,* where cursing is not given poetic expression, but simply told: "He cursed."

Oedipus' powerful curse is of course directed unwittingly against himself cursing. In the *Antigone,* Creon's oaths rebound against him; but the retroactive force of Oedipus' curse is perhaps even more fateful. A dynamic intensification follows his curse, as after Creon's speeches in the *Antigone;* in both cases, a low-keyed beginning is followed by a frenetic rhythm, which may be characterized as the rhythm of illusion. Here we have another reversal, one not expressed in the dialogue, but in the shifting movement of the curse-containing speech itself. The restraint with which the speaker had begun, with which he promised that there would be no punishment for the guilty party—this restraint vanishes once solemn banishment has been proclaimed. The force of the curse and the condemnation possess the speaker as the riddle he wishes to solve draws him ever closer to his own deed:

> So I stand forth a champion of the God
> and of the man who died.
> Upon the murderer I invoke this curse—
> whether he is one man and all unknown,
> or one of many—may he wear out his life
> in misery to miserable doom!
> If with my knowledge he lives at my hearth
> I pray that I myself may feel my curse.

Out of the first unfamiliarity with which the new king has faced the unknown and almost forgotten events, there develops a peculiar intimacy with things unfamiliar to him, as if they were his own. Without suspecting the true state of affairs, he makes himself into the real son of his real father; in the demonic sphere of seeming, he is already gripped magically by his own true being. At the beginning he speaks without real knowledge:

> Hark to me; what I say to you, I say
> as one that is a stranger to the story
> as stranger to the deed. For I would not

194

> be far upon the track if I alone
> were tracing it without a clue. But now,
> since after all was finished, I became
> a citizen among you, citizens—
> now I proclaim to all the men of Thebes:

It is as yet the same lack of knowledge as before:

Creon:
> My lord, before you piloted the state
> we had a King called Laius.

Oedipus:
> I know of him by hearsay. I have not seen him.

But unfamiliarity changes into ever stronger connectedness:

> Since I am now the holder of his office,
> and have his bed and wife that once was his,
> and had his line not been unfortunate
> we would have common children—(fortune leaped
> upon his head)—because of all these things,
> I fight in his defence as for my father,
> and I shall try all means to take the murderer
> of Laius the son of Labdacus
> the son of Polydorus and before him
> of Cadmus and before him of Agenor.

Here at the end, Oedipus mentions all his ancestors; he is the representative of the whole line. It was customary for kings to name all of their ancestors when taking an oath, as does Xerxes in Herodotus:

> For let me not be thought the child of Darius, the son of Hystaspas, the son of Arsames, the son of Ariaramnes, the son of Teispas, nor of Cyrus . . . if I take not vengeance on the Athenians.[1]

There is, to be sure, a tragic-ironic element in both the seeming unfamiliarity and the seeming participation (Oedipus' true participation appears only with his fall). But it is only in the act of appropriating the past—present already in the pretense of appropriating it with a turbulence more excessive than warranted—that being and seeming are ineluctably entwined. It is only from their fusion—no longer external or

----

[1] Rawlinson translation. Modern Library, p. 502.

partial, but comprehending the whole of being, the soul itself, speech itself—that there can arise the tragedy of one who, lost to being, is also hurled from seeming. This is why Oedipus' fate is of such concern to us; and this is how the particular circumstances of his life can be seen as forming, in Sophocles' play; a symbolic whole. The demonic, continuous, and uncalculated transposition from the realm of seeming into the realm of truth is the human element which was not present in the myth and which only Sophocles connected with the figure of Oedipus. And just here lies the ironic element which our academic aesthetics has generalized and inexactly designated as "tragic irony." For here the spectator does not have any knowledge beyond that of the man groping in darkness, and cannot see a meaning in the latter's speeches beyond what is said. Rather, protagonist and spectator are equally perplexed by the puzzle of seeming and being; seeming and being are not distributed any differently to those in the audience than to those on the stage, nor is an exchange of being for seeming between the protagonist and the spectators even conceivable. Here being and seeming encounter each other in every word and gesture of the man who has gone astray. It is not the poet here who uses his own or the theater's power of illusion to play a game with human seeming; it is the invisible gods, working from an invisible background, who do this.

After a secret, unconscious, and preliminary struggle, the open fight between truth and seeming begins in Oedipus' scene with Teiresias. It is not now a battle between truth and error. To speak of error is not to recognize that it is, after all, impossible not to err, and that here there is a failure not of understanding, but rather of the whole human capacity, taken subjectively and objectively. Dianeira in the *Women of Trachis* finds herself in a state of tragic error; she acts in a way which she immediately regrets; in the same play, Hercules' rage is tragic and based also on a misunderstanding. Tragic error is something into which men can indeed fall. But the state of tragic seeming, in which Oedipus finds himself, is undoubtedly something still more profound; it is something that from the start encompasses the character; all that he is and all that he desires, as king, as husband, as leader, as savior; tragic seeming is what conditions him, and also gives him his power and his sureness; he is sustained by nothing else. In the *Antigone*, Creon is driven on and on into semblance, into seeming; Oedipus stands before us, resolute within seeming, and then is hurled out of it.

What the human bearer of truth, the seer Teiresias, has to say is indeed hard to grasp, and it is not only Oedipus who misunderstands. For Teiresias participates both in the superhuman and in the all-too-human; on the one hand, he is the master of secret and infallible knowledge, while on the other he is irresolute and forgetful. He comes, yet he desires to be gone; he conceals, and yet he reveals. An old man, capricious and irritable, his angry disposition is not exactly what it seems: he is a walking riddle, nourishing the riddling nature of truth. One aspect of the puzzling contradiction in the mantic stance, of "neither speaking nor holding back," seems to be personified in him. His contradictoriness clearly goes beyond that exhibited by him in the earlier *Antigone*: the idea of prophecy has been pushed further. There was no longer any need in the *Oedipus* to point up the blindness of Teiresias, by introducing a boy to lead the blind leader of the blind; in place of such a dramatic prop, there is now the pure contradiction of the mantic appearance as such. Taking only character into consideration, such a contradiction presents an incomprehensible fusion of a stubborn, limited existence with a demonic element that, entering from the beyond and aiming at sovereignty, does not thereby endow the man it possesses with an air of ecstasy, or the dignity of a prophet. A similar contradictoriness can be seen in the Oedipus of Sophocles' last play, the work of his old age. Something from beyond overpowers the old Oedipus, commands all his acts, and in the firmness and breadth of its scope raises him into the realm of the mysterious. The magic of this contradictoriness is not yet present in the *Antigone,* from which we may conclude that Sophocles did not feel its force when he wrote that play.

Toward the end of Creon's scene with Teiresias in the *Antigone,* and from out of the timidity and reverence that had been present in the beginning of the scene, invective and accusation break forth; the same thing happens in the *Oedipus.* But here the reversal is more violent, the mood more irrational. Oedipus' very first speech, expressive of royal reverence, recognizes the seer as a person and also the mystery of his office; and both solicitous and trusting, it goes far beyond Creon's acknowledgment of Teiresias in the *Antigone*:

> Teiresias, you are versed in everything,
> things teachable and things not to be spoken,
> things of the heaven and earth-creeping things.

The quarrel in the *Antigone* results from Creon's disdain of the wise warning; then accusations are made which result in the exposure of the accuser; nevertheless, the struggle between Creon and Teiresias takes the form of a debate over right and wrong, *hybris* against *sophrosyne*. In the *Oedipus* however, the protagonist finds himself at grips with a puzzling resistance in the seer himself who darkly refuses to obey, and sets himself up as a barrier against any effort at salvation, against Oedipus' will to confront the very question on which his whole being depends. Here it is not right and wrong, it is nothing less than "dark" and "light" which struggle with each other and engage in mutual recriminations; Oedipus moves from a preliminary darkness to an ever greater, an ever more malicious clarity; Teiresias moves from alertness and receptivity to an ever more passionate deafness; each is carried away by the other as they goad each other on.

The quarrel soon reaches its first peak:

Oedipus:
>You would provoke a stone! Tell us, you villain,
>tell us, and do not stand there quietly
>unmoved and balking at the issue.

The seer, resisting the attack of Oedipus, is of course allied secretly with those forces whose riddling action, ever since the message came from Apollo, have been endangering and threatening the "seeming" in which Oedipus lives. Teiresias is accused by Oedipus of being an accomplice in the crime. And thus a quarrel between two orders ensues, even as in the verbal fencing of the *Antigone*; in that play, in the Teiresias scene, the quarrel was over the word "gain," *kerdos*, which has a double meaning, referring both to salvation and to acquisition, as of worldly goods. In the *Oedipus,* as we saw, there is a similar quarrel—but a much more violent one this time, and also about a word with a double meaning: "truth" or "clarity" to Oedipus is found in what he knows himself to have done, in what he comprehends, in what he has governed by will and knowledge; to Tiresias "truth" and "clarity" are found in what lies beyond human comprehension. To one, the truth is that which lies within human reach; to the other, it is what limits the reach of humans. If one merely considers the situation objectively, one might say that Teiresias, like the spectators, has a knowledge which Oedipus cannot have; so understood, one thinks of the quarrel as tragic-ironic in the conventional sense. But if we look at the quarrel from another perspective, that which has as its object the very being of man, then we see that it is not knowledge and ignorance which are confronting each other, but two different modes of man's being: what is "light" in one of these modes is "darkness" in the other:

Teiresias
I say you are the murderer of the king
whose murderer you seek.

*   *   *

Oedipus
Do you imagine you can always talk
like this, and live to laugh at it hereafter?

Teiresias
Yes, if the truth has anything of strength.

Oedipus
It has, but not for you; it has no strength
for you because you are blind in mind and ears
as well as in your eyes.

Teiresias
                    You are a poor wretch
to taunt me with the very insults which
every one soon will heap upon yourself.

Oedipus
Your life is one long night so that you cannot
hurt me or any other who sees the light.

Oedipus lives in a clarity which "nourishes" him, inwardly and outwardly, a clarity which is the same for him as for all those who "see the light." Without the brightness of this clarity, his quarrel with Teiresias would be a Euripidean argument from contrary postulates. This same clarity must designate as "darkness" all that threatens to obscure it.

Darkness threatens ever more powerfully until the name of Apollo is mentioned:

Teiresias
It is not fate that I should be your ruin,
Apollo is enough; it is his care
to work this out.

Oedipus
                    Was this your own design
    or Creon's?

But Apollo's name is quickly replaced by that of a man,
Creon, and it is thus that the structure of appearance is still
maintained. There has been, to be sure, an attempt to explain
the connection of Apollo with Creon on rational, objective,
and humanly understandable grounds. It had already been
mentioned that it was Creon who advised that Teiresias be
questioned. But the fact that Creon's practical aims could,
for Oedipus, throw suspicion on Teiresias, while telling us
something of the protagonist's character, does not enlighten
us about his situation: suspicion serves him as an excuse, but
once he has become suspicious, he drops all reference to what
occasioned it. Apollo is mentioned at just that critical juncture
where seeming must turn into illusion and madness in order
not to surrender itself to being. On the ground of seeming,
an illusion world order is at once set up: Creon, Teiresias, and
the crime are indissolubly bound together. Indignation now
has a target. Passion can now be discharged in an enigmatic
invocation of all that makes the world worldly and understandable by its very worldliness:

Oedipus
    Wealth, sovereignty and skill outmatching skill
    for the contrivance of an envied life!
    Great store of jealousy fill your treasury chests,
    if my friend Creon, friend from the first and loyal,
    thus secretly attacks me, secretly
    desires to drive me out and secretly
    suborns this juggling, trick devising quack,
    this wily beggar who has only eyes
    for his own gains, but blindness in his skill.

A whole new world system emerges—the past, too, is now
snatched up to confirm the truth of seeming: what good was
the wisdom of Teiresias when he faced the Sphinx. . . . And
is the new view of the world of Oedipus entirely wrong; is it
not right? Who could ever be convinced by "seeming," if
"seeming" did not "seem" true? In the *Antigone,* Creon, too,
appealed to something that was not as such false; but here
there was something brutal and repellent in the true value by
which Creon justifies his ruthless decree. In the *Oedipus* the
disjunction between seeming and being, understood as neces-

sary for self-determination and self-interpretation, belongs to the essence of man.

Teiresias's answer here has again something in common with his prophetic speech in the *Antigone*: both are at once prophecies of the future and interpretations of the present:

Teiresias:
Since you have taunted me with being blind,
here is my word for you.
You have your eyes but see not where you are
in sin, nor where you live, nor whom you live with.
Do you know who your parents are? Unknowing
you are an enemy to kith and kin
in death, beneath the earth, and in this life.
A deadly footed, double striking curse,
from father and mother both, shall drive you forth
out of this land, with darkness on your eyes,
that now have such straight vision.

The phrase "nor where you live," like the words "where you are," serves to designate a place within the general order, wherein a man's deeds have meaning. So these words of Teiresias are not to be understood as a kind of mystifying and artificial paraphrase of what could be said more plainly and more briefly; what Teiresias says does not mean: "Thebes is your home, Jocasta your mother," though if Teiresias had expressed himself thus, he would have said no more than the truth. But origin, place, and associations—the "from where," the "where," and the "with whom"—express the whole content of human existence. Insofar as human existence is tragic in Sophocles, this is always due in some way to its drastic isolation from all natural ties. So it is because of the way human existence is envisaged in this play that the prophetically indefinite is much more suitable than the definite. "You do not know with whom you live. . . ." is an interpretation of the facts. "You do not know that Jocasta is your mother," would be a mere statement of a fact. But the real meaning of Teiresias' remarks is this: You think you have ties, but you are hostile toward everything to which man is tied. "Beneath the earth" and "in this life" stand for the two regions in which one is tied by blood, just as in the prophecies of the *Antigone* "above" and "below," "the living" and "the dead," represent all possible orders. The horror in which Oedipus will find himself at the end of the play, foretold by Teiresias, will do no more than make visible what Oedipus already is. For only from the perspective of the demonic, which enters the situation through the prophet's enigmatic words, can one truly determine the situation in which the hero finds himself. With the enigmatic and indeterminate elements in the prophet's speech, that which in the original fable was only a consequence of the hero's past and a delimitation of his future is, by Sophocles, boldly thrust into the present; as truth it is thrust into that seeming or darkness from which no man can free himself.

The ensuing quarrel between Oedipus and Creon relates to the Teiresias scene even as does the quarrel between Creon and Haimon to the Teiresias scene of the *Antigone*. The causes of Oedipus' quarrel with Teiresias are still hidden, irrational, and dark with prophecy; now there appears a rational man who sees the attack of Oedipus on the seer as a threat to his own person. It is interesting to note that in Sophocles' earlier play, the *Ajax*, the successive quarrel scenes are hardly in contrast with one another: But in the *Oedipus*, the two quarrel scenes are intimately related, the second quarrel being a development of the first. Thus the second scene leads the hero even further away from the aim of his own action and from his task of self-knowledge; we shall see finally that what is wrong humanly, can, supported by the demonic, lead to the required goal. The oracles like to arrive at their goals in just this way; they seem to prefer delays, and are inclined to fulfill their pronouncements at the very moment when it seems these may be proved false. Now in the *Oedipus*, Sophocles is no longer bent on transferring a few archaic and formal elements of the working of the oracular on human lives into a drama, as he still did in the *Women of Trachis;* in the *Oedipus* he directly grasped the experience to which the oracles' pronouncements refer, and made drama out of this. In the *Oedipus* the pronouncements of the oracle do more than provide an incentive to act or an impetus to self-knowledge as in the *Women of Trachis.* Rather, the primal ground of the oracular—as fertile as the soul itself—is the ground from which the drama grows.

However, the continuous crescendo which characterizes the quarrel scenes of the *Antigone* is not repeated in the *Oedipus.* In this play the battle is from the beginning fought in the greatest passion and does not develop out of an initial, though seeming, concord. One man appears on the stage full of indignation, then another even more enraged collides with him. The objective and static element in the play is expressed in the parallelism of equally vehement reproaches by both parties. Nevertheless this kind of duel is quite different from the one we saw in the *Ajax*; between the *Ajax* and the *Oedipus*, there was, after all, the *Antigone*. In the *Oedipus* the conflict at once begins to twist and turn—it is a fight in which one man exhausts himself by hurling himself against his opponent without having a shield to protect him, while the other, well-shielded, parries his blows. Thus it is that Creon is the first to face Oedipus on the stage and it is with him that Oedipus collides:

Oedipus
> You, sir, how is it you come here? Have you so much
> brazen-faced daring that you venture in
> my house although you are proved manifestly
> the murderer of that man, and though you tried,
> openly, highway robbery of my crown?

Oedipus continues his attack. What had been no more than a fleeting suspicion—the unanswered question, Why, after the deed, had the seer kept silent, and why was the inquiry broken off?—is now turned against his enemy in an apparently victorious interrogation. But soon after his first thrust, the questioner yields the initiative to the one he is questioning, and the latter answers with a counterattack by way of a counter question. In so doing, his weapon is his rational clarity, his awareness of his own blameless self. It is easy for him to fight, for he is rooted in no depths, strives toward no heights, has not touched on the frontiers of the human. He has no drive that cannot be mastered by consciousness or find some reasonable fulfillment, he has entered into no purposeless relationships, and is not aware of qualities in himself which are not calculable and for which he would be unable to "render an account." Thus his "rendering an account" has reminded some of the way in which Hippolytus accounts for his actions in Euripides' drama. But in Euripides' play, reason, abstracted by the dramatist from the totality of the human, is posited as belonging to the essence of the human; man is divided into reason and passion. In the *Oedipus*, reason serves only as an impediment, as an obstacle; thus the human as truly understood can collide with and break against it. Facing the man enveloped by an atmosphere of tragedy stands Creon, the rational, enlightened man, the self-conscious representative of the spirit of the times. He is not capable of self-knowledge through suffering, nor does he feel the need of it; he can judge for himself: I am this, I am not that; I am capable of doing this, never that. In these calculations he does not even make mistakes—there are such men. Now in Sophocles, the greatly tragic can only unfold against the untragic—the army and Odysseus against Ajax; Ismene against Antigone; the god who wants to preserve his life against the girl who sacrifices her own. So, too, Creon stands against Oedipus. Against the leader, the ruler, the man of higher strength and first in all things, stands the man of spotless reputation, who draws back from every chance of risk or self-exposure, constantly protecting himself, and content with advantages rather than power, an average man by our standards, born to be second in all things. The victor is clear: it is Creon who has the last word before Jocasta steps between the contestants. Oedipus is already inwardly wounded and bleeding, and rather because of his blind and futile charge against an opposing and resisting world than because he has been touched by anything that was said. Toward the end, cornered, he fights on, scarcely noticing what, when he strikes out, he has hit:

Oedipus
When he that plots against me secretly
moves quickly, I must quickly counterplot.
If I wait taking no decisive measure
his business will be done, and mine be spoiled.

How his defense tells against him! What a contrast there is between it and Creon's account, to which it is a response. Moreover, his threat to punish Creon with death is much more like a paroxysm of anger than a true resolve. It is as though the seeming amid which he stands holds him fast and no longer permits him any effect in the real world. From a forceful king and ruler able to defend himself, he becomes a man left with this one cry: "O city, o city!"

In the *Antigone*, the quarrelers separated at the height of their quarrel. In the *Oedipus* the quarrel is rarefied, almost idealized, in a series of short choral verses and by the influence of rhythm on the surge of feeling. With a strikingly calming effect, Jocasta steps between her brother and her husband. The settling of the final quarrel in the *Ajax* was also achieved by the intervention of a third character. But in the *Oedipus,* the scene is greatly changed. It has been noticed of course that it is with the *Oedipus* that Sophocles first shows the technical mastery needed to order a real dialogue among three characters. In the *Ajax,* in the *Women of Trachis,* and even in the *Antigone,* one can find nothing comparable to the three-way dialogue of Jocasta, Oedipus, and Creon. But the achievement of this "three-way dialogue" signifies a change of style even more than an advance in technique. If we look at comedy, we find the earliest drama of the very young Aristophanes, in the *Acharnians* of 425 B.C., just such a juxtaposition and intermingling of a number of conversations and transactions; one could not wish for anything more varied even on the modern stage. Something of this kind was bound to be done, even without the *Oedipus.* But three-way dialogue, in Sophoclean tragedy, does not have the aim of adding variety. Even in works after the *Oedipus,* Sophocles is not interested in talk for the sake of talk, or for realism, or to indicate the milieu—as in the nineteenth-century drama. Indeed there is no social milieu, no court, which in the plays of the young Shakespeare serves to justify a dialogue among more than two characters. The three-way dialogue in the *Oedipus* is the sign of a distinctive style of scene-construction newly achieved by Sophocles. In the *Ajax,* Odysseus stepped between the quarreling heroes, just as Jocasta does between Oedipus and Creon. But only a two-way dialogue emerged in the Ajax, a third character superseding one of the other two. The static antithesis through which the pathos of the archaic form unfolds would have been weakened rather than enhanced by a dialogue among three characters. Only in a play of fluid motions and changes, where pathos is no longer static but dynamic and demonic, could a three-way dialogue serve to express the content of tragedy; the three-way dialogue, with its changing relationships, is after all best suited to a play about transformation. Here, as everywhere, the outer technical form takes its lead from the form of the soul. The intervention of a third character and the ensuing calm is not an end to the struggle but rather a shift of the conflict toward its reversal. It is not a formal pause but inaugurates a further ascent to the culminating point of the whole episode with its many changes and contrasting levels, its sudden transitions, vagaries, glimmers from obscurity.

The accused, to be sure, goes free; wrath quits its object, but instead of bringing relief, leaves everyone all the more oppressed. The man arraigned and now able to reply freely can say to his persecutor:

Creon

I see you sulk in yielding and you're dangerous
when you are out of temper; natures like yours
are justly heaviest for themselves to bear.

The aggression of Oedipus—who has lost sight of his
goal—becomes a violent consciousness of being the one ag-
gressed against, the victim of a monstrous injustice. Unity
of outer and inner, of acting and feeling, is lost to him.
Seeming, on which certainty rests, persists and perseveres;
however, it has already been undermined from within, even
before the external action, beginning at a point we have
hardly noticed, exerts its destroying power.

Anyone who holds Creon to be without guilt heaps guilt
on Oedipus:

Oedipus

I would have you know that this request of yours
really requests my death or banishment.

This is how it appears to Oedipus: one of the accused must
be the criminal. So deeply has the feeling of persecution
damaged his sense of his worth and his station. Nevertheless,
in letting Creon go free, Oedipus is prepared to shoulder a
guilt he thinks is not his own, and which when he swore to
punish the crime, he could not even conceive as his. An
innocent sufferer, a victim of persecution, he is ready to
pay the price for another's acts as a violent reproach to those
standing by:

Oedipus

Well, let him go then—if I must die ten times for it,
or be sent out dishonoured into exile.

What has happened? Nothing reasonable. But in his shifts
between action and patience, in the shock to his seeming,
this man of wounded soul has grasped the truth without
knowing it. What was first a possibility in the soul now
comes to pass. The demonic does not break into the soul from
without until it has created within, from the soul's own
anticipations and possibilities, the readiness for fate.

Thus the turning point is prepared; thus the truth strikes
home. It no longer appears as an external danger threatening
from afar; it is now at the very center of the protagonist's
inward life. Once again, we have a suspenseful pause. Creon

is gone. Isn't Oedipus going off, too? Isn't the queen about to lead her king, so tormented and perplexed, offstage? But she still has one question: What really happened? Since the chorus refuses to answer, the question is finally directed to the mute Oedipus—now dependent on her, now indeed her son. Here there is a change of mood.

The theme of the blood-tie is not explicitly stated but vibrates in the tone of the dialogue—for instance, in Oedipus' speech to Jocasta:

Oedipus
> It shall not be kept from you, since my mind
> has gone so far with its forebodings. Whom
> should I confide in rather than you, who is there
> of more importance to me who have passed
> through such a fortune?

She is the refuge, he the one who has lost his way. But the more confidently she consoles him, the more violent become his doubts. The very idea that she can console him is in itself a kind of *hybris*, not unlike Creon's in the *Antigone*. Like Creon, Jocasta prides herself on a universal maxim; it is based on an enlightened belief in the divinity. But in this tragedy, catastrophe will not recoil on a too great human arrogance; the danger to the protagonist lies in the *hybris* of his seeming, which is innate in the human essence. Thus what is wrong with Jocasta's consoling words is not their arrogant obstinacy, but that they further veil what is in fact the case. A. W. Schlegel, to be sure, was convinced and able to convince others that Jocasta was "thoughtless" and "irreverent." But how could piety have helped her? Could piety at this point have made her believe that the predictions of the oracle had come to pass? Had she not devoutly sacrificed her son to prevent this consummation? Was she to believe her sacrifice useless? And how could such belief help Laius now, struck down by robbers? If what the seer said was clearly impossible, then why are her doubts "thoughtless"? Is she "godless" when her doubt is not directed against the god but only against his priest? After all that has happened, is not she involved along with with Oedipus, in the objective deceptions of seeming? She is sparing of words, but her tone is firm; she thinks what she says can dissolve suspicions not believed by her but threatening Oedipus:

Jocasta
> Do not concern yourself about this matter;

listen to me and learn that human beings
have no part in the craft of prophecy.
*   *   *
So clear in this case were the oracles.
so clear and false. Give them no heed, I say;
what God discovers need of, easily
he shows to us himself.

The prospect of truth which in the *Oedipus* of Aeschylus
results from the intervention of a witness not involved in the
story, is envisaged here as two persons confide to each other
their real fears, their real faiths. In the *Women of Trachis*,
after the oracle is fulfilled, Sophocles permits his protagonist
to vaunt his knowledge in a pathetic monologue, even as
Aeschylus, in his *Seven Against Thebes*, permits Eteocles
a monologue in which he recognizes and affirms his fate. Now
in Sophocles' *Oedipus*, no monologue could convey the changing effect on one another of two driven souls. The story is
not a pathetic report, but rushes forward in terse phrases;
it wants to get to the heart of the matter and has no time
for metaphors. (Consider the very different rhetoric of the
Women of Trachis, as in the circuitousness of "he is not
alive, but dead," as in the long list of epithets to describe the
holy place, and in the many epithets, pathetic in their effect,
to describe Deianeira's gift; there is nothing of the sort in the
Oedipus.)

To be sure, it is once more an unintended word that leads
to knowledge, just as is the case in the *Women of Trachis*.
There the word is the name "Nessus"; here the word is
"crossroads." Thus, too, in Aeschylus' *Oedipus* "crossroads"
was mentioned: the scholars have attributed it to Sophocles.
But in Aeschylus the word was voiced with much tragic
pomp, requiring three verses:

. . . and thus we moved on a wheel-furrowed street
    to a cleft crossing of paths, where three-fold
    was the road's division, by Potniai. . .

The abundance and even repetition of ornament here has
pathos. It is clear that after this moment there will be no
further questions, doubts, or confirmations. Nothing remains
but for the protagonist to receive the full blow of knowing.
(Anyone who gives the extant three lines to Oedipus instead
of to a witness has surely not considered their rhetoric.)
Something similar occurs in the *Women of Trachis* when

Heracles recognizes his condition after the fateful word has been spoken in response to his own challenge, and in Aeschylus' *Seven Against Thebes* when Eteocles realizes that his father's curses are about to be fulfilled. In the *Oedipus* of Sophocles, the protagonist makes no outcry, he does not indulge in words; there is no longer anything like the tragic outburst belonging to the older form with its interest in the pathetic. Instead, there is an opposition between unsuspiciousness and fearfulness, between ignorance of self and discovery of self, between hesitancy and sureness. For the first time in Greek tragedy, the alternate lines of the dialogue express now security and now the threat to it (how different from the monologue of the *Women of Trachis*); the insecurity here is so uncomprehended and so crippling, that speech is barely possible, rhetoric excluded. Pathos restrained is now stronger than pathos expressed. The hesitant "perhaps," "it seems," the word as yet unspoken, the thing as yet unnamed: these precede the clear revelation of the terrible; and instead of the images and sounds used previously there is now nothing but a naked movement of dialogue:

Oedipus
> I thought I heard you say
> that Laius was killed at a crossroads.

Jocasta
> Yes, that was how the story went and still
> that word goes round.

* * *

Oedipus
> What have you designed, O Zeus, to do with me?

Jocasta
> What is the thought that troubles your heart?

Oedipus
> Don't ask me yet—tell me of Laius—
> How did he look? How old or young was he?

Jocasta
> He was a tall man and his hair was grizzled
> already—nearly white—and in his form
> not unlike you.

Oedipus
> Oh God. I think I have called curses on myself
> in ignorance.

209

Jocasta
What do you mean? I am terrified
when I look at you.

Oedipus
      I have a deadly fear
that the old seer had eyes . . .

Here at last husband and wife appear as visibly tied to each other and attacked by the same fate. But more intimate than their visible tie is the bond between them still in darkness. Both are fighting for the same "semblance" which unites and separates them; and when one wavers, the other, responding to the very same revelation, deludes himself into thinking he is standing firm. The positions of the two in this scene are reversed in the scene which follows. Thus at first Jocasta believes that she and Oedipus have nothing to fear, even as he is plunging into the truth as into an abyss; in the following scene he self-confidently lifts himself up to the very height of "seeming" even as she plunges fatally into her own truth.

What has begun to be unveiled is not yet the whole truth, but only part of it, so that the structure of belief is now even more vulnerable than when there had been complete illusion. Seeming is now like some edifice a part of which has collapsed. Oedipus, frightened by the collapse, tries to support the part still standing: by prayers, by will, by that same resoluteness of spirit he showed when he fled from Corinth.

There still remains one hope, though a feeble one, of perhaps saving seeming in general, that is to say, human seeming. Everything seems likely to lead the protagonist into knowledge of his deed and of himself, except for one thing: there is still an unresolved question of number. According to the witness, more than one person was involved in the murder of Laius. This testimony has led certain scholars to conclude that the *Oedipus* is finally based on a trick. As if it were not by numbers too that we are tied fast to "seeming." As if the structure of appearance, in collapse, could not always find something with which to shore itself up. Isn't it perfectly human for a man in distress to cling tenaciously to the feeblest hope, sustaining it with his ingenuity even to the point of quibbling? Here instinct guides thinking. And surely it is not against human nature in such cases for the feminine instinct to take over and guide the reason of the man:

Jocasta

Be sure, at least, that this was how he told the story. He cannot unsay it now, for every one in the city heard it—not I alone. But, Oedipus, even if he diverges from what he said then, he shall never prove that the murder of Laius squares rightly with the prophecy—for Loxias declared that the king should be killed by his own son. And that poor creature did not kill him surely,—for he died himself first. So as far as prophecy goes, henceforward I shall not look to the right hand or the left.

Not that she has grown more "thoughtless" as some critics have been inclined to assert—why expect her now to be clear about the relation between the prophecy and the prophet? Her earlier words in the same scene express security still unassailed; now she talks the language of the most vehement defensiveness. Emerging from the show of quibbling reason is the distress of existence as such, here embodied in the feminine will to survive and to prevail for the sake of the man; this characterizes Jocasta's action, rather than personal inadequacy. To be sure, she is thus led on to *hybris* against the gods. Nevertheless, her error arises much more from the human essence itself than from her personal nature.

Here doubt and reason are merely means of defense for an existence which has been threatened; doubt and reason do not here spring from any such attitude as that of free spirits in the age of the Sophists—this is shown, if further proof were needed, by the beginning of the third episode. With prayer and sacrificial offerings, Jocasta approaches the same Apollo whose oracle she doubted. For now she is in a state of dread, a dread all the stronger because it is not dread for herself but for Oedipus—she fears because of his fear:

For Oedipus excites himself too much
at every sort of trouble, not conjecturing,
like a man of sense, what will be from what was,
but he is always at the speaker's mercy,
when he speaks terrors.

But instead of discharging her feelings in lamentations and supplications—as do Tecmessa and Deianeira in Sophocles' earlier style—Jocasta begins to perform her silent rite of prayer, and then a messenger enters unannounced and reports the death of Polybus. According to the conventions of Greek

211

drama, to which Sophocles in his *Ajax* and in his *Women of Trachis* still adhered, the messenger's entrance should have been signalled beforehand. But in the *Oedipus* something totally new intrudes, bearing with it the irony of a demonic intervention that most nearly resembles the irony in the *Antigone* when the guard intrudes on Creon's speech of state. Hardly has Jocasta turned to pray when, independently of her wishes, and wonderfully for them, someone appears as by divine command and resolves the distress in her soul:

Jocasta
   O oracles of the Gods, where are you now? It was from this
   man Oedipus fled, lest he should be his murderer! And now
   he is dead, in the course of nature, and not killed by Oedipus.

And now begins a series of developments like the moves in a game of chess. Yet this external confluence of circumstances, not altogether uncontrived, finds a place within the whole, adding a special brightness to the universal gloom, appearing amidst psychic convulsions and against a background of inner confusion. Two-thirds of the drama, almost the whole play in fact, is over before the determining external facts enter the circle of internal dissension. For up to this point Oedipus had received from Creon, Teiresias, Jocasta only solace or mortification for his seeking, erring, seeming: did they not step forward merely because of his own desire to be assuaged by seeming? Now unfamiliar messengers appear, and events, some recent and some long superseded, are brought out; from outside his soul, a circle is cast about Oedipus from which he cannot free himself. The old and kindly messenger goes from amazement to amazement. The news that rule over Corinth has passed to him is not what concerns Oedipus, but only that Polybus is dead: this is the fact he wants proved beyond the peradventure of a doubt. Once proved, he responds with jubilation; it is as though the death of his father is bringing him salvation. And the messenger is puzzled. He hesitates; should he or should he not reveal more? But he is led to imagine that Oedipus would be glad to hear that he is not the dead king's son. Thus his good will impels him to speak and he can speak with pride, for did he not save Oedipus as a foundling?—and thus in his joy, not noticing it, he allows himself to speak familiarly:

Messenger
   Son, it's very plain you don't know what you're doing.

Such an unelevated expression as "Son, it's very plain" would not have been possible in a play like the *Women of Trachis,* where there are also messengers; the play's style would have precluded it. Since the pathos of the *Women of Trachis* is not based on the ironic contrast between outer events and inner suffering, a loss of elevation in that play would have meant a loss of dramatic tension. Here too it differs from both the *Oedipus* and the *Antigone,* even in the presentation of secondary characters.

Two old men have appeared who saved Oedipus as a child. There is a contrast between their attitudes, the joyous advance of the one and the sudden alarm and restraint of the other. In this, there is a repetition, in a popular key, of the very contrast between Oedipus and Jocasta in their tragic recognition scene:

Herdsman

No—
not such that I can quickly call to mind.

Messenger

That is no wonder, master. But I'll make him remember what he does not know. For I know, that he well knows the country of Cithaeron, how he with two flocks, I with one kept company for three years—each year half a year—from spring till autumn time and then when winter came I drove my flocks to our fold home again and he to Laius' steadings. Well—am I right or not in what I said we did?

Herdsman

You're right—although it's a long time ago.

Messenger

Do you remember giving me a child
to bring up as my foster child?

Herdsman

What's this?
Why do you ask this question?

Messenger

Look old man,
here he is—here's the man who was that child!

Herdsman

Death take you! Won't you hold your tongue?

Oedipus

No, no,
do not find fault with him, old man. Your words
are more at fault than his.

Herdsman

O best of masters,
how do I give offense?

Oedipus

When you refuse
to speak about the child of whom he asks you.

Herdsman

He speaks out of his ignorance, without meaning.

Of the two witnesses, one is full of dread, the other is assured; one disavows and the other insists. The contrast between them is very different from that between the two messengers in the *Women of Trachis,* though in that play too one messenger reveals what the other hides: this is the kind of intrigue common in human relations; deception based on good intentions had no place in the *Women of Trachis.* Now in the *Oedipus,* the two messengers show themselves to be good and kindly servants, if not without some interests of their own; but in relation to the whole they are merely the unconscious and lowly instruments of divine destiny. The irony that causes them to confront each other is of the same playful sort by which the divine interweaves the low and the high, so as to disclose itself finally in the impermanence of human greatness.

The third episode falls into two parts which have the same rhythm. First there is an ascent from fear to hope, which lasts until the triumph of seeming certainty—in this part Jocasta leads—and then a new wave of dread begins which again rises apparently to certainty or safety. But now Oedipus leads even as Jocasta retreats, begs him to desist, and finally withdraws. Moreover, an inner reversal takes place between the beginning and the end. At first it was Oedipus who was afraid, and it was Jocasta who advocated trust in "fortune," in what comes by chance, whatever its guise: her words do not urge "frivolity"; they tell Oedipus not to listen to what is sinister and dark, not to slit the fabric of life's questionableness, for it is because of the gods that man is questionable. Soon after, Oedipus, escaping into his final bout with seeming, refers to himself as the "son of fortune" at the very moment that Jocasta, in despair, loses her desire to live. Jocasta, to be sure, is prefigured in this by Deianeira in the *Women of Trachis* when, suddenly silent, and leaving the others ignorant of her purpose, she retires. The chorus, suspecting something, is not informed. The report comes finally, and is told with solemn pathos. In the *Oedipus*, Jocasta is alternately caught in and freed from the grip of her own demon. And just as her retirement signifies her fall from a deceiving security, so too is the misunderstanding she leaves behind her incomparably more drastic and ironic than the misunderstanding after Deianeira's exit. For while in the *Women of Trachis* misunderstanding is due to an unexplained action on the part of a noble person, in the *Oedipus*, we see the ironic eruption of the demonic in man himself; misunderstanding arises from man's inherent tendency to be possessed by seeming, which finds a way to be convincing even after it has failed to convince. It fabricates out of its own substance a new and deceptive motive for hope:

Chorus
Why has the queen gone, Oedipus, in wild
grief rushing from us? I am afraid that trouble
will break out of this silence.
Oedipus
Break out what will! I at least shall be
willing to see my ancestry, though humble.
Perhaps she is ashamed of my low birth,
for she has all a woman's high-flown pride.
But I account myself a child of Fortune,
beneficent Fortune, and I shall not be
dishonoured. She's the mother from whom I spring;
the months, my brother, marked me, now as small,
and now again as mighty. Such is my breeding,
and I shall never prove so false to it,
as not to find the secret of my birth.

In the *Ajax* the deception, a god-sent madness, something foreign to man, something against nature, destroys the hero without his having unravelled it. In the *Women of Trachis*, Deianeira's lamentable error springs from her own loss of hope and from the gloom cast by her frightened, despairing, and passionate nature. In the *Oedipus* deception is viewed as something lurking about, a mood, an atmosphere, as the demonic destiny of man's own nature and world. Is there such a thing as progress in viewing knowledge as futility? Perhaps not; but it would not be easy to think of these plays in reverse order, or to consider the much more limited tragedy of knowledge in the *Women of Trachis* as expressing a more mature view than the tragedy of *Oedipus*.

The two last brief episodes of the *Oedipus* are richer in movement and action than anything else in Sophocles. The final opposition in the final reversal had to be expressed in the contrast between two human beings finally aware of their doom; feminine conduct in the face of fate here stands in the most profound contrast to masculine conduct. For it is not truth that causes Jocasta to hope against what she thinks might be the facts; she hopes in behalf of the man on whom she depends, her hope counters his mood. In security as in dread, her relation to the truth is indirect; she is direct only in relation to the instinctive—even her reason is instinct. While Oedipus, in terms of the old tragedy, conducts himself "pathetically," she conducts herself sym-pathetically. She is lighter in spirit than he and more hopeful, even to the point of hybris; and in defeat, she is less able to endure, and finally takes her life. It is already a victory for her when he merely begins to hope again, though his hope is vain, and her downfall comes not from seeing her own reality, but from the fact that he cannot now avoid his:

Jocasta
> I beg you—do not hunt this out—I beg you,
> if you have any care for your own life.
> What I am suffering is enough.

* * *

> O Oedipus, God help you!
> God keep you from the knowledge of who you are!

Should she be called frivolous? Hardly. The two principals are of course very different, but not in the sense that either is frivolous. They are related to life in opposite ways and it is this that makes possible the intricacy of the tragic net woven about them in the last part of the *Oedipus*. In distress, her dereliction makes her ready to accept seeming, and nothing but seeming, for the sake of life, his life; his dereliction makes him ready to accept such a life, the life of a blinded and accursed man, all for the sake of truth. The real action does not lie in the chess moves of external fates, but in the shifting modes by which two different persons receive the truth that crashes in on them. It is true that the revelation of the *Women of Trachis* has a similarly external character. But in self-knowledge Heracles can remain calm; actually he has learned little more than that he is to die; and though Heracles ascends from this knowledge to his last overcoming, in his ultimately limited heroic existence, he still does not see himself as he really is. Thus, his self-knowledge can only lead him to commiserate with himself, in self-pity and pained subjectivity:

Heracles
Woe, woe is me! This is my miserable end.
Lost! I am lost! I see the light no longer.*

What is called forth from Oedipus, however, is not a subjective yielding to pain. His suffering has a universal meaning which in no way diminishes its force.

Herdsman
          . . . But he saved it
for the most terrible troubles. If you are
the man he says you are, you're bred to misery.

Oedipus
O, O, O, they will all come,
all come out clearly! Light of the sun, let me
look upon you no more after today!
I who first saw the light bred of a match
accursed, and accursed in my living
with them I lived with, cursed in my killing.

Here there is no intensification of suffering by powerful images or outcries, and no self-indulgence in naming the causes of suffering. Instead, we have a meaningful figure of speech, not a play on words but an image of right reason; for a pathetic gesture or unreserved emphasis the poet turns to a kind of understatement. Let us note the likenesses and differences in the endings of the *Oedipus* and of the *Women of Trachis*. In the *Oedipus* the pathos of the ending has a proper fullness, but the expression of suffering is no longer felt to be meaningful as such; suffering here takes on a uni-

* Translated by Michael Jameson, *The Complete Greek Tragedies*, edited by David Grene and Richmond Lattimore, University of Chicago Press.

versal significance, the true quality of the tragic. I am not thinking of the kind of maxim, at the beginning or end of the various speeches, but rather of a universal significance inherent in all that happens. To be sure, the content of the *Women of Trachis* is much more limited, as well as more intimate. But the force of universality in the last part of the *Oedipus* does not indicate in that play any lack of those subjective elements we find in the *Women of Trachis*; at the end of the *Oedipus*, we transcend the special case of the protagonist to a general wonder at our own condition. So that this is not really a story with a particular beginning or end, joining various vicissitudes, told in a tone of high emotion—as is the *Women of Trachis*. The *Oedipus* in its second half is not a drama narrated, and thus revealing what has already happened off-stage, as is the *Antigone*. In the *Oedipus* we come to the limits of the visible: these limits have penetrated into the gestures and accusations of the blinded man who finally can see:

Messenger (of Jocasta, 1. 1242ff.)
When she came raging into the house she went
straight to her marriage bed, tearing her hair
with both her hands, and crying upon Laius
long dead—Do you remember, Laius,
that night long past which bred a child for us
to send you to your death and leave
a mother making children with her son?
And then she groaned and cursed the bed in which
she brought forth husband by her husband, children
by her own child, an infamous double bond.

(of Oedipus, 1. 1268 ff.)

When he saw her, he cried out fearfully
and cut the dangling noose. Then, as she lay,
poor woman, on the ground, what happened after,
was terrible to see. He tore the brooches—
the gold chased brooches fastening her robe—
away from her and lifting them up high
dashed them on his own eyeballs, shrieking out
such things as: they will never see the crime
I have committed or had done upon me!

The event is itself an extended metaphor, even as the language is metaphorical. Every difference between the natural and spiritual is destroyed: surely it is not the physical eye which looks upon the past. "Acting and suffering" are terms that apply to all existence and cannot throw light on either the marriage or the murder lived through in ignorance; rather it is the marriage and murder that throw light on acting and suffering. In the darkness to come there will be "seeing" and "not seeing" as there was when Oedipus had sight: a seeing of those whom he should never have seen with his eyes, and a not-seeing, not-knowing, of those whom he had wished to see when his will drove him to seek his origins. The darkness will be both physical and spiritual, and only thereby will his true seeing begin: that knowledge out of the night of blindness which is self-knowledge. The death of Jocasta had been understood in terms of an enigmatic and paradoxical formula; once again, the paradoxical interweaving of terms points to the complex weaving of the fate of Oedipus, in which blindness and seeing are tangled.

This, too, is expressed finally in lyrical terms, in his last lament. Again the individual instance is shown to contain a universal meaning; the fate of the body is at the same time the fate of the spirit: woe is twofold. In the lament of Ajax in the play of that name, "night" and "light" stand for the opposite spheres of "life" and "death," which are confused by the suffering hero; in appealing to both, he tells all his grievances unrestrainedly. The lament of Oedipus, however, points to a meaning beyond itself, so that "darkness" is not only that of the physical eye but also all which fatefully and demonically envelops him.

Ajax
> O
> Darkness that is my light,
> Murk of the underworld, my only brightness,
> Oh, take me to yourself to be your dweller,
> Receive and keep me . . . .*

In the *Oedipus Rex*, however:

> Darkness!
> Horror of darkness enfolding, resistless, unspeakable visitant sped
>   by an ill wind in haste!
> madness and stabbing pain and memory
> of evil deeds I have done!

* Translated by John Moore, *The Complete Greek Tragedies.*

In the *Ajax* and in the *Women of Trachis,* there is no atmosphere of or contact with the uncanny, as in the *Oedipus*. In the *Ajax,* Athena, who punishes the protagonist, is a familiar figure, known to all the audience. Thus she serves to dissimulate that element of the enigmatic and the uncanny, that "cloudiness" or obscurity we feel in the *Oedipus*; that threat, stemming from no person and hardly even attributable to Apollo, which hangs over the glory of man.

That quality in Attic tragedy which generally appears in the texture of a whole drama, that revelling in the fearful, mingling horror and voluptousness, has in the *Oedipus,* as in no other play, entered into the conduct of the tragic hero himself. In the other plays the strophes and anti-strophes of the chorus do more to make pain bearable than the speeches of the powerless victims in the grip of pleasure-in-pain. In the *Oedipus,* the same person is victim and dithyrambist, the one who writhes and the one who discerns himself, the one who finds himself under torture, the one whose speech is impassioned and the one who sings. Biers, mechanical instruments, are no longer in evidence: from within the house the blinded man calls for the doors to open so that he can be led into the light. But instead of being brought in by others and thus exposed to view, the victim, after his search for himself, rushes into view to exhibit his great find: the blinded man he always was. The traditional act of exhibiting, like the uncovering of the wounded Heracles who thereby can show what has been done to him (*Women of Trachis*) or the uncovering of the bloody dummy that represents Ajax with a sword in his chest—what covered the hero at the start was there to be taken off at the end—this act of exhibiting was never performed in Greek tragedy by the hero himself before the *Oedipus*. While the unveiling of the dead Ajax and the unveiling of the dying Heracles are intended to show what was done to the protagonist, the self-exhibition of Oedipus with his blinded eyes is an act of self-revealing that springs from his situation.

All that surrounded and sustained him, his ancestors and contemporaries, his parents and children, his city and its people, his station, his royal decree, indeed the cosmos itself, all now reject him. How can he look at his children, at his city with its towers and statues of the gods, or think of this people among whom he had gained such glory? Now he will be cast out from the realm of the living as well as from the realm of the dead: even death, as reunion with his kin, would be a kind of coming home to some community. But this possibility he violently rejects with tragic absoluteness:

Chorus
I cannot say your remedy was good;
you would be better dead than blind and living.

Oedipus
What I have done here was best done—don't tell me otherwise, do not give me further counsel.

He is, as it were, the opposite of Ajax; he cannot call upon death to help him. Ajax could look upon and apostrophize the world that had destroyed him: Zeus and the Erinyes, Salamis and Troy, the fields and streams, Hades below and the light above—calling on all of them to hear his last words. The desire of Oedipus, at the end, is to cut himself off from all communication and involvement: now that he cannot see he would also like not to hear.

In other plays after the denouement, the apostrophes were addressed to whatever had been felt as friendly, trustworthy, close—the hero's own arms, bodily strength as in the *Women of Trachis*, the fields of heroism as in the *Ajax*, the dead of the royal line as in the *Antigone*. But Oedipus addresses himself at the end to what at the very beginning was alien, hostile, false:

Oedipus
Cithaeron, why did you receive me? . . .
O Polybus and Corinth and the house
the old house that I used to call my father's . . .
                              crossroads.
and hidden glade . . .
                    O marriage, marriage!
you bred me and again when you had bred
bred children of your child . . .

At this point the verses become tragic even in their ornaments; the words of Oedipus are directed against himself, expressing the pathos of a life that has turned against itself. And the self-disclosure of Oedipus is so deeply tragic because at this moment he is both for and against himself, affirming himself in self-negation, self-destruction. Cursing, he calls on the others to hide him or kill him by throwing him into the sea, to cast him out, to perform on him as they will so long as they prevent him from being seen: but why then had he asked to be led into the light where he could be seen? The contradiction here has the purest kind of tragic pathos, for tragedy delights in affirming the very person whom, by causing his suffering, it negates.

Approaching the man who curses himself is the very apotheosis of the untragic man, Creon. This is the very same Creon who had been unjustly accused by Oedipus in their quarrel, who had proved his integrity, and can now dispose over the defiled and defiling Oedipus. He does so in a matter-of-fact way, with an aptness that is neither inhuman nor calculating; for instance, he makes no decision before consulting the gods. He is a man without a destiny, and even hostile to destiny, and he is the one against whose life the vicissitudes of Oedipus are measured. A short while ago he was the object of Oedipus' profound contempt; now to Oedipus, fallen, and in the mire of self-debasement, he is the best of men where he was once the worst; Creon is the one whose greatest act of mercy would be to allow the now monstrous and blind Oedipus to touch his own daughter. Creon, nonetheless, whatever pity he feels, is rather cold to Oedipus, who in torment reaches out toward those he loves. As the secure and untragic man, his relation to Oedipus— whose companion, opponent, and friend he has been—is much like that of Odysseus to Ajax in the *Ajax* of Sophocles. But once again the moving force of the *Oedipus* is very different from that of the *Ajax*. For there is no development in the *Ajax,* no reversal in the relationship of the characters contrasted: the relationship of Odysseus to Ajax is the same at the end as it was at the beginning of the play. Yet there was nothing in the character of Odysseus as Sophocles took him from the epic which precluded a change in his relationship with his enemy unto death. Thus in every way the *Ajax* is a play of static and the *Oedipus* one of dynamic situations. At the same time, however, the contrast of the characters in the *Oedipus* is deepened to the very limit of the understandable. At the end of the play we perceive the difference between Oedipus and Creon in terms of the protagonists' greatness, sublimity, and humanity; and the difference is of a sort not to be found in any other drama. Nevertheless, this difference cannot be expressed in the language of ethics or of psychology. In his great if rigid heroism, Ajax was opposed by the flexibility, humanity, and intelligence of Odysseus; in the persons of Menelaus and Agamemnon he was opposed by vindictiveness, arrogance, envy, and pettiness. In the *Antigone*, self-sacrifice and youth are opposed by the age and hardened obstinacy of a tyrant. Oedipus is opposed finally only by Creon, who is totally untragic.

One question, however, is not raised in the *Oedipus*, which will be raised by the characters of Euripides: Who is the guilty party? Oedipus indeed refers to himself as a criminal, guilty of another's death. But herein the question of who is really guilty ($a\emph{i}\tau\acute{\iota}a$) is not raised. To be sure, the god is named as the moving force, but this is not done so that Oedipus can fight against the god, or attack himself in the god's presence; he will not wrestle with the god or destroy himself before the god: he does not think of punishing his punisher. The important thing here is that Oedipus and the god are in a strict relationship. The naming of the god is part of the revelation; divine revelation parallels human revelation:

Oedipus
> It was Apollo, friends, Apollo,
> that brought this bitter bitterness, my sorrows to completion.
> But the hand that struck me
> was none but my own.

Pointing to Apollo, as Oedipus does, cannot alter the issue. Apollo is referred to simply to indicate that the justice and injustice expressed in the action touch on the foundations of all life. So here there is no question of assigning guilt. If we could imagine a tribunal of gods and men acquitting Oedipus as Orestes is acquitted in the *Oresteia*, this could hardly help Oedipus in any way. How could such an acquittal resolve the contradiction between what he thought himself to be and what he found himself to be? On the other hand, a judgment of guilty against him would not help him either. Orestes can be found not guilty; but Oedipus cannot be extricated from what he has learned of himself. As was said before, there is no question of assigning responsibility for what has happened; whether the responsibility is to be borne by gods or men or by the order of the world would change nothing. This question of guilt, without which some of the greatest tragedies of Euripides and Aeschylus are hardly thinkable, does not even arise in the *Oedipus*. Nothing is decided in this play about justice or atonement. It would be absurd to think of Oedipus as blinding himself in order to atone for his deeds; nor does the play decide whether we are free or determined. But something is decided in the Oedipus about seeming and truth, those contrary realities in which man is entangled. Caught between seeming and truth, and reaching for what is highest, man consumes and destroys himself.

Translated by Werner Dannhauser

The Opinions of Contemporary
Philosophers

Pragmatism and the Tragic Sense of Life

SIDNEY HOOK

I

"WHAT, if anything, has philosophy to tell us about the human condition, about the fate of man and his works?" This question in all its changes I have heard repeatedly on three major continents. It is asked mostly by philosophical laymen—by students and teachers and men of letters in search of a center, or at least a shelter, in a world become dark and insecure because of the shadows of totalitarianism and war. It is asked at interdisciplinary conferences; and by academic administrators in search of projects to recommend to foundations, projects which, to use an expression in wide use, "are not merely of technical philosophical concern."

The question: What saving message do philosophers bring their fellowmen? I have heard asked even by professional philosophers agonizing over the fact that they have a subject but no apparent subject-matter. It was heard at the XIIth International Congress of Philosophy at Venice—and there the Soviet philosophers undertook to answer it. It is raised periodically by voices in this country and in our own association as a protest against analytic philosophy. It was the central theme of the Third East-West Philosophers' Conference where for six weeks forty older and almost as many young philosophers tried to discover what bearing philosophy had on social practice. At one point we were told to imagine that we had the ear of the statesmen of the world, and were challenged to give them counsel on how to put the world's affair in order. No one recalled Plato's experience at Syracuse or reflected upon the fact that as far as we can judge the only request Aristotle made of Alexander, when he had *his* ear, was that he send back fresh biological specimens from Asia. Indeed, it is not likely that with his views about the essential superiority of the Greeks to the rest of mankind that Aristotle would have given his blessings to Alcxander's enlightened, if premature, attempt to establish a world culture or that he would even have been sympathetic to the purpose of the East-West Philosophers' Conference.

This question, with which I begin, is certainly a large one and may be deemed an appropriate theme for discussion in conjunction with John Dewey's centenary year.

II

For some time now philosophers have been disputing with each other about what philosophy should or should not be. They would be better occupied, it seems to me, doing each what he thinks philosophically worth while instead of objecting either to linguistic analysis or metaphysical speculation, as the case may be. The issue is not one of proper definition or even whether philosophy is a science or a body of knowledge of comparable objectivity, but rather whether it is worth doing, whether there is sufficient illumination and fun in pursuing certain themes, ignored by others, to justify continuing to do so. After all no one really believes that only science is a self-justifying enterprise. But since the subject has become moot and since there has developed a wide concern about what, if anything, philosophy has to say of general human concern, some remarks about it are in order.

As some of you are aware, I have for many years concerned myself with problems of social and political and legal philosophy, with "problems of men" as authentic as any of those recognized by thinkers who would reform modern philosophy. But I find myself increasingly out of sympathy with those who have impugned the whole philosophical enterprise because of its failure to serve as a beacon to mankind in distress. When I ask myself why I feel uncomfortable and at odds with those who attack philosophers because they have nothing of immediate, practical moment to say, I find that my conception of philosophy although stated sometimes in words similar to theirs, differs in important ways. Put most succinctly, although I believe that philosophy is a *quest* for wisdom, many of those who cite this phrase, too, speak and act as if they already had it. The difference may be only of nuance and emphasis but it has a profound bearing on one's conception of the appropriate role of the philosopher in the culture of his time. It is the difference between being a moralist and being a moralizer. The moralizer may be called "the shouting moralist," of whom Santayana somewhere says that he "no doubt has his place but not in philosophy." It is a difference, on the one hand, between *analyzing* specific and basic social problems and conflicts, and *clarifying* the issues in dispute with all the tools at one's command—and, on the other, *proclaiming* solutions and programs on the basis of antecedent commitments which one shares with some faction of his fellowmen. It is the difference between approaching problems of human experience in terms of one's vocation as a philosopher, which is to do intellectual justice to the varied and conflicting interests present or discovered, and one's vocation as a citizen limited by specific duties he must fulfill. It is the difference between intellectual concern which may or may not lead to programs of action and commitment to programs of action which by their very nature estop self-critical thought.

In the course of its history philosophy has been many things. But its distinctive concern at all times *has* been the quest for wisdom. Otherwise there would be no point in including thinkers like Descartes or Leibnitz in the history of philosophy in addition to the history of science or mathematics. What distinguishes the philosopher as a moralist from the philosopher as a mathematician, logician or natural scientist, and from the ordinary man as a philosopher, is his sustained reflective pursuit of wisdom. This means two things. The systematic study of the knowledge which is relevant to wisdom: and the analysis of the commitments we assume and rule out when knowledge is related to policy. All of us know that wisdom and knowledge are not the same thing but we sometimes mistakenly speak as if they are opposed. A man may have knowledge of many things and not be wise but a wise man cannot be ignorant of the things he is wise about. He must have knowledge of the nature and career of values in human experience; knowledge of the nature and history of the situations in which they develop and conflict; knowledge of the minds and emotions of the carriers of value; knowledge of the consequences of actions taken or proposed. The wise man is not one who merely recites moral principles and applies a ready-made schedule of moral obligations to the problems and perplexities of value conflict. He is one who on the basis of what he already knows, or believes he knows, makes fresh inquiry into the situations which define alternatives and exact their costs. "Only the conventional and the fanatical," observes Dewey, "are always immediately sure of right and wrong in conduct." This means that a philosopher must earn his title to be wise not by right of philosophical tradition or philology but by the hard work of acquiring relevant knowledge and by hard thinking about it.

Here lie important tasks for the philosopher. To be wise he must immerse himself in the actual subject matters (not necessarily experiences) out of which life's problems arise. To be wise about economic affairs he must study economics, to be wise about problems of law he must study law, to be wise about politics he must study history, sociology and other disciplines. To be wise about war and peace he must study military technology and the theory and practice of communism including its strategic exploitation of peace movements to disarm the free world. Indeed, these subjects are so interrelated that to be wise about any one of them he must study them all. And I might add, in view of some current writing, to be wise about education it is not enough merely to rebaptize the ends of the good life as ends of a good education, too, as if without operational application to concrete historical situations, they had any but a peripheral bearing on the great, current problems of education. One must study social history, the psychology of learning, the methods and techniques of pedagogy to achieve educational wisdom. To enumerate the ends of the good life is not enough. Nor is a primer on logical analysis which can serve as an introduction to the study of *any* subject, a primer to a philosophy of education.

All of these problems are of tremendous complexity because of the number of independent variables they contain, because they rarely permit of controlled experiment, and because the community must sometimes act upon them in desperate urgency before the analysis is complete. This should make for humility among philosophers even as they bring to the study of these problems the methodological sophistication, the arts and skills of analysis which are the hallmarks of their profession. This is what *I* mean by "the problems of men." It is philosophy not as a quest for salvation but as a pursuit of understanding of great cultural issues and their possible upshot. It does not start from a complete stock of philosophical wisdom which it dispenses to others with hortatory fervor but with an initial sense of concern to meet the challenge of the great unresolved problems of our time, offering analysis of these problems which will win the respect of the specialist and yet command the attention of everyman, e.g. how to preserve peace *and* freedom, achieve adequate production and meaningful vocations for all, design patterns of creative leisure, effect desegregation if possible without coercion, establish a welfare state and a spirit of enterprise, preserve national security and the right to dissent. It is philosophy as *normative* social inquiry. And it is *not* social reform. How could philosophy be identified with social reform in view of the existence of many esteemed philosophers from Aristotle to Santayana whose judgments of wisdom were conservative, hostile to social reform? Such identification would be comparable to defining a physicist as one who was committed to a specific hypothesis in physics.

At this point my inner ear senses unspoken murmurs of surprise. "Surely," some of you must be saying, "this constitutes a repudiation of John Dewey's conception of philosophy, for, after all, does not Dewey call upon philosophers as philosophers to do precisely what is being urged they should not do? Does not Dewey call upon philosophers to play the role of social reformers?" My answer is: "Not as I understand him and not as he is to be understood in the light of all he has written."

Here is not the place to provide the documentation. I content myself merely with saying that Dewey has a very *complex* conception of philosophy. Philosophy is indeed concerned primarily with what I call normative problems of social inquiry. But its function is also to provide leading, speculative ideas in science—natural and social. And a third function is to weave together certain families of ideas into a philosophical synthesis. "There is a kind of music of ideas," he says, "which appeals, apart from any question of verification, to the mind of thinkers!" Nor is this all. The philosopher must bring some perspective or vision to bear upon the world which is related to issues of value and hence makes the analysis of normative problems of social inquiry more sensitive. "Philosophies," declares Dewey, "are different ways of construing life. . . ."

There is more, then, than problems of normative social inquiry which falls within the province of the philosopher's concern. There is the illuminating perspective in which they are seen which is metaphysics. "If philosophy be criticism," Dewey asks in *Experience and Nature*, "what is to be said of the relation of philosophy to metaphysics?" His answer briefly is that metaphysics is a description of those gross features of the world which constitute the backdrop of the theatre of human activity against which men play out their lives. The conduct of life and the analysis of its problems, however indirectly, will reflect what we believe to be the generic features of human experience in the world. In this sense, as ultimately related to the human scene and the adventure of human life, but not to ontology, metaphysics is "a ground map of the province of criticism establishing base lines to be employed in more intricate triangulations."

This brings me finally to my theme of the tragic sense of life as a feature of human experience which provides an illuminating perspective upon the analysis of man's problems. The juxtaposition of the expressions "pragmatism" and "the tragic sense of life" may appear bewildering to those who understand pragmatism as a narrow theory of meaning and "the tragic sense of life" as the hysterical lament that man is not immortal—the theme song of Unamuno's book of that title. To speak of pragmatism and the tragic sense of life is somewhat like speaking of "The Buddhism of John Dewey" or "The Dewey Nobody Knows."

I am not aware that Dewey ever used the phrase "the tragic sense of life" but I know that growing up in the shadow of the Civil War, he felt what I shall describe by it and that it is implied in his account of moral experience. At any rate nothing of moment depends upon whether the view is actually Dewey's or Hegel's or William James' or Nicolai Hartmann's in all of whom it can be found. I take the responsibility of the interpretation and its application. It is a perspective which seems to me to illumine the pragmatic view that problems of normative social inquiry—morals in the broad sense—are the primary—not exclusive—subject matter of philosophy, and that reason or scientific intelligence can and should be used to resolve them.

By the tragic sense of life I do not understand merely sensitivity to the presence of evil or suffering in the world although all tragic situations to some degree involve one or the other. And since I have mentioned Buddha I should like to say that the presence of the evils in the world which led Buddha to surrender his Kingdom in order to seek salvation for himself and mankind are not to me the realities fundamental to the tragic sense of life. There were three things in Buddha's experience, reflection upon which led him to a renunciation of his princely lot and a quest for liberation from desire and incarnate existence—sickness, old age and death. One can very well understand why in the world in which he lived and for many centuries thereafter until our own, these phenomena loomed so large in the overpopulated and poverty-stricken areas of Asia. Nonetheless if we are to distinguish between the sense of the *pitiful* and the sense of the *tragic*—sickness, old age and even many forms of death, despite their numbing effect upon human sensibility, are not necessarily to be classified as tragic.

232

First, given the rapidly expanding horizons of knowledge in our age, there is nothing in the nature of things which requires that the sick, any more than the poor, must always be with us. If scientific medicine develops at the same pace in the next few hundred years as it has in the last century, it is not shallow optimism to anticipate that the most serious forms of sickness will disappear and not be replaced by others. Even where sickness is present it may be the occasion of tragedy but by itself is not an illustration of it. In relation to the forces of nature man's lot may appear pitiful. The tragic is a moral phenomenon.

What is true of sickness is true of old age. The aged arouse our compassion because of their feebleness and fragility—and the multiplicity of their aches and pains. When these are absent—and this, too, is a concern of scientific medicine—there is a chance for serenity, wisdom and beauty of spirit to manifest themselves. There is sometimes a grandeur and stateliness about an old tree which aged persons do not possess because the processes of physical degeneration, and the consequent weakening of the vital powers, make man pitiful. There is no tragedy in growing old biologically but only sorrow; the element of the tragic enters in the defeat of plans or hopes, in the realization that in much grief there is not much wisdom, and that we cannot count merely upon the passage of time alone to diminish our stupidities and cruelties.

But what of death—Buddha's third appalling discovery—preoccupation with which has become so fashionable today among some European existentialist philosophers that their philosophy seems to be more a meditation upon death than upon life? Is not death the ultimate source of whatever is tragic in life? I cannot bring myself to think so. Nor can I convince myself that its nature and significance in life waited to be discovered by Kierkegaard and Heidegger and their modern disciples.

It is the reflective attitude towards death not the popular attitude or the one displayed by those in its last agonies, which throws light on its nature and place in life. The attitude exhibited by Socrates in facing it seems wiser than that expressed by the contemnors of the rational life who not content with talking about what they find when they look into themselves inflate it into a universal trait of the human psyche. So Tolstoy who is quoted by existentialist writers, writes: "If a man has learned to think, no matter what he may think about, he is always thinking of his own death. All philosophers are like that. And what truth can there be, if there is death?" Logically, of course, this makes no more sense than the even more extreme statement of Sartre that "if we must die then our life has no meaning," which to those who solve some problems in life and therefore find some meaning, might be taken as a premise in a new short proof of human immortality. All this it seems to me expresses little more than a fear of death and a craving for immortality. It is a commonplace observation, however, that most human beings who desire immortality desire not unending life but unending youth or other desirable qualities which life makes possible. The fable of Juno and her lover in which Juno petitions the gods to take back the gift of eternal life they had conferred upon a mortal indicates that the Greeks knew that a life without end could be a dubious blessing. In this respect the Hellenes were wiser than the Hebrews whose God drives Adam from Paradise after he had eaten of the fruit of the tree of knowledge to prevent him from eating of the fruit of the tree of eternal life. Agony over death strikes me as one of the unloveliest features of the intellectual life of our philosophic times—and certainly unworthy of any philosophy which conceives itself as a quest for wisdom. It has never been clear to me why those who are nauseated by life, not by this or that kind of life but any kind of life, should be so fearful of death.

Wisdom is knowledge of the uses of life and death. The uses of life are to be found in the consummatory experiences of vision and delight, of love, understanding, art, friendship and creative activity. That is why in a contingent world of finite men, vulnerable to powers they cannot control, which sometimes robs them of the possibility of any justifying consummations, death has its uses, too. For it gives us some assurance that no evil or suffering lasts forever. To anyone aware of the multitude of infamies and injustices which men have endured, of the broken bodies and tortured minds of the victims of these cruelties, of the multiple dimensions of pain in which millions live on mattress graves or with minds shrouded in darkness, death must sometimes appear as a beneficent release, not an inconsolable affliction. It washes the earth clean of what cannot be cleansed in any other way. Not all the bright promises of a future free of these stains of horror can redeem by one iota the lot of those who will not live to see the dawn of the new day.

It is nobler to exist and struggle in a world in which there is always a vital option to live or die. The fear of death, the desire to survive at any cost or price in human degradation, has been the greatest ally of tyranny, past and present. "There are times," says Woodbridge, "when a man ought to be more afraid of living than dying." And we may add, there are situations in which because of the conditions of survival, the worst thing we can know of anyone is that he has survived. We have known such times and situations. They may come again.

Even in a world in which all injustices, cruelties and physical anguish have disappeared, the possibility of withdrawing from it makes the world insofar forth a better and a freer world. So long as we retain possession of our faculties, our decision to remain in the world indicates a participating responsibility on our part for those events within it which our continuance affects. If human beings were unable to die they would to that extent be unfree. Man shares a *conatus sui esse perseverare* with everything else in the world or at least with all other sentient beings. But just because he can on rational grounds give up his being, choose not to be, he differentiates himself most strikingly from his fellow creatures in nature. I conclude therefore that death as such is not a tragic phenomenon and that its presence does not make the world and our experience within it tragic. It would be truer to call tragic a world in which men wanted to die but couldn't.

What, then, do I mean by the tragic sense of life and what is its relevance to pragmatism? I mean by the tragic sense a very simple thing which is rooted in the very nature of the moral experience and the phenomenon of moral choice. Every genuine experience of moral doubt and perplexity in which we ask: "What should I do?" takes place in a situation where good conflicts with good. If we already know what is evil the moral inquiry is over, or it never really begins. "The worst of evil," says Dewey, "is the rejected good" but until we reject it, the situation is one in which apparent good opposes apparent good. "All the serious perplexities of life come back to the genuine difficulty of forming a judgment as to the values of a situation: they come back to a conflict of goods." No matter how we resolve the opposition some good will be sacrificed, some interest, whose immediate craving for satisfaction may be every whit as intense and authentic as its fellows, will be modified, frustrated or even suppressed. Where the goods involved are of a relatively low order, like decisions about what to eat, where to live, where to go, the choice is unimportant except to the mind of a child. There are small tragedies as there are small deaths. At any level the conflict of values must become momentous to oneself or others to convey adequately the tragic quality. Where the choice is between goods that are complex in structure and consequential for the future, the tragic quality of the moral dilemma emerges more clearly. And when it involves basic choices of love, friendship, vocations, the quality becomes poignant. The very nature of the self as expressed in habits, dispositions and character is to some extent altered by these decisions. If, as Hobbes observes, "Hell is truth seen too late," all of us must live in it. No matter how justified in smug retrospect our moral decisions seem to have been, only the unimaginative will fail to see the possible selves we have sacrificed to become what we are. Grant that all regrets are vain, that any other choice would have been equally or more regretted, the selves we might have been are eloquent witnesses of values we failed to enjoy. If we have played it safe and made our existence apparently secure, the fascinating experience of a life of adventure and experience can never be ours, and every thought of a good fight missed will be accompanied by a pang. It is a poor spirit William James reminds us who does not sense the chagrin of the tardy Crillon, who arriving when the battle is over is greeted by Henry IV with the words: "Hang yourself, brave Crillon! We fought at Arques, and you were not there!" On the other hand, if we have scorned to put down our roots, hugged our liberty tightly to ourselves by refusing to give hostages to fortune, become crusaders or martyrs for lost causes, we have thrust from ourselves the warmth of sustained affection, and the comforting regularities which can best heal the bruised spirit.

There is a conflict not only between the good and the good but between the good and the right where the good is a generic term for all the values in a situation and the right for all the obligations. The *concepts* of good and right are irreducible to each other in ordinary use. We are often convinced we must fulfill a certain duty even when we are far from convinced to the same degree that the action or the rule it exemplifies will achieve the greatest good. The "good" is related to the reflective satisfaction of an interest: "the right" to the fulfillment of a binding demand or rule of the community. There is no moral problem when in doing the right thing we can see that it *also* leads to the greatest good or when striving for the greatest good conforms to our sense of what is right. But the acute ethical problems arise when in the pursuit of the good we do things which appear not to be right, as e.g., when in order to avoid the dangers of war a nation repudiates its treaty obligations or when in order to win a war non-combatants are punished who are in no way responsible for the actions of others. They also arise when in doing what is right our actions result in evil consequences, as e.g., when a dangerous criminal, set free on a legal technicality, kills again or when the refusal to surrender to the unjust claims of an aggressor results in wholesale slaughter. Many have been the attempts made to escape the antinomies between the right and the good by defining the good as the object of right or the right merely as the means to the good. All have failed. To act upon the right no matter what its consequences for human weal or woe seems inhuman, at times insane. The thirst for righteousness has too often been an angry thirst satisfied if at all by long draughts of blood. On the other hand, the attempt to do good by *any* means no matter how unjust, is subhuman and usually irrational.

As compared to traditional ethical doctrines, ideal utilitarianism reaches farthest in our quest for an adequate ethics but in the end it, too, must be rejected. And it was the pragmatist and pluralist, William James, long before Pritchard and Ross, who indicated why in the famous question he asked: "If the hypothesis were offered us of a world in which Messrs. Fourier's and Bellamy's and Morris' Utopia should all be outdone, and millions be kept permanently happy on the one simple condition that a certain lost soul on the far off edge of things should lead a life of lonely torture, what except a specifical and independent sort of emotion can it be which would make us immediately feel . . . how hideous a thing would be its enjoyment when deliberately accepted as the fruit of such a bargain?" The situation is unaltered if we recognize that there are other goods besides happiness and that justice is itself a good, because in that case the conflict breaks out again between good and good. In this connection I would venture the statement that it is the failure to see the radical pluralism in the nature of the goods which are reckoned in the consequences of an action which accounts both for Moore's view that it is self-evident that it can *never* be right knowingly to approve an action that would make the world as a whole worse than some alternative action and for Kant's view that there are some duties that it would *always* be right to perform, even if the consequences of the action resulted in a worse world or in no world at all. No specific rule can be laid down as absolutely binding in advance either way. Nothing can take the place of intelligence; the better or the lesser evil in each situation can be best defined as the object of reflective choice. Even the decision in the stock illustration of the text-books whether to execute an innocent man or turn him over to be tortured in order to save the community from destruction—would depend upon a complex of circumstances. It is perfectly conceivable that an unjust act will sometimes produce the greater good or the lesser evil. It is sometimes necessary to burn down a house to save a village. Although when applied to human beings the logic seems damnable, few are prepared to take the position of Kant in those agonizing moral predicaments that are not uncommon in history, especially the history of oppressed minority peoples, in which the survival of the group can be purchased only at the price of the pain, degradation and death of the innocent. No matter how we choose, we must either betray the ideal of the greater good or the ideal of right or justice. In this lies the agony of the choice.

Many have been the attempts to escape the guilt of that choice. I cite one from the past. During the Middle Ages, Maimonides writing on the Laws of the Torah to guide his people discusses what a community is to do when it is beset by enemies who demand the life of one man with the threat to kill all if he be not turned over to them. Maimonides teaches that they are to refuse to turn over any man even if all must die in consequence, except if their enemies call out the name of a specific person. I had heard this teaching defended on the ground that if the community itself had to make the decision who was to die, it would be taking the guilt of an innocent man's death upon itself, which is impermissible. But if the enemy names the man, then he can be turned over because the guilt and sin fall now on *their* heads. By this miserable evasion it was thought that the tragic choice could be avoided. But it turns out that Maimonides has been misread. What Maimonides really taught is that only if the name of the person who has been called out is of one already under the death sentence for his crimes should he be surrendered. But never an innocent man. "Never," however, is a long time. It is problematic whether the Jews would have survived if they had always abided by Maimonides' injunction.

If anything, human beings are more readily inclined to sacrifice the right to the good than the good to the right especially in revolutionary situations which have developed because of grievances too long unmet. It can easily be shown that it was Lenin's conception of Communist ethics which implicitly defined the right action as consisting in doing *anything*—literally anything that would bring victory in the class struggle—which explains the transformation of a whole generation of idealists into hangmen. In fact the health of the revolution whether in the times of Robespierre or Castro never really requires the holocaust of victims offered up to it. But no revolution including our own has ever been achieved without injustice to someone. However the conflict between the principles of right and the values of good be theoretically resolved, in every concrete situation it leads to some abridgement of principle or some diminution of value.

The most dramatic of all moral conflicts is not between good and good, or between good and right, but between right and right. This in its starkest form is the theme of Sophoclean tragedy but the primary locus of the tragic situation is not in a play but in life, in law, and in history. Innocence in personal matters consists in overlooking the conflict of moral duties and obligations. Innocence in political matters, the characteristic of ritualistic liberalism, consists in failing to see the conflicts of rights in our Bill of Rights and the necessity of their intelligent adjustment. In our own country we have witnessed again and again the antinomy of rights revealed in divided loyalties, in the conflict between allegiance to the laws of the state and allegiance to what is called divine law or natural law or the dictates of conscience. On the international scene it is expressed in the conflict of incompatible national claims, each with *some* measure of justification, as in the Israeli-Arab impasse.

One of the noteworthy features of moral intuitionism as illustrated in the doctrines of Ross is this recognition that *prima facie* duties conflict and that every important moral act exhibits at the same time characteristics which tend to make it both *prima facie* right and *prima facie* wrong so that although we may claim certainty about these *prima facie* duties, any particular moral judgment or action is at best only probable or contingent. As Ross says, "There is therefore much truth in the description of the right act as a fortunate act." From this the conclusion to be drawn, it seems to me, is that the most important *prima facie* duty of all in a situation requiring moral decision is that of *conscientiousness,* or reflective assessment of all the relevant factors involved, and the searching exploration of our own hearts to determine what we sincerely want, whether we really wish to do what is right in a situation or to get our own scheming way come what may. As much if not more evil results from confusion of our purposes and ignorance of our motives than from ruthless and clear-eyed resolve to ignore everyone's interests but one's own. This emphasis on the importance of reflective

239

inquiry into the features of the situation which bear on the rightness of an action seems to me to be more important than Ross' conception or interpretation of the intuitive apprehension of our *prima facie* duties. It is easier to doubt that we have this faculty of infallible intuition than that our intelligence has the power to discover our conflicts and mediate between them.

Irony is compounded with tragedy in the fact that many of the rights we presently enjoy we owe to our ancestors who in the process of winning them for us deprived others of their rights. In some regions of the world the very ground on which people stand was expropriated by force and fraud from others by their ancestors. Yet as a rule it would be a new injustice to seek to redress the original injustice by depriving those of their possessions who hold present title to them. Every just demand for reparations against an aggressor country is an unjust demand on the descendants of its citizens who as infants were not responsible for the deeds of aggression. That is why history is the arena of the profoundest moral conflicts in which some legitimate right has always been sacrificed, sometimes on the altars of the God of War.

The Christian and especially the Buddhist ethics of purity which seeks to transcend this conflict and avoid guilt by refusal to violate anyone's right in such situations, can only do so by withdrawing from the plane of the ethical altogether. This may succeed in God's eyes but not in man's. The Buddhist saint or any other who out of respect for the right to life of man or beast refuses ever to use force, or to kill, even when this is the only method, as it sometimes is, that will save multitudes from suffering and death, makes himself responsible for the greater evil, all the more so because he claims to be acting out of compassion. He cannot avoid guilt whether we regard him as more than man or less than man. No more than we does he escape the tragic decision.

There are three generic approaches to the tragic conflicts of life. The first approach is that of history. The second is that of love. The third is that of creative intelligence in quest for ways of mediation which I call here the pragmatic.

The approach of history is best typified by Hegel precisely because he tries to put a gloss of reason over the terrible events which constitute so much of the historical process. Its upshot is woefully inept to its intent. It suggests not only that whatever cause wins and *however* it wins, is more just than the cause which is defeated, but that the loser is the more wicked and not merely the weaker. Further, it calls into question the very fact of tragic conflict from which it so perceptively starts. No one has seen more profoundly into the nature of the tragic situation than Hegel and its stark clash of equally legitimate rights. But his solution, expressed in Schiller's dictum *Die Weltgeschichte ist das Weltgericht,* as Hegel develops it, makes the philosophy of history a theodicy. It thereby vulgarizes tragedy. For it attempts to console man with a dialectical proof that his agony and defeat are not really evils but necessary elements in the goodness of the whole. The position is essentially religious. No monotheistic religion which conceives of God as both omnipotent and benevolent, no metaphysics which asserts that the world is rational, necessary and good has any room for genuine tragedy.

The approach of love is incomplete and ambiguous. It is incomplete because if love is more than a feeling of diffused sympathy but is expressed in action no *man* can love everyone or identify himself with every interest. Empirically love has produced as much disunity as unity in the world—not only in Troy but in Jerusalem. Injustice is often born of love, not only of self-love but of love of some rather than others. Love is not only incomplete but ambiguous. There are various kinds of love and the actions to which they lead may be incompatible. An order of distinction is required. A man's love for his family must be discriminatory: his love of mankind not. He cannot love both in the same way without denying one or the other. The quality of love is altered with the range of its generalization. In one sense love always shows a bias which reinforces some conflicting interest; in another it gives all conflicting values its blessing without indicating any specific mode of action by which conflict can be mediated. Love may enable a person to live with the burden of guilt which he assumes when he sacrifices one right to another. But it is no guide to social conflict as the last two thousand years have shown. Because the Lord loves man equally nothing follows logically about the equality of man before the Law. "The *Agape* quality of love," says Tillich, "sees man as God sees him." But what *man* can tell us how *God* sees man? "Agape," continues Tillich, "loves in everybody and through everybody loves itself." Karl Barth speaks more simply and intelligibly, and with a basic brutality which is the clue to his crude neutralism, when he claims that such love has no bearing whatever for the organization of any human society.

Finally there is the method of creative intelligence. It, too, tries to make it possible for men to live with the tragic conflict of goods and rights and duties, to mediate not by arbitrary fiat but through informed and responsible decision. Whoever uses this method must find his way among all the conflicting claims. He must therefore give each one of them and the interests it represents tongue or voice. Every claimant therefore has a right to be heard. The hope is that as much as possible of each claim may be incorporated in some inclusive or shared interest which is accepted because the alternatives are less satisfactory. To this end we investigate every relevant feature about it, the conditions under which it emerged, its proximate causes and consequences, the costs of gratifying it, the available alternatives and *their* costs. Every mediation entails some sacrifice. The quest for the unique good of the situation, for what is to be done here and now, may point to what is better than anything else available but what it points to is also a lesser evil. It is a lesser evil whether found in a compromise or in moderating the demand of a just claim or in learning to live peacefully with one's differences on the same general principle which tells us that divorce is better for all parties concerned than a murder. In every case the rules, the wisdom, the lessons of the past are to be applied but they have presumptive, not final, validity because they may be challenged by new presumptions. "The pragmatic import of the logic of individualized situations," says Dewey, "is to transfer the attention of theory from pre-occupation with general conceptions to the problem of developing effective methods of inquiry," and applying them. It is a logic which does not preach solutions but explores the suggestions which emerge from the analyses of problems. Its categorical imperative is to inquire, to reason together, to seek in every crisis the creative devices and inventions that will not only make life fuller and richer but tragedy bearable. William James makes essentially the same point as Dewey in the language of ideals. Since in the struggles between ideals "victory and defeat there must be, the victory to be philosophically prayed for is that of the more inclusive side—of the side which even in the hour of triumph will to some degree do *justice* to the ideals in which the vanquished interests lay. . . ." But prayer is not enough. He goes on: "*Invent some manner* of realizing your own ideals which will also satisfy the alien demands—that and that only is the path of peace." To which we must add, provided there is a reciprocal will to peace in

242

the matter. And even then, your own or the alien demands or both must be curtailed.

As you may have gathered by this time, I have been concerned to show that this pragmatic approach to the moral problem can not only be squared with the recognition of tragic conflicts, of troubles, minor and grave, which dog the life of man in a precarious world, but that it gets its chief justification from this recognition. Intelligence may be optimistic when it deals with the control of things but the moral life by its very nature forbids the levity and superficiality which has often been attributed to the pragmatic approach by its unimaginative critics.

Indeed I make bold to claim that the pragmatic approach to tragedy is more serious, even more heroic, than any other approach because it doesn't resign itself to the bare fact of tragedy or take easy ways out at the price of truth. Where death does not result from the tragic situation, there are always consequences for continued living which it takes responsibly without yielding to despair. It does not conceive of tragedy as a pre-ordained doom, but as one in which the plot to some extent depends upon us, so that we become the creators of our own tragic history. We cannot then palm off altogether the tragic outcome upon the universe in the same way as we can with a natural disaster.

Contrast this attitude towards tragedy with the Hegelian fetishism of history which in the end is but the rationalization of cruelty. Contrast it with the Judaic-Christian conception which offers at the price of truth, the hope that the felicities of salvation will both explain and recompense human suffering. Contrast it with the attitude of Unamuno whose hunger for immortality is so intense that he sees in intelligence or reason the chief enemy of life, both in time and eternity. For him the joy and delight of life is the conflict of value and value no matter what the cost. "The very essence of tragedy," he tells us, "is the combat of life with reason." And since the Inquisitor is concerned with the eternal life of his victim's soul, the potential victim must defend the Inquisitor's place in society and regard him as far superior to the merchant who merely ministers to his needs. "There is much more humanity in the Inquisitor," he says. Crazed by this thirst for the infinite, Unamuno glorifies war as the best means of spreading love and knowledge. He illustrates the dialectic of total absurdity and caprice in thought which often prepares the way for atrocity in life. Here is no quest for the better, for the extension of reasonable controls in life and society, for peace in action.

To be sure, Unamuno is so horrified by the flux of things in which all things are ultimately liquefied that he expresses pity for the very "star-strewn heavens" whose light will some day be quenched. But this cosmic sentimentality is disdainful of the vexations, unheroic daily tasks of mediating differences, even of mitigating the consequences of irreconcilable conflicts, of devising ways to limit human suffering whose ubiquitous presence is the alleged cause of spiritual agony.

No two thinkers seem so far removed from each other as Miguel de Unamuno and Bertrand Russell—and as philosophers they are indeed related as a foothill to a Himalayan peak. But this makes all the more significant the similarity of their attitude towards the arts of social control which require the extension of man's power over nature. For Russell, any philosophy, and particularly one like Dewey's, which interprets ideas as implicit guides to activity and behavior, and knowledge as dependent upon experimental reconstructive activity in the situation which provokes it, exhibits "the danger of what may be called cosmic impiety." It is an arrogant power-philosophy whose insolence towards the universe is hardly less objectionable when it stresses social power than individual power.

It is fortunate that Russell's attitude—in which he is not always consistent—towards scientific power and control of our natural environment has not prevailed, otherwise the whole of modern civilization including modern medicine would never have developed. The charge of megalomania against any view of knowledge just because it is not a pure spectator view is absurd. For the pragmatic view accepts the Spinozistic dictum that nature can be changed only by nature's means. The problem is to discover or devise these means. This cannot be intelligently done without experimental activity. According to Russell's own position, power itself is neither good nor bad but only the uses and ends of power. But since he also tells us that there is no such thing as a rational or irrational end, that intelligence or reason is helpless in determining what we should do with our power, one can argue with much better warrant that it is *his* view, *if acted upon*, that increases "the danger of vast social disaster" than the pragmatic view which believes that by changing nature and society, men can to some extent change themselves in the light of rationally determined ends. No humane person can read history without being moved more by man's failures to use the knowledge he has had to remove the evils and sufferings which were remedial than by his attempt to achieve too great a control or power over nature. It was not science which was responsible for the use of the atomic bomb. It was politics—a failure of politics to understand the true situation. The pitiful disparity at any particular time between what we know and don't know is sufficient to inspire a sense of humility in the most intellectually ambitious. But it is only in the most vulgarized sense of the term "pragmatism," a sense which Russell helped to popularize by flagrant misunderstandings, that the adequacy of a theory of knowledge, which regards activity or experiment as integral to the achievement of knowledge of fact, can be judged by its alleged social consequences.

I am more interested tonight in stating a position than establishing it. As I understand the pragmatic perspective on life, it is an attempt to make it possible for men to live in a world of inescapable tragedy,—a tragedy which flows from the conflict of moral ideals,—without lamentation, defiance or make-believe. According to this perspective even in the best of human worlds there will be tragedy—tragedy perhaps without bloodshed but certainly not without tears. It focuses its analysis on problems of normative social inquiry in order to reduce the costs of tragedy. Its view of man is therefore melioristic, not optimistic. Some philosophers belittle man by asking him to look at the immensities without: others belittle him by asking him to look at the perversities and selfishness within. Pragmatism denies nothing about the world or men which one truly finds in them but it sees in men something which is at once, to use the Sophoclean phrase, more wonderful and more terrible than anything else in the universe, viz., the power to make themselves and the world around them better or worse. In this way pragmatic meliorism avoids the romantic pessimism of Russell's free man, shaking his fist in defiance of a malignant universe, and the grandiose optimism of Niebuhr's redeemed man with his delusions of a cosmic purpose which he knows is there but knows in a way in which neither he nor anyone else can possibly understand.

To the meliorist the recognition of the gamut of tragic possibilities is what feeds his desire to find some method of negotiating conflicts of value by intelligence rather than war, or brute force. But this is not as simple as it sounds. There is no substitute for intelligence. But intelligence may not be enough. It may not be enough because of limitations of our knowledge, because of the limited reach of our powers of control. It may not be enough because of the recalcitrance of will—not merely the recalcitrance of will to act upon goods already known and not in dispute, but because of unwillingness to find out what the maximizing good in the situation is. And although we are seeking to settle conflicts of value by the use of intelligence rather than by force, is it not true that sometimes intelligence requires the use of force?

Let us take this last question first. Faced by a momentous conflict of values in which some value must give way if the situation is to be resolved, the rational approach is to find some encompassing value on the basis of some shared interest. This, as we have seen, involves willingness to negotiate—to negotiate honestly. The grim fact, however, is that there is sometimes no desire to reason, no wish to negotiate except as a holding action to accumulate strategic power, nothing but the reliance of one party or the other upon brute force even when other alternatives may exist. In such cases the moral onus rests clearly upon those who invoke force. Their victory no more establishes their claim to be right than a vandal's destruction of a scientist's instruments of inquiry has any bearing on the validity of his assertions, evidence for or against which could have been gathered by the instrument destroyed. The intelligent use of force to *prevent* or crush the use of force where a healthy democratic process, equitable laws and traditions and customs of freedom make it possible to vent differences in a rational and orderly way, is therefore justifiable even if on prudential grounds one may forego such action. This means that tolerance always has limits—it cannot tolerate what is itself actively intolerant.

There is a tendency in modern philosophical thought which, in rejecting too sweeping claims for the role of intelligence in human affairs, settles for too little even when it does not embrace a wholesale skepticism. Of course, a man may know what is right and not do it just as he may know what is true and not publicly assert it. In neither case is this a ground for maintaining that we cannot know what action is more justified than another or what assertion is more warranted than another. The *refusal* to follow a rational method, to give good reasons is one thing: the claim that there are different rational methods, different *kinds* of good reasons each with its own built-in modes of validity, is something else again—and to me unintelligible. To be sure, the acceptance of rational method is not enough. Men must have some non-rational element in common. Hume is on unquestionably solid ground in asserting that reason must always *serve* a human need, interest or passion. But his mistake outweighed his insight when he contended that rational method could only be a servant or slave of what it served and that needs, interests and passions could not be changed or transformed by the use of intelligence. In our flights into space if we encounter other sentient creatures capable of communicating with us, it is more likely that their logical and mathematical judgment will be the same as ours than their ethical judgments, because we can more readily conceive creatures of different needs than of different minds.

At any rate the world we live in is one in which men do not share all their needs and interests and yet it is one in which they have sufficient needs and interests in common to make possible their further extension, and to give intelligence a purchase, so to speak, in its inquiry.

The most difficult of all situations is one in which even the common use of methods of inquiry seems to lead to conclusions which are incompatible with each other although each is objectively justified. There is always an open possibility of ultimate disagreement no matter how far and long we pursue rational inquiry. We can conceive it happening. In such situations we must resign ourselves to living with our differences. Otherwise we must fight or surrender. But it is simply a non-sequitur to maintain that because no guarantee can be given that there will not be ultimate disagreement, penultimate agreements cannot be validly reached and justified.

In any case we cannot in advance determine the limits of reason or intelligence in *human* affairs. So long as we don't know where it lies, it is sensible to press on, at the same time devising the means to curb the effects of the refusal to reason when it manifests itself. Above all, we must avoid oversimplifying the choice of evils and encouraging the hope that to be unreasonable will pay dividends.

We are moving into another period of history in which freedom once more is being readied for sacrifice on the altars of survival. The Munichmen of the spirit are at work again. The stakes are now for the entire world. Our task as philosophers is not to heed partisan and excited calls for action, but rather to think through the problems of freedom and survival afresh. In a famous pronouncement two years ago Bertrand Russell declared that if the Kremlin refused to accept reasonable proposals of disarmament, the West should disarm unilaterally "even if it means the horrors of Communist domination." Although he no longer believes this, there are many others who do. I know that common sense is at a discount in philosophy but in ethics it should not be lightly disregarded. A position like this obviously can have only one effect, viz., to encourage the intransigence of those who wish to destroy the free world without which there cannot be a free philosophy. You cannot negotiate successfully by proclaiming in advance that you will capitulate if the other side persists in being unreasonable. Our alternatives are not limited to surrender and extinction of freedom, on the one hand, and war and the danger of human extermination on the other. There are other alternatives to be explored—all tragic in their costs but not equally extreme. The very willingness, if necessary, to go down fighting in defence of freedom may be the greatest force for peace when facing an opponent who makes a fetish of historical survival. On pragmatic grounds, the willingness to act on a position like Kant's *fiat justitia, pereat mundus* may sometimes—I repeat—sometimes—be the best way of preserving a just and free world—just as the best way of saving one's life is sometimes to be prepared to lose it. The uneasy peace we currently enjoy as a result of "the balance of terror" is tragic. But it may turn out that it is less so than any feasible alternative today. If it endures long enough and it becomes clear to the enemies of freedom that they cannot themselves survive war, they may accept the moral equivalents of war in the making. The pragmatic program is always to find moral equivalents for the expression of natural impulses which threaten the structure of our values.

I have perhaps overstressed the sense of the tragic in human life in an effort to compensate for the distortions to which pragmatism has been subject. There is more in life than the sense of the tragic. There is laughter and joy and the sustaining discipline of work. There are other dimensions of experience besides the moral. There is art and science and religion. There are other uses for intelligence besides the resolution of human difficulties. There is intellectual play and adventure. But until men become Gods—which will never be—they will live with the sense of the tragic in their hearts as they go in quest for wisdom. Pragmatism, as I interpret it, is the theory and practice of enlarging human freedom in a precarious and tragic world by the arts of intelligent social control. It may be a lost cause. I do not know of a better one. And it may not be lost if we can summon the courage and intelligence to support our faith in freedom— and enjoy the blessings of a little luck.

On the Tragic

MAX SCHELER

IN THE following we will speak of no particular art in which tragic is portrayed. It is impossible to arrive at the phenomenon of the tragic through the art product alone, although the results of examining its extant forms might be most fruitful in discovering what it really is. The tragic is rather an essential element of the universe itself. The material made use of by the art product and the tragedian must contain beforehand the dark strain of this element. To determine what makes a tragedy genuine we must first have as precise a notion as possible of the phenomenon.

It is doubtful whether the tragic is essentially an esthetic phenomenon. We are speaking of life and history in general without placing ourselves in any particular esthetic circumstance, no matter how unusually full of tragic events and circumstances. The question of how the tragic works on our emotions or of how we come to "enjoy" the tragic in some art form we are purposely avoiding. These things can not tell us what the tragic is. The usual "psychological" method of observation, proceeding from the investigation of the experiences of one observing a tragic incident to its "objective understanding," tries to discover and describe the evocations of these experiences. Such a method avoids the issue rather than clarifies it.[1] It tells us only what the tragic does, not what it is. The tragic is above all a property which we observe in events, fortunes, characters, and the like, and which actually exists in them. We might say that it is given off by them like a heavy breath, or seems like an obscure glimmering that surrounds them. In it a specific feature of the world's makeup appears before us, and not a condition

[1] Even the famous definition of Aristotle: The tragic is that which arouses pity and fear.

249

of our own ego, nor its emotions, nor its experience of compassion and fear. What goes on in the observer of the tragic as he feels this heavy breath and sees this shimmering darkness that encircles the head of the "tragic hero" is not related to his ability to understand this phenomenon by using his own symbolical way of looking at this feature in the world's makeup. There are people who are blind, or half-blind, to the tragic—like Raphael, Goethe, and Maeterlinck.[2] One must know what the tragic is to depict this experience. Moreover, the experience is historically far more variable than the tragic itself. A tragedy of Aeschylus arouses entirely different emotions today than in his time, although the tragic is just as perceptible to both ages.

The mental processes of understanding the tragic, the inner perception of how it is brought to us, are to be distinguished from what one experiences in observing the tragic. This is not the same as the "experience" theory of the tragic. It has nothing to do with depicting the way it works on us psychologically. However, the former places the problem close to the essence of the tragic and its essential manifestations. Consequently, it should not be disregarded.

How then should we proceed? Should we indiscriminately gather together examples of the tragic, selecting those events that impress men as being such, and then ask what they possess in common? This would be a method of induction that would lend itself well to experimental support. Yet this would bring us only to the observation of our own ego when the tragic works upon us. What right have we to trust men when they call something tragic? A plurality of opinion does not help here. Without knowledge of what the tragic is, must we be forced to decide between the opinions that have weight and those which do not? But even taking this for granted, we would still have to justify ourselves. We would have a confused mass that we would call tragic. What would the common element be that would justify this judgment of ours? Nothing more than the fact that they are all called tragic.

All induction would presuppose that one knows beforehand what the essence of the tragic is, and not just what events are tragic. Our method of procedure will be different. The few examples and statements of others that may be given are not to serve as the basis for abstracting by induction a concept of the tragic. They will rather give us some rough

2 Cf. Maeterlinck's *La Sagesse et la Destinée*.

draft in which to see the basic use of the word and the phenomenon expressed therein, without taking into account who uses the word and to what intent. They will provide the basis for seeing in what experience this phenomenon comes to its given state. We do not assume that the examples are facts in which the tragic adheres as a property. They are only something which will contain the basic manifestations of the tragic. They will provide us with the opportunity of searching out these manifestations and finally of arriving at the tragic itself. It is not a question here of proofs but of indications or signs.

One should also guard against treating the tragic as a phenomenon with its own metaphysical, religious, and otherwise speculative interpretations. The tragic is not the result of an interpretation of the world and the important events of the world. It is a fixed and powerful impression that certain things make and one which can itself be subjected to many different interpretations. Theories like that which Maeterlinck proposes, basically the theory of every Rationalism and Pantheism, are totally wrong. According to these theories the tragic is the result of a false and unstable interpretation of the world. The tragic is attributed to the ways of thinking in uncivilized times with uncontrolled emotions. Or it is a sort of sudden bewilderment in the face of the defects of the world against which one knows of no help, or—what is the simple consequence of this as stated by Maeterlinck—no helper is at hand, no helper to put the matter in order? They obscure rather than clarify the essence of the tragic; their own outlook and times prevent them from seeing it. We, however, reason that these interpretations of the world are wrong because they have no place for the undeniable fact of the tragic and that any age which does not perceive it is insignificant.

Metaphysical interpretations of the tragic are most interesting. But the phenomenon itself is taken for granted by them. Certain metaphysicians like Eduard von Hartmann make God Himself the tragic hero. Others think the tragic lies only on the surface of things and that underneath all tragedies lies an imperceptible harmony, into which they are finally resolved. But to know where the tragic has its source, whether in the basic structure of existence or in human passions and unrest, is to know already what the tragic is.

Every interpretation fails before the inflexibility of reality which reduces it to silence.

This question of the tragic is only one example of the importance of contrasting the changing whims of the times with the facts of reality.

All that can be called tragic is contained within the realm of values and their relationships.

In a universe free of values, such as that constructed by mechanical physics, there are no tragedies.

Only where there is high and low, nobleman and peasant, is there anything like a tragic event.

The tragic is not a value like beautiful, ugly, good, or bad. The tragic appears in objects only through the interplay of their inherent values.

It is always founded on values or connected with values. To repeat, it is found only in that realm where there are objects of value and where these work in one way or another on each other.

Serenity, sadness, grandeur, and earnestness can be classified among the more tranquil values. The tragic is absent here. It appears in the realm of changing values and circumstances. Something must happen for it to appear. There must be a period of time in which something is lost or destroyed.

In empty space—Schiller notwithstanding—dwells much sublimity, but not the tragic. In a spaceless world the tragic might be possible, but never in a timeless world. In its basic connotations the tragic always implies a determined effectiveness in doing and in suffering. The tragic "character" remains such only as long as he has the necessary dispositions for tragic acting and suffering. Even a situation calling for opposition of forces or their reconciliation is only tragic as long as it contains this effectiveness. If the tragic is to appear, however, this effectiveness must take on a definite direction, a direction toward the annihilation of a positive value in a determined hierarchy. The strength which annihilates it must possess this value itself.

To belong to the category of the tragic some value must be destroyed. With regard to man it does not have to be his existence or his life. But at least something of his must be destroyed—a plan, a desire, a power, a possession, a faith. The destruction as such is not tragic. It is rather the course that an object of lower or equal positive values, never of higher values, is able to force upon it. We can hardly call it tragic for a good man to defeat and bring about the downfall of an evil man, nor for a nobleman to do the same to a peasant. Moral approval precludes a tragic impression here. This much is certain. It is also certain that it must be an object of high positive value that destroys a value. (Values such as the honest with respect to the wicked, the good with regard to the bad, and the beautiful compared to the ugly, are here called positive. All values have this opposition and duality, even excluding their degree of "higher" and "lower.") The tragic is apparent only where the strength to destroy a higher positive value proceeds from an object possessing this positive value. The manifestation is, moreover, purest and clearest where objects of equally high value appear to undermine and ruin each other. Those tragedies most effectively portray the tragic phenomenon in which, not only is every one in the right, but where each person and power in the struggle presents an equally superior right, or appears to fulfill an equally superior duty. If an object of higher positive value, let us take for example a good, just man, is overpowered by some insignificant evil object, the tragic is at once senseless and irrational. In place of arousing tragic pity, it arouses painful indignation. Tragic pity can never fall completely into the depths of pain and disgust, but must maintain some semblance of coolness and calmness.

The tragic is first of all a struggle that is occasioned in an object of high positive value, i.e., of a high moral nature, generally treating of the family, marriage, or the state. The tragic is a "conflict" which takes place between the positive value and the very object which possesses it. The great art of the tragedian is to set each value of the conflicting elements in its fullest light, to develop completely the intrinsic rights of each party.

ON THE TRAGIC AND GRIEF

It is true that in some way all tragic events are sad, but in a very definite sense. This is precisely what fate is, an event surrounded by this quality of sadness.[3] On the other hand it arouses sorrow in the feelings of men. It makes the soul sad. Not all sad persons are tragic characters, however. Every

---

[3] That the quality of the sad is definitely not a "feeling," nor a so-called "empathic feeling," cf. the essay, *"Idole der Selbsterkenntnis."*

death is sad and makes those left behind sad as well, but assuredly not every death is tragic. Let us disregard for a moment that type of grief that is produced in us independently of any perception of values, almost as if caused by a "neutral" feeling. We would rather consider the "grieved over something." The nature of a certain event arouses our sentiments and produces this feeling in us. It should not appear to be caused by our individual wishes or aims, but only by the worth of the object. The tragic grief has a double characteristic, one rooted in itself, the other in its subject.

This kind of grief is free from all indignation, anger, reproach, and that accompanying the desire "if it had only been otherwise." It is a calm, quiet fullness; a special kind of peace and composure is characteristic of it.

The atmosphere of tragic grief will be absent if we are aroused to do something about it. Once the event has been completed and brought to its climax, any indication of a compromise or of some chance to avert the catastrophe makes tragic grief impossible.

Tragic grief contains a definite composure. It is thus distinguished from all specifically personal griefs, those which come from a personal experience of being "sad about something." It comes to us from the outside through the soul; it is occasioned by events that are "tragic." The tragedies of Aeschylus show especially well how to awaken this atmosphere of grief in its utmost purity.

We will now point out the twofold characteristic feature of the tragic which causes this atmosphere. One is the very nature of the world's makeup; every individual sad event is thus determined. The other is based on the appearance of an uncompromising inevitability of the destruction of a value, a species of destruction which every tragedy must contain.

In every genuine tragedy we see more than just the tragic event. We see over and above it the permanent factors, associations, and powers which are in the very makeup of the world. It is these which make such a thing possible.[4] In every tragic event we are directly confronted with a definite condition of the world's makeup without deliberation or any sort of "interpretation." This confronts us in the event itself; it does not result from what it does to the things which brought it about. It is only momentarily connected with the event and is independent of the elements that make it up. It is present in the form of a slight presentiment.

[4] We mean "such a thing" in the sense of "a so-constituted value."

Every objective grief like that of a tragic event has its own depth. (I take the word here in a transferred meaning like the "depth" of a room.) It has its own immensity, too, which distinguishes it from a very limited, determined event. The depth is brought about by the fact that its subject is two-fold. One is the element of the event that has been seen by us. The other is that point in the world's makeup that is exemplified by the event of which the event is but an example. Grief seems to pour out from the event into unlimited space. It is not a universal, abstract world-makeup that would be the same in all tragic events. It is rather a definite, individual element of the world's construction. The remote subject of the tragic is always the world itself, the world taken as a whole which makes such a thing possible. This "world" itself seems to be the object immersed in sorrow. In the foreground of this darkness of sorrow we see the specific event and fate standing out all the more clearly.

The element in the world's makeup which produces these situations seems to do so without any warning. In producing them it ignores the peculiarities of the causes of the event and even its normal effects. It is this which causes the second essential element of the tragic, its inevitability.

We will clarify this later. Right now we are interested in the peculiar atmosphere which it lends to the tragedy.

There is a whole category of feelings and affections that can be connected with the destroying of a value. Their essence is in being "preventable," even if in a particular cast they may or may not have been prevented. It doesn't matter what these feelings might be—dread, fear, anger, horror, or the like; they all have in general the characteristic of "excitement." Thinking about the possibility of its turning out otherwise, or even better, causes this excitement. In men it is more frequently caused by the thought, "If so and so had only acted differently." This excitement is able to take hold of a man only because he is a practical being and, as it were, the potential actor in any event.

It softens when the inevitability is seen as an impossibility. The grief does not cease to be what it is, but it assumes the character of the feelings of dissatisfaction, excitement, and pain. These are taken in the same narrow sense as the physical feelings of fear, horror, and the like.

Tragic grief is pure, without physical arousement. In a certain sense even a feeling of "contentment" is joined with it.

There is no desire to do away with the event which led

255

to the destruction of some value. This is abolished by seeing its inevitability.

We see that the tragic seems to have its ultimate roots in the essential makeup of the world itself. It is this which clears away all sense of culpability or responsibility. When we see this in the nature of the event a certain reconciliation takes place. It is a species of reconciliation which fills us with peace and rest and with resignation. This resignation banishes the weakness and pain that would come from contemplating a better-made world.

Thus the specific sadness of the tragic is really an objective character of the event itself. It is independent of the individual circumstances of the beholder. It is free from the feelings provoked by excitement, indignation, blame, and the like. It has a depth and immensity. It is not accompanied by physical feelings or by what can be called real pain. It has a definite resignation, contentment, and a species of reconciliation with the existence which it chances to have.

THE TRAGIC KNOT

We asserted previously that in the tragic a struggle takes place between two objects possessing high positive value and that one of them must be overcome. There is one case where this is fulfilled to the highest degree. It happens when the objects are not different events, persons, or things, but coincide in one event, person, or thing; even better, in one and the same quality, power, or ability.

It would be most tragic if the same power which has brought either itself or another object to a very high positive value becomes its destroyer—especially if this takes place in the very act of its achievement.

If we are observing a certain action which is realizing a high value, and then see in that same action that it is working towards the undermining of the very existence of the being it is helping, we receive the most complete and the clearest of tragic impressions.

The same tragic impression occurs when a special courage or boldness which permits a man to accomplish an heroic deed undermines him because it exposes him to a danger that a moderately prudent man would avoid—"If only I were prudent enough I would not be called Tell." Another example is the man with high ideals toward a spiritual goal who permits them to became shipwrecked on the little things of life. Everyone according to Madame de Staël's dictum has the mistakes of his virtue: the same traits of character which permitted a man to do his best have brought him to catastrophe.

We don't have to talk only of human beings here. An art gallery can be destroyed by the very fire that was kindled to preserve the picture. The event has a sharp tragic character. The flight of Icarus is tragic. The very wax which glued his wings to him melts in the same degree as he flies toward the sun.

The use of the phrase, "the tragic knot," is a pertinent metaphor. It illustrates the inner entanglement between the creation of a value and the destruction of a value as they take place in the unity of the tragic action and the tragic event.

Something else can be deduced from the aforesaid. It is not the relationship between values that constitutes the "stage" for the tragic event, nor is it the connection of causal events which it contains. It is rather a special reference of the value relationships to the causal relationships. It is an essential characteristic of our world—and thus of every world—that the course of the causal events disregards completely the value of things. The exigencies of values as they develop toward a unity or as they unfold themselves toward their ideal fulfillment is not taken into account by the causal series. The simple fact that the sun shines on the good and bad alike makes tragedy possible. At times it may happen that the causal relationships simultaneously coincide with an increase of the values. This is accepted as only accidental. It is not occasioned by intrinsic determination. Nor is it occasioned by a consideration of what the values need to reach their fulfillment or that the causality is at hand to produce them.

Without this basic condition there can be no tragedy.

There would be no tragedy in a world which operated on an established system of laws whereby each thing had the powers and capabilities commensurate with its values, and whereby its activity was directed only towards the exigencies of developing or unifying these values. Tragedy would likewise be impossible in a world operating on a system of laws whereby the powers would be directed against the exigencies of these values, purposely opposing them. The tragic would thrive in a satanic world as well as in a divine—a fact that Schopenhauer forgot in his discussion of the tragic.

We see the tragic only when in one glance we embrace both the causality of things and the exigencies of their immanent values. In this unified glance the mind tries to syn-

257

thetize the conditions in which it finds these values so as to arrive at the unity it is trying to achieve. Then it follows the course of events in their causal sequence. The result is a clear insight into the independence of these two things. It is here that we may see the formal "background" of all tragedies.

Obviously, it is not in the mere knowledge of this circumstance that the tragic exists. The tragic comes into sight only when this independence of the two elements becomes embodied in a concrete event.

What has just been said casts new light on our definition. For never is our insight so clear and so concentrated as when we see that the same action may in some places produce a high value and in others—quite indifferently—destroy this value.

Here then—where we are able to see the unity of an action at a single glance and not by discursive connection, limb by limb—here is a circumstance known previously only by concept which has now come tangibly within our grasp.

What do we mean when we say that in the tragic the destruction of value is "necessary"? Surely not the destruction of causality in general!

Is the question then one of "causal" necessity or is it likely to be one of quite another kind of necessity? Here one might begin to discriminate and say that it is indeed causal necessity but of a particular kind, that is, "inner necessity," and consequently a necessity which depends not on influences breaking in from the outer world but rather on the eternal nature of things and men. Only as such can things and men undergo the tragic fate. Actually, this concept of the tragic—widely held though it may be—is not borne out by the facts.

When a man who seems destined for a certain fate, either by congenital disease or by any sort of natural predisposition, is brought low the first time that external circumstance has a chance to work upon him—such an event does not seem tragic to us even if the highest values inhered in him, values independent of this natural predisposition. Thus Ibsen, with all his artistic genius, has not succeeded in making of Oswald, in *Ghosts,* a tragic figure, since the worm of destruction gnawing at Oswald is the result of a disease he has inherited from his father. We miss here something that belongs to the essence of the tragic hero: that the evil which drives the hero to his downfall pertain to those against whom the struggle is being waged, and also that such a struggle be actually waged.

Both these requirements are missing in *Ghosts*. Nor is the tragic hero to be found in him who immediately surrenders to the inimical, and who at the first dismissive word, immediately abnegates and resigns himself. The "necessity" of which we are now speaking must rather be of such a kind as to take its course even after the performance of all the "free" actions that may be tried in an attempt at flight. When we see the catastrophe opposed by all free efforts of will and means, and can still trace its irruption as "necessary"; when we can even trace, through the turmoil and anguish of this struggle to avert the catastrophe, a species of transcendent necessity: then and then only do we have an example before us of tragic "necessity."

Tragic necessity is not the necessity of the course of nature, a necessity which lies beneath freedom and the power of the will and which may be conceived as the free essence which permits the best linking of events in nature. Rather is tragic necessity of such a kind that it lies *above* freedom: it is to be found only in the conclusion of free acts or of "free causes" in the total sphere of causality, in which may be found even "unfree causes," that is, those which are the results of prior causes.

Wherever men are presented as "milieu-defined," as completely determined by "relationships," as in the naturalist "drama," we have a much less likely source of the tragic than in the drama which gives us the impression that consciously free choices are clearly and conclusively driving the events of the play to its catastrophe. Consequently neither naturalism and determinism on the one hand nor the rationalistic thesis of a "freedom of the human will" limited only by the chances of nature can provide a comprehension of the tragic, or anything more than the beginning of such comprehension. Both these views of the world have no place for the tragic since they make no provision for essential necessity reaching out above the qualities of nature and free choice.

There is still another reason why it is inadequate to define as "inner" that species of necessity we are here discussing. Immanent cause is that which in a thing or in a person exists as latent predisposition, or capacity, or skill, which functions at the inception of true relationships to other things or situations or persons. Wherever we encounter a strictly defined predisposition to the decline of value we must recognize an absence of the true development, of the veridical renewal, of the inner historicity which is needed for the tragic event: in such a situation the catastrophe itself would be predictable if we had a firm and exact picture of the character. The tragic however contains this paradox, that when we behold the destruction of value it seems completely "necessary" and at the same time completely "unpredictable." Though the catastrophe may come closer and closer, driven by all the contributory factors (whether free or not), and each new event is visibly pregnant with danger, yet there must still remain one moment when everything—even by ideal calculation—could still turn out quite differently: whereupon from all this complexity is brought forth a deed which resolves these lurking factors into the unity of one species of reality by a means not rationally predictable.

The seemingly "propitious turn of events" just before the catastrophe, which so many tragic poets have been fond of, is a special means to exclude from the audience even the slightest appearance of "predictability." Even the increase of tension, which every tragedy must arouse, would not be possible if the catastrophe did not seem to us to be well founded from the beginning in the latent inner qualities of the characters and their relationships. It is *concrete* causality, which has nothing to do with "natural law," which governs tragic events as it also governs the irreversible motions of the constellations in their consummation of causality—that species of causality which is rightly called the truly "historical." For this we must return to the assertion of Schopenhauer that tragedy never exhibits true "character development" but only "character revelation," revelation of what was previously latent as disposition and character.

Even the tragic transformation of a character, the alteration of disposition and mentality, the essential and latent diversion from the previous course of life—even this transformation is seldom either the catastrophe itself or even an important part of it. A specifically tragic phenomenon is to be seen in the interruption—even in the midst of external victories—of a course of life directed towards certain values as goals. Tragic necessity is to be seen above all in the ineluctable and inescapable, founded on the eidetic ulations of the universe.

Even these negative definitions indicate that the species of "necessity" we have been talking about becomes apparent only when every conceivable kind of skill seems to be brought into play to halt the destruction of value and to preserve the value in question. Consequently two species of value-destruction are essentially untragic: first, those instances which are tinged with guilt because someone has failed in a duty definitely assigned to him; second, those instances which might have been avoided by the use of available techniques and means. In general, then, the quality of the tragic is lacking when the question "Who is guilty?" has a clear and definite answer.

Only where no such answer can be given does the stuff of tragedy begin to appear. We may use the term "tragic" only when we feel that everyone concerned in the story has hearkened to the demands of his duty with the utmost of his capabilities, and yet the disaster has had to occur. The tragic consists—at least in human tragedies—not simply in the absence of "guilt" but rather in the fact that the guiltiness cannot be localized. Wherever we can substitute, in place of a man who plays a role in the unfolding of a catastrophe, another man who is like the first but morally better— that is, one who has a finer sympathy for moral opportunities as well as a greater energy of the moral will—to the extent that we can perform such substitution the growth of a feeling of tragedy is stunted by the amount of blame we can pin on the responsible person.

In such an instance "necessity" is missing as a quality of the tragic phenomena. Consider, for example, the death of Christ; suppose we were able to have the idea that his death, instead of being an essential relationship between His divine purity and the profaneness and opposition of an obdurate "world," had been brought about by the particular moral laxity of Pontius Pilate, or by the wickedness of an individual named Judas, or by the inimical deeds of the Jews. If we were then able to imagine Jesus of Nazareth surrounded not by these men but by a group morally "better," or if we could place him in a different historical context where he would come to higher recognition and repute—if we could do these things the impression of the tragic would vanish.

The death of Jesus is tragic only when it is presented— everywhere and forever—as the consistent adherence to the higher duty of all the parties concerned. An execution, for example, can never have a tragic culmination. The tragic appears when the idea itself of "justice" appears as leading to the destruction of higher value. An execution, if it is unavoidable, awakens deep sympathy; if it were avoidable it might arouse deep anger or irritation, but never tragic sympathy.[5]

If it is true that a disaster becomes tragic only when everyone has done his duty and, in the usual sense of the word, no one has incurred "guilt," it becomes part of the essence of tragic conflict that this conflict be guiltless and unavoidable even before judges who approach the ideal in wisdom and virtue. The tragic misdeed is even definable as that which silences all possible moral and legal powers of judgment; and, on the other hand, every conflict is essentially untragic when by moral and legal lights it is seen to be obvious and simple. Every essential confusion of the bounds of right and wrong, of good and evil, in the unity of action; every maze of threads, of motives, of views, of duties, so presented as to seem to lead equally well to a judgment of "right" or "wrong"; every complication which is not based on necessary moral and legal wisdom but which instead produces from the circumstances alone an absolute confusion of our moral and legal powers of judgment—every such complication pertains to the subjective side of tragic feeling and thereby transposes us completely from the realm of possible "right" and "wrong," from possible "accusation" and "indignation." "Tragic guilt" is of a kind for which no one can be blamed and for which no conceivable "judge" can be found.

Out of this error of our moral judgments, out of this pardonable search for a subject upon whom to pin this "guilt," a guilt which appears to us as such with crystal clarity—only out of this appears that specific tragic grief and tragic sympathy of which we have been speaking, along with its unique peace and reconciliation of the emotions. Now too the shifting of that which is to be feared to the cosmos itself appears as the essence of the reconciliation of the individual men and wills with the culminating deeds and events in which they have been taking part.

In this way, tragic guilt becomes something other than definable "right" and "wrong," or than "obeying obligation" or "defying obligation."

But individual men have quite different microcosms of values, dependent on the extent of their actual moral awareness and even on the extent of their possible moral aware-

---

[5] It is for this reason that Aeschylus, in his *Eumenides,* furnishes the judges of the Areopagus with both black and white marbles to indicate the guilt or innocence of Orestes.

ness. Only on these bases can be measured their possible "duties" and areas of duty—quite independently of all the peculiarities of their empirical real situations. If every individual does his "duty," to the extent that he does this he behaves *morally;* not otherwise can he do something of equal *value* or *be* in any way of equal value. How deep his gaze thereby penetrates into the macrocosm of moral value, which contains the entire extent of the realm of possible good and evil, and how deep a hold he takes within this macrocosm, are in no way to be decided by the extent to which each individual dutifully produces the "best" of the realm of values with which he has been endowed. It is not duty and the performance of it that "ennoble"—as the Kantian, short-sighted ethic puts it—but rather "noblesse oblige": this is the original nobility of man, which establishes for him quite varied arrays of possible duties—duties which stand in varied relationships to the moral world and are variously "significant" for it.

It makes a difference whether the man doing his duty is a grocer or a noble king; the first one in a vague way obeys a few moral value-distinctions, doing his "duty" with a couple of poor concepts of choice, while the other, living in the fullness of manifold human and other moral relationships, with a finely articulated and higher realm of moral value-distinctions before his eyes, does his "duty" while he demonstrates the highest value given to him, and in will and deed realizes this value. The latter man in this action must conduct himself as occasionally opposed to duty, while the man blind to value blandly performs *his* "duty." If we were now to say that in a true tragic presentation everyone must do his "duty," or at least that it would be prudent so to do, and that—even if everyone has done his duty—the destruction of value and the consequent lessening of the total moral value of the world must nevertheless take place, we would thereby still not know how to exclude this quite different dimension of the moral value-distinction of the individual and of his being taking part in the tragedy. It is rather a quite different species of the tragic which, in this dimension of being, bruises "noble" individuals against the strongly articulated "duties" of the mob. And it appears to be a particular melancholy-ironic glory of this kind of tragedy that the noble individual should accept a moral guilt that his companions do not accept. To the extent that the noble person can more easily become "guilty" than the ignoble—in accord with his richer and higher realm of duties—he is susceptible to a moral "risk" which ever bears with it something potentially tragic, as this risk simultaneously praises and blames his noble nature. The Prometheus of technic, who stole fire from Zeus, is a tragic figure; but even more tragic are the moral Prometheuses in whose eyes a moral world comes with the brilliance of lightning, a moral world that never previously existed . . . While they are realizing values and acquiring duties which the vulgar do not yet know how to see as value or to feel as duty, the vulgar are themselves only doing their "duty" while the noble see as "evil" what may still be "good" for the vulgar. Here is one instance of the tragic "fall" for the "noble," in that his every eventual moral disapproval of the vulgar must necessarily remain silent—to the extent that only through "good consciences" can his sacred "duty" be accomplished.

We can now penetrate more deeply into "tragic guilt" if we are careful to remain clear on the matter of what, in such a case, is the completion of the duty of the noble. Let it be a proposition here—with no attempt at proof—that moral "good" is the relation by which we realize or tend to realize in a given action that a preference indicates a more highly conceived value.[6] To prefer the higher value is always equivalent to depreciating the lower value, that is, to discontinue the realization of this lower value. However, all "moral norms," i.e., all imperative rules of a general type, are only exercises in what to will and what to do, as suggested by the average levelling of values in any given epoch resulting from the "situations" which are typical of and regularly recurring in this epoch; still, even this levelling of values provides "higher" values which must be realized. Every material rule of morality contains the presuppositions of the particular positive world of good appropriate to its level of civilization. What happens then when the "noble" man perceives a value which is higher than the average, a value which is generally trodden under in the levelling of values, and accomplishes his advance in the moral cosmos of value, an advance that the vulgar are not yet ready to grasp? In such a case it must be obvious to him that what appears "good" and "dutiful" according to the ruling morality now becomes wicked and evil—and by the same token becomes for him "opposed to duty." And this realization is not avoidable but rather—to use a term of Kant's—a "necessary perception" ("*notwendiger Schein*"). And since everything that can be generally a

6 Cf. my book, *Der Formalismus in der Ethik und die materiale Wertethik,* vol. I, Niemeyer, Halle, 1914.

"moral law"—even to the most complete codification and strongly logical presentation of these laws—inevitably exhibits the positive material world of values of the "time," the "time" itself being determined by the prevailing system of value-levelling—such a man must violate the prevailing moral precepts and also violate everything in the moral world that comes into the orbit of such precepts. He must necessarily appear "guilty" even before the fairest judge, when he is in fact guiltless and is so seen by God alone. That this is so is not an irregularity but rather part of the essence of all moral development. Here I mean to point out the root of that necessary and "guiltless guilt," which has hitherto been expressed in this paradoxical form only with a feeling for the justice of it. What is essential here is the necessity of the deception into which the most just moralist must blunder when confronted with the "tragic hero." Although the tragic hero with moral awareness[7] is obviously essentially the opposite of a sinner, he cannot be distinguished from a sinner by the age in which he lives. Only to the extent that his newly experienced value becomes established and becomes the prevailing "morality" can he be seen and known—and then only in historical retrospect—as a moral hero. And so there are no present tragedies—there are only tragedies of the past. The tragic man necessarily goes his way in his "present" quiet and speechless. He strides unrecognized through the mob; he may even be there considered a sinner. The error of an instance which separates genius from sinner is here not an accidental but a necessary error. Here, in this tragic fate of the moral genius we can perhaps grasp, in a single species and fashion, the nerve of fate, the complete unpredictability of moral development in man. And even in the absolutely inevitable "fate" and the related absolute loneliness of the moral genius we can see a moment of the type of the tragic, as it may have happened to Jesus in Gethsemane. Here likewise appears the total fate of the world as it appears compressed into the experience of one man, as though in this moment he were standing alone and yet in the "middle," in the center of all the forces that animate the universe. His experience is as though whole epochs of history occurred in him, yet with no one else being aware of his experience—as though everything lay unified in his hand. And perhaps through this something more may become clear: the tragic

---

[7] We are speaking here only of this kind and not of the tragic hero in general.

hero of this kind is not guilty of his guilt, but rather it "happens" to him: this justifiable circumlocution repeats a very characteristic moment of "tragic guilt." That is: that the "guilt" comes to him and not he to the guilt! . . . *"Ihr fuhrt ins Leben ihn hinein . . ."*

Nevertheless this "fall" into guilt does not mean that the tragic hero, either through immoderate passion or through stress and a drive in one direction, is so moved that this drive becomes the central point of his ego and his will consequently is impelled in this same direction. This is also the case in the usual moral guiltiness—at least in great measure; and quantities cannot here serve as a basis for differentiation. Even in the midst of the most powerful stresses the will which "follows" such a direction remains a new action, an action not entirely determined by this stress! The tragic guilt into which the hero "falls" is much more accurately characterized by calling it a "guilty" doing or renunciation of doing which darkens the areas of his possible choices and so makes a certain kind of guilt unavoidable, since the choice of the "best" meaning is necessarily in error.

Moral or "guilty guilt" is based on the act of choice; tragic or unguilty guilt is rather based on the sphere of choice! The act of choice is consequently for the tragic hero free of guilt —just the reverse of what obtains in moral guilt, in which the sphere of choice also entails objectively guiltless possibilities, and only the guilt of the act is important. And so the tragic hero "becomes guilty" while doing a guiltless thing.

The consequence of what has been said is the absurdity of the schoolmasters' theory that a moral guiltiness is to be sought in tragedies, and that the tragic poet instead of being a respectable performer of a tragic phenomenon is made into a moral judge over his heroes, whom he punishes for their deeds while at the same time he animates them to perform those deeds. Only total blindness for the phenomenon of tragedy could hatch out this silliest of all theories.

But we should also fall into error if we should try to make the correct concept of tragic guilt serve as the complete definition of the tragic phenomenon. However, since from its earliest presentations the tragic has been a universal phenomenon, not specifically human or limited to static will, such a definition is self-destructive. However, note this: where a "tragic guilt" is actually portrayed—and it is not the deed of the hero which brings the guilt upon him or is involved in the "catastrophe," nor is his downfall the bearer of the tragic phenomenon, but rather the "guilt of error" itself, and consequently the fact that purity of will falls into guilt—here is the very bearer and root of the tragic.

In this way it is tragic that Othello falls into the guilt of having to kill his beloved, and that guiltless Desdemona should be killed by her beloved who loves her. In his own words, "For, in my sense, 'tis happiness to die," the death of Othello is not punishment for his deed, which as "punishment" must terminate a conscious evil; rather is it deliverance. Tragic guilt is therefore not a condition of the tragic phenomenon— which would indeed be a *circulus in demonstrando*, if the guilt had to be not any sort of "guilt" but only "tragic" guilt— but it is a species of the tragic itself, and to the extent that we are here dealing with moral value, it is therefore a species of absolute value—so to speak, the culminating point of the tragic. Neither death nor any other mischance but only his "fall into guilt" constitutes the tragic fate of the hero.

Translated by Bernard Stambler

On Tragedy

STUART HAMPSHIRE

MR WILLIAMS intends this book[1] to be "about the connections, in modern tragedy, between event and experience and idea, and its form is designed at once to explore and to emphasise these radical connections." The topic is obviously vague. Mr Williams has always used an imaginative sociology of his own. With its aid he sees in contemporary literature a true reflection of the dislocation of private lives, which, he believes, no longer keep a natural connection with a continuing social life in a community, accepted and enjoyed. His vision is of a possible lost Eden, of a wholeness falling away into fragments; the metaphor of a torn social fabric is essential to the vision. The trouble is one must suspect that this particular diagnosis of the disease of modernity is itself part of the condition diagnosed. This kind of imaginative sociology, in the tradition of Carlyle and Ruskin, may itself be an expression of a modern literary temperament, and a con-

1 *Modern Tragedy* by Raymond Williams.

venient myth for intellectuals who are uneasy in an industrial environment.

As one reads, one finds oneself wandering around in a circle, from the imagined social experience to the dramatic literature, and from the literature to the social experience; there is a pattern of interpretation, but no independent confirmation that anything is explained by the pattern. Lukacs's famous studies of Scott and Balzac have opened the way for this strangely intuitive, yet historical, criticism of literature. It amounts to a reversal of Marxism, for a supposed social consciousness replaces any hard, materialistic analysis of social facts as a basis for understanding the decay of literary forms. One may perhaps convince oneself, one may have a dim feeling, that this fragmentation of the social fabric, first suggested by Hegel, is a real feature of modern experience, separately identifiable, and not just a familiar theme, and a recurring fiction, of the imagination. But literary criticism in this style will still seem a prosaic substitute for the original writing which it interprets. Criticism becomes a programme for, or a preface to, a possible fiction, and approaches the condition of fiction itself. It is not inappropriate, therefore, that Mr Williams should end this book with a play of his own.

The historical imaginative style of criticism has become so familiar, as a separate literary genre, that one overlooks the enormity of the assumptions that must be made if it is to be taken literally. Are we to suppose that men's dreams change with changing social relations? Is there not an imagery, and are there not associated themes of fantasy and fiction, which are independent of any adult consciousness of learnt social relations? It has been plausibly suggested that the sources of the interest we take in tragic action on the stage are not unrelated to the religious feelings that surround the doctrines of the Fall, of Judgment, of predestination and salvation. The doctrinal setting of these inchoate ideas may change from period to period; the social setting in which they present themselves will certainly change; the shape and sonority of sentences, the quality of the rhetoric, will change correspondingly. These are changes that touch the surface of the mind, and are a proper part of the history of drama as a history of styles; they may even help to explain its abrupt decays and rebirths. But surely the substance of an interest in tragedy cannot be found here: for the sources of the philosophical ideas that make an action, represented or real, a tragic action are primarily the subject-matter of individual psychology, if not of philosophy.

A tragic disappointment is one that admits of no remedy in social action, or in any alteration of the specific conditions of the action. The disappointment lies in the nature of action itself, as intrinsically liable to accident and mistake, and also in the double face of virtue as carrying its own defect with it, a returning echo that mocks the first intention. Enjoyment of tragedy marks a point of breakdown in the hold that moral ideas have upon us, a breakdown that is the more strongly felt in proportion as moral ideas are clearly defined. This is one place of entry for tragedy, familiar to everyone from their intimate experience. Morality presupposes a relation that is humanly intelligible between intention and achievement, and it therefore also presupposes a kind of inhuman, or real, justice upon which human justice can be built. But even in childhood, this relation is felt to be insecure. Filial and other loyalties are too often seen to be a form of murder and treason, and the clear-sighted repair of wrong in the house too often turns out to be its destruction. So the judgment of action is shifted towards its consequences, where one knows that, from the standpoint of morality, it should not be.

It is not so much that a great ambition, the will to positive action and to repair the disjointed world, fails catastrophically in a tragic situation. Rather, the action fails in a particular way and for a particular reason: the forces used are not, as they seem to be, the forces that really control human fortunes. These are always invisible to the protagonist until it is too late, and are therefore unusable, and appear, to us and to him, as accidents. So the distinction between willed or voluntary evil and involuntary evil is made to seem tenuous and uncertain, a human pretence: and yet any justifiable moral attitude requires the distinction. One may come to think that what one has achieved, not intentionally but seemingly by accident, is more indicative of one's true nature than the original intentions were.

One may be born to be blind, and at the centre of determining forces which remain unrecognised until it is too late, and precisely this may be the condition of resolute action and high intentions. Anna Karenina takes action to escape from a dead life, and finally kills herself, because of the accident, as it seems, of Vronsky's carelessness, restlessness and casual absence. The story becomes a tragedy, because of the uncharted necessities of natural law which are revealed in the lives surrounding hers. The justifiable action that should save her, and repair a loss, becomes a waste and destruction of her life, just because it was too strongly willed, or willed with a single mind. For the tragic consciousness, a strong will to put things right will end in mistake and self-destruction, because the sources of wrong are always too remote, and beyond the reach of any solitary virtue. The sources of evil are in the house and in the family. Once disjointed, house and family are locked together in a natural misfortune, which no individual energy can suddenly break.

Mr Williams has in Ibsen the obvious example of modern tragedy: modern, just because virtue takes the form in his plays of action against a social wrong, or at least against an offence to conscience or to bourgeois freedom. The pride of improvement and liberation ends in waste and destruction, leaving the survivors with their inherited stain, as if it were the shared wrong which had held them together. Within the play there has been single-minded action, and not pathos; but the liberal intentions have been shown to depend upon an ignorance, or an ignoring, of the genealogy of misfortunes, which pass across the generations as an inherited punishment. The family, as Ibsen classically represented it, is not a social unit: its links are more constant and less open to inspection, and, above all, less voluntary and less adjustable at will. Unhappy families are, as Tolstoy wrote, different from each other, fiercely coherent in their attachment to a distinguishing doom. Liberalism and the modern spirit, as Ibsen knew them, try to dismiss tragic inheritances, on the assumption that the quality of an individual life may always be rationally changed in a single generation. Ibsen was on both sides, seeing at once the modern necessity to believe and the old desperate implausibility of the reformers' assumption.

It is at least possible that the criticism that sees literature, unquestioningly, as criticism of society is itself a symptom of the decline which the critics think that they notice. The philosophical idea of tragedy requires a kind of confident individualism which no historically minded critic will retain: the necessary isolation of the individual, alone with his intention and its consequences, will seem untruthful to the historian unless some trailing edges of social analysis are added, as by Sartre. But in the setting of tragedy the social pressures on the individual are uninteresting, because they explain too much, and by the wrong kind of causality. As sometimes in Brecht, the protagonists become pathetic, victims of their historical circumstances, figures in a pageant.

There is a striking consensus in writings about tragedy, which cuts across differences of time and place. It would indeed be strange if the nature of the interest in tragedy changed with changing social conditions, at least within societies which recognise a rational morality, whether secular or religious. The contrast between tragic consequences and the catastrophes that follow imputable errors cannot be ignored, as long as justice and rational reward and punishment are at issue. Mr Williams examines the work of Lawrence, Pirandello, Eliot, Sartre, Brecht, Genet and others in search of what it is that replaces tragic fiction and drama in these representative writers: he has a variety of interesting observations to make, particularly about Lawrence. He is certainly not obliged to write another kind of book, about the philosophical ideas and psychological needs that tragedies embody. The notion of tragedy, so heavily documented, is not strictly essential to his purpose. He is simply continuing that gentle, sincere, discursive meditation—almost a spiritual autobiography—which he began in *Culture and Society*. I think he is trying to imagine the kinds of writing that would both reflect and strengthen an active community of free men, in contemporary conditions. One may respect the vision, even if one believes that an interest in tragedy is an interest in an altogether different kind of freedom.

The Tragic Vision:
The World

LUCIEN GOLDMANN

> It is from our separation and absence from the world that is born the presence and feeling for God (Saint-Cyran: *Maximes*, 263).

THERE are two distinct but complementary planes on which philosophical thought considers the relationship between man and the world: that of historical progress, and that of the ontological reality which both conditions this progress and makes it possible. Thus, men do not see the world as an unchanging unreality given once and for all, since we cannot know what the world is like "in itself," when not seen through the categories of the human mind. There is only one reality which we can gradually come to know through our historical researches, and only one possible starting-point for philosophical investigation: it is the succession of ways in which men have, in the course of history, seen, felt, understood and, above all, changed the world in which they lived, felt and thought. It is only when he studies the way in which different social worlds and different world views have followed one another in history that the philosopher can begin to discover what is common to all the different relationships which man has had with the world and with his fellows. It is this common element which made it possible for these different world views to follow one another in a manner comprehensible to human reason.[1] Yet, even as we attempt to discover the basic and objective element common to all forms of social organisation, we must always remember that we see this in a human and consequently subjective manner; we should therefore resist the strong and permanent temptation to consider our own social world as the world (ontologically speaking), and to look upon it as the one with which men have always been confronted.

This problem, however, goes beyond the immediate limits of this study. What I am here trying to do is to gain a knowledge of a particular historical[2] world, which is paralleled by the particular form of the tragic vision found in seventeenth-century France and eighteenth-century Germany. I shall call the tragedy which forms an essential part of this vision the tragedy of refusal, in order to distinguish it from other forms of tragedy which are based upon fate or upon illusion. Yet in spite of its obvious limits, the study of this particular form of the tragic vision should, if it is valid and in so far as it is historical, be a step towards a solution of the ontological problem of man's relationship with the world; it is also inevitable that, studying the world of the tragic mind, we shall also be led to consider whether or not the vision associated with it offers valid insights into the human predicament, and whether or not it marked a step forward in man's progress towards consciousness and liberty.

I have already pointed out the limitations that prevent us from making out an overall picture of the tragic vision which would include both Greek and Shakespearian tragedy and the tragedy of refusal found in Pascal and Racine. It is nevertheless a fact that all forms of tragic vision have one

[1] Marx sketched out certain elements of this type of knowledge of the foundations of history in his *Theses on Feuerbach* and his preface to his *Critique of Political Economy*.

[2] Historical not in its content but in its reality. One of the most important characteristics of the content of tragic thought is precisely the non-historical character of its world, since history is one of the ways in which one can go beyond and transcend tragedy.

feature in common: they all express a deep crisis in the relationship between man and his social and spiritual world. This is obviously true of Sophocles, who is the only one of the Greek playwrights who can, without any shadow of doubt, be called "tragic" in the now accepted sense of the word. For Aeschylus still wrote trilogies, and the only complete one that we possess ends with the resolution of the conflicts described. We also know that *Prometheus Bound* was followed by a *Prometheus the Torch-Bearer*, which described the reconciliation between Prometheus and Zeus. Moreover, in so far as the word "classical" indicates the idea of a union between man and the world and thus, by implication, the idea of immanence,[3] Aeschylus is still classical in the precise mean-

[3] If we define the classical spirit by the unity between man and the world and the substantial character of the latter, and the Romantic spirit by the complete lack of any satisfactory relationship between man and the world, and by the fact that man places essence and thereby substantial values in a reality that lies outside our world, we can still look upon Aeschylus, like Homer and Sophocles, as a strictly classical author, in spite of the fact that his work is already dominated by the threat of a split between man and the world, which thus makes it foreshadow Sophoclean tragedy.

Moreover, when Hegel in his *Aesthetic* reserves the term classical for Greek art and gives the name of romantic to any art which, since the coming of Christianity, has placed real values elsewhere than in this world, he does nevertheless express a valid idea. We are, admittedly, surprised at a classification which places Shakespeare, Racine and Goethe among Romantic writers, but we must nevertheless consider that, since the unity of man and the world does in fact imply that values are radically immanent, any mind which accepts the existence or possibility of intelligible or transcendent values is romantic in the widest meaning of the word. However, we must try to go beyond this global distinction, and remember that, within the art and philosophy that have been created since the Greeks, there are currents which go in the direction of immanence and others which resolutely turn away from the real and concrete world.

Thus, I shall call the first classical and the second romantic, using the first word in a wider and the second in a narrower sense. Thus, when we bear in mind the fact that even when it aims at being wholly *a priori* and directed towards a universal and intelligible truth, rational thought is still an attempt to understand the real world, it will not be incorrect to use the word classical in its widest sense to describe all literary or philosophical works which aim at a rational understanding of things, and romantic all those which turn away from reason to seek refuge in the passions and the imagination. Thus, in the narrower and more exact sense of the word, Bergson, Schelling, Novalis and Nerval will be romantics, but, in the widest possible sense of the word, Descartes, Corneille and Schiller will be romantic as well. The great writers of Greece, on the other hand—Homer, Aeschylus, Sophocles— will be classical in the narrower and more precise sense of the word, while in the wider sense Aquinas will be classical when compared to

ing of the word. For in spite of the fact that his immanence is threatened in his work, and that he needs a whole trilogy in order to re-establish the balance which has been disturbed by the hubris of both Gods and men, he still remains a writer of radical immanence. What he deals with is the hubris of both Gods and men, and if, in his work, man is never superior to the Gods and to the world, neither are the Gods and the world superior to man. Both Gods and men live within the same world where, in Saint-Evremond's perceptive phrase,[4]

Saint Augustine, Shakespeare, Pascal, Racine, Descartes, Corneille and Goethe will be classical in comparison with all other literary or philosophical writers of the post-Christian era, and, finally, dialectical thinkers will be classical in the strictest and most exact meaning of the term.

What, however, from this point of view is the place of tragic art and thought?

On this particular point, I am entirely in agreement with Lukàcs, who sees tragedy as one of the two peaks of aesthetic expression (the other being the epic, with its representation of the natural, complete and straightforward unity between man and the world). One could thus define tragedy as a universe of agonising questions to which man has no reply. Lukàcs, in contrast, defined the world of the epic as the world where all replies are already given before man's intellectual development or the progress of history have enabled the questions to be formulated. It must nevertheless be added that—still according to Lukàcs—only the works of Homer are true epics. Tragedy expresses those moments when the highest value, the very essence of classical humanism, the unity between man and the world, comes under a threat, so that its importance is felt with a peculiar and urgent acuteness. From this point of view the works of Sophocles, Shakespeare, Pascal, Racine and Kant are, together with those of Homer, Aeschylus, Goethe, Hegel and Marx, peaks in the history of classical thought and art.

4 Saint-Evremond did not like tragedy; in Greek thought he approved of Plato, and in the quarrel over the relative merits of Corneille and Racine he resolutely sided with the supporters of the former.

Nevertheless, he was fully aware of what constitutes the basic feature of the plays both of Racine and of Corneille when they are compared to classical Greek tragedies: the absence of God. Thus, we see him writing that: "The Gods, by their hatreds and protective preferences, brought about all the extraordinary happenings in the theatre of the ancients; and, in the midst of so many supernatural occurrences, the people found nothing incredible or remarkable in the idea that *Gods and men should form a society*. [Here, as later, Monsieur Goldmann's italics.] The Gods almost always acted through the medium of men's passions; men undertook nothing without the Gods' advice, and achieved nothing without their aid. Thus, in this mixture of divinity and humanity, nothing was unbelievable. Today however, we find all these marvels fabulous and unbelievable. *We lack Gods and are lacking to the Gods in our turn*" (Saint-Evremond, *Oeuvres*, Vol. 1, p. 174, of the three-volume edition published by René de Planhal, Cité des Livres, Paris, 1927).

I should add that Saint-Evremond, who is a remarkably perceptive critic, saw quite clearly the non-Christian nature of Corneille's *Polyeucte*. He quite correctly observes that the hero is lacking in Christian they form "a society", and are subject to the same laws of fate. Xerxes is punished because he wanted to rule over nature, to enchain the sea and stretch his authority beyond its valid limits, thereby ruling not only over the forces of nature but also over the Greek world, and especially Athens. Yet when the Erynnies themselves overstep the bounds of moderation they are judged by a human tribunal and made to submit to the laws of the city, in spite of the fact that they are divine. Similarly, when Prometheus is chained to the rock and in torment he still remains stronger than the King of the Gods, since he knows what is going to happen in the future and Zeus does not. This is why, in spite of the bitter conflict that divides them, they are inseparable, and, since neither can conquer or destroy the other, they finally achieve a reconciliation.

humility and that he is wholly self-sufficient. However, his hostility to religious drama in general, linked with his admiration for Corneille, nevertheless leads him to exaggerate the importance of the non-Christian characters in the play: "The spirit of our religion is entirely opposed to that of tragedy, and the humility and patience of our saints are at the furthest remove from the virtues expected of a hero in the theatre. Consider the zeal and strength that the heavens inspire in Néarque and Polyeucte. . . . Unmoved by prayers and entreaties, Polyeucte is more eager to die for God than other men are to live for themselves. Nevertheless, the subject which would have made an excellent sermon would make a very poor tragedy were it not for the fact that the conversations between Pauline and Sévère, both characters being inspired by other feelings and other passions, had maintained for our author the reputation which the Christian virtues of our martyrs would otherwise have taken from him" (op. cit., p. 175).

Similarly, Saint-Evremond has a very clear perception of what we might term the "non-civic" character of tragedy, the conflict between tragic awareness and a wholehearted commitment to the life of the State. "When we consider the normal impression that tragedy made on the souls of the spectators in ancient Athens, we can see that Plato was more justified in his condemnation than was Aristotle in his approval; for since tragedy consisted of excessive feelings of fear and pity, the theatre then surely became a school of terror and compassion, where men learned to be afraid of every danger and to weep over every misfortune.

"I find it difficult to believe that a soul accustomed to be terrified at the sight of other people's misfortunes would be capable of dealing adequately with its own. It was perhaps in this manner that the Athenians became so ready to feel fear, and that the spirit of terror, inspired with so much art in the theatre, became only too natural in the army.

"In Sparta and Rome, where the public showed the citizens only examples of valour and constancy, the people were no less proud and bold in battle than firm and unshakeable in the calamities which beset the Republic" (loc. cit., p. 177).

Authentic tragedy, on the other hand, makes its first appearance with the work of Sophocles. In my view, the basic meaning of his work is to be found in the expression which it gives of the unbridgeable gulf which now separates man—or, more accurately, certain privileged and exceptional men—from the human and divine world. Ajax and Philoctetes, Oedipus, Creon and Antigone all express and illustrate the same truth: the world has become dark and mysterious, the Gods no longer exist side by side with men in the same cosmic totality, and are no longer subject to the same rule of fate or the same demands of balance and moderation. They have cut themselves off from man and taken it upon themselves to rule over him; they speak to him in deceitful terms and from afar off, the oracles which he consults have two meanings, one apparent but false, the other hidden but true, the demands which the Gods make are contradictory, and the world is ambiguous and equivocal. It is an unbearable world, where man is forced to live in error and illusion, and where only those whom a physical infirmity cuts off from normal life can stand the truth when it is revealed to them: the fact that both Teiresias, who knows the will of the Gods and the future of man, and Oedipus,[5] who discovers the truth about himself at the end of the tragedy are both blind is symbolic of this. Their physical blindness is an expression of the separation from the real world which inevitably accompanies a knowledge of the truth; only those who are blind, like the agèd Faust in Goethe, can really live in this world, since as long as they keep their physical sight they can see only illusion and not truth. For the others—Ajax, Creon, Antigone[6]—their discovery of the truth does nothing but condemn them to death.

5 It goes without saying that this refers to *Oedipus Rex,* since *Oedipus at Colonus* is, like *Philoctetes,* an attempt to go beyond tragedy.

6 May I be allowed to formulate a suggestion? In the whole work of Sophocles *Antigone* occupies a quite exceptional position. In spite of all the important differences that I would not for a moment think of denying, Antigone is the character who comes nearest to the modern heroes of the tragedies of refusal. Like Junia and Titus, she knows the truth at the beginning of the play, and does not need to discover it; like them, she acts in a conscious and deliberate way in refusing compromise and accepting death. It is, moreover, this particular quality that has led modern thinkers like Hegel and Kierkegaard to pay special attention to her in their reflections on Greek tragedy. I myself, reading the play, was struck by two facts.

In my view, certain of the Platonic dialogues are directed not only against the Sophists but also against Sophocles; for while Plato is obviously maintaining against the Sophists that objective truth does exist, he is also arguing against another opponent and maintaining that this truth is not only bearable to man but also likely to make him happier and more virtuous. It would thus seem probable that someone had tried to maintain that this was not the case, and such a view is certainly implicit in Sophoclean tragedy.

However, in spite of Plato's argument, the work of Sophocles nevertheless marks the end of a stage in the history of European culture. For when Plato discusses truth, he is not talking about our immediate experience of the external world. Socrates is not interested in truth of this kind, and for him as for the tragic thinker, the external world is illusory and ambiguous. Substance, the eternal values, goodness, happiness and truth are now to be found in an intelligible world which, whether transcendent or not, is opposed to the world of everyday experience. When we take a wider view, and consider philosophy as well as art, it would seem that the transition from the classical to the romantic consciousness which Hegel, basing himself solely on a consideration of art, placed at the beginning of the Christian era, ought really to be put between Sophocles and Plato.

However, this must for the time being remain merely a hypothesis, since in order to grasp the real meaning of a literary or philosophical work we need to situate it in the social and economic circumstances of the time that gave it birth, and our knowledge of classical antiquity is too flimsy to enable this to be done. The same is true of Shakespearian tragedy, which can also be seen as marking the end of the aristocratic and feudal world, and expressing the crisis of the Renaissance and the appearance of the individualistic world of the Third Estate. However, as I pointed out in Chapter II

First of all, from a purely textual and dramatic point of view, the character of Creon is far more important than that of Antigone—he is on the stage much longer, and says much more than she does.

Secondly, Creon is exactly like the other tragic heroes in Sophocles—Ajax, Philoctetes, Oedipus—who live in illusion and discover the truth only at the end of the play, when it kills or blinds them. Would it be too outrageous to suggest that Sophocles began first of all by writing the tragedy of Creon, the man who, in his blindness, infringes the divine laws, and that he then found, in addition, the exceptional character of Antigone, whose novelty and importance he then very rapidly appreciated?

of this book and also elsewhere,[7] we do possess another example of the appearance of the tragic vision: in seventeenth-century France and eighteenth-century Germany the rise of scientific thought and its inevitable concomitant of greater technological efficiency, together with the rise of rationalism and of individualistic morality, produced the alarum cry of Pascal's *Pensées* and the critical philosophy of Kant. Here, once again, it was tragic thought that denounced the symptoms of a deep crisis in man's relationship with the world and his fellows and pointed to the dangers produced—or, rather, about to be produced—by man's progress along a path which had seemed, and which still did seem to many, to be so rich and full of promise. Once again, the danger was avoided and the potential impasse surmounted. The Hegelian and, above all, the Marxist dialectic played the same rôle for the tragic vision of Pascal and Kant that Socratic and Platonic rationalism had played for Greek tragedy, and which modern rationalism and empiricism had played for Shakespearian tragedy: that of going beyond the tragic vision by showing that man is capable of achieving authentic values by his own thoughts and actions.

Naturally, such a parallel is valid in a very general sense, for there are inevitably great differences of detail between the three cases.

After the problems raised by the tragedies of Aeschylus and Sophocles, Socratic and Platonic rationalism based itself upon entirely new foundations, giving up any hope or even desire to rediscover immanent substantiality. In the place of the classical unity between man and the world, it substituted the idea of intelligible truth; it thus separated man from the world of immediate experience, and considered this world either as mere appearance or simply as a potential tool. It is this new attitude which not only explains why Plato refused to allow tragic and epic poets into his ideal state but also why the statement that truth is intelligible—and, implicitly, that it can be transcendent—allowed later thinkers to make Platonism the basis for Augustinianism, one of the three[8] great streams of Christian thought in the Middle Ages. Another aspect of

[7] Cf. Lucien Goldmann, *La Communauté humaine et l'univers chez Kant* (P.U.F., 1949).

[8] I say three, because in addition to Thomism and Augustinianism there is a third eschatological current whose importance is not diminished by the fact that it was partially condemned by the Church: it is represented by the Eternal Gospel of Joachim de Flore, and the spiritualist tendencies of the Franciscans.

Platonism also enabled it to become the basis for one of the two great currents of modern individualism, the rationalism of Descartes and Galileo. It would not, therefore, perhaps be wrong to say that Platonism remained one of the basic positions of Western thought until it was transcended by the first philosophical position which gave up the attempt to seek for values in transcendence and intelligibility in order to return to a new immanence and a new classicism: dialectical materialism.

I do not know English culture well enough to do more than make a suggestion about Shakespearian tragedy:[9] however, it does seem to me that European rationalism and empiricism of the seventeenth, eighteenth and nineteenth centuries was the ideological expression of a class which, as it gained mastery over the physical world and built up a new social order based upon liberalism and respect for the individual, tended increasingly to ignore and pass by the problems raised by Shakespearian tragedy. Rationalism and empiricism had so pauperised man's view of the world that the richness of the Shakespearian universe seemed for a long time to be merely a barbarous creation, admirable or absurd according to the taste of the individual reader, but certainly both foreign and difficult to assimilate. One might possibly see a slender

[9] Readers may perhaps be surprised to find in a work devoted to seventeenth-century tragedy both such an incomplete hypothesis about Greek tragedy and a straightforward confession of ignorance as far as Shakespearian tragedy is concerned. A follower of the analytic method would doubtless have preferred to refrain from any remarks on these particular subjects, and to restrict himself to the immediate field of his research.

For me, such a restriction would have contradicted the very principles of my method. Convinced that the meaning of any element depends upon its relationship to the other elements and on its place in the whole, and that, consequently, research can never go directly from the parts to the whole or from the whole to the parts, I hold that it is very important to avoid the illusion that the study of any partial reality could be self-sufficient in a relative manner, or that general syntheses could dispense with detailed analyses of particular facts.

Research progresses by a constant movement from the parts to the whole and from the whole back to the parts again. This nevertheless implies that we must always point out the immediate aspects of any subject for which we do not have sufficient knowledge, and the points which, by being clarified, could either complete or modify the provisional results obtained. No study of tragedy will ever be complete until we have taken into account the three great forms of tragic awareness and creation that I have indicated—and this without mentioning the fact that tragedy cannot, as a whole, be understood without the study of the psychic forms which it replaced and of those which, in turn, sublated and transcended it.

link between Shakespeare and Montaigne; there was nothing at all in common between him and Hume or Descartes.

The relationship between the tragedy of refusal, expressed in the work of Pascal, Racine and Kant, and dialectical thought is something very different from the hostility which separates tragedy and rationalism. I have said that dialectical thought is characterised by its ability to integrate and go beyond other positions, and it is a fact that both Hegel and Marx both accept and integrate into the very substance of their ideas all the problems raised by the tragic attitude which preceded them. For example, they share its critique of rationalist and empirical philosophy, of both hedonistic and utilitarian dogmatic morality, of the present condition of society, of any form of dogmatic theology and so on. Where they differ from it, however, is in replacing the tragic wager on eternity and a transcendent divinity by an immanent wager on man's future in this world. It is this wager which, for the first time since Plato in the history of Western thought, shows a deliberate break with intelligibility and transcendence, and re-establishes the unity of man with the world, thus raising the hope that we may return to the classicism abandoned since the Greeks.

The fact remains that the tragedy of the seventeenth and eighteenth centuries—and, for the rest of this book, the words "tragedy" and "tragic", except when otherwise stated, will indicate the tragedy of refusal characteristic of these two centuries—does, like other forms of tragic creation and awareness, express a crisis in human relationship between certain groups of men and the cosmic and social world.

I have already said that the central problem of this tragedy is that of discovering whether a man can still live when the eye of God has lighted upon him. This is a real problem, since to live means necessarily to live in this world—a fundamental and universal truth of which phenomenology and existentialism have merely made us more conscious. However, the fact that our attention did need drawing to this truth does indicate that the degree to which we are conscious of it can vary from one historical period to another. These variations cannot, at the present state of our knowledge, be known and studied in detail, but one preliminary observation can be made which will take us to the very centre of the problem we are studying: all forms of consciousness express a provisional and mobile balance between the individual and his social environment; when this balance can be fairly easily established and is relatively stable, or when it can pass fairly easily from one form to another, men tend not to think about the problems raised by their relationship to the external world. On a social as well as on an individual plane, it is the sick organ which creates awareness, and it is in periods of social and political crisis that men are most aware of the enigma of their presence in the world. In the past, this awareness has tended to find its expression in tragedy. At the present day it shows itself in existentialism.

These considerations should help us to see what view the tragic mind takes of the world. Briefly expressed, it is that the world is at one and the same time both nothing and everything. It is nothing, because tragic man lives for ever with God's eye upon him, because he can demand and accept only completely clear, absolute and unequivocal values, because for him "only miracles are real", and because, measured by these standards, the world is essentially confused, ambiguous and therefore non-existent. As Lukàcs writes, the problem of tragic consciousness is

> the problem of the relationship between being and essence— that of knowing whether everything that exists already is by the very fact that it exists. Are there, for example, different degrees of being? Is being a universal property of all things, or is it a value judgment which separates and distinguishes them? . . . Mediaeval philosophy expressed the problem with absolute clarity when it said that the *ens perfectissimum* is also the *ens realissimum*.[10]
>
> In order to enter the universe of tragedy [he continues] men must reach a very high threshold of perfection; anyone who does not reach this level simply does not exist. But everything that does reach it is always both present and absent to the same degree.[11]

It is, in short, because tragic man is aware neither of degrees nor of a transitional plane between nothing and everything, because for him anything which is not perfect does not exist, because he can see no possibility of bringing absence and presence together, that the eye of God makes everything which is not clear and unambiguous, and which does not reach the level of what the young Lukàcs calls "the miracle", completely absent and unimportant. This means that tragic man finds the world as it normally is both non-existent and inauthentic, and that he lives solely for God, finding nothing

[10] Cf. Lukàcs, *Die Seele und die Formen*, pp. 335-6.
[11] Idem, p. 336.

in common between Him and the world. As Pascal wrote, illustrating Lukàcs' thesis in advance:

> The conditions which are most bearable according to this world are the most difficult to endure in the sight of God. For as this world judges, there is nothing more difficult than the Christian life; but in the sight of God, there is no life easier to live than that which keeps His law. For this world, there is nothing easier than to perform great functions and possess great wealth; yet there is nothing more difficult than to live in this world according to God's commandment and without taking love and care for the things it contains (fr. 906, E. 705).

Many other fragments could be quoted from the *Pensées* in order to express this idea, but this one ⌐ 'tract will be enough to show us how the tragic mind views this world. The only condition we must observe is that, in this as in every other case, we must give Pascal's words their fullest possible meaning, even if this means, in this particular instance, extrapolating to the point of saying that everything which God demands is impossible in the eyes of the world, and that everything which is possible when we follow the rules of this world ceases to exist when the eye of God lights upon it.

However, this denial of the reality of the world only presents one aspect of the problem, and the Pascal text which I have just quoted gives us the other complementary but contrasting aspect: for, as I have said, the tragic mind sees the world as nothing and as everything at one and the same time.

The God of tragedy is a God who is always present and always absent. Thus, while his presence takes all value and reality from the world, his equally absolute and permanent absence makes the world into the only reality which man can confront, the only sphere in and against which he can and must apply his demand for substantial and absolute values.

Many forms of religious and revolutionary consciousness have insisted upon the incompatibility between God and the world and between values and reality. Most of them, however, have admitted some possible solution, if only that of an endeavour which can be made in this world to achieve these values, or, alternatively, of the possibility for man of abandoning this world entirely and seeking refuge in the intelligible and transcendent world of values or of God. In its most radical form, tragedy rejects both these solutions as signs of weakness and illusion, and sees them as being either conscious or unconscious attempts at compromise. For tragedy believes neither that the world can be changed and authentic values realised within the framework it provides nor that it can simply be left behind while man seeks refuge in the city of God. This is why tragic man cannot try to spend his wealth or fulfil his duties in the world "well", nor pass over these duties and abandon his wealth completely. Here, as elsewhere, tragic man can find only one valid attitude: that of saying both "*Yes*" and "*No*", of being in the world but not of the world, as "taking neither love nor care for the things which it contains". Living in this world means accepting, in the full sense of the word, that it exists; being in it without being of it means refusing to accept that it has any real existence.

This is the coherent and paradoxical attitude which tragic man must adopt towards the world and towards anything that is in it. It is an attitude which is all the more coherent because of its paradoxical nature and one which, if we understand it correctly, will enable us to dispose of a false problem that has confronted a number of Pascalian scholars. This problem has, in the past, consisted of trying to reconcile two apparently contradictory facts about Pascal's thought. On the one hand, he did not think that "knowledge of the machine"—that is to say, of the reality of the physical world —"was worth an hour's trouble", and said as much in a letter to Fermat on August 8th, 1661. "To be quite frank with you," he wrote, "I consider geometry to be the highest exercise of the mind, but at the same time hold it so useless that I would make little distinction between the man who is a geometer and nothing more and one who is a skilful artisan. Thus, while I call it the finest occupation in the world, it is but an occupation and nothing more; and I have often said that it is useful as a field in which to try out our strength, but not one in which to give it full employment; so that, for my own part, I would not as much as walk down the street for geometry's sake".[12] On the other hand, however, this same Pascal never ceased, at the very time he was writing his letter, to be interested in the life of this world, and especially in problems of geometry, and to devote a large

[12] Letter of August 10th, 1661.

amount of his time to their solution.[13] It is my contention that, looked at correctly, this paradox is not one which either can or should be solved; and that Pascal's attitude is exactly the coherent though paradoxical one which is characteristic of the tragic thinker.

No clearer definition could in fact be given of this dual attitude, which says "*Yes*" and "*No*" at the same time, than the famous passage, written either by Pascal or by someone closely influenced by his ideas, called *On the Conversion of the Sinner*. "On the one hand," writes this author, "the presence of visible objects touches the soul more than does the hope of those invisible; while, on the other, the firmness of those invisible touches it more than the vanity of those visible. So that the presence of the first and the firmness of the second fight for its love, and the vanity of the first and the absence of the second excite its aversion".[14]

Or again, if we want to gain a clearer picture of how the world presents itself to the tragic mind we must once more quote Pascal and once more give his words their full force. His letter to Fermat tells us that he sees "little distinction" between a man who follows "the finest occupation in the world", thus devoting himself to "the highest exercise of the mind", and one who is merely an "artisan". What Pascal's letter tells us is that for the tragic mind there is no such thing as degrees, transitions or approximations; that this mind passes over the concept of "more" or "less" and concentrates solely on that of "All" or "Nothing"; and that when a man who has tragic vision sees "little distinction" between two things, then this means, when we take what he says to its logical conclusion, that he sees no difference at all between the highest and humblest forms of worldly—and therefore relative—forms of existence and activity.

Yet in spite of this, the absence of God deprives tragic man of any right to remain ignorant of the world or to turn his face from it; his refusal remains within the world, both because it is this world that he rejects and because it is only

[13] The letter inviting solutions for the problem of the cycloid dates from June 1658; the *Histoire de la Roulette* from October 1658. A letter from Sluse to Pascal dated April 24th, 1660, mentions that the latter had written to him recently on the subject of the diagrams in Descartes's *Traité de l'Homme*. The document setting up the "carrosses à cinq sous" dates from November 1661, and there is a letter from Huyghens to Hook indicating that the idea of organising the production of spring-type watches was being entertained in 1660.

[14] I have deliberately not quoted the rest of the passage, which I shall be analysing further in a subsequent chapter.

by this movement of rejection that tragic man can know himself and understand his own limits and value. For if the world is too narrow and too ambiguous for man to devote himself to it entirely, and to "give full employment" to his strength in it, it still remains the only place where he can "try out his strength". Thus in every possible aspect of human life, however minute, the reply of both "Yes" and "No" remains the only valid attitude for the man who has become aware of tragedy.

However, this analysis merely introduces us to one of the main difficulties of the subject under discussion: if we try to insert this idea of a simultaneous *"Yes"* and *"No"* into a coherent vision, then we must do so by linking it with practical and theoretical positions that provide an accurate justification and foundation for it. For the complete refusal of a world which offered the chance of achieving authentic values would show just as complete a lack of coherence as the acceptance of a world which was completely absurd and ambiguous. The decision, in Pascal's words, to "try out our strength" in this world should therefore be neither wholly absurd nor wholly meaningful; or, to be more accurate, it should be both absurd and meaningful at one and the same time, an "attempt" which is real in the fullest sense of the word, but one which, by its very nature, can never reach the level of a calling, in the sense of an activity which absorbs all our faculties.

For if we refuse the world absolutely and unilaterally, then we deprive it of any possible meaning, and reduce it to the level of an abstract anonymous obstacle, without form or qualities. Only an attitude which places itself within the world in order to refuse the world can, without abandoning anything of the absolute character of this refusal, still allow tragic man to know the world on which he passes judgment and thus justify his refusal of it by keeping his reasons for doing so constantly in mind. It is these characteristics of extreme rigour and extreme coherence that we find in the expression given to tragic awareness in Racine's *Phèdre*, Pascal's and Kant's philosophical writings and the text from Lukàcs that I have just quoted. It is a paradoxical attitude and one which is very difficult to describe, but it is, in my view, only by reference to it that we shall succeed in understanding the works under discussion.

Before continuing this analysis of the tragic mind, however, I shall now discuss a position which is important both for sociological and historical reasons, and also for an understanding of Pascal. It is a less radical position than the one just described, but one that not only represents a step towards complete coherence but also possesses a relative coherence which renders it autonomous in its own right. I shall call this position—which found its expression in the ideas of most of the more extreme Jansenists—one of complete and unilateral refusal of the world and consequent appeal to God; and I shall contrast it with the attitude to be found in Pascal, which consists of a refusal of the world from within the world and the decision to wager that God exists rather than to call on His presence as something established. The difference between the two positions is the one which lies between Junia and Titus, on the one hand, and Phèdre, on the other, or between Barcos and Mother Angélique and the Pascal who, during the last years of his life, was both discovering the area traced out by the cycloid, creating the first omnibus service and writing the *Pensées*. The importance of this intermediate position can be seen from the fact that, if *Phèdre* and the *Pensées* had not been written, it is the one which we should be tempted to consider as providing the coherent expression of Jansenist thought. It was, indeed, to a very extent the one which Molière made fun of in *Le Misanthrope,* but which also manifested itself in literary works as important as Racine's first three tragedies.

I shall deal with this position in greater detail in Chapter VII when I study Jansenist thought. It should be noted, however, that these two positions do not represent wholly different and autonomous visions. There is a link between them whose existence is proved not only by history—Pascal and Racine both come from Port-Royal—but also by textual analysis. For if the Jansenist doctrine of Grace is carried to its logical conclusions, what we find is the paradoxical notion expressed in the *Pensées* and in *Phèdre*: that of the just man to whom grace has been refused, that of the just man in a state of mortal sin.

Thus, there is an ideological as well as an historical link between Barcos, Pavillon, Singlin, Mother Angélique, on the one hand and, on the other, the Pascal of the *Pensées* and the Racine of *Phèdre*. There is also, in addition, a contrast between them which has found its expression in actual texts. The first time this happened was when Gilberte Pascal tried to explain away her brother's activity in the last years of his life, and the second when Pascal, in a famous fragment of the *Pensées,* reproved the Jansenists for not having "made profession of two opposites".[15]

Gilberte Pascal was indeed faced with a problem when she had to provide a hagiographical account, consistent with Jansenist orthodoxy, of the way in which, in the last years of his life, Pascal returned to science and to life in this world, and came to accept the authority of the Church. In her *Life* she scarcely mentioned the problem of his submission to Rome, talked of his attempt to start the first omnibus service merely as an instance of his concern for the poor of Blois, and explained his return to science by a legend whose naïvety is equalled only by that of the commentators who have accepted it without question as an established fact. It is the story of how Pascal undertook to solve the problem of the cycloid in order to take his mind off his toothache; to which —since this toothache could scarcely explain why Pascal should then publish his solution—she added the account of a "person as distinguished for his piety as for the qualities of his mind" to whom Pascal "owed all kinds of deference both through respect and gratitude" and who "concerned only for the glory of God, considered it fitting that my brother should use his solution as a challenge to his rivals and then have it printed".[16]

It would, in my view, be quite wrong to interpret the change in Pascal's attitude towards the end of his life, his substitution of an attitude of "*Yes*" and "*No*" towards the world for one of absolute refusal, his acceptance of the authority of the Church and his consequent disagreement with Arnauld as to the signing of the *Formulary,* as an indication that he has returned both to the world and to the Church and completely given up Jansenism. What in fact he did was to accept a much more radical and a much more coherent position. Indeed, as Gerberon pointed out, he became "more Jansenist than the Jansenists themselves",[17] and, I would myself add, more Jansenist than even the most radical and extreme among them. For the Jansenists, far from "professing two opposites", simply refused the world, remained outside

---

[15] Cf. fr. 865 (E.947): "If there ever is a time when one should profess both contraries, it is when one is being accused of omitting one. Thus both Jansenists and Jesuits are wrong to disguise them; but the Jansenists are more to blame, for the Jesuits have better professed both."

[16] Cf. Brunschvicg edition of the *Pensées,* p. 24.

[17] Cf. Gerberon. *Histoire du Jansenisme* (Amsterdam, 1700), Vol. II, p. 515.

of it and abolished any link between it and men; or, to be more accurate, they recommended that any such link should be abolished, and called upon God to be the sole judge in these matters. But, for them, the existence of a God who watched all their actions was a certainty, a fixed and immovable point in their intellectual and spiritual make up; the element of doubt, the need to make a decision, the Pascalian idea of the "wager" came only afterwards, when the problem arose of whether or not this God had granted the grace to persevere, of whether a particular person was simply a just man, or "a just man to whom grace has been refused", or a just man who had been damned and had fallen into a state of mortal sin. Pascal carried Jansenism to its logical conclusion when he ceased to wonder whether a particular individual was damned or saved, and introduced doubt as to whether or not God himself really exists. By deliberately choosing the paradoxical position of the "just to whom grace has been refused", by giving up the attempt to be an angel in order to avoid becoming a beast, Pascal, "more Jansenist than the Jansenists themselves", became the creator of dialectical thought and the first philosopher of the tragic vision. For by wagering that God is both continually and permanently absent and present, he transformed the abstract and absolute refusal of the extreme Jansenists into a refusal within the framework of this world. He thus made it a total and concrete refusal of the world by a tragic and absolute being.

I shall discuss the position of the other Jansenists in Chapter VII.[18] For the time being, I am studying the extremist

[18] Let me offer a brief outline of the three principal currents which showed themselves in seventeenth-century Jansenism. Each of them, naturally, contained every imaginable form of mixture and variation, but they nevertheless must be distinguished if we wish to understand the social and intellectual phenomenon of Jansenism.

Thus we have:

(a) The non-tragic current made up of those who could be called "moderates". The principal representatives of this group are, to a certain extent, Saint-Cyran, and especially Arnauld and Nicole. It is to the views of this group that we must link the *Mémorial* and the *Lettres Provinciales*. (A more detailed study should distinguish, within this current, those who were concerned with the spiritual life—the Pascal who wrote the *Mémorial*, Mother Angélique, etc.—and the intellectuals —Arnauld, Nicole, and the Pascal who wrote the *Provinciales*.)

(b) The extremists—Barcos, Pavillon, Singlin, Mother Angélique, Gerberon, etc. Their position tended to be that of the tragic but onesided refusal of the world, and the direct appeal to God. It is to the views of this group that we should link *Andromaque*, *Bérénice* and *Britannicus*.

position, such as it is expressed in *Phèdre* and in *Pensées*.

I have already said that tragic man lives permanently with God's eye upon him, and that for him "only the miracle is real". I have also argued that he confronts the fundamental ambiguity of the world with his own equally fundamental demand for absolute and unambiguous values, for clarity and for the absolute essence of things. Prevented by the presence of God from ever accepting the world, but prevented at the same time by His absence from abandoning it altogether, he is constantly dominated by a permanent and fully justified awareness of the radical incongruity between himself and everything around him, of the unbridgeable gulf which separates him both from any real values and from any possible acceptance of the immediate reality of the ordinary external world. The situation of tragic man is paradoxical, and can be explained only by paradoxes: for he is in the world and conscious of it from within, but at the same time he refuses the world because of its inadequate and fragmentary nature; yet at the same time as he both refuses it and lives in it, he also goes beyond it in an immanent transcendence and a transcendent immanence.

This is why his awareness is first and foremost an awareness of the two complementary inadequacies which (for the historian who studies the mind of tragic man if not for tragic man himself) are mutually self-conditioning and self-reinforcing: man is inadequate and insufficient, he is at one and the same time a king and a slave, a beast and an angel; the world is inadequate because it is ambiguous and unsatisfying, and yet at the same time it is the only realm where man can both try out his strength and yet never put it to use.

"The wisdom brought by the tragic miracle is a wisdom of limits," writes Lukàcs, and Pascal expresses the very essence of tragic awareness when he asks: "Why is my knowledge limited? Why is my stature what it is, and the span of my life one hundred and not one thousand years? Why did nature give me this span of life, choosing it rather than any other from out of the infinite number available, where no compelling reason imposed on her this choice rather than another?" (fr. 208. E.385).

(c) Those who carried Jansenism to its highest degree of coherence, to the position of tragic paradox represented by the refusal of the world from within the world, and the wager on the existence of God, to whose tribunal the final appeal is made. To my knowledge, this position was attained only by the Pascal who wrote the *Pensées,* and the Racine who wrote *Phèdre.*

This is why—as I shall explain later—Lukàcs writes that "tragic life", life dominated exclusively by the divine presence and by the refusal of the world "is the most exclusively terrestrial of all lives".[19]

It is, however, precisely this "Yes" and this "No", both equally complete and equally absolute (the "Yes" in so far as tragic man remains in the world to demand that values be achieved, the "No" in so far as he refuses this world because it is entirely inadequate and offers no scope for the achievement of real values) which allow the tragic mind to achieve, on the plane of knowledge, a degree of accuracy and objectivity of a type never before attained. The man who lives solely in the world, but who remains constantly detached from it, finds that his mind is freed from all the current illusions and limitations which beset his fellows, with the result that the art and ideas which are born of the tragic vision become one of the most advanced forms of realism.

Tragic man never gives up hope, but he does not put his hope in this world; this is why there is no truth either about the structure of this world or about his place in it which can cause him to be afraid. Since he judges all things according to the scale of his own demand for the absolute, and since he finds them all equally wanting, he can look without fear upon their own nature and limitations and upon the limits which beset him personally when he tries out his strength in this world, either in the realm of action or in that of knowledge. Since it seeks only what is necessary, the tragic mind can meet, in this world, only what is contingent; since it acknowledges only the absolute, it will find in this world only what is relative. But as it becomes more aware of these two limitations (both its own and those of this world) and as it refused to accept either of them, it saves human values and goes beyond both this world and its own condition.

What, however, is the concrete meaning of the expression: to refuse this world? The human mind sees the world as a demand for a choice among a number of different possibilities which are all mutually incompatible but none of which is wholly satisfying. To refuse the world while remaining within it means refusing to choose and refusing to be satisfied with any of the possibilities which it offers; it means making a clear and unrestricted judgment of their inadequacy and limitations, and setting up against them a demand for real and unambiguous values; it means setting up against a world

19 Op. cit., p. 345.

290

composed of fragmentary and mutually exclusive elements a demand for totality that inevitably becomes a demand for the reconciliation of opposites. For the tragic mind, authentic values are synonymous with totality, and any attempt at compromise is synonymous with the complete fall from grace and honesty.

This is why tragic man, torn, between "Yes" or "No", will always scorn those who choose an intermediary position, and will remain instead on the only level whose value he recognises to be adequate: that of saying both "Yes" and "No", of attempting to realise a synthesis. Man is "neither beast nor angel", and that is why his real task lies in trying to create the whole and complete man who will bring the two together, the man whose body will be immortal as well as his soul, the man who will unite in his own person the extreme intensities of reason and passion, the man who, on this earth, can never become a reality.[20]

It is from this that spring the two paradoxical elements of the tragic mind ("elements" in the sense that they have to be artificially separated for the purpose of analysis): its extreme realism and its demand for absolute values. Faced with an ambiguous and fragmentary world, the paradoxical nature of the tragic mind becomes a demand for the reconciliation of opposites, a demand in which the two elements reinforce each other. For what the tragic mind accepts as its first absolute value is that of truth, and this demand is inevitably accompanied by the realisation that all the possibilities offered by this world are limited and inadequate.

The fundamental philosophical problem is that of the relationship between value and reality, between what is rational

---

[20] There is no worse mistake than to interpret Pascal, basing oneself on the appearance of certain texts, as recommending a "golden mean" between two extremes, a sceptical position frequently adopted by Montaigne but one which is the complete denial of any tragedy and any dialectical thought. Similarly, the God of the wager (like the God of Kant's practical postulate) is not a God whose existence is probable, but a God who is certain and necessary. However, this certainty and necessity are practical and human, certainties of the heart and not of the reason (or, what is the same thing in Kant, certainties of the reason and not of the understanding).

In an article which, in spite of a number of errors and omissions, nevertheless had the merit of first indicating the dialectical quality of the Pensées and the relationship between this dialectic and paradox as a literary form, Professor Hugo Friedrich gave an excellent analysis of this difference between the notion of "middle" (milieu) in Pascal and Montaigne. (Cf. Hugo Friedrich, Pascals Paradox. Das Sprachbild einer Denform. Zeitschrift fur Romanische Philologie. LVI Band, 1936.)

and what can be perceived, between meaning and individuality and between the soul and the body; on this plane, the tragic mind resembles dialectical thought by the fact that it can recognise as valid only the reconciliation of opposites, the individualisation of essence and the identification between meaning and individuality. Thus, Kant places at the very centre of his epistemology the demand for "integral determination" by the individual being, and Pascal writes, in the *Mystère de Jésus*: "Behold, I have shed these drops of blood for thee" (fr. 553, E. 739).

As the tragic mind becomes aware of the limits prescribing both it and the external world—and the most important of these limits is death—it sees everything in clear and unambiguous outline, even its own paradoxical character and the fundamental ambiguity of the world.[21] And, at the same time, it confronts this ambiguity with its own demand for extreme individuality and extreme essentiality.

Neither tragic nor dialectical thought can accept the idea that clarity should reside solely in ideas while reality remains ambiguous, and that values should not go beyond the stage of being demands and ideas; both reject the idea that the "for itself" should remain empty and the "in itself" blind, and that reality should be foreign or even opposed to value. In this, they are both philosophies of incarnation, not, it is true, in any religious sense, but because both demand that values and meaning should become reality in the real world.

However, while dialectical thought considers that this can come about in the real world of historical experience, tragic thought eliminates this possibility from the world and places it in eternity. It therefore follows that, as far as this world is concerned, tragic thought merely poses the problem of a tension between a radically unsatisfactory world and an individual self that demands absolute authenticity. It does so, as Lukàcs writes,

> with a strength that eliminates and destroys everything until this extreme affirmation of the self, when it reaches the peak of its authenticity, endows everything it meets with a hard, steel-like autonomy; it then goes beyond itself, and in its final tension transcends everything which is purely individual. Its strength has consecrated things by raising them to the level of destiny, but in its great struggle with the destiny it has itself created, the tragic soul rises above itself and becomes a symbol

21 Here again, we are in presence of a paradox: the tragic mind sees the world's ambiguity as clear and unambiguous.

of the ultimate relationship between man and his fate. (loc cit., p. 344).

"Death," continues Lukàcs, "which is an absolute limit, is for tragedy a constantly immanent reality indissolubly linked with everything that the tragic soul experiences", and he adds that it is

> for this reason that the tragic mind is a realisation of concrete essence. With complete assurance and certainty, it solves the most difficult problems of Platonism: that of discovering whether individual things have their own Idea and their own Essence. And the reply which it gives reverses the order in which the question is put, since it shows that it is only when what is individual—that is to say, a particular living individual —is carried to its final limits and possibilities that it conforms to the Idea and begins really to exist.
>
> The universal [he concludes] without form or colour, is, in its generality, too weak to become real. It is too much bound up in itself to possess real being, and to say that it is identical with itself is merely tautological. Thus, as it goes beyond Platonism, tragedy replies to the condemnation which Platonism had earlier laid upon it (loc. cit., pp. 347-8).

And, I will add, it re-opens the way towards the immanent and classical thought which Platonism had abandoned.

With his demand for clarity and for the absolute, tragic man stands confronted with a world that is the only reality against which he can set this demand, the only place where he could live if he were never to give up this demand and his effort to achieve it. But the world can never satisfy him, and this is why the eye of God compels man, for so long as he lives—and for as long as he lives, he lives in the world— never to "love and care for it". Tragic man is absent and present in the world at one and the same time, exactly as God is simultaneously absent and present to man. Even if the smallest and most imperceptible ray of light—of real truth or real justice—were to become visible, tragedy would disappear, and man would be linked with God in a world made humanly habitable. But there stretches before tragic man only "the eternal silence of infinite space"; not even of the narrowest and most insignificant sector of human life can a completely clear and unequivocal statement be made without the opposite and contradictory statement being immediately added; the only answer to every problem is both "Yes" and "No", and paradox is the only valid expression of reality. And, for tragic man, paradox is a constant source of scandal and concern: to accept paradox, to accept human weakness, the ambiguity and confusion of the world, its "sense and nonsense" as Merleau-Ponty puts it, means giving up any attempt to endow life with meaning. Man is a contradictory being, a mixture of strength and weakness, greatness and poverty, living in a world which, like himself, is made up of opposites, of antagonistic forces that fight against one another without hope of truce or victory, of elements that are complementary but permanently unable to form a whole. The greatness of tragic man lies in the fact that he sees and recognises these opposites and inimical elements in the clear light of absolute truth, and yet never accepts that this shall be so. For if he were to accept them, he would destroy the paradox, he would give up his greatness and make do with his poverty and wretchedness (*misère*). Fortunately, however, man remains to the very end both paradoxical and contradictory, "man goes infinitely beyond man", and he confronts the radical and irredeemable ambiguity of the world with his own equal and opposite demand for clarity.

Before continuing this analysis of the tragic mind, however, I should like to make one more point: it is that, as we can see from the popularity of Jean-Paul Sartre and Maurice Merleau-Ponty, the idea of the ambiguity of the world, its "sense and nonsense" has, like that of man's inability to find a clear and unequivocal line of conduct, become once again one of the principal themes of philosophical thought. And, especially when we read their minor works, it is also easy to see what social and historical conditions have led them to the conclusions which they express: once again, the social forces that in the nineteenth century enabled man to go beyond tragedy by using dialectical and revolutionary thought have, for reasons too complicated to analyse here, led to the sacrifice of value to efficiency. And, once again, the most honest thinkers have been compelled to recognise the existence of the dichotomy which had already struck Pascal between justice and force, between man's hopes and the human predicament.[22]

It is also our present historical situation which has not only made us more aware of the ambiguity of the world and of the inauthentic nature of daily life, but which has also revived our interest in the tragic writers and thinkers of the past.

22 This was written in 1952. Since then, the historical situation has changed, and both Sartre and Merleau-Ponty have modified their respective ideological attitudes—in opposite directions, it may be added.

I should like to conclude this chapter by stressing one point: that in spite of the greater interest that we now feel for tragedy, and for the themes of anguish and suffering in Pascalian thought, none of the modern existentialist thinkers can really be linked with Pascal, Hegel and Marx, or to any classical tradition in either the wider or narrower meaning of the term. For it is precisely the fact that it does not accept ambiguity and, instead, keeps alive the demand for reason and clarity, that makes tragedy what it is, and also institutes the essence of the classical spirits. For example, Merleau-Ponty says "sense and nonsense", just as Pascal did before him and as do all the dialectical thinkers who follow Pascal; but they, unlike Merleau-Ponty, insist upon the fact that we must not accept such a universe but rather, if we are men, strive to transcend it. There is a wide gap between these two positions, and I can see no way of bringing them closer together.   Translated by Philip Thody

Notes on Hegel's Theory of Tragedy

ALEXANDRE KOJÈVE

BOUNDED by pagan law, man, that is to say, self-consciousness, could act. But man's consciousness could never individualize itself, for within the horizon of pagan law it could only act criminally. A man could act either in behalf of the state (his action thus having universality) or he could act in behalf of the family (acting as a particular being). And there could be no synthesis or fusion of such actions. So despite its apparent "calm" there was a conflict in pagan society, a *tragic* conflict, ending in the destruction of the particular being and finally in the destruction of society itself, that is to say the pagan state of Masters. The action of the pagan Master, whether on the plane of divine law or on that of human law, was always criminal. For the Master could act only on one plane at a time and the other plane seemed to him to be without value; he denied it in acting, and this was his crime. Here was his tragedy.

The tragic conflict is not a conflict between duty and passion or between two duties. It is a conflict between two planes of existence, one of which is held to be without value by the one who acts, but not by those who do not act. The agent, the tragic actor, does not think he has acted criminally; when punished he has the feeling of submitting to an absolutely unjustifiable "destiny," but one which he accepts without revolt, "without trying to understand it."

The pagan Masters lacked that human particularity necessary to obtain satisfaction in life. Their action, which consisted in giving their lives for their country, realized only the universal in them. The Master could not act as a particular in the state. He had, it is true, particularity inside the family; but inside the family there is no real action, that is to say, no negating action. There is only Sein, that is to say, pure inactive being, which is equivalent to nothingness, to death. Thus the particular being as a particular could only "realize" himself in death. Hence no satisfaction (which exists only in and for the individual) in and by existence. The Master is not "recognized" (venerated) by *all* in his *particularity*, except after his death as an ancestor; only the dead person has *individuality*, which is a synthesis of the particular being (I, and not someone else) and of the universal (recognition of the value of *my* ego by *all*).

The state, in excluding particularity, implies the suppression of the particular being (who is a member of a family); the state suppresses his *Sein* (for the particular being is a natural being, a living being). Thus the essential character of the pagan state is war; the state aims at the destruction of the particular being, his death. But war is criminal with relation to the family, which attributes an absolute value to the particular being, that is to say, to his *Sein,* to his animal life.

The state in punishing the criminal forbids his burial and funeral rites in his honor. Hence once again a destruction of individuality; no *universal recognition* (in the funeral service) of the *particularity* of the dead. Hence what is regarded by the state as punishment is held a crime by the family (the theme of *Antigone*).

First condition of the tragic situation: The People (the Chorus) are passive. Action is not for them. They see the two Heroes (actors) go to their ruin without being able to intervene. They see the conflict but see no possibility of resolving it. All they can do is lament. In a way, the Chorus is the most tragic character in Tragedy. Also the author who solidarizes himself with the Chorus.

The sacrifice of Iphigenia shows the contradiction between the State and the Family. By the murder of Agamemnon, the very principle of Royalty (the State) is suppressed and the Family takes the State's place (Aegisthus is not a king). By destroying the Family (killing his mother), Orestes hopes to restore Royalty to his father, becoming a King himself: for Agamemnon will then become the father of the King and thus will be King again. Orestes will be killed by the infernal gods. There is no solution.

But Aeschylus disavows Agamemnon and domesticates the Erinyes, thus transforming tragedy into comedy.

Hamlet = the Tragedy of the Intellectual. The only modern Tragedies are Tragedies about Intellectuals: Hamlet and Faust. But this kind of Tragedy (bourgeois-Christian) is a Tragedy of inaction. The Tragedy of the pagan Master, on the other hand, is a Tragedy of Action. The Intellectual can be tragic because, since he does not work, he resembles the Master. But he does not fight either, so he has a resemblance to the Slave (he is a Bourgeois, that is to say, a Slave without a Master). Therefore there can be either Tragedy of inaction or Comedy of "pacific," that is pacifist, laziness.

The deception, the imposture of Tragedy: The Master believes and wants others to believe that he is completely the Master, and that through his activity as a Master he exhausts the human essence, including his own. This is an error which turns into a fraud, for his problem is not to eliminate his Particularity but to unite it with his universalizing aims: the life of the Master who excludes Particularity becomes impossible. What does Tragedy finally reveal? That in his Action, universalist in intention, the Master finally acts as a particular being. For evidently the nature of the Master (his "character") is a particular nature. The Master who pretends to the Universal has therefore in him as much of the Particular as he who solidarizes himself openly with the Particular, that is to say, with the Family.

The Master who acts as a Master cannot avoid Tragedy, nor can he avoid the Imposture of Tragedy. The ideal of the Master is not viable: one can only *die* as a Master. The Master who pretends to *live* as a Master is an imposter. Tragically he "plays a role"; this is just so much "hypocrisy." Tragedy cannot continue as such; it has to disappear as a literary genre, giving way to comedy, Roman comedy.

The solution proposed by Aeschylus: peace, the inactivity of the State. . . . Thus: transformation of the warlike State of Masters into a bourgeois "democracy": Comedy.

Let us go back to the pagan state, to the city-state of non-working Warrior-Masters.

This State, like any state, was exclusively interested in and recognized only the Action of its citizens, which Action consisted essentially in Fighting. The pagan State thus recognized in the Citizen only the universal aspect of human existence. However, the particular aspect of human existence could not be absolutely excluded.

In fact, the Master was not only a Master of slaves and the warrior-citizen of a state. He was necessarily the member of a Family, too. And to the Family belonged the *particular* aspect of the pagan Master's existence. Within the Family, Man is not in any sense *a* Master, *a* Citizen, *a* Warrior. He is father, husband, son and he is this *particular* father, *this* husband, *this* son. However, his particularity, recognized in and by the Family, is not truly human. In fact, for the pagan Master, who did not work, human and humanizing Action was reduced to Fighting. But there is no war or risk of life within the Family. Thus there can be no human *Action* recognized by and in the Family; the Family recognizes only the *Sein,* the static and given Being, the biological existence of the man, be he father, husband, brother, or son.

But to attribute an absolute value to a being not by virtue of what he *does,* not because of his acts, but simply because of his *Sein,* of his Being, is to love him. One can therefore also say that it is Love which was realized by and in the Family of the antique world. And since Love does not depend on *acts,* on the *activity* of the loved one, it does not stop, it does not cease, even with the loved one's death. Loving a man in his *inaction,* one regards him as if he were already dead. Death thus cannot change Love, or affect the value attributed to it in and by the Family. And this is why Love and the cult of the dead were the exclusive affair of the pagan Family.

The *particular* and particularist Family was therefore a necessary complement to the *universal* and universalizing State. But the pagan Master was as little "satisfied" (*befreidigt*) by his Family life as by his existence as a citizen. In and by the State his *Human* existence was realized and recognized. But this existence was not truly *his*; *he* was not the one recognized. As to the Family, it recognized his personal, particular existence. But this existence, essentially inactive, was not truly *human*.

Where the human Actions of Warring and Working are not synthesized in a single human being, Man is never fully satisfied. The realization and recognition of uniquely universal

Action for the State satisfies Man as little as the realization and recognition of his particular being within the Family.

For the Family the supreme value is the *Sein*, the natural *Being*, the biological life of its members. But what the State exacted of the Family member was precisely that he risk his life. The State required his death in the interest of all its citizens. To do one's duty as a citizen, it was therefore necessary to violate the law of the Family, and *vice versa*.

In the pagan World this conflict was inevitable and irreconcilable: Man could not renounce the Family since he could not renounce the Particularity of his Being; and he could not renounce the State either, since he could not renounce the Universality of his Action. Thus he was necessarily always *criminal*, either toward the State or toward the Family. Now it was this which made for the *tragic* character of pagan life.

Translated by Lionel Abel

The Limitation of Being

MARTIN HEIDEGGER

WE READ the first chorus from the Antigone of Sophocles (lines 332-75). First we listen to the Greek words in order to get some of the sound into our ears. The translation runs:

> There is much that is strange, but nothing
> that surpasses man in strangeness.
> He sets sail on the frothing waters
> amid the south winds of winter
> tracking through the mountains
> and furious chasms of the waves.
> He wearies even the noblest
> of the gods, the Earth,
> indestructible and untiring,
> overturning her from year to year,
> driving the plows this way and that
> with horses.
> and man, pondering and plotting,
> snares the light-gliding birds
> and hunts the beasts of the wilderness
> and the native creatures of the sea.

With guile he overpowers the beast
that roams the mountains by night as by day,
he yokes the hirsute neck of the stallion
and the undaunted bull.

And he has found his way
to the resonance of the word,
and to wind-swift all-understanding,
and to the courage of rule over cities.
He has considered also how to flee
from exposure to the arrows
of unpropitious weather and frost.

Everywhere journeying, inexperienced and without issue,
he comes to nothingness.
Through no flight can he resist
the one assault of death,
even if he has succeeded in cleverly evading
painful sickness.

Clever indeed, mastering
the ways of skill beyond all hope,
he sometimes accomplishes evil,
sometimes achieves brave deeds.
He wends his way between the laws of the earth
and the adjured justice of the gods.
Rising high above his place,
he who for the sake of adventure takes
the nonessent for essent loses
his place in the end.

May such a man never frequent my hearth;
May my mind never share the presumption
of him who does this.

The following commentary is necessarily inadequate, if
only because it cannot be built up from the poet's entire work
or even from the whole tragedy. Here I shall not be able to
go into the choice of readings or the changes that have been
made in the text. Our interpretation falls into *three phases*,
in each of which we shall consider the whole poem from a
different point of view.

In the first phase we shall set forth the intrinsic meaning of
the poem, that which sustains the edifice of words and rises
above it.

In the second phase we pass through the whole sequence
of stropes and antistrophes and delimit the area that is opened
up by the poem.

In the third phase we attempt to take our stand in the center of the poem, with a view to judging who man is according to this poetic discourse.

First phase. We seek that which sustains the whole and towers above it. Actually we have not far to seek. It is three-fold; it bursts upon us like a triple assault, shattering at the very outset all everyday standards of questioning and definition.

The first is the beginning:

> There is much that is strange, but nothing
> that surpasses man in strangeness.

In these first two verses the poet anticipates. He will spend the rest of the poem in catching up with himself. Man, in *one* word, is *deinotaton,* the strangest. This one word encompasses the extreme limits and abrupt abysses of his being. This aspect of the ultimate and abysmal can never be discerned through the mere description that establishes data, even though thousands of eyes should examine man, searching for attributes and states. Such being is disclosed only to poetic insight. We find no portrayal of existing specimens of man; nor do we find any sort of blind and fatuous inflation of human essence from below, inspired by peevish yearning for some unattained glory; here there is no suggestion of a pre-eminent personality. Among the Greeks there were no personalities (and for this reason no supra-personality). Man is *to deinotaton,* the strangest of the strange. Here we must anticipate an explanation of the Greek word *deinon* and of our translation. This calls for a tacit glance over the whole poem, which alone can provide an appropriate interpretation of the first two verses. The Greek word *deinon* has the strange ambiguity with which Greek discourse cuts across the contending separations (Auseinander-setzungen) of being.

On the one hand *deinon* means the terrible, but not in the sense of petty terrors, and above all not in the decadent, insipid, and useless sense that the word has taken on today, in such locutions as "terribly cute." The *deinon* is the terrible in the sense of the overpowering power which compels panic fear, true fear; and in equal measure it is the collected, silent awe that vibrates with its own rhythm. The mighty, the overpowering is the essential character of power itself. Where it irrupts, it *can* hold its overpowering power in check. Yet this does not make it more innocuous, but *still* more terrible and remote.

301

But on the other hand *deinon* means the powerful in the sense of one who uses power, who not only disposes of power (Gewalt) but is violent (gewalt-tätig) insofar as the use of power is the basic trait not only of his action but also of his being-there. Here we use the word violence in an essential sense extending beyond the common usage of the word, as mere arbitrary brutality. In this common usage violence is seen from the standpoint of a realm which draws its standards from conventional compromise and mutual aid, and which accordingly disparages all violence as a disturbance of the peace.

The essent as a whole, seen as power, is the overpowering, *deinon* in the first sense. Man is *deinon*, first because he remains exposed within this overpowering power, because by his essence he belongs to being. But at the same time man is *deinon* because he is the violent one in the sense designated above. (He gathers the power and brings it to manifestness.) Man is the violent one, not aside from and along with other attributes but solely in the sense that in his fundamental violence (Gewalt-tätigkeit) he uses power (Gewalt) against the overpowering (Überwältigende). Because he is twice *deinon* in a sense that is originally one, he is *to deinotaton,* the most powerful: violent in the midst of the overpowering.

But why do we translate *deinon* as "strange" (unheimlich)? Not in order to hide or attenuate the meaning of powerful, overpowering, violent; quite on the contrary. Because this *deinon* is meant as the supreme limit and link of man's being, the essence of the being thus defined should from the first be seen in its crucial aspect. But, in that case, is the designation of the powerful as the strange and uncanny (unheimlich) not a posterior notion derived from the impression that the powerful makes on us, whereas the essential here is to understand the *deinon* as what it intrinsically is? That is so, but we are not taking the strange in the sense of an impression on our states of feeling.

We are taking the strange, the uncanny (das Unheimliche), as that which casts us out of the "homely," i.e. the customary, familiar, secure. The unhomely (Unheimische) prevents us from making ourselves at home and therein it is overpowering. But man is the strangest of all, not only because he passes his life amid the strange understood in this sense but because he departs from his customary, familiar limits, because he is the violent one, who, tending toward the strange in the sense of the overpowering, surpasses the limit of the familiar (das Heimische).

To understand the full implication of these words of the chorus, we must bear this in mind: to say that man is *to deinotaton*, the strangest of all, is not to impute a particular attribute to man, as though he were also something else; no, the verse says that to be the strangest of all is the basic trait of the human essence, within which all other traits must find their place. In calling man "the strangest of all" it gives the authentic Greek definition of man. We shall fully appreciate this phenomenon of strangeness only if we experience the power of appearance and the struggle with it as an essential part of being-there.

The second passage that sustains the poetic edifice and rises above it is to be found in line 360, in the middle of the second strophe: *Pantoporos aporos ep'ouden erchetai.* "Everywhere journeying, inexperienced and without issue, he comes to nothingness." The essential words are *pantoporos aporos.* The word *poros* means: passage through . . . , transition to . . . , path. Everywhere man makes himself a path; he ventures into all realms of the essent, of the overpowering power, and in so doing he is flung out of all paths. Herein is disclosed the entire strangeness of this strangest of all creatures: not only that he tries the essent in the whole of its strangeness, not only that in so doing he *is* a violent one striving beyond his familiar sphere. No, beyond all this he becomes the strangest of all beings because, without issue on all paths, he is cast out of every relation to the familiar and befallen by *atē,* ruin, catastrophe.

It is not hard to see that this *pantoporos aporos* contains an interpretation of *deinotaton.*

The interpretation is completed in the third salient phrase, line 370: *hypsipolis apolis.* In construction it is similar to *pantoporos aporos,* and its situation in the middle of the antistrophe presents another parallel. But it moves in a different direction. It speaks not of *poros* but of *polis;* not of the paths to all the realms of the essent but of the foundation and scene of man's being-there, the point at which all these paths meet, the *polis.* *Polis* is usually translated as city or city-state. This does not capture the full meaning. *Polis* means, rather, the place, the there, wherein and as which historical being-there is. The *polis* is the historical place, the there *in* which, *out of* which, and *for* which history happens. To this place and scene of history belong the gods, the temples, the priests, the festivals, the games, the poets, the thinkers, the rulers the council of elders, the assembly of the people, the army and the fleet. All this does not first belong to the *polis,* does not become political by entering into a relation with a statesman and a general and the business of the state. No, it is political, i.e. at the site of history, provided there be (for example) poets *alone*, but then really poets, priests *alone*, but then really priests, rulers *alone*, but then really rulers. *Be*, but this means: as violent men to use power, to become pre-eminent in historical being as creators, as men of action. Pre-eminent in the historical place, they become at the same time *apolis*, without city and place, lonely, strange, and alien, without issue amid the essent as a whole, at the same time without statute and limit, without structure and order, because they themselves *as* creators must first create all this.

The first phase shows us the inner design of the essence of the strangest of all beings, the realms and scope of his power and his destiny. Now we go back to the beginning and attempt the second phase of interpretation.

The second phase. In the light of what has been said above we now follow the sequence of the strophes and hear how the being of man, the strangest of beings, unfolds. We shall try to determine when the *deinon* is meant in the first sense, how the *deinon* in the second sense emerges concurrently, and how, in the reciprocal relation between the two, the being of the strangest being is built up before us in its essential form.

The first strophe names the sea and the earth, each of them overpowering (*deinon*) in its way. It does not speak of them in the manner of us moderns who experience them as mere geographical and geological phenomena and then, as though by an afterthought, brush them over with a few faint and fleeting emotions. Here "sea" is said as though for the first time; the poet speaks of the wintry waves that the sea creates as it unceasingly tears open its own depths and unceasingly flings itself into them. Immediately after the main, guiding statement of the first verses, the song begins, hard and powerful, with *touto kai polion*. Man embarks on the groundless deep, forsaking the solid land. He sets sail not upon bright, smooth waters but amid the storms of winter. The account of this departure concerts with the movement of the prosody; the word *chōrei* in line 336 is situated at the point where the meter shifts: *chōrei*, he abandons the place, he starts out—and ventures into the preponderant power of the placeless waves. The word stands like a pillar in the edifice of these verses.

But woven into one with this violent excursion (Aufbruch) upon the overpowering sea is the never-resting incursion (Einbruch) into the indestructible power of the earth. Here the earth is the highest of the gods. Violently, with acts of power (gewalt-tätig) man disturbs the tranquillity of growth, the nurturing and maturing of the goddess who lives without effort. Here the overpowering reigns not in self-consuming wildness but without effort and fatigue; from out of the superior tranquillity of great riches, it produces and bestows the inexhaustible treasure that surpasses all zeal. Into this power bursts the violent one; year after year he breaks it open with his plows and drives the effortless earth into his restless endeavor. Sea and earth, departure and upheaval are joined by the *kai* in line 334, to which corresponds the *te* in line 338.

And now to all this the antistrophe: it names the birds in the air, the denizens of the water, bull and stallion in the mountains. The living things, lightly dreaming, living in their own rhythm and their own precinct, perpetually overflowing into new forms yet remaining in their *one* channel, know the place where they wander and pass the night. As living things, they are embedded in the power of the sea and the earth. Into this life as it rolls along self-contained, extraordinary in its own sphere and structure and ground, man casts his snares and nets; he snatches the living creatures out of their order, shuts them up in his pens and enclosures, and forces them under his yokes. On the one hand eruption and upheaval. On the other capture and constraint.

At this point, before we pass to the second strophe and its antistrophe, it is necessary to insert a note calculated to ward off a misinterpretation of the whole poem—a misinterpretation to which modern man readily inclines and which is indeed frequent. We have already pointed out that this is no description and exposition of the activities and fields of activity of man, an essent among other essents, but a poetic outline of his being, drawn from its extreme possibilities and limits. This in itself precludes the interpretation of this chorus as a narrative of man's development from the savage hunter and primitive sailor to the civilized builder of cities. Such a notion is the product of ethnology and psychological anthropology. It stems from the unwarranted application of a natural science—and a false one at that—to man's being. The basic fallacy underlying such modes of thought consists in the belief that history begins with the primitive and backward, the weak and helpless. The opposite is true. The beginning is the strangest and mightiest. What comes afterward is not development but the flattening that results from mere spreading out; it is inability to retain the beginning; the beginning is emasculated and exaggerated into a caricature of greatness taken as purely numerical and quantitative size and extension. That strangest of all beings *is* what he is *because* he harbors such a beginning in which everything all at once burst from superabundance into the overpowering and strove to master it.

If this beginning is inexplicable, it is not because of any deficiency in our knowledge of history. On the contrary, the authenticity and greatness of historical knowledge reside in an understanding of the mysterious character of this beginning. The knowledge of primordial history is not a ferreting out of primitive lore or a collecting of bones. It is neither half nor whole natural science but, if it is anything at all, mythology.

The first strophe and antistrophe speak of the sea, the earth, the animal, as the overpowering power which bursts into manifestness through the acts of the violent one.

Outwardly the second strophe passes from a description of the sea, the earth, animals to a characterization of man. But no more than the first strophe and antistrophe speak of nature in the restricted sense does the second strophe speak only of man.

No, what is now named—language, understanding, sentiment, passion, building—are no less a part of the overpowering power than sea, earth, and animal. The difference is only that the latter, the power that is man's environment, sustains, drives, inflames him, while the former reigns within him as the power which he, as the essent that he himself is, must take upon himself.

This pervading force becomes no less overpowering because man takes it into his power, which he uses as such. All this merely conceals the uncanniness of language, of the passions, the powers by which man is ordained (gefügt) as a historical being, while it seems to him that it is *he* who disposes (verfügt) of them. The strangeness, the uncanniness of these powers resides in their seeming familiarity. Directly they yield themselves to man only in their nonessence (Unwesen), so driving him and holding him out of his essence. In this way he comes to regard what is fundamentally more remote and overpowering than sea and earth as closest of all to him.

How far man is from being at home in his own essence is revealed by his opinion of himself as he who invented and could have invented language and understanding, building and poetry.

How could man ever have invented the power which pervades him, which alone enables him to *be* a man? We shall be wholly forgetting that this song speaks of the powerful (*deinon*), the strange and uncanny, if we suppose that the poet makes man invent such things as building and language. The word *edidaxato* does not mean: man invented, but: he found his way to the overpowering and therein first found himself: the violent one, the wielder of power. In view of what has been said, the "himself" means at once he who breaks out and breaks up (*ausbricht und umbricht*, departs and plows), he who captures and subjugates.

It is this breaking out and breaking up, capturing and subjugating that opens up the essent *as* sea, *as* earth, *as* animal. It happens only insofar as the powers of language, of understanding, of temperament, and of building are themselves mastered (*bewältigt*) in violence. The violence of poetic speech, of thinking projection, of building configuration, of the action that creates states is not a function of faculties that man has, but a taming and ordering of powers by virtue of which the essent opens up as such when man moves into it. This disclosure of the essent is the power that man must master in order to become himself amid the essent, i.e. in order to be historical. What is meant by *deinon* here in the second strophe must not be misinterpreted as invention or as a mere faculty or attribute of man.

Only if we understand that the use of power in language, in understanding, in forming and building helps to create (i.e. always, to bring forth) the violent act (*Gewalttat*) of laying out paths into the environing power of the essent, only then shall we understand the strangeness, the uncanniness of all violence. For man, as he journeys everywhere, is not without issue in the external sense that he comes up against outward barriers and cannot go on. In one way or another he can always go farther into the etcetera. He is without issue because he is always thrown back on the paths that he himself has laid out: he becomes mired in his paths, caught in the beaten track, and thus caught he compasses the circle of his world, entangles himself in appearance, and so excludes himself from being. He turns round and round in his own circle. He can ward off whatever threatens this limited sphere. He can employ every skill in its place. The violence that originally creates the paths engenders its own mischief of versatility, which is intrinsically issueless, so much so that it bars itself from reflection about the appearance in which it moves.

All violence shatters against *one* thing. That is death. It is an end beyond all consummation (Vollendung), a limit beyond all limits. Here there is no breaking-out or breaking-up, no capture or subjugation. But this strange and alien (unheimlich) thing that banishes us once and for all from everything in which we are at home is no particular event that must be named among others because it, too, ultimately happens. It is not only when he comes to die, but always and essentially that man is without issue in the face of death. Insofar as man *is,* he stands in the issuelessness of death. Thus his being-there is the happening of strangeness. (For us this happening of a strangeness must be initially grounded in human being-there.)

With the naming of *this* strange and powerful thing, the poetic project of being and human essence sets its own limit upon itself.

For the second antistrophe does not go on to name *still* other powers but gathers those already named into their inner unity. The concluding strophe carries the whole back to its basic line. But as we have stressed in the first phase, the basic line of what is actually at the center of the song (the *deinotaton*) resides precisely in the unitary relation between the two meanings of *deinon.* Accordingly the final strophe, in summary, names three things.

1. The power, the powerful, in which the action of the violent one moves, is the entire scope of the machination (Machenschaft), *machanoen,* entrusted to him. We do not take the word "machination" in a disparaging sense. We have in mind something essential that is disclosed to us in the Greek word *technē. Technē* means neither art nor skill, to say nothing of technique in the modern sense. We translate *technē* by "knowledge." But this requires explanation. Knowledge means here not the result of mere observations concerning previously unknown data. Such information, though indispensable for knowledge, is never more than accessory. Knowledge in the authentic sense of *technē* is the initial and persistent looking out beyond what is given at any time. In different ways, by different channels, and in different realms, this transcendence (Hinaussein) effects (setzt ins Werk) what first gives the datum its relative justification, its potential determinateness, and hence its limit. Knowledge is the ability to put into work the being of any particular essent. The Greeks called art in the true sense and the work of art *technē,* because art is what most immediately brings being (i.e. the appearing that stands there in itself) to stand, stabilizes it in something present (the work). The work of art is a work not

primarily because it is wrought (gewirkt), made, but because it brings about (er-wirkt) being in an essent; it brings about the phenomenon in which the emerging power, *physis,* comes to shine (scheinen). It is through the work of art as essent being that everything else that appears and is to be found is first confirmed and made accessible, explicable, and understandable as being or not being.

Because art in a pre-eminent sense stabilizes and manifests being in the work as an essent, it may be regarded as the ability, pure and simple, to accomplish, to put-into-the-work (ins-Werk-setzen), as *techne.* This accomplishment is a manifesting realization (Erwirken) of being *in* the essent. This superior, realizing opening and keeping open is knowledge. The passion of knowledge is inquiry. Art is knowledge and therefore *techne.* Art is not *techne* because it involves "technical" skill, tools, materials.

Thus *techne* provides the basic trait of *deinon,* the violent; for violence (Gewalt-tätigkeit) is the use of power (Gewaltbrauchen) against the overpowering (Überwältigende): through knowledge it wrests being from concealment into the manifest as the essent.

2. Just as *deinon* as violence collects its essence in the fundamental Greek word *techne,* so *deinon* as the overpowering is manifested in the equally fundamental *dikeo.* We translate it as Fug.[1] Here we understand Fug first in the sense of joint and framework (Fuge und Gefüge); then as decree, dispensation, a directive that the overpowering imposes on its reign; finally, as the governing structure (das fügende Gefüge) which compels adaptation (Einfügung) and compliance (Sichfügen).

If *dike* is translated as "justice" taken in a juridical, moral sense, the word loses its fundamental metaphysical meaning. The same applies to the interpretation of *dike* as norm. In all its realms and dominions the overpowering, in respect to its domination, is Fug. Being, *physis,* as power, is basic and original togetherness: *logos;* it is governing order (fügender Fug): *dike.*

Thus the *deinon* as the overpowering (*dike*) and the *deinon* as the violent (*techne*) confront one another, though not as

[1] Heidegger is particularly free to define the word "Fug" as he wishes because the word does not occur in modern literary German except in the combination "mit Fug und Recht"—"with F. and justice," where it conveys no precise meaning but suggests "proper order," "fitness." This is why I have preferred to introduce the word in German. R.M.

two given things. In this confrontation *technē* bursts forth against *dikē,* which in turn, as Fug, the commanding order, disposes (verfügt) of all *technē.* The reciprocal confrontation *is.* It is only insofar as the strangest thing of all, being-human, is actualized, insofar as man is present as history.

3. The basic trait of the *deinotaton* lies in the interrelation between the two meanings of *deinon.* The sapient man sails into the very middle of the dominant order (Fug); he tears it open and violently carries being into the essent; yet he can never master the overpowering. Hence he is tossed back and forth between structure and the structureless, order and mischief (Fug and Un-fug), between the evil and the noble. Every violent curbing of the powerful is either victory or defeat. Both, each in its different way, fling him out of home, and thus, each in its different way, unfold the dangerousness of achieved or lost being. Both, in different ways, are menaced by disaster. The *violent one,* the creative man, who sets forth into the un-said, who breaks into the un-thought, compels the unhappened to happen and makes the unseen appear —this violent one stands at all times in venture (*tolma,* line 371). In venturing to master being, he must risk the assault of the nonessent, *mē kalon,* he must risk dispersion, in-stability, disorder, mischief. The higher the summit of historical being-there, the deeper will be the abyss, the more abrupt the fall into the unhistorical, which merely thrashes around in issueless and placeless confusion.

Arrived at the end of the second phase, we may wonder what purpose can be served by a third.

The third phase. The central truth of the song was set forth in the first phase. The second phase has led us through all the essential realms of the powerful and violent. The final strophe pulls the whole together into the essence of him who is strangest of all. Certain details might be considered and elucidated more fully. But this would provide a mere appendage to what has already been said; it would not necessitate a new phase of interpretation. If we content ourselves with what the poem directly says, the interpretation is at an end. Actually it has just begun. The actual interpretation must show what does not stand in the words and is nevertheless said. To accomplish this the exegete must use violence. He must seek the essential where nothing more is to be found by the scientific interpretation that brands as unscientific everything that transcends its limits.

But here, where we must restrict ourselves to a single poem, we can undertake this third phase only from a limited point of view imposed by our main task, and even here we must confine ourselves to a few steps. Bearing in mind what has been said in the first phase, we start from the results of our explanation of the final strophe in the second phase.

The *deinotaton* of the *deinon*, the strangest of the strange, lies in the conflict between *dikē* and *technē*. The strangest is not the extreme rectilinear intensification of the strange. It is specifically the uniquely strange. The conflict between the overwhelming presence of the essent as a whole and man's violent being-there creates the possibility of downfall into the issueless and placeless: disaster. But disaster and the possibility of disaster do not occur only at the end, when a single act of power fails, when the violent one makes a false move; no, this disaster is fundamental, it governs and waits in the conflict between violence and the overpowering. Violence against the preponderant power of being *must* shatter against being, if being rules in its essence, as *physis,* as emerging power.

But this necessity of disaster can only subsist insofar as what must shatter is driven into such a being-there. Man is forced into such a being-there, hurled into the affliction (Not)[2] of such being, because the overpowering as such, in order to appear in its power, *requires* a place, a scene of disclosure. The essence of being-human opens up to us only when understood through this need compelled by being itself. The being-there of historical man means: to be posited as the breach into which the preponderant power of being hurls man into this breaking-away, which drives him beyond shatter against being.

The strangest (man) is what it is because, fundamentally, it cultivates and guards the familiar, only in order to break out of it and to let what overpowers it break in. Being itself hurls man into this break-away, which drives him beyond himself to venture forth toward being, to accomplish being, to stabilize it in the work, and so hold open the essent as a whole. Therefore the violent one knows no kindness and conciliation (Güte und Begütigung) in the usual sense; he cannot be mollified or appeased by success or prestige. In all this the violent, creative man sees only the semblance of ful-

[2] The dictionary meanings of the German word "Not" are need, want, anguish, distress, affliction, peril, necessity. Insofar as one meaning can be disengaged from the whole, Heidegger's primary meaning is "need," because he has used this word "Not" as a translation for *chre* in the sixth fragment of Parmenides. But the word as used in German speech and poetry carries the primary implication of distress, trouble, affliction.

fillment, and this he despises. In willing the unprecedented, he casts aside all help. To him disaster is the deepest and broadest affirmation of the overpowering. In the shattering of the wrought work, in the knowledge that it is mischief (Unfug) and *sarma* (a dunghill), he leaves the overpowering to its order (Fug). But all this not in the form of "psychic experiences" in which the soul of the creative man wallows, and still less in the form of petty feelings of inferiority, but wholly in terms of the accomplishment itself, the putting-into-the work. *As history* the overpowering, being, is confirmed in works.

Thus the being-there of the historical man is the breach through which the being embodied in the essent can open. As such it is an *in-cident* (Zwischen-fall, a fall-between), the incident in which suddenly the unbound powers of being come forth and are accomplished as history. The Greeks had a profound sense of this suddenness and uniqueness of being-there, forced on them by being itself, which disclosed itself to them as *physis* and *logos* and *dikē*. It is inconceivable that the Greeks should have decided to turn out culture for the benefit of the next few millennia of Western history. In the unique need of their being-there they alone responded solely with violence, thus not doing away with the need but only augmenting it; and in this way they won for themselves the fundamental condition of true historical greatness.

We shall fail to understand the mysteriousness of the essence of being-human, thus experienced and poetically carried back to its ground, if we snatch at value judgments of any kind.

The evaluation of being-human as arrogance and presumption in the pejorative sense takes man out of his essential need as the in-cident. To judge in this way is to take man as something already-there, to put this something into an empty space, and appraise it according to some external table of values. But it is the same kind of misunderstanding to interpret the poet's words as a tacit rejection of being-human, a covert admonition to resign oneself without violence, to seek undisturbed comfort. This interpretation might even find some basis in the concluding lines of the poem.

One who is *thus* (namely the strangest of all) should be excluded from hearth and council. But the final words of the chorus do not contradict what has previously been said about being-human. Insofar as the chorus turns *against* the strangest of all, it says that this manner of being is *not* that of every day. Such being-there is not to be found in the usual bustle

312

and activity. There is nothing surprising about these concluding words; indeed, we should have to be surprised if they
were lacking. Their attitude of rejection is a direct and complete confirmation of the strangeness and uncanniness of human beings. With its concluding words the song swings back
to its beginning.

Nietzsche on Tragedy

The Birth of Tragedy

FRIEDRICH NIETZSCHE

WE NOW approach the real purpose of our investigation, which aims at acquiring a knowledge of the Dionyso-Apollonian genius and his artwork, or at least an anticipatory understanding of the mystery of the aforesaid union. Here we shall ask first of all where that new germ which subsequently developed into tragedy and dramatic dithyramb first makes itself perceptible in the Hellenic world. The ancients themselves supply the answer in symbolic form, when they place *Homer* and *Archilochus* as the forefathers and torch-bearers of Greek poetry side by side on gems, sculptures, etc., in the sure conviction that only these two thoroughly original compeers, from whom a stream of fire flows over the whole of Greek posterity, should be taken into consideration. Homer, the aged dreamer sunk in himself, the type of the Apollonian naïve artist, beholds now with astonishment the impassioned genius of the warlike votary of the muses, Archilochus, violently tossed to and fro on the billows of existence: and modern æsthetics could only add by way of interpretation, that here the "objective" artist is confronted by the first "subjective" artist. But this interpretation is of little service to us, because we know the subjective artist only as the poor artist, and in every type and elevation of art we demand specially and first of all the conquest of the Subjective, the redemption from the "ego" and the cessation of every individual will and desire; indeed, we find it impossible to believe in any truly artistic production, however insignificant, without objectivity, without pure, interestless contemplation. Hence our æsthetics must first solve the problem as to how the "lyrist" is possible as an artist: he who according to the experience of all ages continually says "I" and sings off to us the entire chromatic scale of his passions and desires. This very Archilochus appals us, alongside of Homer, by his cries of hatred and scorn, by the drunken outbursts of his desire. Is not just he then, who has been called the first subjective artist, the non-artist proper? But whence then the reverence which was shown to him—the poet—in very remarkable utterances by the Delphic oracle itself, the focus of "objective" art?

Schiller has enlightened us concerning his poetic procedure by a psychological observation, inexplicable to himself, yet not apparently open to any objection. He acknowledges that as the preparatory state to the act of poetising he had not perhaps before him or within him a series of pictures with co-ordinate causality of thoughts, but rather a *musical mood*. ("The perception with me is at first without a clear and definite object; this forms itself later. A certain musical mood of mind precedes, and only after this does the poetical idea follow with me.") Add to this the most important phenomenon of all ancient lyric poetry, *the union*, regarded everywhere as natural, *of the lyrist with the musician*, their very identity, indeed,—compared with which our modern lyric poetry is like the statue of a god without a head,—and we may now, on the basis of our metaphysics of æsthetics set forth above, interpret the lyrist to ourselves as follows. As Dionysian artist he is in the first place become altogether one with the Primordial Unity, its pain and contradiction, and he produces the copy of this Primordial Unity as music, granting that music has been correctly termed a repetition and a recast of the world; but now, under the Apollonian dream-inspiration, this music again becomes visible to him as in a *symbolic dream-picture*. The formless and intangible reflection of the primordial pain in music, with its redemption in appearance, then generates a second mirroring as a concrete symbol or example. The artist has already surrendered his subjectivity in the Dionysian process: the picture which now shows to him his oneness with the heart of the world, is a dream-scene, which embodies the primordial contradiction and primordial pain, together with the primordial joy, of appearance. The "I" of the lyrist sounds therefore from the abyss of being: its "subjectivity," in the sense of the modern æsthetes, is a fiction. When Archilochus, the first lyrist of the Greeks, makes known both his mad love and his contempt to the daughters of Lycambes, it is not his passion which dances before us in orgiastic frenzy: we see Dionysus and the Mænads, we see the drunken reveller Archilochus sunk down to sleep—as Euripides depicts it in the Bacchæ, the sleep on the high Alpine pasture, in the noonday sun:—and now Apollo approaches and touches him with the laurel. The Dionysomusical enchantment of the sleeper now emits, as it were, picture sparks, lyrical poems, which in their highest development are called tragedies and dramatic dithyrambs.

The plastic artist, as also the epic poet, who is related to him, is sunk in the pure contemplation of pictures. The Dionysian musician is, without any picture, himself just primordial pain and the primordial re-echoing thereof. The lyric genius is conscious of a world of pictures and symbols —growing out of the state of mystical self-abnegation and oneness,—which has a colouring causality and velocity quite different from that of the world of the plastic artist and epic poet. While the latter lives in these pictures, and only in them, with joyful satisfaction, and never grows tired of contemplating them with love, even in their minutest characters, while even the picture of the angry Achilles is to him but a picture, the angry expression of which he enjoys with the dream-joy in appearance—so that, by this mirror of appearance, he is guarded against being unified and blending with his figures;—the pictures of the lyrist on the other hand are nothing but *his very* self and, as it were, only different projections of himself, on account of which he as the moving centre of this world is entitled to say "I": only of course this self is not the same as that of the waking, empirically real man, but the only verily existent and eternal self resting at the basis of things, by means of the images whereof the lyric genius sees through even to this basis of things. Now let us suppose that he beholds *himself* also among these images as non-genius, *i.e.*, his subject, the whole throng of subjective passions and impulses of the will directed to a definite object which appears real to him; if now it seems as if the lyric genius and the allied non-genius were one, and as if the former spoke that little word "I" of his own accord, this appearance will no longer be able to lead us astray, as it certainly led those astray who designated the lyrist as the subjective poet. In truth, Archilochus, the passionately inflamed, loving and hating man, is but a vision of the genius, who by this time is no longer Archilochus, but a genius of the world, who expresses his primordial pain symbolically in the figure of the man Archilochus: while the subjectively willing and desiring man, Archilochus, can never at any time be a poet. It is by no means necessary, however, that the lyrist should see nothing but the phenomenon of the man Archilochus before him as a reflection of eternal being; and tragedy shows how far the visionary world of the lyrist may depart from this phenomenon, to which, of course, it is most intimately related.

Schopenhauer, who did not shut his eyes to the difficulty presented by the lyrist in the philosophical contemplation of art, thought he had found a way out of it, on which, however, I cannot accompany him; while he alone, in his profound metaphysics of music, held in his hands the means whereby this difficulty could be definitely removed: as I believe I have removed it here in his spirit and to his honour. In contrast to our view, he describes the peculiar nature of song as follows[1] (*Welt als Wille und Vorstellung,* I. 295):—"It is the subject of the will, *i.e.,* his own volition, which fills the consciousness of the singer; often as an unbound and satisfied desire (joy), but still more often as a restricted desire (grief), always as an emotion, a passion, or an agitated frame of mind. Besides this, however, and along with it, by the sight of surrounding nature, the singer becomes conscious of himself as the subject of pure will-less knowing, the unbroken, blissful peace of which now appears, in contrast to the stress of desire, which is always restricted and always needy. The feeling of this contrast, this alternation, is really what the song as a whole expresses and what principally constitutes the lyrical state of mind. In it pure knowing comes to us as it were to deliver us from desire and the stress thereof: we follow, but only for an instant; for desire, the remembrance of our personal ends, tears us anew from peaceful contemplation; yet ever again the next beautiful surrounding in which the pure will-less knowledge presents itself to us, allures us away from desire. Therefore, in song and in the lyrical mood, desire (the personal interest of the ends) and the pure perception of the surrounding which presents itself, are wonderfully mingled with each other; connections between them are sought for and imagined; the subjective disposition, the affection of the will, imparts its own hue to the contemplated surrounding, and conversely, the surroundings communicate the reflex of their colour to the will. The true song is the expression of the whole of this mingled and divided state of mind."

Who could fail to see in this description that lyric poetry is here characterised as an imperfectly attained art, which seldom and only as it were in leaps arrives at its goal, indeed, as a semi-art, the essence of which is said to consist

---

[1] *World as Will and Idea*, I. 323, 4th ed. of Haldane and Kemp's translation. Quoted with a few changes.

in this, that desire and pure contemplation, *i.e.*, the unæsthetic and the æsthetic condition, are wonderfully mingled with each other? We maintain rather, that this entire antithesis, according to which, as according to some standard of value, Schopenhauer, too, still classifies the arts, the antithesis between the subjective and the objective, is quite out of place in æsthetics, inasmuch as the subject, *i.e.*, the desiring individual who furthers his own egoistic ends, can be conceived only as the adversary, not as the origin of art. In so far as the subject is the artist, however, he has already been released from his individual will, and has become as it were the medium, through which the one verily existent Subject celebrates his redemption in appearance. For this one thing must above all be clear to us, to our humiliation *and* exaltation, that the entire comedy of art is not at all performed, say, for our betterment and culture, and that we are just as little the true authors of this art-world: rather we may assume with regard to ourselves, that its true author uses us as pictures and artistic projections, and that we have our highest dignity in our significance as works of art—for only as an *æsthetic phenomenon* is existence and the world eternally *justified*:— while of course our consciousness of this our specific significance hardly differs from the kind of consciousness which the soldiers painted on canvas have of the battle represented thereon. Hence all our knowledge of art is at bottom quite illusory, because, as knowing persons we are not one and identical with the Being who, as the sole author and spectator of this comedy of art, prepares a perpetual entertainment for himself. Only in so far as the genius in the act of artistic production colasces with this primordial artist of the world, does he get a glimpse of the eternal essence of art, for in this state he is, in a marvellous manner, like the weird picture of the fairy-tale which can at will turn its eyes and behold itself; he is now at once subject and object, at once poet, actor, and spectator.

With reference to Archilochus, it has been established by critical research that he introduced the *folk-song* into literature, and, on account thereof, deserved, according to the general estimate of the Greeks, his unique position alongside of Homer. But what is this popular folk-song in contrast to the wholly Apollonian epos? What else but the *perpetuum vestigium* of a union of the Apollonian and the Dionysian? Its enormous diffusion among all peoples, still further enhanced by ever new births, testifies to the power of this artistic double impulse of nature: which leaves its vestiges in the popular song in like manner as the orgiastic movements of a people perpetuate themselves in its music. Indeed, one might also furnish historical proofs, that every period which is highly productive in popular songs has been most violently stirred by Dionysian currents, which we must always regard as the substratum and prerequisite of the popular song.

First of all, however, we regard the popular song as the musical mirror of the world, as the original melody, which now seeks for itself a parallel dream-phenomenon and expresses it in poetry. *Melody is therefore primary and universal*, and as such may admit of several objectivations, in several texts. Likewise, in the naïve estimation of the people, it is regarded as by far the more important and necessary. Melody generates the poem out of itself by an ever-recurring process. *The strophic form of the popular song* points to the same phenomenon, which I always beheld with astonishment, till at last I found this explanation. Any one who in accordance with this theory examines a collection of popular songs, such as "Des Knaben Wunderhorn," will find innumerable instances of the perpetually productive melody scattering picture sparks all around: which in their variegation, their abrupt change, their mad precipitance, manifest a power quite unknown to the epic appearance and its steady flow. From the point of view of the epos, this unequal and irregular pictorial world of lyric poetry must be simply condemned: and the solemn epic rhapsodists of the Apollonian festivals in the age of Terpander have certainly done so.

Accordingly, we observe that in the poetising of the popular song, language is strained to its utmost *to imitate music*; and hence a new world of poetry begins with Archilochus, which is fundamentally opposed to the Homeric. And in saying this we have pointed out the only possible relation between poetry and music, between word and tone: the word, the picture, the concept here seeks an expression analogous to music and now experiences in itself the power of music. In this sense we may discriminate between two main currents in the history of the language of the Greek people, according as their language imitated either the world of phenomena and of pictures, or the world of music. One has only to reflect seriously on the linguistic difference with regard to colour, syntactical structure, and vocabulary in Homer and Pindar, in order to comprehend the significance of this contrast; indeed, it becomes palpably clear to us that in the period between Homer and Pindar the *orgiastic flute tones of Olympus* must have sounded forth, which, in an age as late as Aristotle's, when music was infinitely more developed, transported people to drunken enthusiasm, and which, when their influence was first felt, undoubtedly incited all the poetic means of expression of contemporaneous man to imitation. I here call attention to a familiar phenomenon of our own times, against which our æsthetics raises many objections. We again and again have occasion to observe how a symphony of Beethoven compels the individual hearers to use figurative speech, though the appearance presented by a collocation of the different pictorial world generated by a piece of music may be never so fantastically diversified and even contradictory. To practise its small wit on such compositions, and to overlook a phenomenon which is certainly worth explaining, is quite in keeping with this æsthetics. Indeed, even if the tone-poet has spoken in pictures concerning a composition, when for instance he designates a certain symphony as the "pastoral" symphony, or a passage therein as "the scene by the brook," or another as the "merry gathering of rustics," these are likewise only symbolical representations born out of music— and not perhaps the imitated objects of music—representations which can give us no information whatever concerning the *Dionysian* content of music, and which in fact have no distinctive value of their own alongside of other pictorical expressions. This process of a discharge of music in pictures we have now to transfer to some youthful, linguistically productive people, to get a notion as to how the strophic popular song originates, and how the entire faculty of speech is stimulated by this new principle of imitation of music.

If, therefore, we may regard lyric poetry as the effulguration of music in pictures and concepts, we can now ask: "how does music *appear* in the mirror of symbolism and conception?" *It appears as will*, taking the word in the Schopenhauerian sense, *i.e.*, as the antithesis of the æsthetic, purely contemplative, and passive frame of mind. Here, however, we must discriminate as sharply as possible between the concept of essentiality and the concept of phenominality; for music, according to its essence, cannot be will, because as such it would have to be wholly banished from the domain of art— for the will is the unæsthetic-in-itself;—yet it appears as will. For in order to express the phenomenon of music in pictures, the lyrist requires all the stirrings of passion, from the whispering of infant desire to the roaring of madness. Under the impulse to speak of music in Apollonian symbols, he conceives of all nature, and himself therein, only as the eternally willing, desiring, longing existence. But in so far as he interprets music by means of pictures, he himself rests in the quiet calm of Apollonian contemplation, however much all around him which he beholds through the medium of music is in a state of confused and violent motion. Indeed, when he beholds himself through this same medium, his own image appears to him in a state of unsatisfied feeling: his own willing, longing, moaning and rejoicing are to him symbols by which he interprets music. Such is the phenomenon of the lyrist: as Apollonian genius he interprets music through the image of the will, while he himself, completely released from the avidity of the will, is the pure, undimmed eye of day.

Our whole disquisition insists on this, that lyric poetry is dependent on the spirit of music just as music itself in its absolute sovereignty does not *require* the picture and the concept, but only *endures* them as accompaniments. The poems of the lyrist can express nothing which has not already been contained in the vast universality and absoluteness of the music which compelled him to use figurative speech. By no means is it possible for language adequately to render the cosmic symbolism of music, for the very reason that music stands in symbolic relation to the primordial contradiction and primordial pain in the heart of the Primordial Unity, and therefore symbolises a sphere which is above all appearance and before all phenomena. Rather should we say that all phenomena, compared with it, are but symbols: hence *language*, as the organ and symbol of phenomena, cannot at all disclose the innermost essence of music; language can only be in superficial contact with music when it attempts to imitate music; while the profoundest significance of the latter cannot be brought one step nearer to us by all the eloquence of lyric poetry.

We shall now have to avail ourselves of all the principles of art hitherto considered, in order to find our way through the labyrinth, as we must designate *the origin of Greek tragedy*. I shall not be charged with absurdity in saying that the problem of this origin has as yet not even been seriously stated, not to say solved, however often the fluttering tatters of ancient tradition have been sewed together in sundry combinations and torn asunder again. This tradition tells us in the most unequivocal terms, *that tragedy sprang from the tragic chorus,* and was originally only chorus and nothing but chorus: and hence we feel it our duty to look into the heart of this tragic chorus as being the real proto-drama, without in the least contenting ourselves with current art-phraseology—according to which the chorus is the ideal spectator, or represents the people in contrast to the regal side of the scene. The latter explanatory notion, which sounds sublime to many a politician—that the immutable moral law was embodied by the democratic Athenians in the popular chorus, which always carries its point over the passionate excesses and extravagances of kings—may be ever so forcibly suggested by an observation of Aristotle: still it has no bearing on the original formation of tragedy, inasmuch as the entire antithesis of king and people, and, in general, the whole politico-social sphere, is excluded from the purely religious beginnings of tragedy; but, considering the well-known classical form of the chorus in Æschylus and Sophocles, we should even deem it blasphemy to speak here of the anticipation of a "constitutional representation of the people," from which blasphemy others have not shrunk, however. The ancient governments knew of no constitutional representation of the people *in praxi,* and it is to be hoped that they did not so much as "anticipate" it in tragedy.

Much more celebrated than this political explanation of the chorus is the notion of A. W. Schlegel, who advises us to regard the chorus, in a manner, as the essence and extract of the crowd of spectators,—as the "ideal spectator." This view, when compared with the historical tradition that tragedy was originally only chorus, reveals itself in its true character, as a crude, unscientific, yet brilliant assertion, which, however, has acquired its brilliancy only through its concentrated form of expression, through the truly Germanic bias in favour of whatever is called "ideal," and through our momentary astonishment. For we are indeed astonished the moment we compare our well-known theatrical public with this chorus, and ask ourselves if it could ever be possible to idealise something analogous to the Greek chorus out of such a public. We tacitly deny this, and now wonder as much at the boldness of Schlegel's assertion as at the totally different nature of the Greek public. For hitherto we always believed that the true spectator, be he who he may, had always to remain conscious of having before him a work of art, and not an empiric reality: whereas the tragic chorus of the Greeks is compelled to recognise real beings in the figures of the stage. The chorus of the Oceanides really believes that it sees before it the Titan Prometheus, and considers itself as real as the god of the scene. And are we to own that he is the highest and purest type of spectator, who, like the Oceanides, regards Prometheus as real and present in body? And is it characteristic of the ideal spectator that he should run on the stage and free the god from his torments? We had believed in an æsthetic public, and considered the individual spectator the better qualified the more he was capable of viewing a work of art as art, that is, æsthetically; but now the Schlegelian expression has intimated to us, that the perfect ideal spectator does not at all suffer the world of the scenes to act æsthetically on him, but corporeo-empirically. Oh, these Greeks! we have sighed; they will upset our æsthetics! But once accustomed to it, we have reiterated the saying of Schlegel, as often as the subject of the chorus has been broached.

But the tradition which is so explicit here speaks against Schlegel: the chorus as such, without the stage,—the primitive form of tragedy,—and the chorus of ideal spectators do not harmonise. What kind of art would that be which was extracted from the concept of the spectator, and whereof we are to regard the "spectator as such" as the true form? The spectator without the play is something absurd. We fear that the birth of tragedy can be explained neither by the high esteem for the moral intelligence of the multitude nor by the concept of the spectator without the play; and we regard the problem as too deep to be even so much as touched by such superficial modes of contemplation.

An infinitely more valuable insight into the signification of the chorus had already been displayed by Schiller in the celebrated Preface to his Bride of Messina, where he regarded the chorus as a living wall which tragedy draws round herself to guard her from contact with the world of reality, and to preserve her ideal domain and poetical freedom.

It is with this, his chief weapon, that Schiller combats the ordinary conception of the natural, the illusion ordinarily required in dramatic poetry. He contends that while indeed the day on the stage is merely artificial, the architecture only symbolical, and the metrical dialogue purely ideal in character, nevertheless an erroneous view still prevails in the main: that it is not enough to tolerate merely as a poetical license *that* which is in reality the essence of all poetry. The introduction of the chorus is, he says, the decisive step by which war is declared openly and honestly against all naturalism in art.—It is, methinks, for disparaging this mode of contemplation that our would-be superior age has coined the disdainful catchword "pseudo-idealism." I fear, however, that we on the other hand with our present worship of the natural and the real have landed at the nadir of all idealism, namely in the region of cabinets of wax-figures. An art indeed exists also here, as in certain novels much in vogue at present: but let no one pester us with the claim that by this art the Schiller-Goethian "pseudo-idealism" has been vanquished.

It is indeed an "ideal" domain, as Schiller rightly perceived, upon which the Greek satyric chorus, the chorus of primitive tragedy, was wont to walk, a domain raised far above the actual path of mortals. The Greek framed for this chorus the suspended scaffolding of a fictitious *natural state* and placed thereon fictitious *natural beings*. It is on this foundation that tragedy grew up, and so it could of course dispense from the very first with a painful portrayal of reality. Yet it is not an arbitrary world placed by fancy betwixt heaven and earth; rather is it a world possessing the same reality and trustworthiness that Olympus with its dwellers possessed for the believing Hellene. The satyr, as being the Dionysian chorist, lives in a religiously acknowledged reality under the sanction of the myth and cult. That tragedy begins with him, that the Dionysian wisdom of tragedy speaks through him, is just as surprising a phenomenon to us as, in general, the derivation of tragedy from the chorus. Perhaps we shall get a starting-point for our inquiry, if I put forward the proposition that the satyr, the fictitious natural being, is to the man of culture what Dionysian music is to civilisation. Concerning this latter, Richard Wagner says that it is neutralised by music even as lamplight by daylight. In like manner, I believe, the Greek man of culture felt himself neutralised in the presence of the satyric chorus: and this is the most immediate effect of the Dionysian tragedy, that the state and society, and, in general, the gaps between man and man give way to an overwhelming feeling of oneness, which leads back to the heart of nature. The metaphysical comfort,—with which, as I have here intimated, every true tragedy dismisses us—that, in spite of the perpetual change of phenomena, life at bottom is indestructibly powerful and pleasurable, this comfort appears with corporeal lucidity as the satyric chorus, as the chorus of natural beings, who live ineradicable as it were behind all civilisation, and who, in spite of the ceaseless change of generations and the history of nations, remain for ever the same.

With this chorus the deep-minded Hellene, who is so singularly qualified for the most delicate and severe suffering, consoles himself:—he who has glanced with piercing eye into the very heart of the terrible destructive processes of so-called universal history, has also into the cruelty of nature, and is in danger of longing for a Buddhistic negation of the will. Art saves him, and through art life saves him—for herself.

For we must know that in the rapture of the Dionysian state, with its annihilation of the ordinary bounds and limits of existence, there is a *lethargic* element, wherein all personal experiences of the past are submerged. It is by this gulf of oblivion that the everyday world and the world of Dionysian reality are separated from each other. But as soon as this everyday reality rises again in consciousness, it is felt as such, and nauseates us; an ascetic will-paralysing mood is the fruit of these states. In this sense the Dionysian man may be said to resemble Hamlet: both have for once seen into the true nature of things,—they have *perceived,* but they are loath to act; for their action cannot change the eternal nature of things; they regard it as shameful or ridiculous that one should require of them to set aright the time which is out of joint. Knowledge kills action, action requires the veil of illusion—it is this lesson which Hamlet teaches, and not the cheap wisdom of John-a-Dreams who from too much reflection, as it were from a surplus of possibilities, does not arrive at action at all. Not reflection, no!—true knowledge, insight into appalling truth, preponderates over all motives inciting to action, in Hamlet as well as in the Dionysian man. No comfort avails any longer; his longing goes beyond a world after death, beyond the gods themselves; existence with its glittering reflection in the gods, or in an immortal other world is abjured. In the consciousness of the truth he has perceived, man now sees everywhere only the awfulness of the absurdity of existence, he now understands the symbolism in the fate of Ophelia, he now discerns the wisdom of the sylvan god Silenus: and loathing seizes him.

Here, in this extremest danger of the will, *art* approaches, as a saving and healing enchantress; she alone is able to transform these nauseating reflections on the awfulness or absurdity of existence into representations wherewith it is possible to live: these are the representations of the *sublime* as the artistic subjugation of the awful, and the *comic* as the artistic delivery from the nausea of the absurd. The satyric chorus of dithyramb is the saving deed of Greek art; the paroxyms described above spent their force in the intermediary world of these Dionysian followers.

The satyr, like the idyllic shepherd of our more recent time, is the offspring of a longing after the Primitive and the Natural; but mark with what firmness and fearlessness the Greek embraced the man of the woods, and again, how coyly and mawkishly the modern man dallied with the flattering picture of a tender, flute-playing, soft-natured shepherd! Nature, on which as yet no knowledge has been at work, which maintains unbroken barriers to culture—this is what the Greek saw in his satyr, which still was not on this account supposed to coincide with the ape. On the contrary: it was the archetype of man, the embodiment of his highest and strongest emotions, as the enthusiastic reveller enraptured by the proximity of his god, as the fellow-suffering companion in whom the suffering of the god repeats itself, as the herald of wisdom speaking from the very depths of nature, as the emblem of the sexual omnipotence of nature, which the Greek was wont to contemplate with reverential awe. The satyr was something sublime and godlike: he could not but appear so, especially to the sad and wearied eye of the Dionysian man. He would have been offended by our spurious tricked-up shepherd, while his eye dwelt with sublime satisfaction on the naked and unstuntedly magnificent characters of nature: here the illusion of culture was brushed away from the archetype of man; here the true man, the bearded satyr, revealed himself, who shouts joyfully to his god. Before him the cultured man shrank to a lying caricature. Schiller is right also with reference to these beginnings of tragic art: the chorus is a living bulwark against the onsets of reality, because it—the satyric chorus—portrays existence more truthfully, more realistically, more perfectly than the cultured man who ordinarily considers himself as the only reality. The sphere of poetry does not lie outside the world, like some fantastic impossibility of a poet's imagination: it seeks to be the very opposite, the unvarnished expression of truth, and must for this very reason cast aside the false finery of that supposed reality of the cultured man. The contrast between this intrinsic truth of nature and the falsehood of culture, which poses as the only reality, is similar to that existing between the eternal kernel of things, the thing in itself, and the collective world of phenomena. And even as tragedy, with its metaphysical comfort, points to the eternal life of this kernel of existence, notwithstanding the perpetual dissolution of phenomena, so the symbolism of the satyric chorus already expresses figuratively this primordial relation between the thing in itself and phenomenon. The idyllic shepherd of the modern man is but a copy of the sum of the illusions of culture which he calls nature; the Dionysian Greek desires truth and nature in their most potent form;—he sees himself metamorphosed into the satyr.

The revelling crowd of the votaries of Dionysus rejoices, swayed by such moods and perceptions, the power of which transforms them before their own eyes, so that they imagine they behold themselves as reconstituted genii of nature, as satyrs. The later constitution of the tragic chorus is the artistic imitation of this natural phenomenon, which of course required a separation of the Dionysian spectators from the enchanted Dionysians. However, we must never lose sight of the fact that the public of the Attic tragedy rediscovered itself in the chorus of the orchestra, that there was in reality no antithesis of public and chorus: for all was but one great sublime chorus of dancing and singing satyrs, or of such as allowed themselves to be represented by the satyrs. The Schlegelian observation must here reveal itself to us in a deeper sense. The chorus is the "ideal spectator"[2] in so far as it is the only *beholder*,[3] the beholder of the visionary world of the scene. A public of spectators, as known to us, was unknown to the Greeks. In their theatres the terraced structure of the spectators' space rising in concentric arcs enabled every one, in the strictest sense, to *overlook* the entire world of culture around him, and in surfeited contemplation to imagine himself a chorist. According to this view, then, we may call the chorus in its primitive stage in proto-tragedy, a self-mirroring of the Dionysian man: a phenomenon which may be best exemplified by the process of the actor, who, if he be truly gifted, sees hovering before his eyes with almost tangible perceptibility the character he is to represent. The satyric chorus is first of all a vision of the Dionysian throng, just as the world of the stage is, in turn, a vision of the satyric chorus: the power of this vision is great enough to render the eye dull and insensible to the impression of "reality," to the presence of the cultured men occupying the tiers of seats on every side. The form of the Greek theatre reminds one of a lonesome mountain-valley: the architecture of the scene appears like a luminous cloud-picture which the Bacchants swarming on the mountains behold from the

2 Zuschauer.   3 Schauer.

heights, as the splendid encirclement in the midst of which the image of Dionysus is revealed to them.

Owing to our learned conception of the elementary artistic processes, this artistic proto-phenomenon, which is here introduced to explain the tragic chorus, is almost shocking: while nothing can be more certain than that the poet is a poet only in that he beholds himself surrounded by forms which live and act before him, into the innermost being of which his glance penetrates. By reason of a strange defeat in our capacities, we modern men are apt to represent to ourselves the æsthetic proto-phenomenon as too complex and abstract. For the true poet the metaphor is not a rhetorical figure, but a vicarious image which actually hovers before him in place of a concept. The character is not for him an aggregate composed of a studied collection of particular traits, but an irrepressibly live person appearing before his eyes, and differing only from the corresponding vision of the painter by its ever continued life and action. Why is it that Homer sketches much more vividly[4] than all the other poets? Because he contemplates[5] much more. We talk so abstractly about poetry, because we are all wont to be bad poets. At bottom the æsthetic phenomenon is simple: let a man but have the faculty of perpetually seeing a lively play and of constanly living surrounded by hosts of spirits, then he is a poet: let him but feel the impulse to transform himself and to talk from out the bodies and souls of others, then he is a dramatist.

The Dionysian excitement is able to impart to a whole mass of men this artistic faculty of seeing themselves surrounded by such a host of spirits, with whom they know themselves to be inwardly one. This function of the tragic chorus is the *dramatic* proto-phenomenon: to see one's self transformed before one's self, and then to act as if one had really entered into another body, into another character. This function stands at the beginning of the development of the drama. Here we have something different from the rhapsodist, who does not blend with his pictures, but only sees them, like the painter, with contemplative eye outside of him; here we actually have a surrender of the individual by his entering into another nature. Moreover this phenomenon appears in the form of an epidemic: a whole throng feels itself metamorphosed in this wise. Hence it is that the dithyramb is essentially different from every other variety of the choric song. The virgins, who with laurel twigs in

4 Anschaulicher.   5 Anschaut.

their hands solemnly proceed to the temple of Apollo and sing a processional hymn, remain what they are and retain their civic names: the dithyrambic chorus is a chorus of transformed beings, whose civic past and social rank are totally forgotten: they have become the timeless servants of their god that live aloof from all the spheres of society. Every other variety of the choric lyric of the Hellenes is but an enormous enhancement of the Apollonian unit-singer: while in the dithyramb we have before us a community of unconscious actors, who mutually regard themselves as transformed among one another.

This enchantment is the prerequisite of all dramatic art. In this enchantment the Dionysian reveller sees himself as a satyr, *and as satyr he in turn beholds the god,* that is, in his transformation he sees a new vision outside him as the Apollonian consummation of his state. With this new vision the drama is complete.

According to this view, we must understand Greek tragedy as the Dionysian chorus, which always disburdens itself anew in an Apollonian world of pictures. The choric parts, therefore, with which tragedy is interlaced, are in a manner the mother-womb of the entire so-called dialogue, that is, of the whole stage-world, of the drama proper. In several successive outbursts does this primordial basis of tragedy beam forth the vision of the drama, which is a dream-phenomenon throughout, and, as such, epic in character: on the other hand, however, as objectivation of a Dionysian state, it does not represent the Apollonian redemption in appearance, but, conversely, the dissolution of the individual and his unification with primordial existence. Accordingly, the drama is the Apollonian embodiment of Dionysian perceptions and influences, and is thereby separated from the epic as by an immense gap.

The *chorus* of Greek tragedy, the symbol of the mass of the people moved by Dionysian excitement, is thus fully explained by our conception of it as here set forth. Whereas, being accustomed to the position of a chorus on the modern stage, especially an operatic chorus, we could never comprehend why the tragic chorus of the Greeks should be older, more primitive, indeed, more important than the "action" proper,—as has been so plainly declared by the voice of tradition; whereas, furthermore, we could not reconcile with this traditional paramount importance and primitiveness the fact of the chorus' being composed only of humble, ministering beings; indeed, at first only of goatlike satyrs; whereas, finally, the orchestra before the scene was always a riddle to us; we have learned to comprehend at length that the scene, together with the action, was fundamentally and orginally conceived only as a *vision*, that the only reality is just the chorus, which of itself generates the vision and speaks thereof with the entire symbolism of dancing, tone, and word. This chorus beholds in the vision its lord and master Dionysus, and is thus for ever the *serving* chorus: it sees how he, the god, suffers and glorifies himself, and therefore does not itself *act*. But though its attitude towards the god is throughout the attitude of ministration, this is nevertheless the highest expression, the Dionysian expression of *Nature,* and therefore, like Nature herself, the chorus utters oracles and wise sayings when transported with enthusiasm: as *fellow-sufferer* it is also the *sage* proclaiming truth from out the heart of Nature. Thus, then, originates the fantastic figure, which seems so shocking, of the wise and enthusiastic satyr, who is at the same time "the dumb man" in contrast to the god: the image of Nature and her strongest impulses, yea, the symbol of Nature, and at the same time the herald of her art and wisdom: musician, poet, dancer, and visionary in one person.

Agreeably to this view, and agreeably to tradition, *Dionysus,* the proper stage-hero and focus of vision, is not at first actually present in the oldest period of tragedy, but is only imagined as present: *i.e.,* tragedy is originally only "chorus" and not "drama." Later on the attempt is made to exhibit the god as real and to display the visionary figure together with its glorifying encirclement before the eyes of all; it is here that the "drama" in the narrow sense of the term begins. To the dithyrambic chorus is now assigned the task of exciting the minds of the hearers to such a pitch of Dionysian frenzy, that, when the tragic hero appears on the stage, they do not behold in him, say, the unshapely masked man, but a visionary figure, born as it were of their own ecstasy. Let us picture Admetes thinking in profound meditation of his lately departed wife Alcestis, and quite consuming himself in spiritual contemplation thereof—when suddenly the veiled figure of a woman resembling her in form and gait is led towards him: let us picture his sudden trembling anxiety, his agitated comparisons, his instinctive conviction—and we shall have an analogon to the sensation with which the spectator, excited to Dionysian frenzy, saw the god approaching on the stage, a god with whose sufferings he had already become identified. He involuntarily transferred the entire picture of the god, fluttering magically before his soul, to this masked

333

figure and resolved its reality as it were into a phantasmal unreality. This is the Apollonian dream-state, in which the world of day is veiled, and a new world, clearer, more intelligible, more striking than the former, and nevertheless more shadowy, is ever born anew in perpetual change before our eyes. We accordingly recognise in tragedy a thoroughgoing stylistic contrast: the language, colour, flexibility and dynamics of the dialogue fall apart in the Dionysian lyrics of the chorus on the one hand, and in the Apollonian dreamworld of the scene on the other, into entirely separate spheres of expression. The Apollonian appearances, in which Dionysus objectifies himself, are no longer "ein ewiges Meer, ein wechselnd Weben, ein glühend Leben,"[6] as is the music of the chorus, they are no longer the forces merely felt, but not condensed into a picture, by which the inspired votary of Dionysus divines the proximity of his god: the clearness and firmness of epic form now speak to him from the scene, Dionysus now no longer speaks through forces, but as an epic hero, almost in the language of Homer.

Whatever rises to the surface in the dialogue of the Apollonian part of Greek tragedy, appears simple, transparent, beautiful. In this sense the dialogue is a copy of the Hellene, whose nature reveals itself in the dance, because in the dance the greatest energy is merely potential, but betrays itself nevertheless in flexible and vivacious movements. The language of the Sophoclean heroes, for instance, surprises us by its Apollanian precision and clearness, so that we at once imagine we see into the innermost recesses of their being, and marvel not a little that the way to these recesses is so short. But if for the moment we disregard the character of the hero which rises to the surface and grows visible— and which at bottom is nothing but the light-picture cast on a dark wall, that is, appearance through and through,—if rather we enter into the myth which projects itself in these bright mirrorings, we shall of a sudden experience a phenomenon which bears a reverse relation to one familiar in optics. When, after a vigorous effort to gaze into the sun, we turn away blinded, we have dark-coloured spots before our eyes as restoratives, so to speak; while, on the contrary, those light-picture phenomena of the Sophoclean hero,—in short, the Apollonian of the mask,—are the necessary productions

[6] An eternal sea, A weaving, flowing, Life, all glowing. *Faust,* trans. of Bayard Taylor.—Tr.

of a glance into the secret and terrible things of nature, as it were shining spots to heal the eye which dire night has seared. Only in this sense can we hope to be able to grasp the true meaning of the serious and significant notion of "Greek cheerfulness"; while of course we encounter the misunderstood notion of this cheerfulness, as resulting from a state of unendangered comfort, on all the ways and paths of the present time.

The most sorrowful figure of the Greek stage, the hapless *Œdipus*, was understood by Sophocles as the noble man, who in spite of his wisdom was destined to error and misery, but nevertheless through his extraordinary sufferings ultimately exerted a magical, wholesome influence on all around him, which continues effective even after his death. The noble man does not sin; this is what the thoughtful poet wishes to tell us: all laws, all natural order, yea, the moral world itself, may be destroyed through his action, but through this very action a higher magic circle of influences is brought into play, which establish a new world on the ruins of the old that has been overthrown. This is what the poet, in so far as he is at the same time a religious thinker, wishes to tell us: as poet, he shows us first of all a wonderfully complicated legal mystery, which the judge slowly unravels, link by link, to his own destruction. The truly Hellenic delight at this dialectical loosening is so great, that a touch of surpassing cheerfulness is thereby communicated to the entire play, which everywhere blunts the edge of the horrible presuppositions of the procedure. In the "Œdipus at Colonus" we find the same cheerfulness, elevated, however, to an infinite transfiguration: in contrast to the aged king, subjected to an excess of misery, and exposed solely as a *sufferer* to all that befalls him, we have here a supermundane cheerfulness, which descends from a divine sphere and intimates to us that in his purely passive attitude the hero attains his highest activity, the influence of which extends far beyond his life, while his earlier conscious musing and striving led him only to passivity. Thus, then, the legal knot of the fable of Œdipus, which to mortal eyes appears indisolubly entangled, is slowly unravelled—and the profoundest human joy comes upon us in the presence of this divine counterpart of dialectics. If this explanation does justice to the poet, it may still be asked whether the substance of the myth is thereby exhausted; and here it turns out that the entire conception of the poet is nothing but the light picture which healing nature holds up to us after a glance into the abyss. Œdipus, the murderer of his father, the husband of his mother, Œdipus, the interpreter of the riddle of the Sphinx! What does the mysterious triad of these deeds of destiny tell us? There is a primitive popular belief, especially in Persia, that a wise Magian can be born only of incest: which we have forthwith to interpret to ourselves with reference to the riddle-solving and mother-marrying Œdipus, to the effect that when the boundary of the present and future, the rigid law of individuation and, in general, the intrinsic spell of nature, are broken by prophetic and magical powers, an extraordinary counter-naturalness—as, in this case, incest—must have preceded as a cause; for how else could one force nature to surrender her secrets but by victoriously opposing her, *i.e.,* by means of the Unnatural? It is this intuition which I see imprinted in the awful triad of the destiny of Œdipus: the very man who solves the riddle of nature—that double-constituted Sphinx—must also, as the murderer of his father and husband of his mother, break the holiest laws of nature. Indeed, it seems as if the myth sought to whisper into our ears that wisdom, especially Dionysian wisdom, is an unnatural abomination, and that whoever, through his knowledge, plunges nature into an abyss of annihilation, must also experience the dissolution of nature in himself. "The sharpness of wisdom turns round upon the sage: wisdom is a crime against nature": such terrible expressions does the myth call out to us: but the Hellenic poet touches like a sunbeam the sublime and formidable Memnonian statue of the myth, so that it suddenly begins to sound—in Sophoclean melodies.

With the glory of passivity I now contrast the glory of activity which illuminates the *Prometheus* of Æschylus. That which Æschylus the thinker had to tell us here, but which as a poet he only allows us to surmise by his symbolic picture, the youthful Goethe succeeded in disclosing to us in the daring words of his Prometheus:—

> "Hier sitz' ich, forme Menschen
> Nach meinem Bilde,
> Ein Geschlecht, das mir gleich sei,
> Zu leiden, zu weinen,
> Zu geniessen und zu freuen sich,
> Und dein nicht zu achten,
> Wie ich!"[7]

[7] "Here sit I, forming mankind
In my image,

336

Man, elevating himself to the rank of the Titans, acquires his culture by his own efforts, and compels the gods to unite with him, because in his self-sufficient wisdom he has their existence and their limits in his hand. What is most wonderful, however, in this Promethean form, which according to its fundamental conception is the specific hymn of impiety, is the profound Æschylean yearning for *justice*: the untold sorrow of the bold "single-handed being" on the one hand, and the divine need, ay, the foreboding of a twilight of the gods, on the other, the power of these two worlds of suffering constraining to reconciliation, to metaphysical oneness—all this suggests most forcibly the central and main position of the Æschylean view of things, which sees Moira as eternal justice enthroned above gods and men. In view of the astonishing boldness with which Æschylus places the Olympian world on his scales of justice, it must be remembered that the deep-minded Greek had an immovably firm substratum of metaphysical thought in his mysteries, and that all his sceptical paroxysms could be discharged upon the Olympians. With reference to these deities, the Greek artist, in particular, had an obscure feeling as to mutual dependency: and it is just in the Prometheus of Æschylus that this feeling is symbolised. The Titanic artist found in himself the daring belief that he could create men and at least destroy Olympian deities: namely, by his superior wisdom, for which, to be sure, he had to atone by eternal suffering. The splendid "can-ing" of the great genius, bought too cheaply even at the price of eternal suffering, the stern pride of the *artist*: this is the essence and soul of Æschylean poetry, while Sophocles in his Œdipus preludingly strikes up the victory-song of the *saint*. But even this interpretation which Æschylus has given to the myth does not fathom its astounding depth of terror; the fact is rather that the artist's delight in unfolding, the cheerfulness of artistic creating bidding defiance to all calamity, is but a shining stellar and nebular image reflected in a black sea of sadness. The tale of Prometheus is an original possession of the entire Aryan family of races, and documentary evidence of their capacity for the profoundly tragic; indeed, it is not improbable that this myth has the same characteristic significance for the

> A race resembling me,—
> To sorrow and to weep,
> To taste, to hold, to enjoy,
> And not have need of thee,
> As I!"

(Translation in Haeckel's *History of the Evolution of Man*.)

Aryan race that the myth of the fall of man has for the Semitic, and that there is a relationship between the two myths like that of brother and sister. The presupposition of the Promethean myth is the transcendent value which a naïve humanity attach to *fire* as the true palladium of every ascending culture: that man, however, should dispose at will of this fire, and should not receive it only as a gift from heaven, as the igniting lightning or the warming solar flame, appeared to the contemplative primordial men as crime and robbery of the divine nature. And thus the first philosophical problem at once causes a painful, irreconcilable antagonism between man and God, and puts as it were a mass of rock at the gate of every culture. The best and highest that men can acquire they obtain by a crime, and must now in their turn take upon themselves its consequences, namely the whole flood of sufferings and sorrows with which the offended celestials *must* visit the nobly aspiring race of man: a bitter reflection, which, by the *dignity* it confers on crime, contrasts strangely with the Semitic myth of the fall of man, in which curiosity, beguilement, seducibility, wantonness,—in short, a whole series of pre-eminently feminine passions,—were regarded as the origin of evil. What distinguishes the Aryan representation is the sublime view of *active* sin as the properly Promethean virtue, which suggests at the same time the ethical basis of pessimistic tragedy as the *justification* of human evil—of human guilt as well as of the suffering incurred thereby. The misery in the essence of things —which the contemplative Aryan is not disposed to explain away—the antagonism in the heart of the world, manifests itself to him as a medley of different worlds, for instance, a Divine and a human world, each of which is in the right individually, but as a separate existence alongside of another has to suffer for its individuation. With the heroic effort made by the individual for universality, in his attempt to pass beyond the bounds of individuation and become the *one* universal being, he experiences in himself the primordial contradiction concealed in the essence of things, *i.e.,* he trespasses and suffers. Accordingly crime[8] is understood by the Aryans to be a man, sin[9] by the Semites a woman; as also, the original crime is committed by man, the original sin by woman. Besides, the witches' chorus says:

"Wir nehmen das nicht so genau:
Mit tausend Schritten macht's die Frau;

8 *Der* Frevel.   9 *Die* Sunde.

> Doch wie sie auch sich eilen kann
> Mit einem Sprunge macht's der Mann."[10]

He who understands this innermost core of the tale of Prometheus—namely, the necessity of crime imposed on the titanically striving individual—will at once be conscious of the un-Apollonian nature of this pessimistic representation: for Apollo seeks to pacify individual beings precisely by drawing boundary-lines between them, and by again and again calling attention thereto, with his requirements of self-knowledge and due proportion, as the holiest laws of the universe. In order, however, to prevent the form from congealing to Egyptian rigidity and coldness in consequence of this Apollonian tendency, in order to prevent the extinction of the motion of the entire lake in the effort to prescribe to the individual wave its path and compass, the high tide of the Dionysian tendency destroyed from time to time all the little circles in which the one-sided Apollonian "will" sought to confine the Hellenic world. The suddenly swelling tide of the Dionysian then takes the separate little wave-mountains of individuals on its back, just as the brother of Prometheus, the Titan Atlas, does with the earth. This Titanic impulse, to become as it were the Atlas of all individuals, and to carry them on broad shoulders higher and higher, farther and farther, is what the Promethean and the Dionysian have in common. In this respect the Æschylean Prometheus is a Dionysian mask, while, in the aforementioned profound yearning for justice, Æschylus betrays to the intelligent observer his paternal descent from Apollo, the god of individuation and of the boundaries of justice. And so the double-being of the Æschylean Prometheus, his conjoint Dionysian and Apollonian nature, might be thus expressed in an abstract formula: "Whatever exists is alike just and unjust, and equally justified in both."

"Das ist deine Welt! Das heisst eine Welt!"[11]

It is an indisputable tradition that Greek tragedy in its earliest form had for its theme only the sufferings of Dionysus,

---

[10] We do not measure with such care:
    Woman in thousand steps is there,
    But howsoe'er she hasten may,
    Man in one leap has cleared the way.
        Faust, trans. of Bayard Taylor.—Tr.
[11] This is thy world, and what a world!—*Faust*.

and that for some time the only stage-hero therein was simply Dionysus himself. With the same confidence, however, we can maintain that not until Euripides did Dionysus cease to be the tragic hero, and that in fact all the celebrated figures of the Greek stage—Prometheus, Œdipus, etc.—are but masks of this original hero, Dionysus. The presence of a god behind all these masks is the one essential cause of the typical "ideality," so oft exciting wonder, of these celebrated figures. Some one, I know not whom, has maintained that all individuals are comic as individuals and are consequently untragic: from whence it might be inferred that the Greeks in general *could* not endure individuals on the tragic stage. And they really seem to have had these sentiments: as, in general, it is to be observed that the Platonic discrimination and valuation of the "idea" in contrast to the "eidolon," the image, is deeply rooted in the Hellenic being. Availing ourselves of Plato's terminology, however, we should have to speak of the tragic figures of the Hellenic stage somewhat as follows. The one truly real Dionysus appears in a multiplicity of forms, in the mask of a fighting hero and entangled, as it were, in the net of an individual will. As the visible appearing god now talks and acts, he resembles an erring, striving, suffering individual: and that, in general, he *appears* with such epic precision and clearness, is due to the dream-reading Apollo, who reads to the chorus its Dionysian state through this symbolic appearance. In reality, however, this hero is the suffering Dionysus of the mysteries, a god experiencing in himself the sufferings of individuation, of whom wonderful myths tell that as a boy he was dismembered by the Titans and has been worshipped in this state as Zagreus:[12] whereby is intimated that this dismemberment, the properly Dionysian *suffering*, is like a transformation into air, water, earth, and fire, that we must therefore regard the state of individuation as the source and primal cause of all suffering, as something objectionable in itself. From the smile of this Dionysus sprang the Olympian gods, from his tears sprang man. In his existence as a dismembered god, Dionysus has the dual nature of a cruel barbarised demon, and a mild pacific ruler. But the hope of the epos looked for a new birth of Dionysus, which we have now to conceive of in anticipation as the end of individuation: it was for this coming third Dionysus that the stormy jubilation-hymns of the epopts resounded. And it is only this hope

12 See article by Mr. Arthur Symons in *The Academy*, 30th August 1902.

that sheds a ray of joy upon the features of a world torn asunder and shattered into individuals: as is symbolised in the myth by Demeter sunk in eternal sadness, who *rejoices* again only when told that she may *once more* give birth to Dionysus. In the views of things here given we already have all the elements of a profound and pessimistic contemplation of the world, and along with these we have the *mystery doctrine of tragedy*: the fundamental knowledge of the oneness of all existing things, the consideration of individuation as the primal cause of evil, and art as the joyous hope that the spell of individuation may be broken, as the augury of a restored oneness.

It has already been intimated that the Homeric epos is the poem of Olympian culture, wherewith this culture has sung its own song of triumph over the terrors of the war of the Titans. Under the predominating influence of tragic poetry, these Homeric myths are now reproduced anew, and show by this metempsychosis that meantime the Olympian culture also has been vanquished by a still deeper view of things. The haughty Titan Prometheus has announced to his Olympian tormentor that the extremest danger will one day menace his rule, unless he ally with him betimes. In Æschylus we perceive the terrified Zeus, appehensive of his end, in alliance with the Titan. Thus, the former age of the Titans is subsequently brought from Tartarus once more to the light of day. The philosophy of wild and naked nature beholds with the undissembled mien of truth the myths of the Homeric world as they dance past: they turn pale, they tremble before the lightning glance of this goddess—till the powerful fist[13] of the Dionysian artist forces them into the service of the new deity. Dionysian truth takes over the entire domain of myth as symbolism of *its* knowledge, which it makes known partly in the public cult of tragedy and partly in the secret celebration of the dynamic mysteries, always, however, in the old mythical garb. What was the power, which freed Prometheus from his vultures and transformed the myth into a vehicle of Dionysian wisdom? It is the Heracleian power of music: which, having reached its highest manifestness in tragedy, can invest myths with a new and most profound significance, which we have already had occasion to characterise as the most powerful faculty of music. For it is the fate of every myth to insinuate itself into the narrow limits of some alleged historical reality, and to be treated by some later generation

13 Die mächtige Faust.—Cf. *Faust,* Chorus of Spirits.—TR.

as a solitary fact with historical claims: and the Greeks were already fairly on the way to restamp the whole of their mythical juvenile dream sagaciously and arbitrarily into a historico-pragmatical *juvenile history*. For this is the manner in which religions are wont to die out: when of course under the stern, intelligent eyes of an orthodox dogmatism, the mythical presuppositions of a religion are systematised as a completed sum of historical events, and when one begins apprehensively to defend the credibility of the myth, while at the same time opposing all continuation of their natural vitality and luxuriance; when, accordingly, the feeling for myth dies out, and its place is taken by the claim of religion to historical foundations. This dying myth was now seized by the new-born genius of Dionysian music, in whose hands it bloomed once more, with such colours as it had never yet displayed, with a fragrance that awakened a longing anticipation of a metaphysical world. After this final effulgence it collapses, its leaves wither, and soon the scoffing Lucians of antiquity catch at the discoloured and faded flowers which the winds carry off in every direction. Through tragedy the myth attains its profoundest significance, its most expressive form; it rises once more like a wounded hero, and the whole surplus of vitality, together with the philosophical calmness of the Dying, burns in its eyes with a last powerful gleam.

What meantest thou, oh impious Euripides, in seeking once more to enthral this dying one? It died under thy ruthless hands: and then thou madest use of counterfeit, masked myth, which like the ape of Heracles could only trick itself out in the old finery. And as myth died in thy hands, so also died the genius of music; though thou couldst covetously plunder all the gardens of music—thou didst only realise a counterfeit, masked music. And because thou hast forsaken Dionysus, Apollo hath also forsaken thee; rout up all the passions from their haunts and conjure them into thy sphere, sharpen and polish a sophistical dialectics for the speeches of thy heroes—thy very heroes have only counterfeit, masked passions, and speak only counterfeit masked music.

Greek tragedy had a fate different from that of all her older sister arts: she died by suicide, in consequence of an irreconcilable conflict; accordingly she died tragically, while they all passed away very calmly and beautifully in ripe old age. For if it be in accordance with a happy state of things to depart this life without a struggle, leaving behind a fair posterity, the closing period of these older arts exhibits such a happy state of things: slowly they sink out of sight, and before their dying eyes already stand their fairer progeny, who impatiently lift up their heads with courageous mien. The death of Greek tragedy, on the other hand, left an immense void, deeply felt everywhere. Even as certain Greek sailors in the time of Tiberius once heard upon a lonesome island the thrilling cry, "great Pan is dead": so now as it were sorrowful wailing sounded through the Hellenic world: "Tragedy is dead! Poetry itself has perished with her! Begone, begone, ye stunted, emaciated epigones! Begone to Hades, that ye may for once eat your fill of the crumbs of your former masters!"

But when after all a new Art blossomed forth which revered tragedy as her ancestress and mistress, it was observed with horror that she did indeed bear the features of her mother, but those very features the latter had exhibited in her long death-struggle. It was *Euripides* who fought this death-struggle of tragedy; the later art is known as the *New Attic Comedy*. In it the degenerate form of tragedy lived on as a monument of the most painful and violent death of tragedy proper.

This connection between the two serves to explain the passionate attachment to Euripides evinced by the poets of the New Comedy, and hence we are no longer surprised at the wish of Philemon, who would have got himself hanged at once, with the sole design of being able to visit Euripides in the lower regions: if only he could be assured generally that the deceased still had his wits. But if we desire, as briefly as possible, and without professing to say aught exhaustive on the subject to characterise what Euripides has in common with Menander and Philemon, and what appealed to them so strongly as worthy of imitation: it will suffice to say that the *spectator* was brought upon the stage by Euripides. He who has perceived the material of which the Promethean tragic writers prior to Euripides formed their heroes, and how remote from their purpose it was to bring the true mask of reality on the stage, will also know what to make of the wholly divergent tendency of Euripides. Through him the commonplace individual forced his way from the spectators' benches to the stage itself; the mirror in which formerly only great and bold traits found expression now showed the painful exactness that conscientiously reproduces even the abortive lines of nature. Odysseus, the typical Hellene of the Old Art, sank, in the hands of the new poets, to the figure of the Græculus, who, as the good-naturedly cunning domestic slave, stands henceforth in the centre of dramatic interest. What Euripides takes credit for in the Aristophanean "Frogs," namely, that by his household remedies he freed tragic art from its pompous corpulency, is apparent above all in his tragic heroes. The spectator now virtually saw and heard his double on the Euripidean stage, and rejoiced that he could talk so well. But this joy was not all: one even learned of Euripides how to speak: he prides himself upon this in his contest with Æschylus: how the people have learned from him how to observe, debate, and draw conclusions according to the rules of art and with the cleverest sophistications. In general it may be said that through this revolution of the popular language he made the New Comedy possible. For it was henceforth no longer a secret, how—and with what saws—the commonplace could represent and express itself on the stage. Civic mediocrity, on which Euripides built all his political hopes, was now suffered to speak, while heretofore the demigod in tragedy and the drunken satyr, or demiman, in comedy, had determined the character of the language. And so the Aristophanean Euripides prides himself on having portrayed the common, familiar, everyday life and dealings of the people, concerning which all are qualified to pass judgment. If now the entire populace philosophises, manages land and goods with unheard-of circumspection, and conducts law-suits, he takes all the credit to himself, and glories in the splendid results of the wisdom with which he inoculated the rabble.

It was to a populace prepared and enlightened in this manner that the New Comedy could now address itself, of which Euripides had become as it were the chorus-master; only that in this case the chorus of spectators had to be trained. As soon as this chorus was trained to sing in the Euripidean key, there arose that chesslike variety of the drama, the New Comedy, with its perpetual triumphs of cunning and artfulness. But Euripides—the chorus-master—was praised incessantly: indeed, people would have killed themselves in order to learn yet more from him, had they not known that tragic poets were quite as dead as tragedy. But with it the Hellene had surrendered the belief in his immortality; not only the belief in an ideal past, but also the belief in an ideal future. The saying taken from the well-known epitaph, "as an old man, frivolous and capricious," applies also to aged Hellenism. The passing moment, wit, levity, and caprice, are its highest deities; the fifth class, that of the slaves, now attains to power, at least in sentiment: and if we can still speak at all of "Greek cheerfulness," it is the cheerfulness of the slave who has nothing of consequence to answer for, nothing great to strive for, and cannot value anything of the past or future higher than the present. It was this semblance of "Greek cheerfulness" which so revolted the deep-minded and formidable natures of the first four centuries of Christianity: this womanish flight from earnestness and terror, this cowardly contentedness with easy pleasure, was not only contemptible to them, but seemed to be a specifically anti-Christian sentiment. And we must ascribe it to its influence that the conception of Greek antiquity, which lived on for centuries, preserved with almost enduring persistency that peculiar hectic colour of cheerfulness—as if there had never been a Sixth Century with its birth of tragedy, its Mysteries, its Pythagoras and Heraclitus, indeed as if the art-works of that great period did not at all exist, which in fact—each by itself—can in no wise be explained as having sprung from the soil of such a decrepit and slavish love of existence and cheerfulness, and point to an altogether different conception of things as their source.

The assertion made a moment ago, that Euripides introduced the spectator on the stage to qualify him the better to pass judgment on the drama, will make it appear as if the old tragic art was always in a false relation to the spectator: and one would be tempted to extol the radical tendency of Euripides to bring about an adequate relation between art-work and public as an advance on Sophocles. But, as things are, "public" is merely a word, and not at all a homogeneous and constant quantity. Why should the artist be under obligations to accommodate himself to a power whose strength is merely in numbers? And if by virtue of his endowments and aspirations he feels himself superior to every one of these spectators, how could he feel greater respect for the collective expression of all these subordinate capacities than for the relatively highest-endowed individual spectator? In truth, if ever a Greek artist treated his public throughout a long life with presumptuousness and self-sufficiency, it was Euripides, who, even when the masses threw themselves at his feet, with sublime defiance made an open assault on his own tendency, the very tendency with which he had triumphed over the masses. If this genius had had the slightest reverence for the pandemonium of the public, he would have broken down long before the middle of his career beneath the weighty blows of his own failures. These considerations here make it obvious that our formula —namely, that Euripides brought the spectator upon the stage in order to make him truly competent to pass judgment—was but a provisional one, and that we must seek for a deeper understanding of his tendency. Conversely, it is undoubtedly well known that Æschylus and Sophocles during all their lives, indeed, far beyond their lives, enjoyed the full favour of the people, and that therefore in the case of these predecessors of Euripides the idea of a false relation between artwork and public was altogether excluded. What was it that thus forcibly diverted this highly gifted artist, so incessantly impelled to production, from the path over which shone the sun of the greatest names in poetry and the cloudless heaven of popular favour? What strange consideration for the spectator led him to defy the spectator? How could he, owing to too much respect for the public—dis-respect the public?

Euripides—and this is the solution of the riddle just propounded—felt himself, as a poet, undoubtedly superior to the masses, but not to two of his spectators: he brought the masses upon the stage; these two spectators he revered as the only competent judges and masters of his art: in compliance with their directions and admonitions, he transferred the entire world of sentiments, passions, and experiences, hitherto present at every festival representation as the invisible chorus on the spectators' benches, into the souls of his stage-heroes; he yielded to their demands when he also sought for these new characters the new word and the new tone; in their voices alone he heard the conclusive verdict on his work, as also the cheering promise of triumph when he found himself condemned as usual by the justice of the public.

Of these two spectators the one is—Euripides himself, Euripides *as thinker*, not as poet. It might be said of him, that his unusually large fund of critical ability, as in the case of Lessing, if it did not create, at least constantly fructified a productively artistic collateral impulse. With this faculty, with all the clearness and dexterity of his critical thought, Euripides had sat in the theatre and striven to recognise in the masterpieces of his great predecessors, as in faded paintings, feature and feature, line and line. And here had happened to him what one initiated in the deeper arcana of Æschylean tragedy must needs have expected: he observed something incommensurable in every feature and in every line, a certain deceptive distinctness and at the same time an enigmatic profundity, yea an infinitude, of background. Even the clearest figure had always a comet's tail attached to it, which seemed to suggest the uncertain and the inexplicable. The same twilight shrouded the structure of the drama, especially the significance of the chorus. And how doubtful seemed the solution of the ethical problems to his mind! How questionable the treatment of the myths! How unequal the distribution of happiness and misfortune! Even in the language of the Old Tragedy there was much that was objectionable to him, or at least enigmatical; he found especially too much pomp for simple affairs, too many tropes and immense things for the plainness of the characters. Thus he sat restlessly pondering in the theatre, and as a spectator he acknowledged to himself that he did not understand his great predecessors. If, however, he thought the understanding the root proper of all enjoyment and productivity, he had to inquire and look about to see whether any one else thought as he did, and also acknowledged this incommensurability. But most people, and among them the best individuals, had only a distrustful smile for him, while none could explain why the great masters were still in the right in face of his scruples and objections. And in this painful condition he found *that other spectator*, who did not comprehend, and therefore did not esteem, tragedy. In alliance with him he could venture, from amid his lonesomeness, to begin the prodigious struggle against the art of Æschylus and Sophocles—not with polemic writings, but as a dramatic poet, who opposed *his own* conception of tragedy to the traditional one.

Before we name this other spectator, let us pause here a moment in order to recall our own impression, as previously described, of the discordant and incommensurable elements in the nature of Æschylean tragedy. Let us think of our own astonishment at the *chorus* and the *tragic hero* of that type of tragedy, neither of which we could reconcile with our practices any more than with tradition—till we rediscovered this duplexity itself as the origin and essence of Greek tragedy, as the expression of two interwoven artistic impulses, *the Apollonian and the Dionysian.*

To separate this primitive and all-powerful Dionysian element from tragedy, and to build up a new and purified form of tragedy on the basis of a non-Dionysian art, morality, and conception of things—such is the tendency of Euripides which now reveals itself to us in a clear light.

In a myth composed in the eve of his life, Euripides himself most urgently propounded to his contemporaries the question as to the value and signification of this tendency. Is the Dionysian entitled to exist at all? Should it not be forcibly rooted out of the Hellenic soil? Certainly, the poet tells us, if only it were possible: but the god Dionysus is too powerful; his most intelligent adversary—like Pentheus in the "Bacchæ"

347

—is unwittingly enchanted by him, and in this enchantment meets his fate. The judgment of the two old sages, Cadmus and Teiresias, seems to be also the judgment of the aged poet: that the reflection of the wisest individuals does not overthrow old popular traditions, nor the perpetually propagating worship of Dionysus, that in fact it behooves us to display at least a diplomatically cautious concern in the presence of such strange forces: where however it is always possible that the god may take offence at such lukewarm participation, and finally change the diplomat—in this case Cadmus—into a dragon. This is what a poet tells us, who opposed Dionysus with heroic valour throughout a long life—in order finally to wind up his career with a glorification of his adversary, and with suicide, like one staggering from giddiness, who, in order to escape the horrible vertigo he can no longer endure, casts himself from a tower. This tragedy—the Bacchæ—is a protest against the practicability of his own tendency; alas, and it has already been put into practice! The surprising thing had happened: when the poet recanted, his tendency had already conquered. Dionysus had already been scared from the tragic stage, and in fact by a demonic power which spoke through Euripides. Even Euripides was, in a certain sense, only a mask: the deity that spoke through him was neither Dionysus nor Apollo, but an altogether new-born demon called *Socrates*. This is the new antithesis: the Dionysian and the Socratic, and the art-work of Greek tragedy was wrecked on it. What if even Euripides now seeks to comfort us by his recantation? It is of no avail: the most magnificent temple lies in ruins. What avails the lamentation of the destroyer, and his confession that it was the most beautiful of all temples? And even that Euripides has been changed into a dragon as a punishment by the art-critics of all ages—who could be content with this wretched compensation?

Let us now approach this *Socratic* tendency with which Euripides combated and vanquished Æschylean tragedy.

We must now ask ourselves, what could be the ulterior aim of the Euripidean design, which, in the highest ideality of its execution, would found drama exclusively on the non-Dionysian? What other form of drama could there be, if it was not to be born of the womb of music, in the mysterious twilight of the Dionysian? Only *the dramatised epos*: in which Apollonian domain of art the *tragic* effect is of course unattainable. It does not depend on the subject-matter of the events here represented; indeed, I venture to assert that it would have been impossible for Goethe in his projected "Nausikaa" to have rendered tragically effective the suicide of the idyllic being with which he intended to complete the fifth act; so extraordinary is the power of the epic-Apollonian representation, that it charms, before our eyes, the most terrible things by the joy in appearance and in redemption through appearance. The poet of the dramatised epos cannot completely blend with his pictures any more than the epic rhapsodist. He is still just the calm, unmoved embodiment of Contemplation whose wide eyes see the picture *before* them. The actor in this dramatised epos still remains intrinsically rhapsodist: the consecration of inner dreaming is on all his actions, so that he is never wholly an actor.

How, then, is the Euripidean play related to this ideal of the Apollonian drama? Just as the younger rhapsodist is related to the solemn rhapsodist of the old time. The former describes his own character in the Platonic "Ion" as follows: "When I am saying anything sad, my eyes fill with tears; when, however, what I am saying is awful and terrible, then my hair stands on end through fear, and my heart leaps." Here we no longer observe anything of the epic absorption in appearance, or of the unemotional coolness of the true actor, who precisely in his highest activity is wholly appearance and joy in appearance. Euripides is the actor with leaping heart, with hair standing on end; as Socratic thinker he designs the plan, as passionate actor he executes it. Neither in the designing nor in the execution is he an artist pure and simple. And so the Euripidean drama is a thing both cool and fiery, equally capable of freezing and burning; it is impossible for it to attain the Apollonian effect of the epos, while, on the other hand, it has severed itself as much as possible from Dionysian elements, and now, in order to act at all, it requires new stimulants, which can no longer lie within the sphere of the two unique art-impulses, the Apollonian and the Dionysian. The stimulants are cool, paradoxical *thoughts*, in place of Apollonian intuitions—and fiery *passions*—in place of Dionysian ecstasies; and in fact, thoughts and passions very realistically copied, and not at all steeped in the ether of art.

Accordingly, if we have perceived this much, that Euripides did not succeed in establishing the drama exclusively on the Apollonian, but that rather his non-Dionysian inclinations deviated into a naturalistic and inartistic tendency, we shall now be able to approach nearer to the character of *æsthetic Socratism*, the supreme law of which reads about as follows: "to be beautiful everything must be intelligible," as the parallel to the Socratic proposition, "only the knowing one is virtuous." With this canon in his hands Euripides measured all the separate elements of the drama, and rectified them according to his principle: the language, the characters, the dramaturgic structure, and the choric music. The poetic deficiency and retrogression, which we are so often wont to impute to Euripides in comparison with Sophoclean tragedy, is for the most part the product of this penetrating critical process, this daring intelligibility. The Euripidean *prologue* may serve us as an example of the productivity of this rationalistic method. Nothing could be more opposed to the technique of our stage than the prologue in the drama of Euripides. For a single person to appear at the outset of the play telling us who he is, what precedes the action, what has happened thus far, yea, what will happen in the course of the play, would be designated by a modern playwright as a wanton and unpardonable abandonment of the effect of suspense. Everything that is about to happen is known beforehand; who then cares to wait for it actually to happen?—considering, moreover, that here there is not by any means the exciting relation of a predicting dream to a reality taking place later on. Euripides speculated quite differently. The effect of tragedy never depended on epic suspense, on the fascinating uncertainty as to what is to happen now and afterwards: but rather on the great rhetoro-lyric scenes in which the passion and dialectics of the chief hero swelled to a broad and mighty stream. Everything was arranged for pathos, not for action: and whatever was not arranged for pathos was regarded as objectionable. But what interferes most with the hearer's pleasurable satisfaction in such scenes is a missing link, a gap in the texture of the previous history. So long as the spectator has to divine the meaning of this or that person, or the presuppositions of this or that conflict of inclinations and intentions, his complete absorption in the doings and sufferings of the chief persons is impossible, as is likewise breathless fellow-feeling and fellow-fearing. The Æschyleo-Sophoclean tragedy employed the most ingenious devices in the first scenes to place in the hands of the spectators as if by chance all the threads requisite for understanding the whole: a trait in which that noble artistry is approved, which as it were masks the *inevitably* formal, and causes it to appear as something accidental. But nevertheless Euripides thought he observed that during these first scenes the spectator was in a strange state of anxiety to make out the problem of the previous history, so that the poetic beauties and pathos of the exposition were lost to him. Accordingly he placed the prologue even before the exposition, and put it in the mouth of a person who could be trusted: some deity had often as it were to guarantee the particulars of the tragedy to the public and remove every doubt as to the reality of the myth: as in the case of Descartes, who could only prove the reality of the empiric world by an appeal to the truthfulness of God and His inability to utter falsehood. Euripides makes use of the same divine truthfulness once more at the close of his drama, in order to ensure to the public the future of his heroes; this is the task of the notorious *deus ex machina*. Between the preliminary and the additional epic spectacle there is the dramatico-lyric present, the "drama" proper.

Thus Euripides as a poet echoes above all his own conscious knowledge; and it is precisely on this account that he occupies such a notable position in the history of Greek art. With reference to his critico-productive activity, he must often have felt that he ought to actualise in the drama the words at the beginning of the essay of Anaxagoras: "In the beginning all things were mixed together; then came the understanding and created order." And if Anaxagoras with his "*voῦς*" seemed like the first sober person among nothing but drunken philosophers, Euripides may also have conceived his relation to the other tragic poets under a similar figure. As long as the sole ruler and disposer of the universe, the *voῦς*, was still excluded from artistic activity, things were all mixed together in a chaotic, primitive mess;—it is thus Euripides was obliged to think, it is thus he was obliged to condemn the "drunken" poets as the first "sober" one among them. What Sophocles said of Æschylus, that he did what was right, though unconsciously, was surely not in the mind of Euripides: who would have admitted only thus much, that Æschylus, *because* he wrought unconsciously, did what was wrong. So also the divine Plato speaks for the most part only ironically of the creative faculty of the poet, in so far as it is not conscious insight, and places it on a par with the gift of the soothsayer and dream-interpreter; insinuating that the poet is incapable of composing until he has become unconscious and reason has deserted him. Like Plato, Euripides undertook to show to the world the reverse of the "unintelligent" poet; his æsthetic principle that "to be beautiful everything must be known" is, as I have said, the parallel to the Socratic "to be good everything must be known." Accordingly we may regard Euripides as the poet of æsthetic Socratism. Socrates, however, was that *second spectator* who did not comprehend and therefore did not esteem the Old Tragedy; in alliance with him Euripides ventured to be the herald of a new artistic activity. If, then, the Old Tragedy was here destroyed, it follows that æsthetic Socratism was the murderous principle; but in so far as the struggle is directed against the Dionysian element in the old art, we recognise in Socrates the opponent of Dionysus, the new Orpheus who rebels against Dionysus; and although destined to be torn to pieces by the Mænads of the Athenian court, yet puts to flight the overpowerful god himself, who, when he fled from Lycurgus, the king of Edoni, sought refuge in the depths of the ocean —namely, in the mystical flood of a secret cult which gradually overspread the earth.

That Socrates stood in close relationship to Euripides in the tendency of his teaching, did not escape the notice of contemporaneous antiquity; the most eloquent expression of this felicitous insight being the tale current in Athens, that Socrates was accustomed to help Euripides in poetising. Both names were mentioned in one breath by the adherents of the "good old time," whenever they came to enumerating the popular agitators of the day: to whose influence they attributed the fact that the old Marathonian stalwart capacity of body and soul was more and more being sacrificed to a dubious enlightenment, involving progressive degeneration of the physical and mental powers. It is in this tone, half indignantly and half contemptuously, that Aristophanic comedy is wont to speak of both of them—to the consternation of modern men, who would indeed be willing enough to give up Euripides, but cannot suppress their amazement that Socrates should appear in Aristophanes as the first and head *sophist*, as the mirror and epitome of all sophistical tendencies; in connection with which it offers the single consolation of putting Aristophanes himself in the pillory, as a rakish, lying Alcibiades of poetry. Without here defending the profound instincts of Aristophanes against such attacks, I shall now indicate, by means of the sentiments of the time, the close connection between Socrates and Euripides. With this purpose in view, it is especially to be remembered that Socrates, as an opponent of tragic art, did not ordinarily patronise tragedy, but only appeared among the spectators when a new play of Euripides was performed. The most noted thing, however, is the close juxtaposition of the two names in the Delphic oracle, which designated Socrates as the wisest of men, but at the same time decided that the second prize in the contest of wisdom was due to Euripides.

Sophocles was designated as the third in this scale of rank; he who could pride himself that, in comparison with Æschylus, he did what was right, and did it, moreover, because he *knew* what was right. It is evidently just the degree of clearness of this *knowledge,* which distinguishes these three men in common as the three "knowing ones" of their age.

The most decisive word, however, for this new and unprecedented esteem of knowledge and insight was spoken by Socrates when he found that he was the only one who acknowledged to himself that he *knew nothing*; while in his critical pilgrimage through Athens, and calling on the greatest statesmen, orators, poets, and artists, he discovered everywhere the conceit of knowledge. He perceived, to his astonishment, that all these celebrities were without a proper and accurate insight, even with regard to their own callings, and practised them only by instinct. "Only by instinct": with this phrase we touch upon the heart and core of the Socratic tendency. Socratism condemns therewith existing art as well as existing ethics; wherever Socratism turns its searching eyes it beholds the lack of insight and the power of illusion; and from this lack infers the inner perversity and objectionableness of existing conditions. From this point onwards, Socrates believed that he was called upon to correct existence; and, with an air of disregard and superiority, as the precursor of an altogether different culture, art, and morality, he enters single-handed into a world, of which, if we reverently touched the hem, we should count it our greatest happiness.

Here is the extraordinary hesitancy which always seizes upon us with regard to Socrates, and again and again invites us to ascertain the sense and purpose of this most questionable phenomenon of antiquity. Who is it that ventures single-handed to disown the Greek character, which, as Homer, Pindar, and Æschylus, as Phidias, as Pericles, as Pythia and Dionysus, as the deepest abyss and the highest height, is sure of our wondering admiration? What demoniac power is it which would presume to spill this magic draught in the dust? What demigod is it to whom the chorus of spirits of the noblest of mankind must call out: "Weh! Weh! Du hast sie zerstört, die schöne Welt, mit mächtiger Faust; sie stürzt, sie zerfällt!"[14]

14 Woe! Woe!
   Thou hast it destroyed,
   The beautiful world;

With powerful fist;
In ruin 'tis hurled!
Faust, trans. of Bayard Taylor.—Tr.

A key to the character of Socrates is presented to us by the surprising phenomenon designated as the "daimonion" of Socrates. In special circumstances, when his gigantic intellect began to stagger, he got a secure support in the utterances of a divine voice when then spake to him. This voice, whenever it comes, always *dissuades.* In this abnormal nature instinctive wisdom only appears in order to hinder the progress of conscious perception here and there. While in all productive men it is instinct which is the creatively affirmative force, consciousness only comporting itself critically and dissuasively; with Socrates it is instinct which becomes critic, it is consciousness which becomes creator—a perfect monstrosity *per defectum!* And we do indeed observe here a monstrous *defectus* of all mystical aptitude, so that Socrates might be designated as the specific *non-mystic,* in whom the logical nature is developed, through a superfoetation, to the same excess as instinctive wisdom is developed in the mystic. On the other hand, however, the logical instinct which appeared in Socrates was absolutely prohibited from turning against itself; in its unchecked flow it manifests a native power such as we meet with, to our shocking surprise, only among the very greatest instinctive forces. He who has experienced even a breath of the divine naïveté and security of the Socratic course of life in the Platonic writings, will also feel that the enormous driving-wheel of logical Socratism is in motion, as it were, *behind* Socrates, and that it must be viewed through Socrates as through a shadow. And that he himself had a boding of this relation is apparent from the dignified earnestness with which he everywhere, and even before his judges, insisted on his divine calling. To refute him here was really as impossible as to approve of his instinct-disintegrating influence. In view of this indissoluble conflict, when he had at last been brought before the forum of the Greek state, there was only one punishment demanded, namely exile; he might have been sped across the borders as something thoroughly enigmatical, irrubricable and inexplicable, and so posterity would have been quite unjustified in charging the Athenians with a deed of ignominy. But that the sentence of death, and not mere exile, was pronounced upon him, seems to have been brought about by Socrates himself, with perfect knowledge of the circumstances, and without the natural fear of death: he met his death with the calmness with which, according to the description of Plato, he leaves the symposium at break of day, as the last of the revellers, to begin a new day; while the sleepy companions remained behind on the benches and the floor, to dream of Socrates, the true eroticist. *The dying Socrates* became the new ideal of noble Greek youths,—an ideal they had never yet beheld,—and above all, the typical Hellenic youth, Plato, prostrated himself before this scene with all the fervent devotion of his visionary soul.

Let us now imagine the one great Cyclopean eye of Socrates fixed on tragedy, that eye in which the fine frenzy of artistic enthusiasm had never glowed—let us think how it was denied to this eye to gaze with pleasure into the Dionysian abysses —what could it not but see in the "sublime and greatly lauded" tragic art, as Plato called it? Something very absurd, with causes that seemed to be without effects, and effects apparently without causes; the whole, moreover, so motley and diversified that it could not but be repugnant to a thoughtful mind, a dangerous incentive, however, to sensitive and irritable souls. We know what was the sole kind of poetry which he comprehended: the *Æsopian fable*: and he did this no doubt with that smiling complaisance with which the good honest Gellert sings the praise of poetry in the fable of the bee and the hen:—

> "Du siehst an mir, wozu sie nützt,
> Dem, der nicht viel Verstand besitzt,
> Die Wahrheit durch ein Bild zu sagen."[15]

But then it seemed to Socrates that tragic art did not even "tell the truth": not to mention the fact that it addresses itself to him who "hath but little wit"; consequently not to the philosopher: a twofold reason why it should be avoided. Like Plato, he reckoned it among the seductive arts which only represent the agreeable, not the useful, and hence he required of his disciples abstinence and strict separation from such unphilosophical allurements; with such success that the youthful tragic poet Plato first of all burned his poems to be able to become a scholar of Socrates. But where unconquerable native capacities bore up against the Socratic maxims, their power, together with the momentum of his

[15] In me thou seest its benefit,—
To him who hath but little wit,
Through parables to tell the truth.

mighty character, still sufficed to force poetry itself into new and hitherto unknown channels.

An instance of this is the aforesaid Plato: he, who in the condemnation of tragedy and of art in general certainly did not fall short of the naïve cynicism of his master, was nevertheless constrained by sheer artistic necessity to create a form of art which is inwardly related even to the then existing forms of art which he repudiated. Plato's main objection to the old art—that it is the imitation of a phantom,[16] and hence belongs to a sphere still lower than the empiric world—could not at all apply to the new art: and so we find Plato endeavouring to go beyond reality and attempting to represent the idea which underlies this pseudo-reality. But Plato, the thinker, thereby arrived by a roundabout road just at the point where he had always been at home as poet, and from which Sophocles and all the old artists had solemnly protested against that objection. If tragedy absorbed into itself all the earlier varieties of art, the same could again be said in an unusual sense of Platonic dialogue, which, engendered by a mixture of all the then existing forms and styles, hovers midway between narrative, lyric and drama, between prose and poetry, and has also thereby broken loose from the older strict law of unity of linguistic form; a movement which was carried still farther by the *cynic* writers, who in the most promiscuous style, oscillating to and fro betwixt prose and metrical forms, realised also the literary picture of the "raving Socrates" whom they were wont to represent in life. Platonic dialogue was as it were the boat in which the shipwrecked ancient poetry saved herself together with all her children: crowded into a narrow space and timidly obsequious to the one steersman, Socrates, they now launched into a new world, which never tired of looking at the fantastic spectacle of this procession. In very truth, Plato has given to all posterity the prototype of a new form of art, the prototype of the *novel*: which must be designated as the infinitely evolved Æsopian fable, in which poetry holds the same rank with reference to dialectic philosophy as this same philosophy held for many centuries with reference to theology: namely, the rank of *ancilla*. This was the new position of poetry into which Plato forced it under the pressure of the demon-inspired Socrates.

Here *philosophic thought* overgrows art and compels it to cling close to the trunk of dialectics. The *Apollonian* ten-

16 *Scheinbild*=εἴδολον.—Tr.

dency has chrystalised in the logical schematism; just as
something analogous in the case of Euripides (and moreover
a translation of the *Dionysian* into the naturalistic emotion)
was forced upon our attention. Socrates, the dialectical hero
in Platonic drama, reminds us of the kindred nature of the
Euripidean hero, who has to defend his actions by arguments and counter-arguments, and thereby so often runs the
risk of forfeiting our tragic pity; for who could mistake the
optimistic element in the essence of dialectics, which celebrates
a jubilee in every conclusion, and can breathe only in cool
clearness and consciousness: the optimistic element, which,
having once forced its way into tragedy, must gradually over-
grow its Dionysian regions, and necessarily impel it to self-
destruction—even to the death-leap into the bourgeois drama.
Let us but realise the consequences of the Socratic maxims:
"Virtue is knowledge; man only sins from ignorance; he who
is virtuous is happy": these three fundamental forms of
optimism involve the death of tragedy. For the virtuous hero
must now be a dialectician; there must now be a necessary,
visible connection between virtue and knowledge, between
belief and morality; the transcendental justice of the plot in
Æschylus is now degraded to the superficial and audacious
principle of "poetic justice" with its usual *deus ex machina*.

How does the *chorus,* and, in general, the entire Dionysomusical substratum of tragedy, now appear in the light of
this new Socrato-optimistic stage-world? As something accidental, as a readily dispensable reminiscence of the origin of
tragedy; while we have in fact seen that the chorus can be
understood only as the *cause* of tragedy, and of the tragic
generally. This perplexity with respect to the chorus first manifests itself in Sophocles—an important sign that the Dionysian
basis of tragedy already begins to disintegrate with him. He
no longer ventures to entrust to the chorus the main share of
the effect, but limits its sphere to such an extent that it now
appears almost co-ordinate with the actors, just as if it were
elevated from the orchestra into the scene: whereby of
course its character is completely destroyed, notwithstanding
that Aristotle countenances this very theory of the chorus,
which Sophocles at any rate recommended by his practice,
and, according to tradition, even by a treatise, is the first
step towards the *annihilation* of the chorus, the phases of
which follow one another with alarming rapidity in Euripides,
Agathon, and the New Comedy. Optimistic dialectics drives
music out of tragedy with the scourge of its syllogisms: that
is, it destroys the essence of tragedy, which can be explained

only as a manifestation and illustration of Dionysian states, as the visible symbolisation of music, as the dream-world of Dionysian ecstasy.

If, therefore, we are to assume an anti-Dionysian tendency operating even before Socrates, which received in him only an unprecedentedly grand expression, we must not shrink from the question as to what a phenomenon like that of Socrates indicates: whom in view of the Platonic dialogues we are certainly not entitled to regard as a purely disintegrating, negative power. And though there can be no doubt whatever that the most immediate effect of the Socratic impulse tended to the dissolution of Dionysian tragedy, yet a profound experience of Socrates' own life compels us to ask whether there is *necessarily* only an antipodal relation between Socratism and art, and whether the birth of an "artistic Socrates" is in general something contradictory in itself.

For that despotic logician had now and then the feeling of a gap, or void, a sentiment of semi-reproach, as of a possibly neglected duty with respect to art. There often came to him, as he tells his friends in prison, one and the same dream-apparition, which kept constantly repeating to him: "Socrates, practise music." Up to his very last days he solaces himself with the opinion that his philosophising is the highest form of poetry, and finds it hard to believe that a deity will remind him of the "common, popular music." Finally, when in prison, he consents to practise also this despised music, in order thoroughly to unburden his conscience. And in this frame of mind he composes a poem on Apollo and turns a few Æsopian fables into verse. It was something similar to the demonian warning voice which urged him to these practices; it was because of his Apollonian insight that, like a barbaric king, he did not understand the noble image of a god and was in danger of sinning against a deity—through ignorance. The prompting voice of the Socratic dream-vision is the only sign of doubtfulness as to the limits of logical nature. "Perhaps"—thus he had to ask himself—"what is not intelligible to me is not therefore unreasonable? Perhaps there is a realm of wisdom from which the logician is banished? Perhaps art is even a necessary correlative of and supplement to science?"

*   *   *   *

Dionysian art, too, seeks to convince us of the eternal joy of existence: only we are to seek this joy not in phenomena, but behind phenomena. We are to perceive how all that comes into being must be ready for a sorrowful end; we are compelled to look into the terrors of individual existence—yet we are not to become torpid: a metaphysical comfort tears us momentarily from the bustle of the transforming figures. We are really for brief moments Primordial Being itself, and feel its indomitable desire for being and joy in existence; the struggle, the pain, the destruction of phenomena, now appear to us as something necessary, considering the surplus of innumerable forms of existence which throng and push one another into life, considering the exuberant fertility of the universal will. We are pierced by the maddening sting of these pains at the very moment when we have become, as it were, one with the immeasurable primordial joy in existence, and when we anticipate, in Dionysian ecstasy, the indestructibility and eternity of this joy. In spite of fear and pity, we are the happy living beings, not as individuals, but as the *one* living being, with whose procreative joy we are blended.

The history of the rise of Greek tragedy now tells us with luminous precision that the tragic art of the Greeks was really born of the spirit of music: with which conception we believe we have done justice for the first time to the original and most astonishing significance of the chorus. At the same time, however, we must admit that the import of tragic myth as set forth above never became transparent with sufficient lucidity to the Greek poets, let alone the Greek philosophers; their heroes speak, as it were, more superficially than they act; the myth does not at all find its adequate objectification in the spoken word. The structure of the scenes and the conspicuous images reveal a deeper wisdom than the poet himself can put into words and concepts: the same being also observed in Shakespeare, whose Hamlet, for instance, in an analogous manner talks more superficially than he acts, so that the previously mentioned lesson of Hamlet is to be gathered not from his words, but from a more profound contemplation and survey of the whole. With respect to Greek tragedy, which of course presents itself to us only as word-drama, I have even intimated that the incongruence between myth and expression might easily tempt us to regard it as shallower and less significant than it really is, and accordingly to postulate for it a more superficial effect than it must have had according to the testimony of the ancients: for how easily one forgets that what the word-poet did not succeed in doing, namely realising the highest spiritualisation and ideality of myth, he might succeed in doing every moment as creative musician! We require, to be sure, almost by philological method to reconstruct for ourselves the ascendency of musical influence in order to receive something of the incomparable comfort which must be characteristic of true tragedy. Even this musical ascendency, however, would only have been felt by us as such had we been Greeks: while in the entire development of Greek music—as compared with the infinitely richer music known and familiar to us—we imagine we hear only the youthful song of the musical genius intoned with a feeling of diffidence. The Greeks are, as the Egyptian priests say, eternal children, and in tragic art also they are only children who do not know what a sublime plaything has originated under their hands and—is being demolished.

That striving of the spirit of music for symbolic and mythical manifestation, which increases from the beginnings of lyric poetry to Attic tragedy, breaks off all of a sudden immediately after attaining luxuriant development, and disappears, as it were, from the surface of Hellenic art: while the Dionysian view of things born of this striving lives on in Mysteries and, in its strangest metamorphoses and debasements, does not cease to attract earnest natures. Will it not one day rise again as art out of its mystic depth?

Here the question occupies us, whether the power by the counteracting influence of which tragedy perished, has for all time strength enough to prevent the artistic reawaking of tragedy and of the tragic view of things. If ancient tragedy was driven from its course by the dialectical desire for knowledge and the optimism of science, it might be inferred that there is an eternal conflict between *the theoretical* and *the tragic view of things*, and only after the spirit of science has been led to its boundaries, and its claim to universal validity has been destroyed by the evidence of these boundaries, can we hope for a re-birth of tragedy: for which form of culture we should have to use the symbol *of the music-practising Socrates* in the sense spoken of above. In this contrast, I understand by the spirit of science the belief which first came to light in the person of Socrates,—the belief in the fathomableness of nature and in knowledge as a panacea.

He who recalls the immediate consequences of this restlessly onward-pressing spirit of science will realise at once that *myth* was annihilated by it, and that, in consequence of this annihilation, poetry was driven as a homeless being from her natural ideal soil. If we have rightly assigned to music the capacity to reproduce myth from itself, we may in turn expect to find the spirit of science on the path where it inimically opposes this mythopoeic power of music. This

takes place in the development of the *New Attic Dithyramb,*
the music of which no longer expressed the inner essence,
the will itself, but only rendered the phenomenon insuffi-
ciently, in an imitation by means of concepts; from which
intrinsically degenerate music the truly musical natures
turned away with the same repugnance that they felt for the
art-destroying tendency of Socrates. The unerring instinct
of Aristophanes surely did the proper thing when it comprised
Socrates himself, the tragedy of Euripides, and the music
of the new Dithyrambic poets in the same feeling of hatred,
and perceived in all three phenomena the symptoms of a
degenerate culture. By this New Dithyramb, music has in an
outrageous manner been made the imitative portrait of phenomena, for instance, of a battle or a storm at sea, and has
thus, of course, been entirely deprived of its mythopoeic
power. For if it endeavours to excite our delight only by
compelling us to seek external analogies between a vital or
natural process and certain rhythmical figures and characteristic sounds of music; if our understanding is expected
to satisfy itself with the perception of these analogies, we
are reduced to a frame of mind in which the reception of
the mythical is impossible; for the myth as a unique exemplar
of generality and truth towering into the infinite, desires to be
conspicuously perceived. The truly Dionysian music presents
itself to us as such a general mirror of the universal will:
the conspicuous event which is refracted in this mirror ex-
pands at once for our consciousness to the copy of an eternal
truth. Conversely, such a conspicious event is at once divested
of every mythical character by the tone-painting of the New
Dithyramb; music has here become a wretched copy of the
phenomenon, and therefore infinitely poorer than the phenomenon itself: through which poverty it still further reduces
even the phenomenon for our consciousness, so that now, for
instance, a musically imitated battle of this sort exhausts itself in marches, signal-sounds, etc., and our imagination is
arrested precisely by these superficialities. Tone-painting is
therefore in every respect the counterpart of true music with
its mythopoeic power: through it the phenomenon, poor in
itself, is made still poorer, while through an isolated Dionysian
music the phenomenon is evolved and expanded into a picture
of the world. It was an immense triumph of the non-Dionysian
spirit, when, in the development of the New Dithyramb, it
had estranged music from itself and reduced it to be the slave
of phenomena. Euripides, who, albeit in a higher sense, must
be designated as a thoroughly unmusical nature, is for this
very reason a passionate adherent of the New Dithyrambic

Music, and with the liberality of a freebooter employs all its effective turns and mannerisms.

In another direction also we see at work the power of this un-Dionysian, myth-opposing spirit, when we turn our eyes to the prevalence of *character representation* and psychological refinement from Sophocles onwards. The character must no longer be expanded into an eternal type, but, on the contrary, must operate individually through artistic by-traits and shadings, through the nicest precision of all lines, in such a manner that the spectator is in general no longer conscious of the myth, but of the mighty nature-myth and the imitative power of the artist. Here also we observe the victory of the phenomenon over the Universal, and the delight in the particular quasi-anatomical preparation; we actually breathe the air of a theoretical world, in which scientific knowledge is valued more highly than the artistic reflection of a universal law. The movement along the line of the representation of character proceeds rapidly: while Sophocles still delineates complete characters and employs myth for their refined development, Euripides already delineates only prominent individual traits of character, which can express themselves in violent bursts of passion; in the New Attic Comedy, however, there are only masks with *one* expression: frivolous old men, duped panders, and cunning slaves in untiring repetition. Where now is the mythopoeic spirit of music? What is still left now of music is either excitatory music or souvenir music, that is, either a stimulant for dull and used-up nerves, or tone-painting. As regards the former, it hardly matters about the text set to it: the heroes and choruses of Euripides are already dissolute enough when once they begin to sing; to what pass must things have come with his brazen successors?

The new un-Dionysian spirit, however, manifests itself most clearly in the *dénouements* of the new dramas. In the Old Tragedy one could feel at the close the metaphysical comfort, without which the delight in tragedy cannot be explained at all; the conciliating tones from another world sound purest, perhaps, in the *Œdipus at Colonus*. Now that the genius of music has fled from tragedy, tragedy is, strictly speaking, dead: for from whence could one now draw the metaphysical comfort? One sought, therefore, for an earthly unravelment of the tragic dissonance; the hero, after he had been sufficiently tortured by fate, reaped a well-deserved reward through a superb marriage or divine tokens of favour. The hero had turned gladiator, on whom, after being liberally battered about and covered with wounds, freedom was occasionally bestowed. The *deus ex machina* took the place of metaphysical comfort. I will not say that the tragic view of things was everywhere completely destroyed by the intruding spirit of the un-Dionysian: we only know that it was compelled to flee from art into the under-world as it were, in the degenerate form of a secret cult. Over the widest extent of the Hellenic character, however, there raged the consuming blast of this spirit, which manifests itself in the form of "Greek cheerfulness," which we have already spoken of as a senile, unproductive love of existence; this cheerfulness is the counterpart of the splendid "naïveté" of the earlier Greeks, which, according to the characteristic indicated above, must be conceived as the blossom of the Apollonian culture growing out of a dark abyss, as the victory which the Hellenic will, through its mirroring of beauty, obtains over suffering and the wisdom of suffering. The noblest manifestation of that other form of "Greek cheerfulness," the Alexandrine, is the cheerfulness of the *theoretical man*: it exhibits the same symptomatic characteristics as I have just inferred concerning the spirit of the un-Dionysian:—it combats Dionysian wisdom and art, it seeks to dissolve myth, it substitutes for metaphysical comfort an earthly consonance, in fact, a *deus ex machina* of its own, namely the god of machines and crucibles, that is, the powers of the genii of nature recognised and employed in the service of higher egoism; it believes in amending the world by knowledge, in guiding life by science, and that it can really confine the individual within a narrow sphere of solvable problems, where he cheerfully says to life: "I desire thee: it is worth while to know thee."

Hegel on Tragedy

The Concrete Development of Dramatic Poetry and Its Types

HEGEL

Within the essential distinctions of conception and poetical achievement which we have just considered the different types of dramatic art assert themselves, and, for the first time in such association, and in so far as their development follows either one or the other direction, attain a really genuine completeness. We have, therefore, in concluding the present work, still to concentrate our inquiry upon the concrete mode under which they receive such a configuration.

(a) Excluding as we shall do for the reasons already given from our subject-matter the origins of such poetry in Oriental literature, the material of first and fundamental importance which engages our attention, as the most valuable phase of genuine tragedy no less than comedy, is the dramatic poetry of the *Greeks*. In other words, in it for the first time we find the human consciousness illuminated with that which in its general terms the tragic and comic situation essentially is; and after these opposed types of dramatic outlook upon human action have been securely and beyond all confusion separated from each other, we mark first in order tragedy, and after that comedy, rise in organic development to the height of their achievement. Of such a successful result the dramatic art of Rome merely returns a considerably attenuated reflection, which does not indeed reach the point secured by the similar effort of Roman literature in epic and lyrical composition. In my examination of the material thus offered my object will be merely to accentuate what is most important, and I shall therefore limit my survey to the tragic point of view of Aeschylus and Sophocles, and to Aristophanes so far as comedy is concerned.

(aa) Taking, then, tragedy first, I have already stated that the fundamental type which determines its entire organization and structure is to be sought for in the emphasis attached to the substantive constitution of final ends and their content, as also of the individuals dramatized and their conflict and destiny.

In the tragic drama we are now considering, the general basis or background for tragic action is supplied, as was also the case in the Epos, by that world-condition which I have already indicated as the *heroic*. For only in heroic times, when the universal ethical forces have neither acquired the independent stability of definite political legislation or moral commands and obligations, can they be presented in their primitive jocundity as gods, who are either opposed to each other in their personal activities, or themselves appear as the animated content of a free and human individuality. If, however, what is intrinsically ethical is to appear throughout as the substantive foundation, the universal ground, shall we say, from which the growth of personal action arrests our attention with equal force in its disunion, and is no less brought back again from such divided movement into unity, we shall find that there are two distinct modes under which the ethical content of human action is asserted.

First, we have the simple consciousness, which, in so far as it wills its substantive content wholly as the unbroken identity of its particular aspects, remains in undisturbed, uncriticized, and neutral tranquillity on its own account and as related to others. This undivided and, we may add, purely formal state of mind in its veneration, its faith, and its happiness, however, is incapable of attaching itself to any definite action; it has a sort of dread before the disunion which is implied in such, although it does, while remaining itself incapable of action, esteem at the same time that spiritual courage which asserts itself resolutely and actively in a self-proposed object, as of nobler worth, yet is aware of its inability to undertake such enterprise, and consequently considers that it can do nothing further for such active personalities, whom it respects so highly, than contrast with the energy of their decision and conflict the object of its own wisdom, in other words, the substantive ideality of the ethical Powers.

The *second* mode under which this ethical content is asserted is that of the individual pathos, which urges the active characters with moral self-vindication into opposition to others, and brings them thereby into conflict. The individuals subject to this pathos are neither what, in the modern use of the term, we describe as characters, nor are they mere abstractions. They are rather placed in the vital midway sphere between both, standing there as figures of real stability, which are simply that which they are, without aught of collision in themselves, without any fluctuating recognition of some other pathos, and in so far—in this respect a contrast to our modern irony—elevated, absolutely determinate characters, whose definition, however, discovers its content and basis in a particular ethical power. Forasmuch as, then, the tragic situation first appears in the *antagonism* of individuals who are thus empowered to act, the same can only assert itself in the field of actual human life. It results from the specific character of this alone that a particular quality so affects the substantive content of a given individual, that the latter identifies himself with his entire interest and being in such a content, and penetrates it throughout with the glow of passion. In the blessed gods, however, it is the divine Nature, in its indifference, which is what is essential; in contrast to which we have the contradiction, which in the last instance is not treated seriously, rather is one which, as I have already noticed when discussing the Homeric Epos, becomes eventually a self-resolving irony. These two modes or aspects—of which the one is as important for the whole as the other—namely, the unsevered consciousness of the godlike, and the combating human action, asserted, however, in godlike power and deed, which determines and executes the ethical purpose—supply the two fundamental elements, the mediation of which is displayed by Greek tragedy in its artistic compositions under the form of *chorus* and *heroic figures* respectively.

In modern times, considerable discussion has been raised over the significance of the Greek chorus, and the question has been raised incidentally whether it can or ought to be introduced into modern tragedy. In fact, the need of some such substantial foundation has been experienced; but critics have found it difficult to prescribe the precise manner in which effect should be given to such a change, because they failed to grasp with sufficient penetration the nature of that in which true tragedy consists and the necessity of the chorus as an essential constituent of all that Greek tragedy implies. Critics have, no doubt, recognized the nature of the chorus to the extent of maintaining that in it we find an attitude of tranquil meditation over the whole, whereas the characters of the action remain within the limits of their particular objects and situations, and, in short, receive in the chorus and its observations a standard of valuation of their characters and actions in much the same way as the public discovers in it, and within the drama itself, an objective representative of its own judgment upon all that is thus represented. In this view we have to this extent the fact rightly conceived, that the chorus is, in truth, there as a substantive and more enlightened intelligence, which warns us from irrelevant oppositions, and reflects upon the genuine issue. But, granting this to be so, it is by no means, like the spectator, a wholly disinterested person, at leisure to entertain such thoughts and ethical judgments as it likes which, uninteresting and tedious on its own account, could only be attached for the sake of such reflections. The chorus is the actual substance of the heroic life and action itself: it is, as contrasted with the particular heroes, the common folk regarded as the fruitful earth, out of which individuals, much as flowers and towering trees from their native soil, grow and whereby they are conditioned in this life. Consequently, the chorus is peculiarly fitted to a view of life in which the obligations of State legislation and settled religious dogmas do not, as yet, act as a restrictive force in ethical and social development, but where morality only exists in its primitive form of directly animated human life, and it is merely the equilibrium of unmoved life which remains assured in its stability against the fearful collisions which the antagonistic energies of individual action produces. We are made aware of the fact that an assured asylum of this kind is also a part of our actual existence by the presence of the chorus. It does not, therefore, practically co-operate with the action; it executes no right, actively, as against the contending heroes; it merely expresses its judgment as a matter of opinion; it warns, commiserates, or appeals to the divine law, and the ideal forces imminent in the soul, which the imagination grasps in external guise as the sphere of the gods that rule. In this self-expression it is, as we have already seen, lyrical; for it does not act and there arc no events for it to narrate in epical form. The content, however, retains at the same time the epic character of substantive universality; and its lyric movement is of such a nature that it can, and in this respect in contrast to the form of the genuine ode, approach at times that of the paean and the dithyramb. We must lay emphatic stress upon this position of the chorus in Greek tragedy. Just as the theatre itself possesses its external ground, its scene and environment, so, too, the chorus, that is the general community, is the spiritual scene; and we may compare it to the architectural temple which surrounds the image of the god, which resembles the heroes in the action. Among ourselves, statues are placed under the open sky without such a background, which also modern tragedy does not require, for the reason that its actions do not depend on this substantive basis, but on the personal volition and personality, no less than the apparently external contingency of events and circumstances.

In this respect it is an entirely false view which regards the chorus as an accidental piece of residuary baggage, a mere remnant from the origins of Greek drama. Of course, it is incontestable that its source is to be traced to the circumstance that, in the festivals of Bacchus, so far as the artistic aspect is concerned, the choral song was of most importance until the introduction and interruption of its course by one reciter, whose relation finally was transformed into and exalted by the real figures of dramatic action. In the blossoming season of tragedy, however, the chorus was not by any means merely retained in honour of this particular phase of the festival and ritual of the god Bacchus; rather it became continuously more elaborate in its beauty and harmonious measures by reason of the fact that its association with the dramatic action is essental and, indeed, so indispensable to it that the decline of tragedy is intimately connected with the degeneration of the choruses, which no longer remain an integral member of the whole, but are degraded to a mere embellishment. In contrast to this, in romantic tragedy, the chorus is neither intrinsically appropriate nor does it appear to have originated from choric songs. On the contrary, the content is here of a type which defeats from the first any attempt to introduce choruses as understood by Greek dramatists. For, even if we go back to the most primitive of those so-called mysteries, morality plays, and farces of a similar character, from which the romantic drama issued, we find that these present no action in that original Greek sense of the term, no outbreak, that is, of opposing forces from the undivided consciousness of life and the god-like. To as little extent is the chorus adapted to the conditions of chivalry and the dominion of kings, in so far as, in such cases, the attitude of the folk is one of mere obedience, or it is itself a party, involved together with the interest of its fortune or misfortune in the course of the action. And in general the chorus entirely fails to secure its true position where the main subject-matter consists of particular passions, ends, and characters, or where any considerable opportunity is admitted to intrigue.

In contrast to the chorus, the *second* fundamental feature of dramatic composition is that of the *individuals* who act in *conflict* with each other. In Greek tragedy it is not at all bad will, crime, worthlessness, or mere misfortune, stupidity, and the like, which act as an incentive to such collisions, but rather, as I have frequently urged, the ethical right to a definite course of action. Abstract evil neither possesses truth in itself, nor does it arouse interest. At the same time, when we attribute ethical traits of characterization to the individuals of the action, these ought not to appear merely as a matter of opinion. It is rather implied in their right or claim that they are actually there as essential on their own account. The hazards of crime, such as are present in modern drama, the useless, or quite as much the so-called noble criminal, with his empty talk about fate, we meet with in the tragedy of ancient literature, rarely, if at all, and for the good reason that the decision and deed depends on the wholly personal aspect of interest and character, upon lust for power, love, honour, or other similar passions, whose justification has its roots exclusively in the particular inclination and individuality. A resolve of this character, whose claim is based upon the content of its object, which it carries into execution in one restricted direction of particularization, violates, under certain circumstances, which are already essentially implied in the actual possibility of conflicts, a further and equally ethical sphere of human volition, which the character thus confronted adheres to, and, by his thus stimulated action, enforces, so that in this way the collision of powers and individuals equally entitled to the ethical claim is completely set up in its movement.

The sphere of this content, although capable of great variety of detail, is not in its essential features very extensive. The principal source of opposition, which Sophocles in particular, in this respect following the lead of Aeschylus, has accepted and worked out in the finest way, is that of the *body politic*, the opposition, that is, between ethical life in its social universality and the family as the natural ground of moral relations. These are the purest forces of tragic representation. It is, in short, the harmony of these spheres and the concordant action within the bounds of their realized content, which constitute the perfected reality of the moral life. In this respect I need only recall the "Seven before Thebes" of Aeschylus and, as a yet stronger illustration, the "Antigone" of Sophocles. Antigone reverences the ties of blood-relationship, the gods of the nether world. Creon alone recognizes Zeus, the paramount Power of public life and the commonwealth. We come across a similar conflict in the "Iphigenia in Aulis," as also in the "Agamemnon," the "Choephorae," and "Eumenides" of Aeschylus, and in the "Electra" of Sophocles. Agamemnon, as king and leader of his army, sacrifices his daughter in the interest of the Greek folk and the Trojan expedition. He shatters thereby the bond of love as between himself and his daughter and wife, which Clytemnestra retains in the depths of a mother's heart, and in revenge prepares an ignominious death for her husband on his return. Orestes, their son, respects his mother, but is bound to represent the right of his father, the king, and strikes dead the mother who bore him.

A content of this type retains its force through all times, and its presentation, despite all difference of nationality, vitally arrests our human and artistic sympathies.

Of a more formal type is that second kind of essential collision, an illustration of which is the tragic story of Oedipus the Greek tragedians especially favoured. Of this Sophocles has left us the most complete example in his "Oedipus Rex," and "Oedipus at Colonus." The problem here is concerned with the claim of alertness in our intelligence, with the nature of the obligation implied in that which a man carries out with a volition fully aware of its acts as contrasted with that which he has done in fact, but unconscious of and with no intention of doing what he has done under the directing providence of the gods. Oedipus slays his father, marries his mother, begets children in this incestuous alliance, and nevertheless is involved in these most terrible of crimes without active participation either in will or knowledge. The point of view of our profounder modern consciousness of right and wrong would be to recognize that crimes of this description, inasmuch as they were neither referable to a personal knowledge or volition, were not deeds for which the true personality of the perpetrator was responsible. The plastic nature of the Greek on the contrary adheres to the bare fact which an individual has achieved, and refuses to face the division implied by the purely ideal attitude of the soul in the self-conscious life on the one hand and the objective significance of the fact accomplished on the other.

For ourselves, to conclude this survey, other collisions, which either in general are related to the universally accepted association of personal action to the Greek conception of Destiny, or in some measure to more exceptional conditions, are comparatively speaking less important.

In all these tragic conflicts, however, we must above all

place on one side the false notion of *guilt* or *innocence*. The heroes of tragedy are quite as much under one category as the other. If we accept the idea as valid that a man is guilty only in the case that a choice lay open to him, and he deliberately decided on the course of action which he carried out, then these plastic figures of ancient drama are guiltless. They act in accordance with a specific character, a specific pathos, for the simple reason that they are this character, this pathos. In such a case there is no lack of decision and no choice. The strength of great characters consists precisely in this that they do not choose, but are entirely and absolutely just that which they will and achieve. They are simply themselves, and never anything else, and their greatness consists in that fact. Weakness in action, in other words, wholly consists in the division of the personal self as such from its content, so that character, volition and final purpose do not appear as absolutely one unified growth; and inasmuch as no assured end lives in the soul as the very substance of the particular personality, as the pathos and might of the individual's entire will, he is still able to turn with indecision from this course to that, and his final decision is that of caprice. A wavering attitude of this description is alien to these plastic creations. The bond between the psychological state of mind and the content of the will is for them indissoluble. That which stirs them to action is this very pathos which implies an ethical justification and which, even in the pathetic aspects of the dialogue, is not enforced in and through the merely personal rhetoric of the heart and the sophistry of passion, but in the equally masculine and cultivated objective presence, in the profound possibilities, the harmony and vitally plastic beauty of which Sophocles was to a superlative degree master. At the same time, however, such a pathos, with its potential resources of collision, brings them to deeds that are both injurious and wrongful. They have no desire to avoid the blame that results therefrom. On the contrary, it is their fame to have done what they have done. One can in fact urge nothing more intolerable against a hero of this type than by saying that he has acted innocently. It is a point of honour with such great characters that they are guilty. They have no desire to excite pity or our sensibilities. For it is not the substantive, but rather the wholly personal deepening of the personality which stirs our individual pain. His securely strong character, however, coalesces entirely with his essential pathos, and this indivisible accord inspires wonder, not compassion. The drama of Euripides marks the transition to that.

The final result, then, of the development of tragedy conducts us to this issue and only this, namely, that the two-fold vindication of the mutually conflicting aspects is no doubt retained, but the *one-sided* mode is cancelled, and the undisturbed ideal harmony brings back again that condition of the chorus, which attributes without reserve equal honour to all the gods. The true course of dramatic development consists in the annulment of *contradictions* viewed as such, in the reconciliation of the forces of human action, which alternately strive to negate each other in their conflict. Only so far is misfortune and suffering not the final issue, but rather the satisfaction of spirit, as for the first time, in virtue of such a conclusion, 'the necessity of all that particular individuals experience, is able to appear in complete accord with reason, and our emotional attitude is tranquillized on a true ethical basis; rudely shaken by the calamitous result to the heroes, but reconciled in the substantial facts. And it is only in so far as we retain such a view securely that we shall be in a position to understand ancient tragedy. We have to guard ourselves therefore from concluding that a *dénouement* of this type is merely a moral issue conformably to which evil is punished and virtue rewarded, as indicated by the proverb that "when crime turns to vomit, virtue sits down at table." We have nothing to do here with this wholly personal aspect of a self-reflecting personality and its conception of good and evil, but are concerned with the appearance of the affirmative reconciliation and the equal validity of both powers engaged in conflict, if the collision is complete. To as little extent is the necessity of the issue a blind destiny, or in other words a purely irrational, unintelligible fate, identified with the classical world by many; rather it is the rationality of destiny, albeit it does not as yet appear as self-conscious Providence, the divine final end of which in conjunction with the world and individuals appears on its own account and for others, depending as it does on just this fact that the highest Power paramount over particular gods and mankind cannot suffer this, namely, that the forces, which affirm their self-subsistence in modes that are abstract or incomplete, and thereby overstep the boundary of their warrant, no less than the conflicts which result from them, should retain their self-stability. Fate drives personality back upon its limits, and shatters it, when it has grown overweening. An irrational compulsion, however, an

375

innocence of suffering would rather only excite indignation in the soul of the spectator than ethical tranquillity. From a further point of view, therefore, the reconciliation of *tragedy* is equally distinct from that of the *Epos*. If we look at either Achilles or Odysseus in this respect we observe that both attain their object, and it is right that they do so; but it is not a continuous happiness with which they are favoured; they have on the contrary to taste in its bitterness the feeling of finite condition, and are forced to fight wearily through difficulties, losses and sacrifices. It is in fact a universal demand of truth that in the course of life and all that takes place in the objective world the nugatory character of finite conditions should compel attention. So no doubt the anger of Achilles is reconciled; he obtains from Agamemnon that in respect of which he had suffered the sense of insult; he is revenged upon Hector; the funeral rites of Patroclus are consummated, and the character of Achilles is acknowledged in all its glory. But his wrath and its reconciliation have for all that cost him his dearest friend, the noble Patroclus; and, in order to avenge himself upon Hector for this loss, he finds himself compelled to disengage himself from his anger, to enter once more the battle against the Trojans, and in the very moment when his glory is acknowledged receives the prevision of his early death. In a similar way Odysseus reaches Ithaca at last, the goal of his desire; but he does so alone and in his sleep, having lost all his companions, all the war-booty from Ilium, after long years of endurance and fatigue. In this way both heroes have paid their toll to finite conditions and the claim of nemesis is evidenced in the destruction of Troy and the misfortunes of the Greek heroes. But this nemesis is simply justice as conceived of old, which merely humiliates what is everywhere too exalted, in order to establish once more the abstract balance of fortune by the instrumentality of misfortune, and which merely touches and affects finite existence without further ethical signification. And this is the justice of the Epic in the field of objective fact, the universal reconciliation of simple accommodation. The higher conception of reconciliation in tragedy is on the contrary related to the resolution of specific ethical and substantive facts from their contradiction into their true harmony. The way in which such an accord is established is asserted under very different modes; I propose therefore merely to direct attention to the fundamental features of the actual process herein involved.

First, we have particularly to emphasize the fact, that if it is the one-sidedness of the pathos which constitutes the real basis of collisions this merely amounts to the statement that it is asserted in the action of life, and therewith has become the unique pathos of a particular individual. If this one-sidedness is to be abrogated then it is this individual which, to the extent that his action is exclusively identified with this isolated pathos, must perforce be stripped and sacrificed. For the individual here is merely this single life, and, if this unity is not secured in its stability on its own account, the individual is shattered.

The most complete form of this development is possible when the individuals engaged in conflict relatively to their concrete or objective life appear in each case essentially involved in one whole, so that they stand fundamentally under the power of that against which they battle, and consequently infringe that, which, conformably to their own essential life, they ought to respect. Antigone, for example, lives under the political authority of Creon; she is herself the daughter of a king and the affianced of Haemon, so that her obedience to the royal prerogative is an obligation. But Creon also, who is on his part father and husband, is under obligation to respect the sacred ties of relationship, and only by breach of this can give an order that is in conflict with such a sense. In consequence of this we find immanent in the life of both that which each respectively combats, and they are seized and broken by that very bond which is rooted in the compass of their own social existence. Antigone is put to death before she can enjoy what she looks forward to as bride, and Creon too is punished in the fatal end of his son and wife, who commit suicide, the former on account of Antigone's death, and the latter owing to Haemon's. Among all the fine creations of the ancient and the modern world—and I am acquainted with pretty nearly everything in such a class, and one ought to know it, and it is quite possible—the "Antigone" of Sophocles is from this point of view in my judgment the most excellent and satisfying work of art.

The tragic issue does not, however, require in every case, as a means of removing both over-emphasized aspects and the equal honour which they respectively claim, the downfall of the contestant parties. The "Eumenides" ends, as we all know, not with the death of Orestes, or the destruction of the Eumenides, these avenging spirits of matricide and filial affection, as opposed to Apollo, who seeks to protect unimpaired the worth of and reverence for the family chief and king, who prompted Orestes to slay Clytemnestra, but with

Orestes released from the punishment and honour bestowed on both divinities. At the same time we cannot fail to see in this adjusted conclusion the nature of the authority which the Greeks attached to their gods when they presented them as individuals contending with each other. They appear, in short, to the Athenian of everyday life merely as definite aspects of ethical experience which the principles of morality viewed in their complete and harmonious coherence bind together. The votes of the Areopagus are equal on either side. It is Athene, the goddess, the life of Athens, that is, imagined in its essential unity, who adds the white pebble, who frees Orestes, and at the same time promises altars and a cult to the Eumenides no less than Apollo. As a contrast to this type of objective reconciliation the settlement may be, *secondly,* of a more personal character. In other words, the individual concerned in the action may in the last instance surrender his one-sided point of view. In this betrayal by personality of its essential pathos, however, it cannot fail to appear destitute of character; and this contradicts the masculine integrity of such plastic figures. The individuals, therefore, can only submit to a higher Power and its counsel or command, to the effect that while on his own account he adheres to such a pathos, the will is nevertheless broken in its bare obstinacy by a god's authority. In such a case the knot is not loosened, but, as in the case of Philoctetes, it is severed by a *deus ex machina.*

But as a *further* and final class, and one more beautiful than the above rather external mode of resolution, we have the reconciliation more properly of the soul itself, in which respect there is, in virtue of the personal significance, a real approach to our modern point of view. The most perfect example of this in ancient drama is to be found in the ever admirable "Oedipus at Colonus" of Sophocles. The protagonist here has unwittingly slain his father, secured the sceptre of Thebes, and the bridal bed of his own mother. He is not rendered unhappy by these unwitting crimes; but the power of divination he has of old possessed makes him realize, despite himself, the darkness of the experience that confronts him, and he becomes fearfully, if indistinctly, aware of what his position is. In this resolution of the riddle in himself he resembles Adam, losing his happiness when he obtains the knowledge of good and evil. What he then does, the seer, is to blind himself, then abdicate the throne and depart from Thebes, very much as Adam and Eve are driven from Paradise. From henceforward he wanders about a helpless old man. Finally a god calls the terribly afflicted man to himself, the man, that is, who refusing the request of his sons that he should return to Thebes, prefers to associate with the Erinyes; the man, in short, who extinguishes all the disruption in himself and who purifies himself in his own soul. His blind eyes are made clear and bright, his limbs are healed, and become a treasure of the city which received him as a free guest. And this illumination in death is for ourselves no less than for him the more truly visible reconciliation which is worked out both in and for himself as individual man, in and through, that is, his essential character. Critics have endeavoured to discover here the temper of the Christian life; we are told we have here the picture of a sinner, whom God receives into His grace; and the fateful misfortunes which expire in their finite condition are made good with the seal of blessedness in death. The reconciliation of the Christian religion, however, is an illumination of the soul, which, bathed in the everlasting waters of salvation, is raised above mortal life and its deeds. Here it is the heart itself, for in such a view the spiritual life can effect this, which buries that life and its deed in the grave of the heart itself, counting the recriminations of earthly guilt as part and parcel of its own earthly individuality; and which, in the full assuredness of the eternally pure and spiritual condition of blessedness, holds itself in itself calm and steadfast against such impeachment. The illumination of Oedipus, on the contrary, remains throughout, in consonance with ancient ideas, the restoration of conscious life from the strife of ethical powers and violations to the renewed and harmonious unity of this *ethical content itself.*

There is a further feature in this type of reconciliation, however, and that is the *personal* or ideal nature of the satisfaction. We may take this as a point of transition to the otherwise to be the contrasted province of *comedy*.

(bb) That which is comic is, as we have already seen, in general terms the subjective or personal state, which forces and then dissolves the action which issues from it by its own effect into and in contradiction, remaining throughout and in virtue of this process tranquil in its own self-assurance. Comedy possesses, therefore, for its basis and point of departure that with which it is possible for tragedy to terminate, that is, a soul to the fullest extent and eventually reconciled, a joyous state, which, however much it is instrumental in the marring of its volitional power, and, indeed, in itself comes to grief, by reason of its asserting voluntarily what is in conflict with its aim, does not therefore lose its general equanimity. A personal self-assurance of this character, however, is, from a further point of view, only possible in so far as the ends proposed, and withal the characters include nothing that is on its own account essentially substantive; or, if they do possess such an intrinsic worth, it is adopted and carried out intentionally under a mode which is totally opposed to the genuine truth contained, in a form, therefore, that is destitute of such truth, so that in this respect, as in the previous case, it is merely that which is itself essentially of no intrinsic importance, but a matter of indifference which is marred, and the individual remains just as he was and unaffected.

Such a view is, too, in its general lines the conception of the old classic comedy, in so far as tradition reflects it in the plays of Aristophanes. We should, however, be careful to notice the distinction whether the individuals in the play are aware that they are comic, or are so merely from the spectator's point of view. It is only the first class that we can reckon as part of the genuine comedy in which Aristophanes was a master. Conformably to such a type, a character is only placed in a ridiculous situation, when we perceive that he himself is not in earnest about the earnestness of his purpose and voluntary effort, so that this earnestness is throughout the means of his own undoing, inasmuch as throughout such a character is unable to enter into any more noble and universally valid interest, which necessarily involves it in a situation of conflict; and, even assuming that he does actually partake of it, merely does so in a way that shows a nature, which, in virtue of its practical existence, has already annihilated that which it appears to strive to bring into operation, so that after all one sees such a coalescence has never been really effected. The comic comes, therefore, rather into play among classes of a lower social order in actual conditions of life, among men who remain much as they are, and neither are able or desire to be anything else; who, while incapable of any genuine pathos, have no doubt whatever as to what they are and do. At the same time the higher nature that is in them is asserted in this that they are not with any seriousness attached to the finite conditions which hem them in, but remain superior to the same and in themselves essentially steadfast and self-reliant against mishap and loss. This absolute freedom of spirit, which brings its own essential comfort from the first in all that a man undertakes, this world of subjective serenity is that to which Aristophanes conducts us. Without a reading of him it is hardly possible to imagine what a wealth of exuberance there is in the human heart.

The interests among which this type of comedy moves are not necessarily taken from spheres opposed to religion, morality, and art. On the contrary the old Greek comedy remains no doubt within the limits of this positive and substantive content of human life; but it is the individual caprice, the vulgar folly and perversity, by reason of which the characters concerned bring to nought activities which in their aim have a finer significance. And in this respect an ample and very pertinent material is supplied Aristophanes partly by Greek gods, and partly by the life of the Athenian people. In other words, the configuration of the divine in human impersonation itself possesses, in its mode of presentation and its particularization, to the extent at least that it is further enforced in opposition to that which is merely one-sided and human, the contradiction that is opposed to the nobility of its significance; it is thus permitted to appear as a purely empty extension of this personal life which is inadequate wholly to express it. More particularly, however, Aristophanes revels in the follies of the common folk, the stupidities of its orators and statesmen, the blockheadedness of war, and is eager, above all, and with all the politeness of his satire and the full weight of his ridicule, but also not without the profoundest meaning, to hand over the new tendencies of the tragedies of Euripides to the laughter of his fellow-citizens. The characters he has imported into the substance of his amazing artistic creations he runs into the mould of fool from that start with a sportive fancy that seems inexhaustible, so that the very idea of a rational result is imposible. He treats all alike, whether it be a Strepsiades, who will join the ranks of philosophers in order to be rid of his debts, or a Socrates, who offers to instruct the aforesaid Strepsiades and his son, or Bacchus, whom he makes descend into the lower world, in order to bring up a genuine tragic poet, and in just the same way Cleon, the women, and the Greeks, who would like to pump up the goddess of Peace from the well. The key-note that we find in all these various creations is the imperturbable self-assurance of such characters one and all, which becomes all the more emphatic in proportion as they prove themselves incapable of carrying into effect that which they project. Our fools here are so entirely unembarrassed in their folly, and also the more sensible among them possess such a tincture of that which runs contrary to the very course upon which they are set, that they all, the more sensible with the rest, remain fixed to this personal attitude of prodigious imperturbability, no matter what comes next or where it carries them. It is in fact the blessed laughter of the Olympian gods, with their untroubled equanimity, now at home in the human breast, and prepared for all contingencies. And withal we never find Aristophanes merely a cold or evil-disposed mocker. He was a man of the finest education, a most exemplary citizen, to whom the weal of Athens was of really deep importance, and who through thick and thin shows himself to be a true patriot. What therefore is in the fullest sense resolved in his comedies is, as already stated, not the divine and what is of ethical import, but the thoroughgoing upside-down-ness which inflates itself into the semblance of these substantive forces, the particular form and distinctive mode of its manifestation, in which the essential thing or matter is already from the first no longer present, so that it can without restriction be simply handed over to the unconcerned play of unqualified personal caprice. But for the very reason that Aristophanes makes explicit the absolute contradiction between the essential nature of the gods, or that of political and social life, and the personal activities of individual persons or citizens, who ought to endow such substantive form with reality, we find in this very triumph of purely personal self-assertion, despite all the profounder insight which the poet displays, one of the greatest symptoms of the degeneracy of Greece. And it is on account of this that these pictures of a wholly unperturbed sense of fundamental well-being are as a matter of fact the last important harvest which we have from the poetry created by the exuberant genius, culture, and wit of the Greek nation.

(B) I shall now direct attention to the dramatic art of the modern world, and here, too, I only propose to emphasize the more general and fundamental features which we find of importance, whether dealing with tragedy or the ordinary drama and comedy.

(aa) Tragedy, in the nobility which distinguishes it in its ancient plastic form, is limited to the partial point of view that for its exclusive and essential basis it only enforces as effective the ethically substantive content and its necessary laws; and, on the other hand, leaves the individual and subjective self-penetration of the dramatic characters essentially unevolved; while comedy on its part, to complete what we may regard as the reversed side of such plastic construction, exhibits subjectivity in the unfettered abandonment of its topsy-turvydom and ultimate dissolution.

Modern tragedy accepts in its own province from the first the principle of subjectivity. It makes, therefore, the personal intimacy of character—the character, that is, which is no purely individual and vital embodiment of ethical forces in the classic sense—its peculiar object and content. It, moreover, makes, in a type of concurrence that is adapted to this end, human actions come into collision through the instrumentality of the external acident of circumstances in the way that a contingency of a similar character is also decisive in its effect on the consequence, or appears to be so decisive.

In this connection we would subject to examination the following fundamental points:

First, the nature of the varied *ends* which ought to come into the executive process of the action as the content of the characters therein.

Secondly, the nature of the tragic *characters* themselves, as also of the collisions they are compelled to face.

Thirdly, the nature of the final *issue* and tragic reconciliation, as these differ from those of ancient tragedy.

To start with, we may observe that, however much in romantic tragedy the subjectivity of suffering and passions, in the true meaning of these words, is the focal centre, yet, for all that, it is impossible in human activity that the ground basis of definite ends in the concrete worlds of the family, the State, the Church, and others should be dispensed with, for with activity, man passes wholly into the sphere of true particularity. In so far, however, as the drama under discussion, it is not the substantive content as such in these spheres of life which constitutes the main interest of individuals, such ends are from a certain point of view particularized in a breadth of extension and variety, as also in exceptional modes of presentment, in which it often happens that what is truly essential is only able to force itself on our attention with attenuated strength. And over and above this fact, these ends receive an entirely altered form. In the province of religion, for example, the content which preeminently is asserted is no longer the particular ethical powers exhibited imaginatively under the mode of divine individuals, either in their own person or in the pathos of human heroes. It is the history of Christ, or of saints and the like, which is now set before us. In the political community it is mainly the position of kingship, the power of vassal chiefs, the strife of dynasties, or the particular members of one and the same ruling family which forms the content of the varied picture. Nay, if we take a step further we find as the principal subject-matter questions of civic or private right and other relations of a similar character; and, further, we shall find a similar attention paid to features in the family life which were not yet within the reach of ancient drama. And the reason of this is that, inasmuch as in the spheres of life above-mentioned the principle of the personal life in its independence has asserted its claim, novel phases of existence make their inevitable appearance in each one of them, which the modern man claims to set up as the end and directory of his action.

And, from a further point of view in this drama, it is the right of subjectivity, as above defined, absolutely unqualified, which is retained as the dominating content; and for this reason personal love, honour, and the rest make such an exclusive appeal as ends of human action that, while in one direction other relations cannot fail to appear as the purely external background on which these interests of our modern life are set in motion, in another such relations on their own account actively conflict with the requirements of the more individual state of emotion. Of more profound significance still is wrong and crime, even if a particular character does not deliberately and to start with aim at either, yet does not avoid them to attain his original purpose.

And, furthermore, in contrast to this particularization and individual standpoint, the ends proposed may likewise either in one direction expand to cover the universality and all-inclusive embrace of the content, or they are in another apprehended and carried into execution as themselves intrinsically substantive. In the first respect, I will merely recall to memory that typically philosophical tragedy, the "Faust" of Goethe, in which, on the one hand, a spirit of disillusion in the pursuit of science, and, on the other, the vital resources of a worldly life and earthly enjoyment—in a word, the attempted mediation in the tragic manner of an individual's wisdom and strife with the Absolute in its essential significance and phenomenal manifestation, offers a breadth of content such as no other dramatic poet has hitherto ventured to include in one and the same composition. The "Carl Moor" of Schiller is something of the same fashion. He rebels against the entire order of civic society and the collective condition of the world and the humanity of his time, and fortifies himself as such against the same. Wallenstein in the same way conceives a great and far-reaching purpose, the unity and peace of Germany, an object he fails to carry into effect by the means which, in virtue of the fact that they are welded together in an artificial manner, and one that lacks essential coherence, break in pieces and come to nought precisely in the direction where he is most anxious of their success; and he fails in the same way by reason of his opposition to the imperial authority, upon which he himself and his enterprise are inevitably shattered. Such objects of a world-wide policy, such as a Carl Moor or a Wallenstein pursue, are as a rule not accomplished at the hands of a single individual for whom others become obedient instruments; they carry themselves into effect partly with the will of many, partly against and without their knowledge. As an illustration if a conception of objects viewed in their essential significance, I will merely instance certain tragedies of Calderon, in which love, honour, and similar virtues are respectively to the rights and obligations in which they involve the characters of the action, treated as so many unyielding laws of independent force with all the stringency of a code. We find also frequently much the same thing assumed in Schiller's tragic characters, though the point of view is no doubt wholly different, at least to the extent that such individuals conceive and combat for their ends with the assumption they are universal and absolutely valid human rights. So in the early play of "Kabale und Liebe" Major Ferdinand seeks to defend the rights of Nature against the conveniences of fashionable society, and, above all, claims of the Marquis Posa freedom of thought as an inalienable possession of humanity.

Generally speaking, however, in modern tragedy it is not the substantive content of their object in the interest of which men act, and which is maintained as the stimulus of their passion; rather it is the inner experience of their heart and individual emotion, or the particular qualities of their personality, which insist on satisfaction. For even in the examples already referred to we find that to a real extent in those heroes of Spanish honour and love the content of their ultimate ends is so essentially of a personal character that the rights and obligations deducible from the same are able to fuse in direct concurrence with the individual desires of the heart, and to a large extent, too, in the youthful works of Schiller this continual insistence upon Nature, rights of man, and a converted world somewhat savours of the excess of a wholly personal enthusiasm. And if it came about that Schiller in later years endeavoured to enforce a more mature type of pathos, this was simply due to the fact that it was his main idea to restore once again in modern dramatic art the principle of ancient tragedy.

In order to emphasize still more distinctly the difference which in this respect obtains between ancient and modern tragedy, I will merely refer the reader to Shakespeare's "Hamlet." Here we find fundamentally a collision similar to that which is introduced by Aeschylus into his "Choephorae" and by Sophocles into his "Electra." For Hamlet's father, too, and the King, as in these Greek plays, has been murdered, and his mother has wedded the murderer. That which, however, in the conception of the Greek dramatists possesses a certain ethical justification—I mean the death of Agamemnon—in the contrasted case of Shakespeare's play, can only be viewed as an atrocious crime, of which Hamlet's mothers is innocent; so that the son is merely concerned in his vengeance to direct his attention to the fratricidal king, and there is nothing in the latter's character that possesses any real claim to his respect. The real collision, therefore, does not turn on the fact that the son, in giving effect to a rightful sense of vengeance, is himself forced to violate morality, but rather on the particular personality, the inner life of Hamlet, whose noble soul is not steeled to this kind of energetic activity, but, while full of contempt for the world and life, what between making up his mind and attempting to carry into effect or preparing to carry into effect its resolves, is bandied from pillar to post, and finally through his own procrastination and the external course of events meets his own doom.

If we now turn, in close connection with the above conclusions, to our *second* point of fundamental importance in modern tragedy—that is to say, the nature of the characters and their collisions—we may summarily take a point of departure from the following general observations.

The heroes of ancient classic tragedy discover circumstances under which they, so long as they irrefragably adhere to the *one* ethical state of pathos which alone corresponds to their own already formed personality, must infallibly come into conflict with an ethical Power which opposes them and possesses an equal ethical claim to recognition. Romantic characters, on the contrary, are from the first placed within a wide expanse of contingent relations and conditions, within which every sort of action is possible; so that the conflict, to which no doubt the external conditions presupposed supply the occasion, essentially abides within the *character* itself, to which the individuals concerned in their passion give effect, not, however, in the interests of the ethical vindication of the truly substantive claims, but for the simple reason that they are the kind of men they are. Greek heroes also no doubt act in accordance with their particular individuality; but this individuality, as before noted, if we take for our examples the supreme results of ancient tragedy, is itself necessarily identical with an ethical pathos which is substantive. In modern tragedy the peculiar character in its real significance, and to which it as a matter of accident remains constant, whether it happens to grasp after that which on its own account is on moral grounds justifiable, or is carried into wrong and crime, forms its resolves under the dictate of personal wishes and necessities, or among other things purely external considerations. In such a case, therefore, though we may have a coalescence between the moral aspect of the object and the character, yet, for all that, such a concurrence does not constitute, and cannot constitute—owing to the divided character of ends, passions, and the life wholly personal to the individual—the *essential* basis and objective condition of the depth and beauty of the tragic drama.

In view of the great variety of differences which further separates particular characters in this type of poetry, it is impossible to say much in the way of generalization. I will, therefore, restrict myself to a reference to the following fundamental points of view. A primary opposition which at once invites notice is that of an *abstract*, and consequently formal, characterization in its contrast with the actual individuals whom we are accustomed to meet in the concrete living world. As example of this type, we may with exceptional pertinency cite the tragic characters of the French and Italians, which, originating in the imitation of ancient drama, to a greater or less degree merely amount to pure personifications of specific passions, such as love, honour, fame, ambition, tyranny, and so forth, and which, while they present the motives of their actions as also the gradation and quality of their emotions to the best advantage with a lavish display of declamation, and all the arts of rhetoric, none the less by doing so rather resemble the dramatic failures of Seneca than the dramatic masterpieces of the Greeks. Spanish tragedy also receives the stamp of this abstract style of character-drawing. In this case, however, the pathos of love, in its conflict with honour, friendship, royal prerogative, and the rest is itself of so abstract a subjective character that in the case where the intention is to make this equally subjective substantiality stand out as the genuine object of interest, a more complete particularization of characters is hardly feasible. The characters of Spanish drama, however, often possess a certain kind of solidity, and, if I may use the expression, inflexible personality, however wanting in content it may be, a feature that is absent from French work; and at the same time Spanish writers, here also in contrast to the cold simplicity which the movement of French tragedies exhibits even in their tragic composition, know how to make up with the cleverly invented abundance of interesting situations and developments the deficiency referred to in the matter of characterization.

In contrast to both these schools, and in their mastery of the exposition of fully developed human characters and personality, the English are exceptionally distinguished; and among them, and soaring above the rest at an almost unapproachable height, stands Shakespeare. For even in the cases where a purely formal passion, as for instance ambition in Macbeth, or jealousy in Othello, claims as its field the entire pathos of his tragic hero, such an abstraction impairs by no fraction the full breadth of the personality. Despite this restriction the characters remain throughout entire men. In fact, the more Shakespeare on the infinite embrace of his world-stage, proceeds to develop the extreme limits of evil and folly, to that extent, as I have already observed, on these very boundaries—of course, not without real wealth of poetic embellishment—he concentrates these characters in their limitations. While doing so, however, he confers on them intelligence and imagination; and, by means of the image in which they, by virtue of that intelligence, contemplate themselves objectively as a work of art, he makes them free artists of themselves, and is fully able, through the complete virility and truth of his characterization, to awaken our interest in criminals, no less than in the most vulgar and weak-witted lubbers and fools. Of a similar nature is the style of expression he makes his tragic characters adopt. It is at once individual, realistic, emphatically vital, extraordinarily various, and, moreover, where it seems advisable, it can rise to sublimity and is marked by an overwhelming force of utterance. Its ideal intensity and its qualities of invention are displayed in images and similes that flash from each other with lightning rapidity. Its very rhetoric, here the barren child of no school, but the growth of genuine emotion and penetration into human personality, is such that, if we take into account this extraordinary union of the directness of life itself and ideal greatness of soul, we shall find it hard indeed to point to a single other dramatic poet among the moderns whom we are entitled to rank in his company. No doubt Goethe in his youth made a real effort to achieve some approach to a like natural truth and detailed characterization; but in the ideal force and exaltation of passion his rivalry collapses. Schiller, again, has shown an increasing tendency toward violence, the tempestuous expatiation of which lacks a true core of reality.

Modern characters also differ in the nature of their *constancy* or their spiritual *vacillation* and distraction. We find, no doubt, the weakness of indecision, the fluctuations of reflection, the weighing of reasons, conformably to which a resolve should be directed, here and there in classic drama, and more particularly in the tragedies of Euripides. But Euripides is a writer whose tendency is already to forsake the wholly plastic completeness of characterization and action and to develop exceptional aspects of personal sensibility. In modern tragedy we meet yet more frequently such vacillating characters, more particularly on the ground that they are essentially under the sway of two opposed passions, which make them fluctuate from one resolve or one kind of deed to another. I have already made some observations on this attitude of vacillation in another context, and now merely supplement this by stating that, although the tragic action must depend on colliding factors, yet where we find such a division in *one* and the same individual such a concurrence is always attended with precarious consequences. And the reason is that this disruption into interests, which are opposed to each other, is due in part to an obscurity and obtuseness of the intelligence, and in some measure, too, to weakness and immaturity. We come across characters of this type in the creations of Goethe's younger days, notably Weislingen, Fernando in "Stella," and above all Clavigo. They are, as we may say, double men, who are unable to secure a ready, and so stable, individuality. It is wholly another matter when two opposed spheres of life or moral obligation are equally sacred to a character which, on its own account, is not deficient in stability, and such a person is under the necessity of ranking himself on *one* side to the exclusion of the other. In a case of that kind, the vacillation is merely a moment of passage, and does not itself constitute, as it were, the nervous system of the character. Again, of a somewhat similar kind, is the tragic case where the spiritual life is seduced, despite its nobler purpose, into objects of passion which are contradictory to the same, as in the case of Schiller's "Holy Maid," and are then forced to seek a recovery from this division of the soul in their own intimate or objective life, or pay the penalty. At the same time, this personal tragedy of inward division, when it is made the pivot on which the tragic action revolves, contains, as a rule, what is merely pitiful and painful, or, from another standpoint, exasperating; and the poet will rather do better to avoid it than go out of his way to find it and develop it. The worst case is that, however, where such a vacillation and veering round of character and the entire personality is—the very dialectic of art being thrown awry for this purpose—made the principle of the entire presentation, as though the truth of all importance was to demonstrate that no character is in itself firmly rooted and self-assured. The one-sided ends of specific passions, it is true, ought not to bring about a realization which is secured without a battle; and also, in everyday life, they cannot fail to experience, through the reactionary power of conditions and individuals which oppose them, their finite character and lack of stability. An issue of this kind, however, before the appearance of which we are unable to get the pertinent conclusion, ought not to be introduced as a dialectical piece of wheel adjustment in the personality itself; if it is, the person concerned, viewed as *this* personal state of the soul, is a wholly empty and undefined form, whose collective living growth is found, no less in respect to its objects than in its character, to be wholly wanting in definition. In much the same way the case, also, is otherwise, where the change in the spiritual condition of the entire man itself appears as a direct consequent of just this, its own kind of self-detachment, so that only that is developed and emphasized which essentially and from the first lay secured in the character. As an example, we find in Shakespeare's Lear that the original folly of the old man is intensified to the point of madness much in the same way that Gloster's spiritual blindness is converted into actual physical blindness, in which for the first time his eyes are opened to the true distinction in the love he entertains for his two sons respectively. It is precisely Shakespeare who, as a contrast to that exposition of vacillating and essentially self-divided characters, supplies us with the finest examples of essentially stable and consequential characters, who go to their doom precisely in virtue of this tenacious hold upon themselves and their ends. Unsupported by the sanction of the moral law, but rather carried onward by the formal necessity of their personality, they suffer themselves to be involved in their acts by the coil of external circumstances, or they plunge blindly therein and maintain themselves there by sheer force of will, even where all that they do is merely done because they are impelled to assert themselves against others, or because they have simply come to the particular point they have reached. The rise of insurgent passion, one essentially consonant with a certain type of character, one which has not as yet fully emerged, but now secures its utmost expansion, this onward movement and process of a great soul, with all the intimate traits of its evolution, this picture of its self-destructive conflict with circumstances, human and objective conditions and results, is the main content of some of Shakespeare's most interesting tragedies.

The last of the subjects which we have still to discuss as proposed is the nature of the *tragic issue* which characters in our present drama have to confront, as also the type of tragic *reconciliation* compatible with such a standpoint. In ancient tragedy it is the eternal justice which, as the absolute might of destiny, delivers and restores the harmony of substantive being in its ethical character by its opposition to the particular forces which, in their strain to assert an independent subsistence, come into collision, and which, in virtue of the rational ideality implied in its operations, satisfies us even where we see the downfall of particular men. In so far as a justice of the same kind is present in modern tragedy, it is necessarily, in part, more abstract on account of the closer differentiation of ends and characters, and, in part, of a colder nature and one that is more akin to that of a criminal court, in virtue of the fact that the wrong and crime into which individuals are necessarily carried, in so far as they are intent upon executing their designs, are of a profounder significance. Macbeth, for instance, the elder daughters of Lear and their husbands, the president in "Kabale und Liebe," Richard III, and many similar examples, on account of their atrocious conduct, only deserve the fate they get. This type of *dénouement* usually is presented under the guise that individuals are crushed by an actual force which they have defied in order to carry out their personal aims. Wallenstein, for example, is shattered on the adamantine wall of the imperial power; but the old Piccolomini, who, in order to maintain the lawful régime, betrays a friend and misuses the rights of friendship, is punished through the death and sacrifice of his son. Götz von Berlichingen, too, attacks a dominant and securely founded political order, and goes to ground, as also Weislingen and Adelheid, who range themselves, no doubt, on the side of this organized power, but, through wrongful deed and disloyalty, prepare the way to disaster. And along with this we have the demand emphasized, in virtue of the personal point of view of such characters, that these should of necessity appear themselves to acknowledge the justice of their fate. Such a state of acceptance may either be of a religious nature, in which case the soul becomes conscious of a more exalted and indestructible condition of blessedness with which to confront the collapse of its mundane personality; or it may be of a more formal, albeit more worldly, type, in so far, that is, as the strength and equanimity of the character persists in its course up to the point of overthrow without breaking asunder; and in this way, despite all circumstances and mischances, preserves with unimpaired energy its personal freedom. Or, as a final alternative, where the substance of such acceptance is of more real value, by the recognition that the lot which the individual receives is the one, however bitter it may be, which his action merits.

From another point of view, however, we may see the tragic issue also merely in the light of the effect of unhappy circumstances and external accidents, which might have brought about, quite as readily, a different result and a happy conclusion. From such a point of view we have merely left us the conception that the modern idea of individuality, with its searching definition of character, circumstances, and developments, is handed over essentially to the contingency of the earthly state, and must carry the fateful issues of such finitude. Pure commiseration of this sort is, however, destitute of meaning; and it is nothing less than a frightful kind of external necessity in the particular case where we see the downfall of essentially noble natures in their conflict thus assumed with the mischance of purely external accidents. Such a course of events can insistently arrest our attention; but in the result it can only be horrible, and the demand is direct and irresistible that the external accidents ought to accord with that which is identical with the spiritual nature of such noble characters. Only as thus regarded can we feel ourselves reconciled with the grievous end of Hamlet and Juliet. From a purely external point of view, the death of Hamlet appears as an accident occasioned by his duel with Laertes and the interchange of the daggers.

But in the background of Hamlet's soul, death is already present from the first. The sandbank of finite condition will not content his spirit, As the focus of such mourning and weakness, such melancholy, such a loathing of all the conditions of life, we feel from the first that, hemmed within such an environment of horror, he is a lost man, whom the surfeit of the soul has well-nigh already done to death before death itself approaches him from without. The same thing may be observed in the case of Romeo and Juliet. The ground on which these tender blossoms have been planted is alien to their nature; we have no alternative left us but to lament the pathetic transiency of such a beautiful love, which, as some tender rose in the vale of this world of accident, is broken by rude storms and tempests, and the frangible reckonings of noble and well-meaning devices. This pitiful state of our emotions is, however, simply a feeling of reconciliation that is painful, a kind of *unhappy blessedness* in misfortune.

(bb) Much as poets present to us the bare downfall of particular people they are also able to treat the similar contingency of the development of events in such a way, that, though the circumstances in all other respects would appear to give them little enough support, a happy issue of such conditions and characters is secured, in which they elicit our interest. No doubt the favour of such a destiny of events has at least an equal claim upon us as the disfavour. And so far as the question merely concerns the nature of this difference, I must admit that I prefer a happy conclusion. How could it be otherwise? I can myself discover no better ground for the preference of misfortune, simply on its own account as such, to a happy resolution than that of a certain condition of fine sensibility, which is devoted to pain and suffering, and experiences more interest in their presence than in painless situations such as it meets with every day. If therefore the interests are of such a nature, that it is really not worth the trouble to sacrifice the men or women concerned on their altar, it being possible for them either to surrender their objects, without making such surrender as is equivalent to a surrender of their individuality, or to mutually come to an agreement in respect thereof, there is no reason why the conclusion should be tragic. The tragic aspect of the conflicts and their resolution ought in principle merely to be enforced in the cases where it is actually necessary in order to satisfy the claim of a superior point of view. If this necessity is absent there is no sufficient ground for mere suffering and unhappiness. And it is simply due to this fact that social *plays* and *dramas* originate which form, as it were, an intermediate link between tragedies and comedies. I have already in a previous passage explained the poetical standpoint of this class of composition. Among us Germans we find it to some extent appropriating what readily moves us in the world of the citizen and family life; in another direction it is preoccupied with chivalry, a movement to which the "Götz" of Goethe has given a decided stimulus; mainly, however, we may call it the triumph of *ordinary morality,* which in the large majority of cases is the main thing celebrated. The subject-matter of such plays most in vogue are questions of finance or property, differences of status, unfortunate love affairs, examples of spiritual baseness in the more restricted conditions and affairs of life and so on. In one word, what we have here is that which otherwise is already before our eyes, only with this difference, that in such moral dramas, virtue and duty obtain the victory, and crime is shamed and punished, or betakes itself to repentance, so that in a moral conclusion of this kind the reconciliation ought to centre in this, namely, that whatever happens good is the result. Thereby the fundamental interest is concentrated in the personal or spiritual quality of views held and a good or evil heart. The more, however, the abstractly moral state of mind or heart supplies the pivot on which all turns, so much the less can it be the pathos of a particular matter, or an intrinsically essential object, to which the personality in question is attached. And add to this, from a further point of view, so much the less ultimately is the definite character able to maintain itself and persist in such self-assertion. If all is to be finally focused in the purely moral aspects of the psychological state, or the condition of the heart, from a subjective point of view such as this, with its dominating emphasis on ethical reflection, no standing ground remains for any other definite characteristics, or at least specific ends to be proposed. Let the heart break and change its views. Such seems to be the idea. Pathetic dramas of this type, notably Kotzebue's "Menschenhass und Reue," and also too many moral offences in the dramas of Iffland, strictly speaking, have therefore an issue which we can neither call good or bad. I mean by this that the main thing is as a rule the question of pardon and the promise of moral improvement, and we are therefore confronted with that possibility of spiritual conversion and surrender of the self. No doubt in this fact we discover the exalted nature and greatness of Spirit.

When, however, the jolly dog, as the heroes of Kotzebue are for the most part, and not infrequently Iffland's too, after being a scap and a rascal, suddenly promises to turn over a new leaf, it is frankly impossible with a good-for-nothing chap of this sort that his conversion can be otherwise than mere pretence, or of so superficial a character that it merely affects his skin, and merely supplies a momentary conclusion to the course of events that has no substantial basis, but rather, by all ordinary reckoning, will take the knave to disreputable quarters, if we will only acquaint ourselves with his subsequent history.

(cc) As regards our *modern comedy* I must draw particular attention to one point of difference, to which I have already alluded when discussing the old Attic comedy. The point is this—whether the folly and restricted outlook of the characters appears ridiculous to others only, or also to themselves; whether in short the comic figures are an object of laughter only for the audience, or also for themselves. Aristophanes, that creator of genuine comedy, exclusively accepted as the main principle of his plays the latter alternative. Already, however, in Greek comedy of a later date, and subsequently in the hands of Plautus and Terence, the opposite principle came into vogue; and in our modern examples of comedy it has been carried to such a length that we find a large number of comic compositions the inclination of which is more or less the subject-matter which is ridiculous in a purely prosaic sense, or rather we might say matters that leave a sour taste in the mouth of and are repugnant to the comic characters. This is the standpoint of Molière in particular in his best comedies, which have no right to be regarded as farces. The prosaic quality here is justified on the ground that the object aimed at by such characters is a matter of bitter earnest. They are deadly serious in the pursuit of it; they are therefore quite unable to join with satisfaction in the laughter, when they are finally deceived, or themselves are responsible for its failure. They are in short merely the disillusioned objects of a laughter foreign to themselves and generally damaging to themselves. As an example, Molière's "Tartuffe," *le faux dévot,* viewed as the unmasking of a really damned rascal has nothing funny in it, but is a very earnest business, and the deception of the deluded Orgon amounts to a sheer intensity of misfortune, which can only be resolved by the *deus ex machina*, in reference to whom the official of the court of justice utters the following exhortation:

Remettez-vous, monsieur, d'une alarme si chaude.
Nous vivons sous un prince, ennemi de la fraude,
Un prince dont les yeux se font jour dans les cœurs,
Et que ne peut tromper tout l'art des imposteurs.

We may add, too, that the odious abstract excess of characters so stable as, for example, Molière's "Miser," the absolutely stolid and serious subjection of whom to his idiotic passion renders any emancipation from such fetters impossible, contains in it nothing that is genuinely comic.

It is pre-eminently in this field that for compensation of such defects a fine artistic power in the accurate and exhaustive delineation of character is manifested, or a true mastery of the craft discovers its best opportunity for an admirably thought-out intrigue. As a rule the occasion for such an intrigue is supplied by the circumstance that some character or other endeavours to secure his objects by deluding some one else, such a course appearing to harmonize with these interests and advance them. As a matter of fact, however, it only results in the contradictory situation that it is through this pernicious demand they are self-destructive. In opposition to such a plot we find as a rule a similar plot of dissembled appearances put in motion, which has for its object the like confusion of the original plotter. Such a general scheme admits of an infinite number and degree of ups and downs in the interweaving of its situations which are adapted to every conceivable subtlety. The Spaniards are, in particular, the most consummate masters in the invention of such intrigues and developments, and have composed much that is delightful and excellent in this class of work. The subject-matter generally consists of the attractive incidents of love or affairs of honour and the like. These, which in tragedy bring about the profoundest collisions, in comedy, by contrast—as, for example, pride, love of long standing that doesn't wish to reveal itself, yet directly betrays itself in the end—prove themselves fundamentally without substance and dissolve in the comic. A word in conclusion as to the characters who hatch and carry out such intrigues. Such are usually, following the example of the slaves in the Roman comedy, servants or menials, who have no respect for the objects of their superiors, but rather make them subordinate to their own advantage or bring them to nought, and merely present us with the amusing position, that the real masters are the servants and the masters the slaves, or at least give rise to all kinds of comic situation, which come about accidentally, or are directly the result of intention. We of course, as audience, are in the know about such mysteries, and can fortify ourselves against every sort of cunning and deceit, which often carries the most serious consequences to fathers, uncles, aunts, and the rest, all of the most respectable antecedents; and we may laugh as we please over the contradictory situations that appear before us, or are involved in such ingenious deceptions.

In this kind of way our modern comedy, generally speaking, gives play on the stage to private interests and personalities of the social life I have mentioned in their accidental vagaries, laughable features, abnormal habits and follies, partly by means of character delineation, and partly with the help of comic developments of situations and circumstances. A joviality so frank and genial as that which persists in the Aristophanic comedy as the mediating element of its resolution, does not animate this kind of comedy; or rather cases occur where it can be actually repulsive, that is to say, where that which is essentially evil, the tricks of menials, the treachery of sons and wards towards worthy men, fathers and guardians is triumphant, always assuming that the persons deluded have in no way themselves been influenced by false prejudices or eccentricities of such a kind that there is some reason why they should be made to appear ridiculous in their helpless stupidity and handed over as the sport of the aims of others.

In a converse way, however, and in contrast as such to the above generally prosaic type of treatment, the modern world, too, has elaborated a world of comedy which is both truly comic and poetical in its nature. The fundamental note here again is the cheeriness of disposition, the inexhaustible resources of fun, no matter what may be the nature of miscarriage or bad luck, the exuberance and dash of what is at bottom nothing better than pure tomfoolery, and, in a word, exploited self-assurance. We have here as a result, in yet profounder expatiation, and yet more intense display of humour, whether the sphere of it be more restricted or capacious, and whether the mode of it be more or less important, what runs on parallel lines with that which Aristophanes in the ancient world and in his own field created beyond all rivalry. As the master, who in a similar way outshines all others in his field, or rather the particular portion to which I now refer, I will, though without now further entering into detail, once again emphasize the name of William Shakespeare.

Tragedy and the Attacks on Socrates

HEGEL

With this Genius of Socrates as one of the chief parts of
his indictment, we now enter upon the subject of his fate,
which ends with his condemnation. We may find this fate out
of harmony with his professed business of instructing his
fellow-citizens in what is good, but taken in connection with
what Socrates and his people were, we shall recognize the
necessity of it. The contemporaries of Socrates, who came
forward as his accusers before the Athenian people, laid
hold on him as the man who made known that what was
held as absolute was not absolute. Socrates, with this new
principle, and as one who was an Athenian citizen whose
express business was this form of instruction, came, through
this his personality, into relationship with the whole Athenian people; and this relationship was not merely with a
certain number or with a commanding number, but it was
a living relationship with the spirit of the Athenian people.
The spirit of this people in itself, its constitution, its whole
life, rested, however, on a moral ground, on religion, and
could not exist without this absolutely secure basis. Thus
because Socrates makes the truth rest on the judgment of
inward consciousness, he enters upon a struggle with the
Athenian people as to what is right and true. His accusation
was therefore just, and we have to consider this accusation
as also the end of his career. The attacks which Socrates
experienced are well known, and were from two sources;
Aristophanes attacked him in the "Clouds," and then he was
formally accused before the people.

Aristophanes regarded the Socratic philosophy from the
negative side, maintaining that through the cultivation of reflecting consciousness, the idea of law had been shaken, and
we cannot question the justice of this conception. Aristophanes' consciousness of the one-sidedness of Socrates may
be regarded as a prelude to his death; the Athenian people

likewise certainly recognized his negative methods in condemning him. It is known that Aristophanes brought upon the stage along with Socrates, not only such men as Aeschylus, and more specially Euripides, but also the Athenians generally and their generals—the personified Athenian people and the gods themselves—a freedom which we would not dream of were it not historically authenticated. We have not here to consider the real nature of the Comedy of Aristophanes, nor the wanton way in which he was said to have treated Socrates. As to the first, it should not startle us, nor do we require to justify Aristophanes or to excuse him. The Comedy of Aristophanes is in itself as real a part of the Athenian people, and Aristophanes is as essential a figure, as were the sublime Pericles, the happy Alcibiades, the divine Sophocles, and the moral Socrates, for he belongs as much as any other to this circle of luminaries. Thus much can alone be said, that it certainly goes against our German seriousness to see how Aristophanes brings on the boards men living in the State, by name, in order to make a jest of them; and we feel this specially in regard to so upright a man as Socrates.

By chronological considerations, some have tried hard to refute the fact that Aristophanes' representations had no influence on the condemnation of Socrates. It is seen that, on the one hand, Socrates was treated quite unjustly; but then we must recognize the merit of Aristophanes, who in his "Clouds" was perfectly right. This poet, who exposed Socrates to scorn in the most laughable and bitter way, was thus no ordinary joker and shallow wag who mocked what is highest and best, and sacrificed all to wit with a view to making the Athenians laugh. For everything has to him a much deeper basis, and in all his jokes there lies a depth of seriousness. He did not wish merely to mock; and moreover to mock what is worthy of honour would be perfectly bald and flat. It is a pitiful wit which has no substance, and does not rest on contradictions lying in the matter itself. But Aristophanes was no bad jester. It is, generally speaking, not possible to joke in an external way about what does not contain matter for joking or irony in itself. For what really is comic is to show a man or a thing as they disclose themselves in their extent; and if the thing is not itself its contradiction, the comic element is superficial and groundless. Hence, when Aristophanes makes merry over the Democracy, there is a deep political earnestness at heart, and from all his works it appears what a noble, excellent, true Athenian citizen he was. We thus have a real patriot before us, who, though it involved the punishment of death, did not fear in one of his works to counsel peace. In him, as one who had a patriotism of the most enlightened kind, we find the blissful self-satisfied enjoyment of a people giving free rein to itself. There is, in what is humorous, a self-security which, though with all seriousness it strives after some particular thing, while the opposite of what it aims at always comes to pass, never has for that reason any doubts nor any reflection about itself, since it remains perfectly certain of itself and of what concerns it. We enjoy in Aristophanes this side of the free Athenian spirit, this perfect enjoyment of itself in loss, this untroubled certainty of itself in all miscarriage of the result in real life, and this is the height of humour.

In the "Clouds" we do not indeed see this natural humour, but a contradiction with definite intention. Aristophanes indeed depicts Socrates humorously too, for he brings forth in his moral works the opposite of that from which he starts, and his scholars derive delight from the far-extending discoveries reached through him, which they think are made by their own good luck, but which afterwards turn hateful to them, and become the very opposite of what they intended. The wonderful perception which the followers of Socrates are here represented as having attained is just a perception of the nullity of the laws of the determinate good as it is to the natural consciousness. Aristophanes made fun of the fact that Socrates occupied himself with elementary researches as to how far fleas spring, and of his putting wax on their feet in order to discover this. This is not historic, but it is well known that Socrates had in his philosophy the side which Aristophanes showed up with such acrimony. Shortly, the fable of the "Clouds" is this: Strepsiades, an honourable Athenian citizen of the old school, had great trouble with his new-fashioned extravagant son, who, spoiled by mother and uncle, kept horses and led a life out of keeping with his position. The father thus got into trouble with his creditors, and went in distress to Socrates, and became his disciple. There the old man learned that not this or that, but another is the right, or rather he learned the stronger *kreitton* and weaker reasons *hetton logus*. He learned the dialectic of laws, and how, by reasoning, the payment of debts can be disregarded, and he then required that his son should go to the School of Socrates; and the latter likewise profited from his wisdom. But we find the result ensuing from the universal which has now through the Socratic dialectic become empty, in the private interest or the wrong spirit of

Strepsiades and his son, which spirit is merely the negative consciousness of the content of laws. Equipped with this new wisdom of reasons, and the discovery of reasons, Strepsiades is armed against the chief evil that presses on him, as regards his threatening creditors. These now come one after another to obtain payment. But Strepsiades knows how to put them off with excellent reasons, and to argue them away, for he pacifies them by all sorts of *titulos,* and shows them that he does not need to pay them; indeed he even mocks them, and is very glad that he learned all this from Socrates. But soon the scene changes, and the whole affair alters. The son comes, behaves in a very unseemly way to his father, and finally beats him. The father cries to the supreme power, as if this were the last indignity, but the son shows him, with equally good reasons, obtained by the method derived by him from Socrates, that he had a perfect right to strike him. Strepsiades ends the comedy with execrations on the Socratic dialectic, with a return to his old ways, and with the burning of Socrates' house. The exaggeration which may be ascribed to Aristophanes is that he drove this dialectic to its bitter end, but it cannot be said that injustice is done to Socrates by this representation. Indeed we must admire the depth of Aristophanes in having recognized the dialectic side in Socrates as being a negative, and—though after his own way—in having presented it so forcibly. For the power of judging in Socrates' method is always placed in the subject, in conscience, but where this is bad, the story of Strepsiades must repeat itself.

With regard to the formal public accusation of Socrates, we must not, like Tennemann (Vol. II., p. 39 seq.), say of Socrates' treatment, that "it is revolting to humanity that this excellent man had to drink the cup of poison as a sacrifice to cabals—so numerous in democracies. A man like Socrates, who had made right" (right is not being discussed, but we may ask what right? The right of moral freedom) "the sole standard of his action, and did not stray from the straight path, must necessarily make many enemies" (Why? This is foolish; it is a moral hypocrisy to pretend to be better than others who are then called enemies) "who are accustomed to act from quite different motives. When we think of the corruption, and of the rule of the thirty tyrants, we must simply wonder that he could have worked on to his sixtieth year unmolested. But since the Thirty did not venture to lay hands on him themselves, it is the more to be wondered at that in the reconstituted and just rule and freedom which followed the overthrow of despotism"—in that very way the danger in which their principle was, came to be known—"a man like Socrates could be made a sacrifice to cabals. This phenomenon is probably explained by the fact that the enemies of Socrates had first of all to gain time in order to obtain a following, and that under the rule of the Thirty, they played too insignificant a part," and so on.

Now, as regards the trial of Socrates, we have to distinguish two points, the one the matter of the accusation, the judgment of the court, and the other the relation of Socrates to the sovereign people. In the course of justice there are thus these two parts—the relation of the accused to the matter on account of which he is accused, and his relation to the competency of the people, or the recognition of their majesty. Socrates was found guilty by the judges in respect of the content of his accusation, but was condemned to death because he refused to recognize the competency and majesty of the people as regards the accused.

(1) The accusation consisted of two points: "That Socrates did not consider as gods those who were held to be such by the Athenian people, but introduced new ones; and that he also led young men astray."[1] The leading away of youth was his casting doubt on what was held to be immediate truth. The first accusation has in part the same foundation, for he made it evident that what was usually so considered, was not acceptable to the gods; and in part it is to be taken in connection with his Daemon, not that he called this his god. But with the Greeks this was the direction which the individuality of judgment took; they took it to be a contingency of the individual, and hence, as contingency of circumstances is an external, they also made the contingency of judgment into something external, i.e. they consulted their oracles—conscious that the individual will is itself a contingent. But Socrates, who placed the contingency of judgment in himself, since he had his Daemon in his own consciousness, thereby abolished the external universal Daemon from which the Greeks obtained their judgments. This accusation, as also Socrates' defence, we wish now to examine further; Xenophon represents both to us, and Plato has also supplied us with an Apology. Meanwhile we may not rest content with saying that Socrates was an excellent man who suffered innocently, etc., for in this accusation it was

1 Xenoph. "Apologia Socrat." § 10; "Memorab." I. c.1, § 1 Plato "Apologia Socrat." p. 24 (p. 104).

the popular mind of Athens that rose against the principle which became fatal to him.

(a) As regards the first point of the accusation, that Socrates did not honour the national gods, but introduced new ones, Xenophon[2] makes him answer that he always brought the same sacrifices as others to the public altars, as all his fellow-citizens could see—his accusers likewise. But as to the charge that he introduced new Daemons, in that he heard the voice of God showing him what he should do, he appealed to them whether by soothsayers the cry and flight of birds, the utterances of men (like the voice of Pythia), the position of the entrails of sacrificial animals, and even thunder and lightning were not accepted as divine revelations. That God knows the future beforehand, and, if He wishes, reveals it in these ways, all believe with him; but God can also reveal the future otherwise. He could show that he did not lie in maintaining that he heard the voice of God, from the testimony of his friends, to whom he often announced what was said; and in its results this was always found to be true. Xenophon ("Memorab." I. c. 1, § 11) adds, "No one ever saw or heard Socrates do or say anything godless or impious, for he never tried to find out the nature of the Universe, like most of the others, when they sought to understand how what the Sophists called the world began." That is, from them came the earlier atheists, who, like Anaxagoras, held that the sun was a stone.[3]

The effect which the defence against this part of the accusation made on the judges is expressed thus by Xenophon:[4] "One section of them was displeased because they did not believe what Socrates said, and the other part because they were envious that he was more highly honoured of the gods than they." This effect is very natural. In our times this also happens in two ways. Either the individual is not believed when he boasts of special manifestations, and particularly of manifestations which have to do with individual action and life; it is neither believed that such manifestations took place at all, or that they happened to this subject. Or if anyone does have dealings with such divinations, rightly enough his proceedings are put an end to, and he is shut up. By this it is not denied in a general way that God foreknows everything, or that He can make revelations to individuals;

[2] "Apologia Socrat." §§ 11-13; "Memorab." I. c. 1, §§ 2-6; 19.
[3] Plat. "Apol. Socrat." p. 26.
[4] "Apologia Socrat." § 14 (cf. "Memorab." I. c. 1, § 17).

this may be admitted *in abstracto,* but not in actuality, and it is believed in no individual cases. Men do not believe that to him, to this individual, there has been a revelation. For why to him more than to others? And why just this trifle, some quite personal circumstances—as to whether someone should have a successful journey, or whether he should converse with another person, or whether or not he should in a speech properly defend himself? And why not others amongst the infinitely many things which may occur to the individual? Why not much more important things, things concerning the welfare of whole States? Hence it is not believed of an individual, in spite of the fact that if it is possible, it must be to the individual that it happens. This unbelief, which thus does not deny the general fact and general possibility, but believes it in no particular case, really does not believe in the actuality and truth of the thing. It does not believe it because the absolute consciousness—and it must be such—certainly knows nothing of a positive kind of trivialities such as form the subject of these divinations and also those of Socrates; in spirit such things immediately vanish away. The absolute consciousness does not know about the future as such, any more than about the past; it knows only about the present. But because in its present, in its thought, the opposition of future and past to present becomes apparent, it likewise knows about future and past, but of the past as something which has taken shape. For the past is the preservation of the present as reality, but the future is the opposite of this, the Becoming of the present as possibility, and thus the formless. From out of this formlessness the universal first comes into form in the present; and hence in the future no form can be perceived. Men have the dim feeling that when God acts it is not in a particular way, nor for particular objects. Such things are held to be too paltry to be revealed by God in a particular case. It is acknowledged that God determines the individual, but by this the totality of individuality, or all individualities, is understood; hence it is said that God's way of working is found in universal nature.

Now while with the Greeks judgment had the form of a contingency externally posited through the flight and cries of birds, in our culture we decide by an inward contingency, because I myself desire to be this contingency, and the knowledge of individuality is likewise a consciousness of this contingency. But if the Greeks, for whom the category of the contingency of consciousness was an existent, a knowledge of it as an oracle, had this individuality as a universal knowledge of which everyone could ask counsel, in Socrates—in whom what was here externally established had become inward consciousness, as with us, though not yet fully, being still represented as an actual voice, and conceived of as something which he separated from his individuality—the decision of the single individual had the form of personality as a particular, and it was not a universal individuality. That his judges could not in justice tolerate, whether they believed it or not. With the Greeks such revelations had to have a certain nature and method; there were, so to speak, official oracles (not subjective), such as Pythia, a tree, etc. Hence when this appeared in any particular person like a common citizen, it was considered incredible and wrong; the Daemon of Socrates was a medium of a different kind to any formerly respected in the Greek Religion. It is individuality. This his judges could not in justice tolerate, of the Delphian Apollo, Pythia, declared Socrates to be the wisest Greek.[5] Socrates it was who carried out the command of the god of knowledge, "Know Thyself," and made it the motto of the Greeks, calling it the law of the mind, and not interpreting it as meaning a mere acquaintanceship with the particular nature of man. Thus Socrates is the hero who established in the place of the Delphic oracle, the principle that man must look within himself to know what is Truth. Now seeing that Pythia herself pronounced that utterance, we find in it a complete revolution in the Greek mind, and the fact that in place of the oracle, the personal self-consciousness of every thinking man has come into play. This inward certainty, however, is undoubtedly another new god, and not the god of the Athenians existing hitherto, and thus the accusation of Socrates was quite just.

(b) If we now consider the second point of the accusation, that Socrates led youth astray, we find that he first sets against it the fact that the oracle of Delphi declared that none could be nobler, juster or wiser than he.[6] And then he sets against this accusation his whole manner of life, and asks whether by the example that he gave, particularly to those with whom he went about, he ever led any into evil.[7] The general accusation had to be further defined and witnesses came forward. "Meletus said that he knew some whom he advised to obey him rather than their parents."[8] This

5 Plato. "Apol. Socrat." p. 21.
6 Xenoph. "Apol. Socrat." § 14.
7 Xenoph. "Apol. Socrat." §§ 16-19; "Memorab." I. c. 2, §§ 1-8.
8 Xenoph. "Apol. Socrat." § 20; cf. "Memorab." I. c.2, § 49 seq.

point of the accusation principally related to Anytus, and since he made it good by sufficient testimony, the point was undoubtedly proved in accordance with law. Socrates explained himself further on this point when he left the court. For Xenophon tells us (Apol. Socr. §§ 27, 29-31) that Anytus was inimical to Socrates, because he said to Anytus, a respected citizen, that he should not bring up his son to the trade of a tanner, but in manner befitting a free man. Anytus was himself a tanner, and although his business was mostly conducted by slaves, it was in itself not ignominious, and Socrates' expression was hence wrong, although, as we have seen, quite in the spirit of Greek thought. Socrates added that he had made acquaintance with this son of Anytus and discovered no evil in him, but he prophesied that he would not remain at this servile work to which his father kept him. Nevertheless, because he had no rational person near to look after him, he would come to have evil desires and be brought into dissolute ways. Xenophon added that Socrates' prophecy had come to pass literally, and that the young man gave himself up to drink, and drank day and night, becoming totally depraved. This can be easily understood, for a man who feels himself to be fit for something better (whether truly so or not) and through this discord in his mind is discontented with the circumstances in which he lives, yet capable of attaining to no other, is led out of this disgust into listlessness, and is thus on the way to the evil courses which so often ruin men. The prediction of Socrates is thus quite natural.

To this definite accusation that he led sons into disobedience to their parents, Socrates replied by asking the question whether in selecting men for public offices, such as that of general, parents, or those experienced in war, were selected. Similarly in all cases those most skilful in an art or science are picked out. He demanded whether it was not a matter of astonishment that he should be brought before a judge because he was preferred to parents by the sons in their aspirations after the highest human good which is to be made a noble man.[9] This reply of Socrates is, on the one hand, quite just, but we see at the same time that we cannot call it exhaustive, for the real point of the accusation is not touched. What his judges found unjust was the intrusion morally of a third into the absolute relation between parents

9 Xenoph. "Apol. Socrat." §§ 20, 21; "Memorab." I. c. 2, §§ 51-55; Plat. "Apol. Socrat." pp. 24-26.

and children. On the whole not much can be said on this point, for all depends on the mode of intervention, and if it is necessary in certain cases, it need not take place generally, and least of all when some private individual takes that liberty. Children must have the feeling of unity with their parents; this is the first immediately moral relationship; every teacher must respect it, keep it pure, and cultivate the sense of being thus connected. Hence, when a third person is called into this relation between parents and children, what happens through the new element introduced is that the children are for their own good prevented from confiding in their parents, and made to think that their parents are bad people who harm them by their intercourse and training; and hence we find this revolting. The worst thing which can happen to children in regard to their morality and their mind, is that the bond which must ever be held in reverence should become loosened or even severed, thereby causing hatred, disdain, and ill-will. Whoever does this, does injury to morality in its truest form. This unity, this confidence, is the mother's milk of morality on which man is nurtured; the early loss of parents is therefore a great misfortune. The son, like the daughter, must indeed come out of his natural unity with the family and become independent, but the separation must be one which is natural or unforced, and not defiant and disdainful. When a pain like this has found a place in the heart, great strength of mind is required to overcome it and to heal the wound. If we now speak of the example given us by Socrates, he seems, through his intervention, to have made the young man dissatisfied with his position. Anytus' son might, indeed, have found his work generally speaking uncongenial, but it is another thing when such dislike is brought into consciousness and established by the authority of a man such as Socrates. We may very well conjecture that if Socrates had to do with him, he strengthened and developed in him the germ of the feeling of incongruity. Socrates remarked on the subject of his capacities, saying that he was fit for something better, and thus established a feeling of dissatisfaction in the young man, and strengthened his dislike to his father, which thus became the reason of his ruin. Hence this accusation of having destroyed the relationship of parents and children may be regarded as not unfounded, but as perfectly well established. It was also thought very bad in Socrates' case particularly, and made a matter of reproach that he had such followers as Critias and Alcibiades, who brought Athens almost to the brink of ruin.

For when he mixed himself in the education which others gave their children, men were justified in the demand that the result should not belie what he professed to do for the education of youth.

The only question now is, how the people came to take notice of this, and in how far such matters can be objects of legislation and be brought into court. In our law, as regards the first part of the accusation, divination such as Cagliostro's is illegal, and it would be forbidden as it formerly was by the Inquisition. Respecting the second point, such a moral interference is no doubt more recognized with us, where there is a particular office having this duty laid upon it; but this interference must keep itself general, and dare not go so far as to call forth disobedience to parents, which is the first immoral principle. But should such questions come before the court? This first of all brings up the question of what is the right of the State, and here great laxity is now allowed. Nevertheless, when some professor or preacher attacks a particular religion, the legislature would certainly take notice of it, and it would have a complete right to do so, although there would be an outcry when it did it. There is undoubtedly a limit which in liberty of thought and speech is difficult to define and rests on tacit agreement; but there is a point beyond which we find what is not allowed, such as direct incitement to insurrection. It is indeed said, that "bad principles destroy themselves by themselves and find no entrance." But that is only true in part, for with the populace the eloquence of sophistry stirs up their passions. It is also said, "This is only theoretic, no action follows." But the State really rests on thought, and its existence depends on the sentiments of men, for it is a spiritual and not a physical kingdom. Hence it has in so far maxims and principles which constitute its support, and if these are attacked, the Government must intervene. Added to this, it was the case that in Athens quite a different state of things was present than with us; in order to be able to judge rightly of Socrates' case we must first consider the Athenian State and its customs. According to Athenian laws, i.e. according to the spirit of the absolute State, both these things done by Socrates were destructive of this spirit, while in our constitution the universal of the states is a stronger universal, which last undoubtedly permits of individuals having freer play, since they cannot be so dangerous to this universal. Hence it would undoubtedly in the first place mean the subversion of the Athenian State, if this

408

public religion on which everything was built and without which the State could not subsist, went to pieces; with us the State may be called an absolute and independent power. The Daemon is now, in fact, a deity differing from any known, and because it stood in contradiction to the public religion, it gave to it a subjective arbitrariness. But since established religion was identified with public life so closely that it constituted a part of public law, the introduction of a new god who formed self-consciousness into a principle and occasioned disobedience, was necessarily a crime. We may dispute with the Athenians about this, but we must allow that they are consistent. In the second place, the moral connection between parents and children is stronger, and much more the moral foundation of life with the Athenians than with us, where subjective freedom reigns; for family piety is the substantial key-note of the Athenian State. Socrates thus attacked and destroyed Athenian life in two fundamental points; the Athenians felt and became conscious of it. Is it then to be wondered at that Socrates was found guilty? We might say that it had to be so. Tennemann (Vol. II., p. 41) says: "Though these charges contained the most palpable untruths, Socrates was condemned to death because his mind was too lofty for him to descend to the common unworthy means, by which the judgment of the court was usually perverted." But all this is false; he was found guilty of these deeds, but not for that reason condemned to death.

(2) We here come to the second occurrence in his history. In accordance with Athenian laws, the accused had, after the Heliasts (resembling the English jury) pronounced him guilty, the liberty of suggesting (*antitimasthai*) a penalty different from the punishment which the accuser proposed; this implied a mitigation of the punishment without a formal appeal—an excellent provision in Athenian law, testifying to its humanity. In this penalty the punishment in itself is not brought into question, but only the kind of punishment; the judges had decided that Socrates deserved punishment. But when it was left to the accused to determine what his punishment should be, it might not be arbitrary, but must be in conformity with the crime, a money or bodily punishment (*o ti chre pathein e apotithai*).[10] But it was implied in the guilty person's constituting himself his own judge, that he submitted himself to the decision of the court and

[10] Meier und Schömann: "Der Attische Prozess," pp. 173-77.

acknowledged himself to be guilty. Now Socrates declined to assign a punishment for himself consisting either of fine or banishment, and he had the choice between these and death, which his accusers proposed. He declined to choose the former punishment because he, according to Xenophon's account (Apol. Socr. § 23), in the formality of the exchange-penalty (*nupotimasthai*), as he said, would acknowledge guilt; but there was no longer any question as to the guilt, but only as to the kind of punishment.

This silence may indeed be considered as moral greatness, but, on the other hand, it contradicts in some measure what Socrates says later on in prison, that he did not wish to flee, but remained there, because it seemed better to the Athenians and better to him to submit to the laws. But the first submission would have meant that as the Athenians had found him guilty, he respected this decision, and acknowledged himself as guilty. Consistently he would thus have held it better to impose his punishment, since thereby he would not only have submitted himself to the laws, but also to the judgment. We see in Sophocles (Antig., verses 925, 926), the heavenly Antigone, that noblest of figures that ever appeared on earth, going to her death, her last words merely stating—

> "If this seems good unto the gods,
>   Suffering, we may be made to know our error."

Pericles also submitted himself to the judgment of the people as sovereign; we saw him going round the citizens entreating for Aspasia and Anaxagoras. In the Roman Republic we likewise find the noblest men begging of the citizens. There is nothing dishonouring to the individual in this, for he must bend before the general power, and the real and noblest power is the people. This acknowledgment the people must have direct from those who raise themselves amongst them. Here, on the contrary, Socrates disclaims the submission to, and humiliation before the power of the people, for he did not wish to ask for the remission of his punishment. We admire in him a moral independence which, conscious of its own right, insists upon it and does not bend either to act otherwise, or to recognize as wrong what it itself regards as right. Socrates hence exposed himself to death, which could not be regarded as the punishment for the fault of which he was found guilty; for the fact that he would not himself determine the punishment, and thus disdained the juridical power of the people, was

410

foremost in leading to his condemnation. In a general way he certainly recognized the sovereignty of the people, but not in this individual case; it has, however, to be recognized, not only in general, but in each separate case. With us the competency of the court is presupposed, and the criminal judged without further ado; to-day the whole matter is also open to the light of day and accepted as an acknowledged fact. But with the Athenians we find the characteristic request that the prisoner should, through the act of imposing on himself a penalty, sanction the judge's sentence of guilt. In England this is certainly not the case, but there still remains a like form of asking the accused by what law he wishes to be judged. He then answers, by the law of the land and by the judges of his country. Here we have the recognition of legal operations.

Socrates thus set his conscience in opposition to the judges' sentence, and acquitted himself before its tribunal. But no people, and least of all a free people like the Athenians, has by this freedom to recognize a tribunal of conscience which knows no consciousness of having fulfilled its duty excepting its own consciousness. To this government and law, the universal spirit of the people, may reply: "If you have the consciousness of having done your duty, we must also have the consciousness that you have so done." For the first principle of a State is that there is no reason or conscience or righteousness or anything else, higher than what the State recognizes as such. Quakers, Anabaptists, etc., who resist any demands made on them by the State, such as to defend the Fatherland, cannot be tolerated in a true State. This miserable freedom of thinking and believing what men will, is not permitted, nor any such retreat behind personal consciousness of duty. If this consciousness is no mere hypocrisy, in order that what the individual does should be recognized as duty, it must be recognized as such by all. If the people can make mistakes the individual may do so much more easily, and he must be conscious that he can do this much more easily than the people. Now law also has a conscience and has to speak through it; the law-court is the privileged conscience. Now if the miscarriage of justice in a trial is shown by every conscience clamouring for something different, the conscience of the court alone possesses any value as being the universal legalized conscience, which does not require to recognize the particular conscience of the accused. Men are too easily convinced of having fulfilled their duty, but

411

the judge finds out whether duty is in fact fulfilled, even if men have the consciousness of its being so.

We should expect nothing else of Socrates than that he should go to meet his death in the most calm and manly fashion. Plato's account of the wonderful scene his last hours presented, although containing nothing very special, forms an elevating picture, and will be to us a permanent representation of a noble deed. The last dialogue of Plato is popular philosophy, for the immortality of the soul is here first brought forward; yet it brings no consolation, for, as Homer makes Achilles say in the nether world, he would prefer to be a ploughboy on the earth.

But though the people of Athens asserted through the execution of this judgment the rights of their law as against the attacks of Socrates, and had punished the injury caused to their moral life by Socrates, Socrates was still the hero who possessed for himself the absolute right of the mind, certain of itself and of the inwardly deciding consciousness, and thus expressed the higher principle of mind with consciousness. Now because, as has been said, this new principle, by effecting an entrance into the Greek world, has come into collision with the substantial spirit and the existing sentiments of the Athenian people, a reaction had to take place, for the principle of the Greek world could not yet bear the principle of subjective reflection. The Athenian people were thus, not only justified, but also bound to react against it according to their law, for they regarded this principle as a crime. In general history we find that this is the position of the heroes through whom a new world commences, and whose principle stands in contradiction to what has gone before and disintegrates it: they appear to be violently destroying the laws. Hence individually they are vanquished, but it is only the individual, and not the principle, which is negated in punishment, and the spirit of the Athenian people did not in the removal of the individual, recover its old position. The false form of individuality is taken away, and that, indeed, in a violent way, by punishment; but the principle itself will penetrate later, if in another form, and elevate itself into a form of the world-spirit. This universal mode in which the principle comes forth and permeates the present is the true one; what was wrong was the fact that the principle came forth only as the peculiar possession of one individual. His own world could not comprehend Socrates, but posterity can, in as far as it stands above both. It may be conceived that the life of Socrates had no need to have such an end, for Socrates might have lived and died a private philosopher, and his teaching might have been quietly accepted by his disciples, and have spread further still without receiving any notice from State or people; the accusation thus would seem to have been contingent. But it must be said that it was through the manner of that event that this principle became so highly honoured. The principle is not merely something new and peculiar to itself, but it is an absolutely essential moment in the self-developing consciousness of self which is designed to bring to pass as a totality, a new and higher actuality. The Athenians perceived correctly that this principle not only meant opinion and doctrine, for its true attitude was that of a direct and even hostile and destructive relation to the actuality of the Greek mind; and they proceeded in accordance with this perception. Hence, what follows in Socrates' life is not contingent, but necessarily follows upon this principle. Of the honour of having recognized that relation, and indeed of having felt that they themselves were tinged with this principle, is due to the Athenians.

(3) The Athenians likewise repented of their condemnation of Socrates, and punished some of his accusers with death itself, and others with banishment; for according to Athenian laws, the man who made an accusation, and whose accusation was found to be false, usually underwent the same punishment that otherwise the criminal would have borne. This is the last act in this drama. On the one hand the Athenians recognized through their repentance the individual greatness of the man; but on the other (and this we find by looking closer) they also recognized that this principle in Socrates, signifying the introduction of new gods and disrespect to parents, has—while destructive and hostile to it— been introduced even into their own spirit, and that they themselves are in the dilemma of having in Socrates only condemned their own principle. In that they regretted the just judgment of Socrates, it seems to be implied that they wished that it had not occurred. But from the regret it does not follow that in itself it should not have occurred, but only tha it should not have happened for their consciousness. Both together constitute the innocence which is guilty and atones for its guilt; it would only be senseless and despicable if there were no guilt. An innocent person who comes off badly is a simpleton; hence it is a very flat and uninteresting matter when tyrants and innocent persons are represented in tragedies, just because this is an empty contingency. A great

413

man would be guilty and overcome the great crisis that ensues; Christ thus gave up his individuality, but what was brought forth by him remained.

The fate of Socrates is hence really tragic, not in the superficial sense of the word and as every misfortune is called tragic. The death of an estimable individual must, in such a sense, be specially tragic, and thus it is said of Socrates, that because he was innocent and condemned to death, his fate was tragic. But such innocent suffering would only be sad and not tragic, for it would not be a rational misfortune. Misfortune is only rational when it is brought about by the will of the subject, who must be absolutely justified and moral in what he does, like the power against which he wars—which must therefore not be a merely natural power, or the power of a tyrannic will. For it is only in such a case that man himself has any part in his misfortune, while natural death is only an absolute right which nature exercises over men. Hence, in what is truly tragic there must be valid moral powers on both the sides which come into collision; this was so with Socrates: His is likewise not merely a personal, individually romantic lot; for we have in it the universally moral and tragic fate, the tragedy of Athens, the tragedy of Greece. Two opposed rights come into collision, and the one destroys the other. Thus both suffer loss and yet both are mutually justified; it is not as though the one alone were right and the other wrong. The one power is the divine right, the natural morality whose laws are identical with the will which dwells therein as in its own essence, freely and nobly; we may call it abstractly objective freedom. The other principle, on the contrary, is the right, as really divine, of consciousness or of subjective freedom; this is the fruit of the tree of the knowledge of good and evil, i.e. of self-creative reason; and it is the universal principle of Philosophy for all successive times. It is these two principles which we see coming into opposition in the life and the philosophy of Socrates.

The Athenian people had come into a period of culture, in which this individual consciousness made itself independent of the universal spirit and became for itself. This was perceived by them in Socrates, but at the same time it was felt that it meant ruin, and thus they punished an element which was their own. The principle of Socrates is hence not the transgression of one individual, for all were implicated; the crime was one that the spirit of the people committed against itself. Through this perception the condemnation of

414

Socrates was retracted; Socrates appeared to have committed no crime, for the spirit of the people has now generally reached the consciousness which turns back from the universal into itself. This meant the disintegration of this people, whose mind and spirit consequently soon disappeared from the world, but yet out of its ashes a higher spirit took its rise, for the world-spirit had raised itself into a higher consciousness. The Athenian State, indeed, endured for long, but the bloom of its character soon faded. It is characteristic of Socrates that he grasped the principle of the inwardness of knowledge, not practically merely, as did Critias and Alcibiades, but in thought, making it valid to thought, and this is the higher method. Knowledge brought about the Fall, but it also contains the principle of Redemption. Thus what to others was only ruin, to Socrates, because it was the principle of knowledge, was also a principle of healing. The development of this principle, which constitutes the content of all successive history, is explicitly the reason that the later philosophers withdrew from the affairs of the State, restricted themselves to cultivating an inner world, separated from themselves the universal aim of the moral culture of the people, and took up a position contrary to the spirit of Athens and the Athenians. From this it came to pass that particularity of ends and interests now became powerful in Athens. This has, in common with the Socratic principle, the fact that what seems right and duty, good and useful to the subject in relation to himself as well as to the State, depends on his inward determination and choice, and not on the constitution and the universal. This principle of self-determination for the individual has, however, become the ruin of the Athenian people, because it was not yet identified with the constitution of the people; and thus the higher principle must in every case appear to bring ruin with it where it is not yet identified with the substantial of the people. The Athenian life became weak, and the State outwardly powerless, because its spirit was divided within itself. Hence it was dependent on Laodaemon, and we finally see the external subordination of these States to the Macedonians.

We are done with Socrates. I have been more detailed here because all the features of the case have been so completely in harmony, and he constitutes a great historic turning point. Socrates died at sixty-nine years of age, in Olympiad 95, 1 (399-400 B.C.), an Olympiad after the end of the Peloponnesian war, twenty-nine years after the death of Pericles, and forty-four years before the birth of Alexander. He saw Athens in its greatness and the beginning of its fall; he ex-from the world, but yet out of its ashes a higher spirit took its misfortunes.

Translated by E. S. Haldane